BURMA OR MYANMAR?

The Struggle for National Identity

BURMA OR MYANMAR?

The Struggle for National Identity

editor

Lowell Dittmer
University of California, Berkeley, USA

World Scientific

NEW JERSEY · LONDON · SINGAPORE · BEIJING · SHANGHAI · HONG KONG · TAIPEI · CHENNAI

Published by

World Scientific Publishing Co. Pte. Ltd.

5 Toh Tuck Link, Singapore 596224

USA office: 27 Warren Street, Suite 401-402, Hackensack, NJ 07601

UK office: 57 Shelton Street, Covent Garden, London WC2H 9HE

British Library Cataloguing-in-Publication Data
A catalogue record for this book is available from the British Library.

First published 2010 (Hard cover)
Reprinted 2015 (in paperback edition)
ISBN 978-981-4730-36-5

BURMA OR MYANMAR? THE STRUGGLE FOR NATIONAL IDENTITY

ISBN-13 978-981-4313-64-3
ISBN-10 981-4313-64-5

Typeset by Stallion Press
Email: enquiries@stallionpress.com

Contents

Preface

Later this year (2010) the self-selected leadership of Burma has credibly promised to hold nation's first elections in 20 years, though they have not yet announced the date or electoral rules, and we can only wish the country well. Having been ruled for more than 50 years by an unbroken series of military dictatorships, it is difficult to imagine how Burma can function with a mere civilian government — the army monopolizes not only the instruments of violence more effectively than ever before (thanks to a series of cease-fire agreements with the ethnic armies and consistent budgetary preference), the educational, civil service, and welfare systems beyond it have all atrophied badly over the years. But then a Chile-style sweeping displacement of the junta is not a very realistic option. The State Peace and Development Council has taken every precaution to structure the forthcoming election to ensure the *Tatmadaw*'s continued dominance, and a 1990-style democratic surprise is highly unlikely. Not only are a quarter of parliamentary seats reserved for the military, the main opposition party has been disbanded and its leaders remain under house arrest. Yet the shift to constitutional rule may still prove a meaningful one, marking perhaps the first step of a "pacted transition" to less arbitrary if not democratic rule.

I first became interested in Burma through its connection to China, the giant neighbor to the north with which it shares not only a long border but many other features as well. Both have adopted a form of socialism (which both have since revised extensively based on "national characteristics"), both legitimate themselves in terms of tutelary developmentalism heavily augmented by state coercion. To be sure, China is still "communist" in the sense that it is ruled by a communist party, but the Burman junta now seems to be emulating the ruling party model as well, first in the form of Ne Win's Burmese Socialist Programme Party, later as the Union Solidarity and Development Association. Yet the differences are far more striking. In contrast to China's Promethean GDP growth, Burma is a developmental dictatorship without much development, a form of socialism exhibiting some of the world's highest rates of poverty, disease, illiteracy and corruption. The transportation infrastructure remains primitive, economic development (beyond the extractive sector) extremely modest. Weberian assumptions about "legitimacy" to the contrary notwithstanding, a leadership that is neither rationally-legally competent, credibly "traditional," nor led by charismatic personalities and can claim a popular mandate neither domestically nor abroad has proved highly durable over time and is now stronger than ever. On the other hand the democratic and ethnic opposition forces, though currently in eclipse, have proved amazingly resilient over past decades as well.

Our purpose in this volume is to explain how this could be true, to depict the problems that beset this unhappy country and the forces underlying its calm and beautiful façade at a time of incipient transition. We begin with mass politics, encompassing the forthcoming electoral context, the ethnic cleavages, and the humanitarian crisis inflicted on the nation's masses. We then turn to elite politics, focusing in turn on military rule, with its monomaniacal focus on personnel chess-playing at the top and sycophantic loyalty at the bottom, and then in counterpoint to a study of the tragic symbol of democratic opposition to the military, Daw Aung San Suu Kyi. In the next section we turn to the national political economy, finding surprisingly that the country is not at all a "hermit kingdom" but one with a thriving trade sector and a seemingly bright fiscal outlook based on escalating international demand for hydrocarbons and other natural resources — though of course such an endowment is no unmixed blessing. Last but by no means least, we turn to foreign policy, showing how the junta has managed to chart a perilous course among their most powerful and influential neighbors, China, India and the Association of Southeast Asian Nations.

I wish to express my sincere appreciation to my research assistant, Min Zin. A former leader of the democratic resistance in exile from Burma, now an advanced graduate student at the University of California at Berkeley and a brilliant and dedicated scholar, he knows far more about the country than I will ever know. As ever, I am also indebted to the Center for Chinese Studies and the Political Science Department of the University of California at Berkeley for financial support. An earlier version of this project appeared in the form of a special issue of Asian Survey (vol. 48, no. 6, November–December 2008), and we would like to express our collective gratitude to that distinguished journal for permission to use considerably revised and updated versions of those articles first published there. Early versions of the chapters by Jalal Alamgir, Renaud Egreteau, Ian Holliday, Stephen McCarthy, Win Min, and Sean Turnell first appeared in that context.

Contributors

Jalal Alamgir is Assistant Professor of Political Science at the University of Massachusetts, Boston, and a fellow at the South Asia Initiative at Harvard University. His research focuses on the intersection between democracy/democratization and economic globalization in South and Southeast Asia, particularly India, Bangladesh, and Burma. His book, *India's Open-Economy Policy: Globalism, Rivalry, Continuity* (London: Routledge, 2009), was selected by *Asia Policy* as part of its recommended Policymaker's Library. He holds a PhD in political science from Brown University. He may be reached at Jalal.Alamgir@umb.edu.

Lowell Dittmer is Professor of Political Science at the University of California, Berkeley, and editor of *Asian Survey*. Recent works include (with Haruhiro Fukui and Peter N.S. Lee, eds.) *Informal Politics in East Asia* (Cambridge: Cambridge University Press, 2000), *South Asia's Nuclear Security Dilemma: India, Pakistan, and China* (Armonk: M. E. Sharpe, 2005), (with Guoli Liu, eds.) *China's Deep Reform: Domestic Politics in Transition* (Lanham, MD: Rowman & Littlefield, 2006), (with George T. Yu), *China, the Developing World, and the New Global Dynamic* (Boulder, CO: Lynne Rienner, 2010), and many scholarly articles. He can be reached at dittmer@berkeley.edu.

Renaud Egreteau holds three degrees in Political Science and in Oriental Studies (in Hindi, National Institute of Oriental Languages and Civilizations, INALCO-Paris), as well as a PhD in Political Science (Sciences Po Paris, 2006). His dissertation dealt with the

Sino-Indian rivalry through Burma/Myanmar and its limits since 1988. In 2009, he took up a Research Assistant Professor position at The University of Hong Kong, where he coordinates the China-India Project of the Hong Kong Institute for the Humanities and Social Sciences (inc. Centre of Asian Studies). Also a Research Associate at the Bangkok-based Institute of Research on Contemporary South East Asia (IRASEC), he has been focusing his academic research on India's foreign policy, the intricacies of the Sino-Indian dyad, the instability of India's Northeastern frontier, Burma's political affairs, and the Indian and Chinese diaspora. His latest publications in English include contributions to *India Review*, *Asian Survey*, *East Asia*, and other scholarly journals. He can be contacted at regreteau@hotmail.com.

Christina Fink is an anthropologist and lecturer at the International Sustainable Development Studies Institute in Chiang Mai, Thailand. She is the author of *Living Silence in Burma: Surviving under Military Rule* (London: Zed Books, 2009, second edition) and the co-editor of *Converging Interests: Traders, Travelers, and Tourists in Southeast Asia* (Berkeley: University of California at Berkeley, 1999). She has written chapters and journal articles on the 2007 monks' movement and militarization in eastern Burma. She can be reached cfink@pobox.com

Daniel Gomà is a researcher at the Department of Contemporary History, University of Barcelona, Spain. He was a visiting scholar at Columbia University between 2007 and 2009. He has written articles about contemporary Burma and is currently working on the role of the military in the politics of Southeast Asian nations. His email address is dgoma@ub.edu.

Ian Holliday is Dean of Social Sciences at the University of Hong Kong. Previously he was Dean of Humanities and Social Sciences at City University of Hong Kong. He has written about Burma/Myanmar for the past five years, and has undertaken intermittent teaching and field research in Tak Province, Thailand, over the past two years. His email address is ian.holliday@hku.hk.

Tom Kramer (1968) is a political scientist with over 15 years of working experience in the field of Burma and its border regions, which he has visited regularly since 1993. He has carried out field research and written reports for a wide range of international NGOs, institutes, and UN organizations. He is also a researcher for the Drugs & Democracy programme (with a focus since 2005 on Afghanistan) of the Transnational Institute in Amsterdam. Apart from his work for TNI, he is also a writer and freelance consultant, specializing on ethnic conflict and civil society in Burma. He can be reached at Tom.Kramer@c2i.net.

Kyaw Yin Hlaing is Assistant Professor of Asian and International Studies at City University of Hong Kong. His area of specialization is mainland Southeast Asia. A native of Burma, he received a BA from Mandalay University and an MA and PhD from Cornell University. He can be reached at YH.Kyaw@cityu.edu.hk.

Stephen McCarthy is a Senior Lecturer in the Department of International Business and Asian Studies at Griffith University, Australia. His research interests include political theory, comparative politics, and international relations in Southeast Asia and more generally the Asia Pacific region. He has authored a book and numerous articles on Burma in international journals, and is currently researching on political stability and modes of governance in the Asia Pacific. Cf. He can be reached at S.Mccarthy@griffith.edu.au.

Min Zin is an advanced graduate student in political science at the University of California, Berkeley. As an activist-turned-journalist, Min Zin is a contributor to print and radio media and is also a teaching fellow responsible for the International Visiting Scholars' Program at UC Berkeley's Graduate School of Journalism. He holds an MA degree from the Asian Studies Graduate Program at UC Berkeley. He can be reached at Min_Zin@berkeley.edu.

Based at the Economics Department at Macquarie University in Sydney, Australia, Sean Turnell has been a Visiting Fellow at the

University of Cambridge, Cornell University, and the Paul H. Nitze School of Advanced International Studies, Johns Hopkins University. A former senior analyst at the Reserve Bank of Australia, Sean has maintained a long-term research interest in Burma and its economy, especially its financial system. Sean has been an advisor and consultant on Burma to a number of government departments, agencies, and NGOs around the world, and in 2006 and 2009 he testified on the country's economy before US Senate and House Foreign Relations and Human Rights Committees. He is co-founder and editor of Burma Economic Watch (BEW), and the author of numerous academic papers on Burma, as well as many articles on the country in the press and elsewhere. His book on Burma's monetary and financial history, *Fiery Dragons: Banks, Moneylenders and Microfinance in Burma*, was published in 2009 by the Nordic Institute of Asian Studies. He can be reached at sturnell@efs.mq.edu.au.

Win Min is a lecturer on contemporary Burma/Myanmar at the Thai and Southeast Asian Studies Program at Payap University in Chiang Mai (Thailand). He also lectures at various Burmese education programs at Chiang Mai University. He is a member of the Vahu Development Institute as well From 2001 to 2005, he was a researcher at the Burma Fund, a think tank for the Burmese government in exile. He received a Masters degree in Public Administration from the Kennedy School of Government at Harvard University in 2001. He was a student activist in Burma in 1988 and a member of the All Burma Students' Democratic Front from 1988 to 2000. The focus of his research is comparative studies of civil–military relations for a democratic transition in Burma. He is the co-author of *Assessing Burma's Ceasefire Accords* (Washington DC: East-West Center, 2007), and has contributed articles to *Asian Survey* and other journals and scholarly anthologies. He can be reached at winmin@post.harvard.edu.

Chapter 1

Burma vs. Myanmar: What's in a Name?

Lowell Dittmer

Abstract

Burma or Myanmar? The introduction of new English nomenclature for the country (and for other places within it) by Burma's military leadership has been controversial, not because of the names per se, but because the two sets of names have come to symbolize two diverging national identity trajectories for the country: one democratic and federalist, one militarily enforced hierarchical unity. The resulting cleavage has greatly complicated national political and economic development.

Keywords: Adaptation of expressions law; ethnic minorities; *Tatmadaw*.

The then State Law and Order Restoration Council (SLORC) decreed in the 1989 Adaptation of Expressions Law, three years after the UN had adopted pinyin for the spelling of Chinese place names, that their country, hitherto known as Burma, would henceforth be referred to as Myanmar in English, that Rangoon would be called Yangon, and so forth. The new name is taken from the literary form of the language, which first appears in 12th-century inscriptions, while the term "Burma" was derived from the spoken form in Bamar, the language of the majority Burmese ethnic group. Although the Burmese-language name for the country has included some version of "Myanmar" since independence, some organizations, including Aung San Suu Kyi's National League for Democracy (NLD), took exception to the change, preferring the spoken form "Burma" (which was also used by the independence movement prior to 1948) and continue to use it, signaling their refusal to recognize either the legitimacy of the ruling military government or its authority to rename the country. Some non-Burman ethnic groups, on the other hand, prefer the new name as it is less associated with the Burman (or Bamar) majority ethnic group. Since the political rechristening came in the wake of the 1988 coup, this has given rise to a division between linguistic nominalists (who believe names are simply a matter of arbitrary convenience) and realists (who think names must mean something). This cleavage aligns the United Nations, ASEAN, China, India and Japan among the nominalists (for whom Burma becomes Myanmar) and the United States, Australia, Canada and the United Kingdom among the "realists" — metaphysical, not political — who continue to adhere to the old usage as a way of denying the legitimacy of the ruling junta. This seems to have since hardened into an almost principled semantic stance among some analysts, as if the choice of names could in some way strengthen or undermine that unhappy nation's military dictatorship. Neither they nor we have been able to resolve either this terminological controversy or Burma's political troubles linguistically, and the contributors to this volume will use the two names interchangeably — sometimes "Burma," sometimes "Myanmar," sometimes resorting to the European Union's catch-all solution: "Myanmar/Burma." Linguistically, we can live and let live.

So much for our title — would that the political reality underlying this lexicographical cleavage might prove equally tractable! For behind this apparently petty linguistic dispute, a long struggle for national identity has raged since the founding of the state in 1948. These two names have come to symbolize two quite different historical experiences and political trajectories, each upholding its own claim to legitimacy and political loyalty. Actually there are more than two — only the military government's steadfast suppression of any voice but its own has produced the illusory dualism that stems from forced bipolarity. Though there has not been an official census since March 1983 (and even that was rendered incomplete by ongoing civil war), according to best estimates the Burman (or Bamar) people make up only about 68% of the populace, the other 32% consisting of some 135 "distinct" ethnic groups, the main ones being Shan (9%), Kayin or Karen (7%), Rakhine or Arakan (4%), Mon (2%),

Kayah (1.75%) or Karenni (1.25%), and Kachin (1.5%). Though in the minority, these ethnic groups occupy nearly 60% of the land area, much of it along the borders. Intra-ethnic relations have long been tense, exacerbated by the British during the colonial era and by Japanese invaders during World War II. Although an attempt was made to reconcile these tensions by guaranteeing ethnic autonomy at the February 1947 Panglong meeting, perceived failure to honor these pledges resulted in the explosion of strife that helped topple the first Burmese attempt at democracy in 1958–1962. Ne Win's subsequent imposition of the "Burmese way to socialism" was legitimated by the assumption that only the army (the *Tatmadaw*) could hold the nation together.

The grounding assumption of this book is that the quest for national identity, a developmental "crisis" usually resolved fairly early in the nation-building process with the establishment of national borders, a national language, constitution, armed forces, capital, currency, and so forth, was never achieved in Burma's case but only forced underground by suppression — from which it would burst forth again whenever the opportunity arose. Certainly national identity is not the most immediately obvious issue in one of the poorest and least developed countries on earth (e.g., the world's lowest GDP per capita, estimated at $98 per annum). Yet identity discord has created a frozen set of cleavages around which a cumulative series of supplementary troubles have clustered along the interstices of identity, as it were, sustaining and exacerbating national fragmentation. Thus the enduring mistrust between democratic forces and the military establishment, coinciding as it does with a split between the educated middle classes and the security apparatus, has resulted in gutting the country's once respected education system and thrown many idealistic political entrepreneurs in jail or out of the country; the ethnic splits have made room for and given incentive to the cultivation of opium crops and the drug trade, making Burma the world's second-largest exporter of opium and a leading manufacturer of methamphetamine — and so forth. National fragmentation has also contributed to egregious human rights violations with attendant spillover effects complicating relations with neighboring countries. Until the national identity dilemma can be resolved, the quest for national development is likely to falter — or at best take a contorted, imbalanced form, threatening future unity and stability.

In the following chapters some of the world's leading Burma specialists consider various dimensions of the problems that have clustered around the identity issue to hold the country back, developmentally as well as politically. The book is divided into three sections: the first and longest section is on domestic politics, the second is on political economy, while the third focuses on foreign policy. Our analysis of domestic politics is then further subdivided into a first part on "mass" politics and a second on "high," or elite politics. In each section we seek to show how these problems have coagulated in the gaps or interstices of identity to impede healthy political and economic development.

Ian Holliday not only provides an excellent historical overview of the country's political experience from independence to the present but undertakes an insightful analysis of the prospects for democratization — the demand for which (despite limited empirical experience) has obviously taken inveterate root in Burmese society.[1] He does so within a comparative theoretical framework of successful democratic transitions, with particular focus on the disruptive impact of nationalist violence — a disease of the transition particularly endemic to Burma. Although nationalism typically arises in the course of democratization, "when political identities are up for grabs," in Burma's case it was already a disputatious issue during the colonial period, which the British manipulated to maintain their control. They drew the boundaries of the new nation quite arbitrarily, often bisecting ethnic groups. Although, fortunately, Burma has not been afflicted by trans-boundary movements fighting for separatism or irredenta, ethnic spillover has given adjoining states the basis for special access and leverage against the central government. Against this

---

[1] Despite its mixed empirical record, the democratic dream has proved remarkably resilient in Burma, sparking mass demonstrations in 1962, 1969–1970, 1974, 1988, 1996 and 2007.

background, the country's abortive early experience with democratization might have been anticipated, as nationalist rivalries quickly spun out of control, undermining democracy and leading to half a century of Burman-dominated military dictatorship. Viewing future prospects for democratization from this theoretical perspective, Holliday finds a mixed picture: On the one hand, a "pacted transition" under the aegis of the current SPDC leadership seems to have acquired considerable momentum, and both leading opposition camps — the NLD and a majority of the ethnic minorities who have made ceasefire arrangements — seem to be willing to go along with the "road map to democracy."[2] On the other hand, the current constitution vouchsafes only a democratic sham thinly masking continued military dominance, and the SPDC seems at this point ill-inclined to make the minimal concessions for civil rights demanded by the NLD or for ethnic autonomy demanded by the ethnic minorities. The "tripartite dialogue" suggested in 1994 by the UN General Assembly and still demanded by both oppositions, though seemingly

---

[2] The "road map to democracy" was introduced on August 30, 2003, and has since been adhered to by the SPDC despite the purge of Prime Minister Khin Nyunt in 2004. It consists of seven points:

1. Reconvening of the National Convention that has been adjourned since 1996.
2. After the successful holding of the National Convention, step-by-step implementation of the process necessary for the emergence of a genuine and disciplined democratic system.
3. Drafting of a new constitution in accordance with detailed basic principles laid down by the National Convention.
4. Adoption of the constitution through a national referendum.
5. Holding of free and fair elections for *Pyithu Hluttaws* [legislative bodies] according to the new constitution.
6. Convening of *Hluttaws* [assemblies] attended by *Hluttaw* members in accordance with the new constitution.
7. Building a modern, developed and democratic nation by the state leaders elected by the *Hluttaw*, and the government and other central organs formed by the *Hluttaw* (*New Light of Myanmar*, August 31, 2003). As of December 2009, the first four points had been fulfilled and legislative elections are scheduled for 2010.

sine qua non for any workable compromise, has been steadfastly rejected by the SPDC. From a theoretical perspective some of these missing pieces seem dispensable, according to Holliday, such as the temporary deferral of the full conspectus of liberal human rights, or a consociational mechanism to accommodate minority demands for autonomy. Whether the opposition will continue to play a game in which they have so little stake is another question. Given their position, they might accept a provisional deal if they could see light at the end of the tunnel. Hopes for a successful pacted transition may thus be contingent upon the SPDC's willingness to compromise. For instance, more politically realistic provisions for future constitutional revision would be reassuring to all but beneficiaries of the status quo (the 2008 Constitution requires 75% legislative approval and, for many of the more significant provisions, passage of a national referendum by 50% of eligible voters — either of which will be very difficult to achieve, given the likelihood of continued military dominance).

The plight of Burma's ethnic minorities gained additional salience in the summer of 2009 as a result of the SPDC's attempt to integrate forcibly the tiny Kokang minority into the border guard before the 2010 elections, precipitating the latter's violent resistance and the subsequent flight of some 35,000 refugees into China's Yunnan Province (much to Beijing's dismay, preoccupied at the time with staging their "harmonious" 60th national anniversary). But according to Tom Kramer, a Dutch political scientist who has long focused on ethnic minority politics and civil society in Burma, this was only the tip of the iceberg. Burma's ca. 135 ethnic minorities, though bewildering in their diversity and internecine alliances and rivalries, are quite united in their basic demand for a certain realm of federal autonomy — yet this has never been fully granted in any of the state's three constitutions. They reached perhaps the acme of their power around 1988, when most of the border areas were dominated by well-armed ethnic coalitions, from the West-leaning National Democratic Front (NDF) along the Thai border to the Communist Party of Burma (which had formed coalitions with several minority ethic groups, mainly the Wa) along the border with China. But from 1989 to the mid-1990s, SLORC Secretary 1 Khin Nyunt succeeded in forming ceasefire alliances with 17 of the 18 largest ethnic armies (25, by 2009), bringing civil war under (relative) control. These ceasefire alliances are all strictly bilateral, the center's discretionary silence keeping inter-ethnic relations invidious, and the ethnic armies retained their weapons. Thus ethnic divisiveness has been suspended but not really resolved. Though they comprise only 35–40% of the total population, the ethnic minorities occupy nearly 60% of the land, much of it strategically situated along Burma's borders (the longest land borders in Southeast Asia), where Burma's neighbors (Thailand, China, India) have not been above playing them off against the center or one minority group against another in order to gain marginal advantage, as in logging or mining operations, gas or oil pipelines or illegal immigration. For their part, the minorities too have exploited national fragmentation and cross-border ethnic connections for drug manufacture, gambling emporiums, arms or drug smuggling and other clandestine activity. Civil society is marred by inter-ethnic suspicion, and there is even a certain distance between the ethnics and the (mostly Burman) NLD. Only the United Nationalities Alliance has been able thus far to build a tenable coalition bridging this gap. Yet the SPDC, having built its legitimacy on Burman nationalism, has consistently opposed federalism as the first step toward national disintegration, preferring to govern using bilateral divide-and-rule tactics. In April 2009, with the end of the road map in view and the truces set to expire, the junta demanded that the minority armies disarm and place their troops under central command in a new Border Guard Force. A few of the smaller ceasefire groups have acquiesced, but at least four of the major forces have thus far rebuffed the offer and regrouped as the Myanmar Peace and Democracy Front.[3] Whether the SPDC's 2009 attack on Kokang is a harbinger of moves against the more formidable groups is an issue relevant not only to domestic

---

[3] The four are the United Wa State Army (15,000–20,000 troops), the Kachin Independence Organization (5,000–6,000 troops), the Mongla-based National Democratic Alliance Army—Eastern Shan State (under 2,000 troops), and the Kokang ceasefire group (1,000–1,500 troops).

tranquility but to Burma's relations with China, its main patron. Though the SPDC has been keen to absorb the ethnic armies before the 2010 elections, by force if necessary, China as the country's biggest foreign investor (since 2008), with a stake in border stability, has had a pacifying effect.

The series of choices made by the country's leadership has had devastating humanitarian consequences for the Burmese people, as clearly documented in Christina Fink's chapter. This seems of little concern to the military leadership, as became clear in May 2008, when Cyclone Nargis hit and the SPDC barred international human rights nongovernmental organizations (INGOs) from providing aid because they might interfere with the national referendum on the new constitution — to which the SPDC gave top priority, even evicting Nargis refugees from schools to be used as polling stations. Most authoritarian systems, including the Soviet Union, even Nazi Germany, do have social welfare packages to compensate for infringements on liberty.[4] But in Burma, the junta's comprehensive focus on potential threats to national security is ironically accompanied by a minimalist view of the state's obligation to promote the general welfare — the economy seems to be seen as self-sufficient, or at least self-reliant. Education, health and welfare all receive derisory fractions of the budget. The populace is swept by malaria, tuberculosis and HIV/AIDS pandemics, poverty is currently estimated at 26%; and there are thousands of internal displaced persons (IDPs) as people are shifted from one place to another to bolster national security. Poverty seems to have affected even the military, which is more generously provided for, throwing the lower ranks upon the local populace for their upkeep. These social disfunctions are not only a domestic time bomb but complicate relations with Burma's neighbors, spilling over in the form of drug exports, disease epidemics, gambling emporiums and massive refugee flows (e.g., 2–4 million illegal migrants in Thailand alone). Skewed fiscal priorities (ca. 40% of the budget to the military, a nonproductive allocation) result in a large external debt and a big

---

[4] David Schoenbaum, *Hitler's Social Revolution; Class and Status in Nazi Germany, 1933–1939* (Garden City, NY: Doubleday, 1966).

budget deficit. This has been financed largely by printing money, resulting in chronic double-digit inflation (est. 20–30% since 2000). About 70% of the economy remains agricultural, but the combination of low procurement prices for grain (to ensure food supplies to the military), ill-advised and arbitrary agricultural policies, and special exactions (including corvée labor) for roads, bridges and other mer-etricious public works have resulted in a per capita income (in 2006) less than half that of Bangladesh or Laos, high percentages of which must be expended on food and shelter.[5] The humanitarian crisis is linked to national identity more as a functional consequence of the leadership's priorities than a causal factor, though certainly it has become part of the identity of the regime and its long-suffering citizenry and the nation they have built together (since 1987 the UN has relegated the country to the world's "least developed countries").

To the world, Aung San Suu Kyi personifies her country more than any other human being, living or dead, as Kyaw Yin Hlaing illustrates. While symbolizing Burma, she is at the same time very much a global citizen: educated abroad and married to an English don, she was engaged in work on an Oxford PhD on Burmese literature when first drawn into Burmese politics during the 1988 uprising. At this time she was known only as the daughter of General Aung San, Leader of the Anti-Fascist People's Freedom League and martyr-founder of the Burmese Army (*Tatmadaw*) and the Union of Burma. Her instant name recognition, lack of political baggage, personal courage in confronting the junta on behalf of the oppressed, and finally Burma's only Nobel Peace Prize (1991) all helped to vault her to the forefront of the democracy movement where she was exalted as the "goddess of democracy." Her democratic crusade has indeed

---

[5] In 2005 the United Nations Development Program report, carried out in consultation with the government, found that 90% of the population lived on less than 65 cents per day. The average household thus spends three-quarters of its budget on food. UNDP/Myanmar and Ministry of National Planning (Myanmar), "Integrated Household Living Conditions Survey in Myanmar: Vulnerability-Related Information," March 8, 2006, as cited in Mary Callahan, "Myanmar's Perpetual Junta," *New Left Review* 60 (November–December 2009), pp. 27–63.

been implacable, sometimes even reckless, never succumbing to unprincipled compromise, not even leaving the country for her husband's funeral lest the military deny her return. Yet this combination of dedication to principle and international renown has made her *persona non grata* to the xenophobic military leadership, which used her marriage as a pretext to bar her from politics. Though reportedly difficult to work with, she has remained head of the NLD despite being under house arrest for 14 of the past 20 years, still politically indispensable to any meaningful settlement. While her principled opposition has helped dramatize her country's plight, an integrated national identity will require reconciliation with a leadership she once called fascist — yet she cannot compromise too much without losing her constituency. In September and November 2009 she reportedly wrote two letters to the SPDC, offering to work for the lifting of economic sanctions and possible further collaborative endeavors. In response, she was allowed to discuss the lifting of sanctions with representatives of the US, the EU and Australia and to meet briefly with the aging leadership of the NLD (but not with Than Shwe). Yet the SPDC made no concessions, and sanctions seem likely to remain in place at least for the time being. Whether the West will agree and, if so, whether the SPDC will in any way reciprocate remain of course to be seen.

On the other side of this symbolic dualism is the nation's military dictatorship which, however lacking in charisma, has maintained its collective solidarity and iron grip on power for half a century. Based on interviews and other primary sources, Win Min provides rare insight into the internal workings of this secretive regime. The leadership is not as cohesive as might appear, as various factions based on *saya–tapyit* (patron–client, teacher–student) ties form along vertical formal hierarchies and vie for power, particularly as a leadership succession approaches. But so far it has avoided crippling splits — partly through prophylactic purges of suspected dissidents, fostering a corporate culture of subservient conformity. The *Tatmadaw* conceives its legitimacy as the sole reliable pillar of national unity, and since the civil wars of the 1940s–1980s the rank and file (particularly the officer corps) have been monochromatically Burman in ethnic origin. Aside from that they seem to have no particular guiding ideology or international mission, as has typically characterized fascist or communist party-states, nor has the military ever articulated a very coherent or effective plan to put the economy on a self-sustaining growth trajectory. Like the PRC or the DPRK at the time, Ne Win's "Burmese way to socialism" bought into the dependency theory argument that the only way to escape perpetual underdevelopment was to sever all ties with capitalist markets, practicing an extreme form of "self-reliance" that was to prove economically disastrous. The subsequent SLORC and SPDC governments have sought to encourage more outside trade and investment, but security priorities have severely limited any real opening. Though highly sensitive to perceived threats, to which it reacts with considerable brutality, the leadership's intolerance of dissent insulates it from negative feedback. This enhances self-confidence at the cost of impairing learning capacity, allowing a number of quaint superstitions to persist, such as astrology and numerology.

The military leadership has not shrunk from redefining Burma's national identity, as in the 1989 Adaptation of Expressions Law, which changed the name of the country to Myanmar as well as the names of the capital and many other cities. Western observers were even more taken aback when, in November 2005, it suddenly moved the administrative capital of the country from Rangoon (now Yangon) to a new city to be named Naypyidaw ("great city of the sun" or "abode of kings") on the outskirts of Pyinmana, a remote logging town some 200 miles (320 km) to the north of Yangon. Though the leadership never explained these moves (aside from attesting that the more central location was in the national interest), Daniel Goma has educed several plausible reasons for this strange move. National identity always embeds some narrative, however mythical, of national origin. Pyinmana has some historical significance for the *Tatmadaw* as the pre-war headquarters of the Burma Independence Army (renamed the Burma Defense Army by the Japanese, then the Burma National Army after it switched sides and supported the allied offensive against the Japanese). But long before that, Burma's Cakravartin Kings or "Universal Monarchs," such as Anawrahta, Bayinnaung or Hsinbyushin (with whom Senior General

Than Shwe is said to identify), would create their own Mandala or field of power and move the capital to commemorate each reign. The transplanted capital thus might, Daniel Gomá concedes, make sense as a final step in the junta's nationalistic quest to efface all traces of colonialism and form a bridge to its precolonial, cosmo-logical origins. But the main reason for the move was probably less grandiose and more strategic — the country's large cities had become staging grounds for protests against the regime, and rather than respond with reforms the regime deemed potentially destabiliz-ing, it retreated to a fortress mentality. University campuses have also been relocated to the countryside in self-enclosed compounds that can promptly be shut down in case of unrest. Moreover, the new capital is deemed less vulnerable to a US naval attack, which the SPDC has feared since the 2003 Iraq invasion. The cost, of course, is increasing isolation from what is actually going on in the country, irrespective of the leadership's preferences.

However lofty the leadership's nationalist aspirations, they must be realized in today's most widely accepted currency of national vali-dation, namely, GDP growth. Once the most prosperous country in Southeast Asia and the world's biggest rice exporter, Burma, since the introduction of the "Burmese way to socialism," has become one of the poorest nations in the world, with a GDP growth rate averag-ing 2.9% annually — the lowest in the Greater Mekong Subregion.[6] By 1987 the UN had categorized it among the world's least devel-oped countries. In 1988 the SLORC assayed an opening to interna-tional market forces by courting trade and investment, but reform plans soon gave way to security priorities and market opening fell athwart Western trade sanctions invoked in response to human rights

[6] "Burma," *The World Factbook*, Central Intelligence Agency. Retrieved January 13, 2007. There is a gross discrepancy between IMF estimates, reflecting the more opti-mistic official statistics and the more skeptical CIA estimates. Here are the IMF estimates (CIA estimates in brackets) for 2003–2009: 2003: 13.8% (3.3%), 2004: 13.56% (−0.5%), 2005: 13.57% (−1.3%), 2006: 13% (5.2%), 2007: 11.9% (3%), 2008: 4% (3.8%), 2009: 4.3% (1.1%). The more optimistic growth estimates of course beg the question of why the nation's GDP per capita ($1,200 in 2008, PPP) ranks 206th in the world.

violations. Some of the consequences of years of economic misman-agement are spelled out in Christina Fink's chapter — chronic budget deficits, a dilapidated public sector, poverty, ill health, illiteracy, and so forth. The combination of generous arms spending and a woefully underdeveloped tax collection capability (only 4.4% of GDP in 2008) has given rise to chronic fiscal deficits. Yet according to Sean Turnell, Burma is now, for the first time in half a century, "moving to a sce-nario in which the *means* exists for effective capital accumulation" (Chapter 8). Thus this once bankrupt regime has recently displayed indications of great wealth, including big infrastructure projects (e.g., nuclear reactors — possibly to build weapons), the move to a new capital, and a comfortable cushion of foreign exchange earnings (over $5 billion, as of fall 2009).[7] The largest (legal) source of revenue derives from the export of natural gas and other hydrocarbons.[8] Thanks to recent discoveries, the country boasts proven reserves of 510 billion cubic meters out of an estimated total of 2.54 trillion cubic meters of offshore and onshore natural gas, while its recoverable crude oil reserves are estimated at 3.2 billion barrels. Surely, by any objective standard, this must be deemed an opulent resource endowment. But of course winning the lottery does not necessarily imply the jackpot will be prudently invested. In fact, many of the new projects on which the regime has lavished its new wealth seem unlikely to make a significant contribution to sustainable devel-opment. Professor Turnell thus invokes the "resource curse" theory, both to discount the value of this windfall to the Burmese people and to point out the considerable risk it poses to balanced future eco-nomic development. Yet he also concedes that the distorted priorities of the SLORC/SPDC regime were clearly evident long before it struck oil, and hence the resource curse theory can function not as a cause of these distortions but at most as a factor enabling the regime

[7] See David I. Steinberg, "The Burma Road Ahead," in PacNet Newsletter, No. 76 (December 3, 2009), in pacnet@hawaiibiz.rr.com, accessed December 7, 2009.
[8] In 1999–2000, natural gas accounted for less than 1% of all export earnings, but it was over 40% by 2006–2007; by late 2007, hundreds of millions of dollars had rolled in. Callahan, "Junta," p. 48.

to maintain its current course for the indefinite future without too much concern for the economic consequences.

The SPDC's new wealth also complicates any effort by the international community to influence the country's evolving national identity via economic incentives. The problem is no longer strictly that of economic isolationism, Jalal Alamgir points out; though Burma may not have the trade to GDP ratio of the East Asian "Tigers" or its Southeast Asian neighbors, the regime welcomes trade "under its terms," and commerce has been growing since the 1990s — in any case, trade statistics tabulate only official, legal trade, about half the total. One might say the economy has been globalized in both positive and negative senses: as the US and the EU have imposed trade sanctions for human rights abuses, neighboring trade partners such as Thailand, China and India have escalated trade correlatively. The international market has thus been politically bifurcated into ineligible and eligible trade partners, with the former (democracies) demanding political reform and the latter (mostly nondemocracies) professing overriding respect for Burma's sovereignty. Alamgir concedes that even this partial embargo has had an inhibiting effect on the nation's involvement in international trade. If the purpose of sanctions was to punish its leadership by constraining trade and thereby restraining economic growth (which correlates strongly with trade) below what might have otherwise been expected, they may thus have succeeded — though not enough to topple the regime, or even to force it to change course. To the question of whether sanctions can achieve their political purpose if they are not universal and hence not prohibitive, Alamgir's answer is not very promising: so far they have only moved the SPDC to confine trade to that small number of countries eager to trade and invest without political preconditions. In terms of trade composition, the imports that Burma's politically indiscriminate trade partners are most interested in importing or investing in are the extractive industries, hydrocarbons in particular, but also gems and timber — and these are the businesses the regime (or its cronies) monopolizes. Those most damaged by the sanctions, on the other hand, include agriculture and light industry (e.g., textiles), whose growth might have most benefited private landowners and entrepreneurs and the affiliated rural and industrial workforce while having minimal impact on the state-owned, capital-intensive extractive industries from which the regime derives support. Thus in structural terms, Alamgir clearly implies, trade sanctions have achieved the exact opposite of their political objectives, whether taken in the aggregate or decomposed sectorally.

Would it then be politically advisable to lift the sanctions? This is an issue with which the incoming Obama administration has been wrestling. It is important to bear in mind that Alamgir's is a structural economic analysis that leaves political agency aside — but the use of sanctions is ultimately a political issue. The politics of lifting sanctions has two components, one for the party imposing the sanctions (the sanctioner) and one for the target of the sanctions (the sanctionee, if you will). For the sanctioners to lift them (without reciprocal concessions) would involve a loss of "face" and likely domestic electoral backlash. While a liberal leadership would risk alienating its human rights constituency, a conservative one might well lose its nationalistic constituency. For either, lifting sanctions would incur not only congressional criticism in the US case but that of international human rights advocacy groups and the Burman exile community. Thus lifting them will require a bold (i.e., risk-tolerant) leadership with a relatively firm domestic support base. As for the sanctionees, lifting the sanctions might have two conceivable outcomes: First, it might persuade them that the former sanctioners no longer constitute a threat and they could thus open up to international markets and perhaps even domestic dissent. This is the assumption, for example, of Kim Dae-jung's "Sunshine Policy" based on Aesop's fable illustrating that carrots are more effective than sticks (to switch metaphors). The second possibility is, however, that the sanctionee simply accepts this free gift and makes no reciprocal concessions. After all, the SPDC might well feel vindicated, inferring that it could now resume all the practices that had triggered the sanctions in the first place with perfect impunity. That would be a bitter pill to swallow for the NLD, the ethnic minorities and the several thousand political dissidents still languishing in Burma's prisons. But even assuming the second, worst-case scenario, lifting the sanctions may draw Burma into international markets and economic integration may have political cultural spillover effects in the long run (as in China). To be sure, the military elite (like their PRC counterparts) may also be expected to be alert to such spillover effects, undertaking various preventive measures to forestall them. The efficacy of such tactics in the long term may be debated. But probably the biggest hurdle to lifting sanctions gratuitously, in view of the calculated long-term but uncertain "payoff" (in terms of political impact on the sanctionee), is the short-term penalty of domestic political backlash.

National identity is by no means exclusively a domestic phenomenon: the nation-state must exist in the world, and an identity is determined in part by its international environment — by the countries with which the national leadership identifies its national interests and by those it regards as categorical threats to those interests. The three essential external reference points on the SPDC's international horizon are its immediate neighbors, China, India and the Association of Southeast Asian Nations (ASEAN) whose roles are insightfully analyzed in chapters by Min Zin, Renaud Egreteau, and Stephen McCarthy respectively. The most important of these is China, an imposing neighbor that invaded Burma at least twice in the pre-colonial era and the only country outside the West interested in molding Burma's national identity in its own image — if only to make a troublesome neighbor less of an international embarrassment and source of refugee, disease and drug flows. Then, too, the two have a certain moral solidarity as fellow victims of Western humanitarian sanctions imposed after Burma's Four Eights (1988) and China's Tiananmen (1989) crackdowns, respectively. Building goodwill with its "soft" policies (especially non-interference in internal affairs), China has already so thoroughly penetrated the country that, according to Min Zin, "the Burmese military regime finds itself lacking the capacity to steer the country away from China's orbit." China is Burma's second-largest trade partner (bilateral trade grew more than one quarter in 2008, to around US$2.63 billion)[9] and fourth-largest source of FDI,

---

[9]Total trading volume is much higher when adding the illegal trade in drugs and marble, which contributes to the military leaders' personal incomes. Xu Ben Qin, "Sino–Burmese Political and Economic Relations: Strategic and Economic Dimensions," *Southeast Asian Affairs* 12(1) (2005), p. 39.

and it provides weaponry and training to the military, financial support in the form of condition-free loans, and finally it defends the country's human rights record in international forums. Yet PRC support is not entirely disinterested. In October 2009 China's CNPC started building a crude oil port in Sittwe, part of a pipeline project to Kunming in China's Sichuan Province aimed at cutting the long detour oil tankers take through the strategically vulnerable Malacca Strait; a natural gas pipeline is projected to be built as well. Chinese economic immigrants have been pouring into the "golden land," often illegally (it is currently estimated that over 2 million residents are Chinese, ca. 4% of the population, including some 20% of the population of Mandalay). There are risks and draw-backs on either side of this asymmetrical dependency. Though they call each other "brothers" (*paukphaw*), the feeling of the military leadership towards the Chinese is hardly one of unalloyed admiration: aside from historically based mistrust traceable to three decades of sporadic civil war against the Communist Party of Burma (CPB), always closely allied to the CCP (which provided weapons and strate-gic advice) and made up largely of ethnically Sinitic Burmans strategic advice, the SPDC deems the current dependency excessive and dan-gerously one-sided. So far as one can tell, given official constraints on public opinion polling, the Burmese people are even less enthusiastic. The SPDC has undertaken to balance its relationship with China by cultivating contacts with India, Russia, ASEAN and North Korea, but none of these is fully qualified to supplant China's patronage. From Beijing's perspective, the SPDC's seeming inability to maintain polit-ical control without periodic crackdowns that send refugees fleeing into China and incense the international community, leading to pleas for China to somehow make the SPDC behave, is both peripherally destabilizing (with potential spillover on its own minorities) and a diplomatic embarrassment — still more aggravating when the SPDC declines its advice. Thus, while Beijing has taken pains not to publicly criticize the Burmese regime or to allow official criticism or sanctions to emanate from any international organizations in which it has veto power, it would not oppose reform in Burma — indeed (as with

North Korea) quite the contrary, so long as reform does not go so far
as to disenchant the country from its "fraternal" Chinese embrace.
Yet China's influence over Burma is probably even less than in North
Korea, a more effectively centralized dictatorship, as implicitly
acknowledged in their far less vigorous efforts to promote Chinese-
style reform" there.[10]

The Indo–Burmese relationship is to both countries somewhat
evocative of the colonial era, a memory of which Indians are however
more fond than Burmans. India shares a colonial legacy with Burma
as part of the Raj, a "golden land" of opportunity for a sizable Indian
expatriate community, a merchant and professional elite that Burmans
have however distrusted. While relations were quite cordial during
the 1947–1987 period, when U Nu joined Nehru and Sukarno in
support of a "third way" between the two Cold War "camps," in the
wake of the SLORC's Four Eights crackdown, India was disposed to
join the chorus of regional critics, for example, by awarding the
Nehru Prize for International Understanding to Aung San Suu Kyi in
1995 (after all, she had been educated in New Delhi, where her family was close to the Nehru–Gandhi family). But India in the mid-
1990s shifted with its "Look East" policy to a more pragmatic
position, henceforth refusing to endorse sanctions and attempting to
cultivate trade, investment and security cooperation with the SPDC
and to negotiate a joint effort against border insurgencies by ethnic
minorities who found sanctuary in Burma. India saw Burma as a strategic land bridge to Southeast Asia — a bridge the growing Chinese
presence there threatened to block. But according to Renaud
Egreteau, "wooing the generals" has in practice met with "more frustration than success" — India's trade and investment thrust has failed
to make serious inroads on the massive Chinese head start. Nor can
India compete on the same ground diplomatically, given China's
Security Council seat. India's frustration is partly attributable to its
own ambivalence — impugned moral credibility seems to have left a

---

[10] Hak Yin Li and Yongnian Zheng, "Re-interpreting China's Non-Intervention
Policy towards Myanmar: Leverage, Interest and Intervention," *Journal of
Contemporary China* 18(61) (September 2009), pp. 617–637.

bad conscience, voting for example in 2007 in favor of a resolution by the UN Human Rights Council calling for the release of Aung San Suu Kyi and condemning the SPDC's "violent repression" of the so-called "Saffron Uprising" while still refusing to endorse sanctions. The greatest success of New Delhi's Burma initiative has ironically been in the strategic realm, where it has been able to put to rest fears that the PRC had established a "strategic corridor" to the Bay of Bengal where it was constructing listening posts and naval bases in an India-containment scheme — all quite groundless. There has even been some collaboration between the two navies. But all things considered, if India's Burma policy since 1995 is taken as an example of what a more "realist" diplomacy can achieve, it is hardly an inspiring one.

The junta became interested in ASEAN as a way of normalizing its relations with the newly dynamic Southeast Asian subregion and partaking in the investment and growth boom of the 1990s. Despite US opposition, ASEAN was for its part interested in expanding the IGO to include the authoritarian northern tier of the region: since the end of the Cold War, ideological aversions were no longer deemed relevant, and it might be easier to negotiate various authoritarian externalities (drug traffic, refugees) with a fellow member. ASEAN's slogan was "constructive engagement," hoping to socialize these authoritarian regimes by assimilating them to the "ASEAN way." Yet Burma was to prove even harder for ASEAN to assimilate than the Indochinese communist party-states. For its part, the SPDC seems to have hoped to broaden its strategic and economic options and to lure foreign direct investment (FDI), which then had such telling effect in neighboring China, not to mention Malaysia and Thailand. But, alas, Burma's accession to ASEAN coincided with the Asian financial crisis (1997–1998), when FDI was moving out rather than into the region. And given that the junta saw no connection between joining ASEAN and improving its human rights record, participation did not legitimate but only exposed its internal governance to critical scrutiny. Indeed it would seem that Burma's membership (continuing human rights abuses) affected ASEAN more than the reverse, pushing the forum ever further to the left. Only six years after Burma's ASEAN accession, "Black Friday" (viz., the 30 May

1962 Depayin incident) occurred, when a party of leading NLD politicians came under fire and were later arrested, arousing international outcry and prompting ASEAN to issue a joint statement calling for Aung San Suu Kyi's release. This was the first time ASEAN had jointly criticized a fellow member. Yet it may not be the last, as the new ASEAN Charter adopted in 2008 provides for the establishment of a ASEAN Human Rights Board (HRB) for this express purpose (though the Charter is nonbinding, with no enforcement mechanism). Although the SPDC would no doubt appreciate an ASEAN endorsement of their 2010 inaugural elections, if it proceeds as planned with a 90%-plus ratification of a military puppet show, the response is likely to be mixed at best.

In the following chapters the reader will find a comprehensive conspectus of Burma's misadventures in modernization — hampered, we submit, largely by difficulties in forming a coherent national identity. Identity formation is normally achieved early in the developmental process, but Burma was afflicted by unusually deep and intransigent ethnic and religious divisions, aggravated by an inability to reach a consensus on how to deal with them. These divisions, never successfully resolved during the colonial era, were then simply suppressed or papered over by the military regime, creating a superficial and highly fragile unity. Through careful analysis of these splits and their consequences, we hope to illuminate how the formation of a consensual national identity might eventually be achieved, after which the nation can perhaps finally unite and begin to deal constructively with its many other developmental hindrances.

Part A
Mass Politics

Chapter 2

Voting and Violence in Myanmar: Nation Building for a Transition to Democracy

Ian Holliday

Abstract

Democratization studies now highlight potentially derailing problems such as warlike nationalism and violent ethnic conflict. In Myanmar, where ethnic tension runs deep, the risks are especially great. Political reformers should work with the grain of the military junta's planned 2010 general elections and pay close attention to nation building.

Keywords: Burma; democracy; democratisation; Myanmar; nationalism.

A prominent feature of the pessimistic turn recently taken by democratization studies is heightened scrutiny of the problem of transitional violence. In a stream of work published since the mid-1990s, Edward D. Mansfield and Jack Snyder warn of the danger of war in early phases of political reform. Acknowledging that mature democracies are characterized by internal stability and external order, they hold democratizing states to exhibit more belligerent traits. Noting further that transitional violence is generally fueled by aggressive nationalism, they seek through detailed empirical analysis to determine why conflict arises and how it can be minimized or even averted. Their argument is that nationalism is usually not a pre-transitional given that should, as a first priority, be managed through political devices such as federalism and consociationalism or, worse, social mechanisms such as population transfer and ethnic cleansing. Rather, it is a product of elite competition and strategizing in the transition process itself. Once present, it marks a society for generations. Their policy prescription calls for close attention to social foundations before a transition is attempted. In the short run, steps should be taken to contain nationalist conflict. In the long run, a thick network of bonding civic institutions should be created. Only then should a nation turn to democracy.

These themes are of direct relevance to Myanmar. Established as a functioning democracy at independence from Britain in 1948, Burma (as it was then called) saw a barely constitutional caretaker government take office for 18 months in the late 1950s, and witnessed a full-blown military coup in 1962. For nearly half a century since then, it has not succeeded in restoring democracy, though nationwide protests in 1988, a general election in 1990 and a monk-led "Saffron Uprising" in 2007 indicated there was ample support for doing so. Indeed, democracy talk now dominates political debate to such an extent that the military junta has made its own plans for a general election of sorts in 2010. At the same time, the country has long been prone to nationalist conflict. Within months of independence in 1948, Burma was torn apart by ethnic rebellion. For the rest of the period down to the 1962 coup, ethnic issues were so pressing that army leaders used them to justify their power grab. Under successive authoritarian regimes, nationalism has remained a central feature of the political landscape, and to this day low-grade civil war continues to scar peripheral regions. For six decades of this sovereign state, the political agenda has thus been dominated by problems of democratization and nationalist conflict.

In these circumstances, one question that arises is whether the policy recommendations advanced by Mansfield and Snyder might be useful to Myanmar. To answer it, this chapter is divided into six main parts. The first reviews the literature on transitions to democracy, paying particular heed to debates about nationalist violence. It develops prescriptions for peaceful and sustainable change. The second examines democracy in sovereign Burma since the late 1940s. It demonstrates that the country has a searing knowledge of both nationalism and democracy. The third looks at the junta's current road map to democracy in 2010. It shows that the main aim of this road map is to build a façade for entrenched military rule. The fourth considers the applicability to Myanmar of the prescriptions advanced by Mansfield and Snyder. It reveals that there is some support for reading them into a future transition, but also good reason not to. The fifth floats a democratization proposal. It holds nation building to be critical, and considers how appropriate policies might be implemented in the wake of the 2010 general election. The sixth thinks through how outsiders might facilitate a transition to democracy in Myanmar. It makes a case for targeted and sustained intervention.

The argument is that the work of Mansfield and Snyder is centrally relevant to Myanmar. A unitary democracy, though favored by the military junta and designed for implementation through the flawed 2010 general election, is not viable in the long run. Indeed, the generals' polity will be democratic only in name, and will lack much necessary substance. Nevertheless, the political system instituted in 2010 can form the basis for a real transition further down the line. It should be used as a platform for nation-building efforts designed to graft a common national identity on to regional and local affiliations. The chapter therefore focuses on the roles both insiders and outsiders might play in a post-2010 process that seeks first to contain nationalist conflict, second to construct a national civic safety net, and third to make a sustainable transition to democracy.

Voting and Violence

The optimism generated by the breaking of democratization's third wave across East-Central Europe in 1989 has latterly been challenged by more pessimistic analyses. Five years after the George W. Bush administration's attempt to roll out democracy across the Middle East through the triggering effect of regime change in Baghdad, popular sovereignty is viewed as a difficult implant in uncultivated terrain. Moreover, several writers now argue that it is not only in Iraq that problems are found, and posit a general association between democratization and violence.[1] While concerns of this kind reach back at least as far as the early 1970s, they are raised more insistently today by Mansfield and Snyder, who urge policymakers to look beyond democracy's long-term benefits, found internally in ordered societies and externally in the democratic peace.[2] Equally important are short-term costs, notably warlike nationalism and violent ethnic conflict. Transitional societies often erupt into inter-ethnic conflict, as in the former Yugoslavia in the 1990s and Iraq in the present decade. They can also threaten their neighbors. The force that drives this belligerence is usually nationalism.

Snyder's *From Voting to Violence* presents two accounts of why democratization entails a heightened risk of nationalist violence.[3] The popular-rivalries view focuses on atavistic ethnic tensions unleashed by a transition. By contrast, the elite-persuasion view rejects the notion of raw ethnic divisions, holding conflict to be fomented by transitional elites seeking political gain. It is critical to determine which view is correct, for while one points to separating ethnic groups prior to a transition or building ethnic safeguards into a democratic settlement, the other argues for inclusive civic identities and cross-ethnic political alignments during the fluid, early phases of democratization.

---

[1] Samuel P. Huntington, *The Third Wave: Democratization in the Late Twentieth Century* (Norman, OK: University of Oklahoma Press, 1991). Larry Diamond, *Squandered Victory: The American Occupation and the Bungled Effort to Bring Democracy to Iraq* (New York: Times Books, 2005). Amy Chua, *World on Fire: How Exporting Free Market Democracy Breeds Ethnic Hatred and Global Instability* (New York: Doubleday, 2003).

[2] Robert A. Dahl, *Polyarchy: Participation and Opposition* (New Haven, CT: Yale University Press, 1971). Alvin Rabushka and Kenneth A. Shepsle, *Politics in Plural Societies: A Theory of Democratic Instability* (Stanford, CA: Stanford University Press, 1972). Edward D. Mansfield and Jack Snyder, "Democratization and the Danger of War," *International Security* 20:1 (Summer 1995), pp. 5–38. Edward D. Mansfield and Jack Snyder, "Democratization and War," *Foreign Affairs* 74:3 (May 1995), pp. 79–97. Edward D. Mansfield and Jack Snyder, *Electing to Fight: Why Emerging Democracies Go to War* (Cambridge: MIT Press, 2005).

[3] Jack Snyder, *From Voting to Violence: Democratization and Nationalist Conflict* (New York, NY: W.W. Norton, 2000), pp. 31–3.

Snyder himself favors the elite-persuasion argument, contending that mass nationalism has rarely been well developed prior to democratization. Although individuals in non-democratic states may be aware of racial differences, that does not give them political salience for politics is chiefly an elite business. Rather, mass nationalism typically emerges when the bulk of the population gains a political voice in the initial stages of reform. At this point, when political identities are up for grabs, allegiance may develop a nationalist tinge. If it does, it is generally because political leaders seek to mobilize mass support without conceding political power. Whether a nationalist turn actually takes place then depends on their motivation and opportunity to do so. Snyder argues that elite motivation varies in direct proportion to the threat posed by full democracy. He holds that elite opportunity varies in inverse proportion to the strength of political institutions. Militant nationalism is likely to emerge when a political elite feels deeply threatened by popular sovereignty, and political institutions are weak.

On these grounds, Snyder argues against the shortcut of instant mechanical democracy, holding that the social context must be attended to first. At the same time, he rejects early institutionalization of ethnic divisions through devices such as federalism and consociationalism. These, he maintains, should be adopted only as a last resort, for they run the risk of politicizing and locking in inimical cultural distinctions. Similarly, ethnic cleansing should not be a starting point, but rather a reluctant final expedient. In addition, he makes a case for accommodating authoritarian rulers and including them in the transition process in order to minimize their fear and reduce their incentive to play the ethnic card. He also contends that rapid creation of a free press is likely to be counterproductive because open media can readily become vehicles for nationalism.

In short, this prescription for successful democratic transition holds that at the outset all possible means, including coercion, should be used to contain nationalist conflict. At the same time, sustained moves should be made to create a thick network of civic institutions capable of defusing motives for belligerent nationalist mobilization. Only when this social safety net is securely in place should elites embark on a transition. This "sequencing" approach is not without critics. In a recent exchange, Thomas Carothers attacked what he calls the sequencing fallacy, arguing instead for gradualism in tough contexts. "Never put off democracy" is his core message. Similarly, Sheri Berman wrote of the vain hope for "correct" timing, holding that most democracies have difficult beginnings, and noting that democratization will not be completed unless a start is made somewhere. Nonetheless, there is widespread endorsement of the turbulent democratization argument advanced by Mansfield and Snyder, and clear concern about what they term "the lasting birth defects of untimely democratic transitions".[4]

Democracy in Burma

Myanmar is no stranger to democracy, though most of the relevant experience came during its prior incarnation as Burma. An initial transition took place during the decolonization process in the late 1940s, and was sustained for the best part of a decade and a half to the early 1960s. Arguably, a second democratization attempt was made in the mass uprising of 1988, and an echoing third attempt could be found in the monk-led protests of 2007. Any future transition will therefore take place not on virgin territory, but rather on terrain marked and scarred by historical struggles that remain alive in the hearts and minds of the people. Critical to an analysis of the form democratization might take in the future is then an understanding of the past.

Burma's transition in the late 1940s had a pre-history in British attempts to broaden the popular base of the colonial polity and, later, prepare the Burmese for self-rule. In local government, voting was instituted on a limited basis in 1882 and expanded notably through

---

[4] Thomas Carothers, "The 'Sequencing' Fallacy," *Journal of Democracy* 18:1 (January 2007), pp. 12–27. Thomas Carothers, "Misunderstanding Gradualism," *Journal of Democracy* 18:3 (July 2007), pp. 18–22. Sheri Berman, "The Vain Hope for 'Correct' Timing," *Journal of Democracy* 18:3 (July 2007), pp. 14–17. Edward D. Mansfield and Jack Snyder, "The Sequencing 'Fallacy'," *Journal of Democracy* 18:3 (July 2007), pp. 5–9, p. 7.

reforms undertaken in 1921. In national government, the principle of election was introduced in 1909, when the Rangoon Chamber of Commerce was allowed to elect one individual to the 15-member Legislative Council. In 1923, the Legislative Council was expanded to 103 members, of whom 79 were elected through household suffrage at age 18 with no gender discrimination. A further extension of popular control took place in 1937, when Burma was separated from India and became a free-standing British colony. An assessment made by colonial official and scholar J.S. Furnivall in the late 1940s was nevertheless scathing: "the Council had no root among the people ... in reality it represented only the western superstructure divorced from national life." Driving this contempt was a famous analysis that ascribed to colonial rule the creation of a plural society in which a "medley of peoples ... mix but do not combine". For Furnivall, the four main racial groups in British Burma — European, Chinese, Indian and native — were held together solely by an economic nexus and had no social or cultural ties. It was therefore impossible for a national will to develop. As early as 1931 he argued for social reconstruction: "Nationalism in Burma is morally right." However, as events unfolded before and after independence in January 1948, it was not an inclusive Burmese nationalism that emerged. Rather, ethnic divisions came to the fore.[5]

The first elections to the legislature of a sovereign state, held in April 1947, were won by a landslide by the Anti-Fascist People's Freedom League (AFPFL). Led by war hero General Aung San, this was a popular front party built on inter-ethnic alliances formed in 1945 to drive Japan from Burma. An agreement reached with ethnic minority leaders at Panglong in February 1947, and later fed into constitutional clauses, gave Aung San a fair claim to lead the nation. In July 1947, however, he was assassinated alongside several members of his cabinet-in-waiting. In April 1948 a Communist revolt was

---

[5] J. S. Furnivall, *Colonial Policy and Practice: A Comparative Study of Burma and Netherlands India* (Cambridge: Cambridge University Press, 1948), pp. 71–2, 160, 165, 304. J. S. Furnivall, *An Introduction to the Political Economy of Burma* (Rangoon: Burma Book Club, 1931), p. ix.

launched, and soon after ethnic tensions exploded in Karen and other ethnic uprisings. In its early years, sovereign Burma teetered on the verge of collapse as rebel forces threatened the capital Rangoon. "There is little danger that Burma will go Communist, but great danger that it may go to pieces," Furnivall wrote in August 1949.[6]

Ethnic division in Burma in the late 1940s was chiefly the product of British colonial practice in ruling Burma Proper directly, and other parts of the territory indirectly. In those parts lived a set of minority ethnic groups generally held to constitute about one third of the total population. Even constitutional reforms introduced by the British to prepare the colony for self-government were ethnically segregated. "Burma was fitted up with the machinery of responsible government on the fashionable model of western democracy ..." wrote Furnivall; "this however was restricted to Burma proper, excluding the Shan States, Karenni and Tribal Hills."[7] Partial democratization of colonial Burma was thus discriminatory in its effects, as were associated developments in mass political culture. Political evolution ran at different speeds on separate tracks. Notwithstanding initiatives taken at Panglong and elsewhere in the independence phase, those tracks had not been fused by the time of the sovereignty transfer in January 1948.

During Burma's first democratization, nationalist politics derived chiefly from the elite persuasion that Snyder prioritizes. Colonial divide-and-rule tactics, supplemented by often petty squabbling and maneuvering on the part of ethnic leaders, ensured that communal rivalries came to the fore. Violence was then intensified and prolonged by the historical accident that saw part of the Chinese Revolution migrate to Burmese soil in a contingent of 12,000 Kuomintang (KMT) soldiers. Taking refuge in ethnic minority areas, notably Kachin and Shan States on the border with Yunnan Province, KMT troops were supported by US technical advisers employed by the Central Intelligence Agency. In response, as Mary Callahan puts

---

[6] J. S. Furnivall, "Communism and Nationalism in Burma," *Far Eastern Survey* 18:17 (August 24, 1949), pp. 193–7.
[7] Furnivall, *Colonial Policy and Practice*, p. 159.

it, "military and civilian leaders had few choices but to reinvigorate and redeploy the colonial security apparatus to hold together a disintegrating country during the formative period of postcolonial state transformation."[8] Thus came about the rise of a nationalist Burman army — the *Tatmadaw* — as the critical institution within the state. At the same time, the disruption and militarization of Burmese politics prompted ethnic claims made above all by Karens in the late 1940s to surface in Arakan and Shan States and elsewhere in the mid-1950s. Hostility to AFPFL Burmanization policies was a contributory factor.[9]

By the late 1950s, Burmese ethnic divisions were assuming the character of deep popular rivalries. In 1958, constitutional clauses enabling some minority states to trigger autonomy provisions provoked an upswing in revolt. At much the same time, the *Tatmadaw* had its first taste of power through an 18-month caretaker government headed by Chief of Staff General Ne Win. In the early 1960s, when a return to civilian rule generated not only renewed elite bickering and incompetence, but also federation talks, Ne Win's nationalist Burman army seized power in a near-bloodless coup performed on March 2, 1962. His Revolutionary Council soon created a one-party state under the Burmese Socialist Program Party (BSPP). At this point, Burma's experience of functioning democracy ceased, and ethnic divisions intensified still further.

What was arguably a second democratization attempt came more than 25 years later in a national movement for political reform. Following months of upheaval, the Four Eights uprising was launched on 8-8-88, and in bouts of military repression was utterly crushed. In its final crackdown on September 18, 1988, the *Tatmadaw* dissolved the BSPP and created a formal military junta, the State Law and Order Restoration Council (SLORC), chaired by Chief of Staff

---

[8] Mary P. Callahan, *Making Enemies: War and State Building in Burma* (Ithaca, NY: Cornell University Press, 2003), p. 5.

[9] Hugh Tinker, "Burma's Northeast Borderland Problems," *Pacific Affairs* 29:4 (December 1956), pp. 324–46. Geoffrey Fairbairn, "Some Minority Problems in Burma," *Pacific Affairs* 30:4 (December 1957), pp. 299–311.

General Saw Maung. Within days, he publicly committed the regime to organizing national elections. Decrees enabling parties to organize and polling to take place were also issued. However, when the general election eventually held on May 27, 1990, was won by a landslide by the opposition National League for Democracy party (NLD), no power transfer was made.[10]

This second attempt at democratization substantially developed civil society, prompting mass mobilization in urban centers across the land and the formation of more than 200 political parties. However, even though charismatic NLD leader Aung San Suu Kyi followed her father in projecting an image of national unity, deep popular rivalries continued to define the political landscape.[11] Some 40 years on from the first experiment with democracy, and more than 25 years after an aggressively Burman nationalist coup, the country's ethnic divisions were no longer merely the product of elite persuasion. They marked society much more thoroughly than that.

Democratization in Myanmar

The subjugation of Burma's democracy movement in 1988 and the voiding of the election result in 1990 did not remove democratization from the political agenda of the country (renamed Myanmar in July 1989). Rather, they diverted it onto a long and winding road mapped by the military junta. The first major milestone was reached on January 9, 1993, when a National Convention charged with devising principles for the drafting of a new constitution was launched. Despite undertakings given in 1989 and 1990 that its membership would reflect the election results, most of the 700 or so delegates were

[10] Bertil Lintner, *Outrage: Burma's Struggle for Democracy* (Hong Kong: Review Publishing Company, 1989). Derek Tonkin, "The 1990 Elections in Myanmar: Broken Promises or a Failure of Communication?" *Contemporary Southeast Asia* 29:1 (April 2007), pp. 33–54.

[11] Martin Smith, *Burma: Insurgency and the Politics of Ethnicity*, 2nd ed (London: Zed Books, 1999).

nominated by the SLORC.[12] For more than three years they met sporadically to debate constitutional questions within a tight framework imposed by the ruling generals. However, an NLD boycott in November 1995, which the SLORC turned into an expulsion for breach of discipline, plus problems with ethnic representatives regarding government offers on territorial status and autonomy, prompted drafting work to be suspended in April 1996.[13] For years there was little public progress on constitutional matters, though the convention's steering committee met frequently for deliberations.[14]

The issue of democratization returned to the public agenda in August 2003, when military intelligence chief and incoming Prime Minister General Khin Nyunt unveiled a seven-point road map to democracy.[15] This traced a route from the writing of a new charter to a popular referendum and on to democratic elections. On this basis, the National Convention was reassembled in May 2004, this time with more than 1,000 delegates corralled in an isolated facility north of Yangon. Although in October 2004 Khin Nyunt was purged from the junta, now known as the State Peace and Development Council (SPDC), and placed under a long term of house arrest, the road map remains in place and the constitutional process continues to unfold. State suppression of the 2007 Saffron Uprising underscored that the junta would retain control of the democratization process.[16] Subsequently, a constitutional referendum

---

[12] David I. Steinberg, "Myanmar in 1992: Plus Ça Change ...?" *Asian Survey* 33:2 (February 1993), pp. 175–83.

[13] Mary P. Callahan, "Burma in 1995: Looking Beyond the Release of Aung San Suu Kyi," *Asian Survey* 36:2 (February 1996), pp. 158–64, 160.

[14] Tin Maung Maung Than, *State Dominance in Myanmar: The Political Economy of Industrialization* (Singapore: Institute of Southeast Asian Studies, 2007), p. 343.

[15] Kyi Kyi Hla, "Road Map to Democracy in Myanmar," http://www.myanmar.gov. mm/Perspective/persp2003/8-2003/map.htm, accessed November 26, 2009.

[16] Human Rights Watch, *The Resistance of the Monks: Buddhism and Activism in Burma* (New York: Human Rights Watch, 2009). Human Rights Watch, *Burma's Forgotten Prisoners* (New York: Human Rights Watch, 2009). Human Rights Documentation Unit, *Bullets in the Alms Bowl: An Analysis of the Brutal SPDC Suppression of the September 2007 Saffron Revolution* (National Coalition Government of the Union of Burma, 2008).

held in May 2008 in the immediate wake of the devastation wrought by Cyclone Nargis was said to have generated 92% support on a 98% turnout. This paved the way for an SPDC announcement that elections for a "peaceful, modern, developed and discipline-flourishing democratic nation" would take place, as already scheduled, in 2010.

Few are under any illusion about the SPDC's reform process. From the outset the National Convention was constrained by six guiding objectives: "non-disintegration of the Union; non-isintegration of national sovereignty; consolidation and perpetuation of sovereignty; emergence of a genuine multiparty system; development of the eternal principles of justice, liberty, and equality in the state; and participation of the *Tatmadaw* in the leading role of national politics in the state."[17] Later, 104 fixed principles were unveiled: the state president must have military experience; the army will make nominations to 25% of parliamentary seats; military policy and budgets will be beyond executive and legislative control; and so on. All of these key provisions were present in the draft constitution put to the nation in May 2008, and adopted as soon as the referendum had been successfully completed. Considered together, it is clear that their main effect will be to entrench *Tatmadaw* power behind a façade of democracy. At the same time, however, the 2010 general election will constitute the greatest change in domestic politics in more than 20 years. While much of the substance of democracy will be lacking, some form of it will be present in a set of national and regional democratic institutions. Moreover, although these institutions will certainly be controlled by the military, they will nevertheless enable other figures to enter the political arena and make their voices heard.[18]

Debating Democracy in Myanmar

Faced with a sham democratization sponsored by the military junta, opposition forces are currently engaged in fierce internal debate

---

[17] Steinberg, "Myanmar in 1992," p. 178.

[18] International Crisis Group, *Myanmar: Towards the Elections*, Asia Report No. 174 (Brussels: International Crisis Group, 2009).

about how to react and, in particular, whether to participate in the 2010 general election. Throughout 2009, this was a staple of political discourse inside the country. In the course of their debates, groups such as the exiled National Council of the Union of Burma (NCUB) and the Ethnic Nationalities Council (Union of Burma) (ENC) often harked back to proposals long floated for a full democratic transition.[19] Others in the opposition camp also held firm to established positions. Notwithstanding the junta's plans for 2010 and its intention to institute a form of democracy in its own image, it is clear that debate in Myanmar will continue to be informed by these themes.

Looking at proposals made by opposition groups, the core themes can be said to overlap with those of Mansfield and Snyder in four key areas. First, while democracy groups such as the NLD and organizations that developed out of the 1988 student uprising look back to 1990 rather than forward to a fresh poll, a clear priority is still given to elections.[20] Analysts such as Andrew Reynolds *et al.* also take this position.[21] Second, and not necessarily in conflict with this, major groups are generally willing to engage the SPDC in the kind of pacted transition seen in many successful democratizations in recent decades.[22] This is most obviously the case among organizations that accepted the junta's invitation to

---

[19] National Council of the Union of Burma, *(Future) Constitution of the Federal Union of Burma*, http://www.blc-burma.org/pdf/Constitution/ncubcon_e.pdf. Ethnic Nationalities Council (Union of Burma), "Publications," http://www. encburma.org/, accessed November 26, 2009. The ENC was launched as the Ethnic Nationalities Solidarity and Cooperation Committee in August 2001. It changed its name in January 2004.

[20] Central Executive Committee National League for Democracy, "NLD Statement 35/1998," August 21, 1998, http://old.ncgub.net/NLD_Statements/NLD%20 Statement%20%2035,1998.htm, accessed November 26, 2009.

[21] Andrew Reynolds, Alfred Stepan, Zaw Oo and Stephen Levine, "How Burma Could Democratize," *Journal of Democracy* 12:4 (October 2001), pp. 95–108.

[22] Guillermo O'Donnell and Philippe C. Schmitter, *Transitions from Authoritarian Rule: Tentative Conclusions about Uncertain Democracies* (Baltimore, MD: Johns Hopkins University Press, 1986).

attend the National Convention, notably some 20 ethnic minority groups that signed ceasefire deals after 1989 and have since maintained sporadic dialogue channels with the SPDC. However, it is also the case for the NLD, which for many years has espoused a willingness to talk to army leaders without preconditions.[23] Pleas for tripartite dialogue were a uniform response to the 2007 crackdown, and were reiterated by Aung San Suu Kyi during and after the long saga of the trial prompted by John Yettaw's nocturnal swim to her villa in May 2009. Third, opposition groups tend to demand a rapid restoration of liberal freedoms prior to democratization, with Aung San Suu Kyi for instance arguing that the country urgently needs a set of basic human rights.[24] Fourth, opposition leaders insist on institutional safeguards for all major ethnic groups. Here, the outstanding instance is a series of constitutional proposals issued by the ENC, which states that the "ultimate goal ... is to establish a genuine Federal Union of Burma based on the principles of the Panglong Agreement".[25] Its position papers reflect this commitment.

Comparing the positions taken by Myanmar's main opposition forces with the policy prescriptions advanced by Mansfield and Snyder, there is both agreement and disagreement. On engaging authoritarian rulers in a pacted transition, dissent in Myanmar tends to be confined to the small number of ethnic groups that have not yet "returned to the legal fold". It thus seems safe to say that most major opposition groups subscribe to a big tent, broad dialogue approach, and seek tripartite talks embracing key figures from the military led by the SPDC, democracy groups clustered around the NLD, and ethnic nationalities represented by the ENC. This is also the position

---

[23] Aung Shwe, *Letters to a Dictator: Correspondence from NLD Chairman Aung Shwe to the SLORC's Senior General Than Shwe* (Bangkok: All Burma Students' Democratic Front, 1997).

[24] Aung San Suu Kyi, "In Quest of Democracy," in *Freedom from Fear: And Other Writings*, ed. Aung San Suu Kyi, revised edition (London: Penguin, 1995), pp. 167–79.

[25] Ethnic Nationalities Council (Union of Burma), "Objective," http://www.encburma.org/, accessed November 26, 2009.

regularly endorsed by the UN General Assembly since 1994.[26] In the other three areas, however, opposition groups disagree with Mansfield and Snyder. Contrary to the proposal that instant elections be forsworn, they demand a rapid return to the electoral process, by which they mean genuinely free and fair elections and not the managed election scheduled by the junta for 2010. As opposed to the notion that moves to create space for a vibrant media be delayed, they take a maximalist free speech position. This was raised, for instance, as a key demand during the junta's May 2008 constitutional referendum.[27] Instead of the idea that early recourse to institutional devices designed to entrench ethnic divisions be avoided, they promote federalism as a starting point for constitution drafting. Close attention therefore needs to be paid to these issues.

With regard to early elections that conform fully to global democratic standards, the concern is that they may result in ethnic mass mobilization. In the Myanmar case, it might be noted that just as the broad-based AFPFL and successor parties swept the board in elections held during Burma's democratic phase, so the NLD won by a landslide in 1990 with 392 seats from 485 constituencies. Placed second and third were NLD affiliates, the Shan Nationalities League for Democracy (23) and the Arakan League for Democracy (11).[28] However, it would be prudent not to rely too heavily on history repeating itself. The aura of Aung San that hung over many polls in the early independence phase, and the spell cast by her in 1990, may not always be so powerful. Indeed, even before constrained elections take place in 2010, the junta proceeded to precipitate the disbandment of the NLD by in effect barring its loading candidates from contesting the election. While this

---

[26] Note, however, that Reynolds *et al.* hold Myanmar to be an unpromising environment for a pacted transition. Reynolds *et al.*, "How Burma Could Democratize," p. 106.

[27] Mizzima News, "Opposition in Burma Calls for Free Referendum," BurmaNet News, February 21, 2008, http://www.burmanet.org/news/2008/02/21/mizzima-news-opposition-in-burma-calls-for-free-referendum/, accessed November 26, 2009.

[28] Tonkin, "The 1990 Elections in Myanmar," p. 35.

will not eradicate the ideas or individuals that made the NLD such a potent force nearly two decades ago, it could trigger the fragmentation of the opposition movement so clearly desired by the SPDC. Ethnic mass mobilization would then become more probable.

As for the rapid restoration of liberal freedoms, the concern is that a politically immature citizenry served by a jejune media corps could feed nationalist demagogues. In the Myanmar context it is hard to know how to respond to this. On the one hand, the mass of the population is not wholly untutored in democratic norms, and while press freedom in the early independence phase was transformed into rigid censorship soon after the 1962 coup, there was a burst of popular debate in the 1980s that went some way to reviving mass political communication. On the other hand, the unvarying diet of regime propaganda on which citizens have long been force-fed is already so nationalistic that it is hard to see how things could get worse. Notwithstanding the negative connotations of the Maoist historical analogy, the best policy would thus seem to be letting a hundred flowers bloom and a hundred schools of thought contend. In this way, people across the land can take collective ownership of democracy. Moreover, the stories and pictures transmitted from Yangon during the 2007 Saffron Uprising suggest that technological advance has made such a policy unavoidable. At the same time, of course, it would be advisable as a matter of urgency to train up a fresh cohort of professional journalists capable of making objective and responsible contributions to political debate.

Regarding early recourse to ethnic safeguards, such as federalism and consociationalism, the concern is that a transition should not begin by entrenching social divisions. Rather, the first step should be to build an inclusive nation embracing all ethnic communities. Only if this fails should institutional protections be put in place. In the Myanmar context, this is the most contentious matter of all. Ever since the British decided at the time of final annexation in 1886 to rule Burma Proper directly and the Frontier Areas indirectly, the territory has been parceled out along ethnic lines. The parcels have changed over time, and the seven states and seven divisions created by

the socialist constitution of 1974, still in place today, bear little relation to ethnic areas established by the British. Nevertheless, the principle of institutional separation by ethnicity was ingrained during the
colonial period. It was reinforced by traumatic events in World War II
that saw Burma's ethnic groups fighting each other. It was reified by
the agreement struck at Panglong in 1947 and inscribed in the blood
of fallen comrades as low-intensity civil war broke out across the
country after independence. Only with the spread of ceasefire deals
from 1989 was a fragile peace established between majority and
minority ethnic groups.[29] Today, even the military junta subscribes to
a form of symmetrical federalism for Myanmar.[30] It would therefore
seem that popular rivalries are now too entrenched, and ethnic separatism already too institutionalized, for this concern to be relevant.

A Democratization Proposal

Policy prescriptions derived from elsewhere cannot be read directly
into the Myanmar context. Rather, its democratization agenda needs
to be both informed by comparative experience, and sensitive to the
local context. Broadly, the proposal that emerges is for a pacted transition based on tripartite talks between elites drawn from the military,
democracy groups and ethnic nationalities. While issues such as
democracy and federalism can be placed on the table from the outset,
elites should as a first priority attend to social underpinnings and seek
to create an inclusive national polity.

   In a context of ethnic tension sparked by elite persuasion in the
colonial period and hardened into popular rivalry in the independence phase, a multifaceted nation-building project will be needed.
On a defensive note, it should do all it can to contain ethnic conflict.
On a constructive note, it should comprise humanitarian programs
to address the worst forms of human suffering, economic programs
to oversee national economic renewal, social programs to embed

---

[29] Ashley South, "Political Transition in Myanmar: A New Model for Democratization,"
Contemporary Southeast Asia 26:2 (August 2004), pp. 233–55.
[30] Reynolds *et al.*, "How Burma Could Democratize," pp. 103–4.

cultural diversity and respect within a unified national community, and political programs to foster real national reconciliation through a truth commission and lustration system.[31] Together, these strands should seek to create a civic safety net articulated around the concept of one nation, within which subsidiary ethnic identities and commitments are couched. A re-examination of the modern nation's founding myth in renewed debate about the "spirit of Panglong", for which Matthew J. Walton calls, should be central to this exercise.[32]

Paralleling elite activity in the country's pacted transition, the critical role of an already emergent civil society should be recognized.[33] To boost popular participation, shackles that currently restrict civil actors should be removed, and rights to free speech and a free press restored. Quality training programs for journalists should be rapidly launched in order to build a professional media corps. A core theme should be bonding the nation, with a reassessment of Panglong again placed at the heart of public debate. Only within this overarching framework should subsidiary loyalties be encouraged to develop. The discipline and unity regularly demanded by both military and opposition leaders should be cast as a key theme of national reconciliation and renewal.[34]

The broad expectation should be that no early attempt will be made to reform the legislature slated for election in 2010, and that genuinely free and fair national polls will only be held several years

[31] Roman David and Ian Holliday, "Set the Junta Free: Pre-Transitional Justice in Myanmar's Democratization," *Australian Journal of Political Science* 41:1 (March 2006), pp. 91–105.
[32] Matthew J. Walton, "Ethnicity, Conflict, and History in Burma: The Myths of Panglong," *Asian Survey* 48:6 (November/December 2008), pp. 889–910.
[33] South, "Political Transition in Myanmar." Brian Heidel, *The Growth of Civil Society in Myanmar* (Bangalore: Books for Change, 2006). David I. Steinberg, "Civil Society and Legitimacy: The Basis for National Reconciliation in Burma/Myanmar," in *Myanmar's Long Road to National Reconciliation*, ed. Trevor Wilson (Singapore: Institute of Southeast Asian Studies, 2006), pp. 149–76.
[34] Aung San Suu Kyi, "Speech to a Mass Rally at the Shwedagon Pagoda," in *Freedom from Fear: And Other Writings*, ed. Aung San Suu Kyi, pp. 192–8.

into the transition process. From the outset, elites should urge citizens to be patient and constructive in jointly committing to the preparatory civic work that will enable full democratization to take place. At the same time, it should be widely understood that when proper elections eventually are held, they will be for a polity that institutionalizes both power-sharing mechanisms and safeguards for minority groups. As Reynolds *et al.* argue, these requirements point to a parliamentary system informed by principles of proportional representation and asymmetrical federalism.[35]

This, then, is the proposal in outline. The key question is whether it is feasible. While there are multiple reasons to think not, there are also grounds for believing it just might be. Among the three major sets of stakeholders, the *Tatmadaw* is clearly critical.[36] Snyder holds that belligerent nationalism is most likely to emerge when an established elite feels threatened by popular sovereignty, and restraining and channeling political institutions are weak. This precisely captures the situation of Myanmar's officer corps. Ideologically, it is defined by a commitment to one nation. In the turbulent years of the 1940s it set itself up as defender of the nation, and today it seeks aggressively to impose concepts of unity on a subject population.[37] It seems unlikely under any future leadership to retreat from a position that runs so deep in its culture. Top generals also have extensive economic interests at stake. In addition, they see little reason to change course when on the one hand they believe themselves to be winning, and on the other they fear oblivion should they relinquish control. Small wonder, then, that the junta showed during and after the Saffron Uprising of 2007 that it has no intention of opening up the political process. As Information Minister Brigadier-General Kyaw Hsan put it in

---

[35] Reynolds *et al.* "How Burma Could Democratize."

[36] Mary Callahan, "Myanmar's Perpetual Junta," *New Left Review* 60 (November/December 2009), pp. 27–63.

[37] Ian Holliday, "National Unity Struggles in Myanmar: A Degenerate Case of Governance for Harmony in Asia," *Asian Survey* 47:3 (May/June 2007), pp. 374–92.

December 2007, "no assistance or advice from other persons is required".[38]

It thus seems probable that at least for as long as Senior General Than Shwe remains paramount leader, no change in state policy can be expected. At the same time, however, it is necessary to prepare for the moment when this ageing leader quits the stage, and a window of opportunity cracks open. Then, the notion of a robust parliamentary system informed by principles of proportional representation and asymmetrical federalism will certainly be seen as a challenge to the military leaders' ideological bottom line. At the same time, however, they will take comfort from the insistence that nation building be undertaken first, and that thoroughgoing review of the limited democracy they plan to bring into being in 2010 be held in abeyance for several years. Furthermore, the concern that existing leaders might play the nationalist card when threatened by full democracy is addressed by making them central to the transition process. Indeed, this policy prescription is clearly an extension of the junta's road map to democracy, for even the elections scheduled for 2010 will institute a very limited form of power sharing between the military, the democratic opposition and ethnic nationalities. In these circumstances, there is a chance that the next generation of military leaders will view this proposal as the best hope for securing their interests in the long run.

Among the democracy groups, the NLD retains a core position and consistently indicates a willingness to reach out to the junta in implementing a transition to democracy. In special statements released in February and April 2006, for instance, it first held that if the 1990 parliament were convened it would recognize the junta as an interim government charged with overseeing a transition, and then appealed to military leaders to work with it to facilitate humanitarian aid flows

---

[38] New Light of Myanmar, "Minister for Information Brig-Gen Kyaw Hsan Speaks at Press Conference 2/2007," BurmaNet News, December 3, 2007, http://www.burmanet.org/news/2007/12/03/new-light-of-myanmar-minister-for-information-brig-gen-kyaw-hsan-speaks-at-press-conference-22007/#more-10269, accessed November 26, 2009.

to the population. In a statement released by Aung San Suu Kyi through UN envoy Ibrahim Gambari in November 2007, similar commitments were visible.[39] In remarks made during and after the Yettaw trial in 2009, the NLD leader's position remained the same. By and large, each of these initiatives was dismissed by the SPDC. Nevertheless, they demonstrate a degree of flexibility on the part of the NLD that could enable it to sign up for the post-2010 proposal sketched here, particularly as civil rights and, eventually, free elections form major parts of it.

Among the ethnic nationalities, the ENC is likely to react negatively to the proposal to prioritize overarching nation-building and delay the introduction of both full democracy and federalism until this has been at least partially accomplished. Indeed, the junta's attempts in 2009 to turn ethnic militias into Border Guard Force battalions integrated into *Tatmadaw* command structures generated considerable friction in eastern Myanmar, and triggered outbreaks of fighting along the borders with both Thailand and China. More widely, in any transition there is certain to be tension between local ethnic elites and expatriate ethnic groups, which will substantially complicate any nation-building project. However, if talk of national reconciliation is to have any meaning, ideas along the lines of this proposal must be considered. The key point is that nationalism cannot be expected to come out in the wash of a transition to democracy. Rather, early and sustained efforts have to be made to avert conflict. In the Myanmar context, where ethnic divisions already run deep,

---

[39] Aung Hla Tun, "Myanmar Opposition Offers to Recognize Military Rule," Reuters, February 14, 2006, http://www.burmanet.org/news/2006/02/14/reuters-myanmar-opposition-offers-to-recognize-military-rule-aung-hla-tun/#more-1784. National League for Democracy Central Executive Committee, "Special Statement," BurmaNet News, April 21, 2006, http://www.burmanet.org/news/2006/04/21/national-league-for-democracy-central-executive-committee-special-statement/#more-3221. Associated Press, "Text of Aung San Suu Kyi's Statement," BurmaNet News, November 9, 2007, http://www.burmanet.org/news/2007/11/09/associated-press-text-of-aung-san-suu-kyis-statement/#more-9888, accessed November 26, 2009.

attending to ways of managing and channeling nationalist conflict is a critical first step.

Furthermore, looking beyond elite positions to the situation currently faced by ordinary people, it seems that a constituency might exist for the proposal sketched here. While circumstances are diverse, three features are common to the lives of almost all citizens. First, as Callahan noted in a recent analysis of ethnic minority states, "Political power is in the hands of specialists in violence." Her earlier work showed this also to be true of the country as a whole.[40] Second, poverty is rife and human security is low.[41] Third, identity is contested at many levels, with the result that internal debates take place even among members of the same broad ethnic group.[42] It is thus necessary to develop a set of incentives capable of drawing many actors, both elite and mass, into a transition articulated around the twin themes of peace and democracy. The greatest incentives lie in a project that releases individuals from oppressive violence and helps them rebuild shattered communities. Only a multifaceted nation-building project can do this.

The power of such incentives is clear from individual testimony. Particularly among ethnic minority groups, so many years of civil war have made peace and development core demands. Alan Saw U testifies, for instance, that "Many Karen people in Myanmar have become very weary and fed up with the prolonged civil war and its consequences. They are of the opinion that it is imperative to get beyond their frustration, anger and helplessness and to direct their energies to mobilizing their cultural wisdom, religious knowledge and social

---

[40] Mary P. Callahan, *Political Authority in Burma's Ethnic Minority States: Devolution, Occupation, and Coexistence* (Washington, DC: East-West Center Washington, 2007), p. 3. Callahan, *Making Enemies.*

[41] Helen James, *Security and Sustainable Development in Myanmar* (London: Routledge, 2006). Tin Maung Maung Than, "Mapping the Contours of Human Security Challenges in Myanmar," in *Myanmar: State, Society and Ethnicity*, eds. Narayanan Ganesan and Kyaw Yin Hlaing (Singapore: Institute of Southeast Asian Studies, 2007), pp. 172–218.

[42] Ashley South, "Karen Nationalist Communities: The 'Problem' of Diversity," *Contemporary Southeast Asia* 29:1 (April 2007), pp. 55–76.

understanding so as to constructively work towards a better future."[43] Reports produced by indigenous NGOs also articulate a crying need for peace as the foundation for change. Aung San Suu Kyi has long written of the pervasive fear that stalks the land.[44] There is thus a possibility that the linked prospects of peaceful reconstruction at the local level, cultural renaissance at the regional level and genuine reconciliation at the national level could persuade even the leaders of ethnic nationalities to sit at the negotiating table. The political space created by ceasefire deals, which is already opening up new opportunities in Myanmar's borderlands, indicates that this possibility is real.[45]

Many objections can be raised. There is always a chance that even the post-Than Shwe army elite will be obdurate and defensive. At the same time, however, preparations must be made for a scenario in which the officer corps starts to explore new ways forward. Equally, it is possible that democrats will refuse to delay a shift from the junta's sham democracy to free and fair elections, and that ethnic minorities will dismiss a nation-building project. Yet neither broad group has taken a definitive position, and each has indeed expressed a willingness to compromise. Space thus exists to learn from elsewhere. Comparative work undertaken by Mansfield and Snyder shows that before embarking on a full transition, it is critically important to contain nationalist conflict. While any actual process of political reform will be dynamic and unpredictable, the probability of success will grow if early energies are devoted to forging popular commitment to one nation.

---

[43] Alan Saw U, "Reflections on Confidence-building and Cooperation among Ethnic Groups in Myanmar: A Karen Case Study," in *Myanmar: State, Society and Ethnicity*, eds. Narayanan Ganesan and Kyaw Yin Hlaing, pp. 219–35.

[44] Aung San Suu Kyi, "Freedom from Fear." Also see Christina Fink, *Living Silence: Burma under Military Rule* (London: Zed Books, 2001).

[45] Martin Smith, "Ethnic Participation and National Reconciliation in Myanmar: Challenges in a Transitional Landscape," in *Myanmar's Long Road to National Reconciliation*, ed. Trevor Wilson (Singapore: Institute of Southeast Asian Studies, 2006), pp. 38–74. Ashley South, "Conflict and Displacement in Burma/Myanmar," in *Myanmar: The State, Community and the Environment*, eds. Monique Skidmore and Trevor Wilson (Canberra: ANU E Press and Asia Pacific Press, 2007), pp. 54–81. Callahan, *Political Authority in Burma's Ethnic Minority States*.

Inside Myanmar, then, opposition forces should participate in the 2010 general election, and use the framework of institutions formed as a platform for roundtable nation-building efforts conducted in conjunction with the still dominant military elite. Initially, issues concerning reform of the discipline-flourishing democracy that will come into being in 2010 should be set to one side while nation-building holds center stage. Only when real progress has been registered here should attention turn to a full transition.

A Role for Outsiders

If this proposal is pursued, outsiders must play a major facilitative role.[46] To date, such actors have divided into two broad camps. Engagers, often located in Asia, prefer to maintain dialogue channels and create incentives for the junta to take the path of reform. Isolationists, often based in North America and Europe, seek through political and economic sanctions to force reform on the junta. While there are nuances on both sides, the key point is that neither has registered much progress to date, and in the aftermath of the Saffron Uprising of 2007 neither looks like doing so in the foreseeable future. The question is therefore whether this proposal offers a better way forward. If it does, the issue is how outsiders might best become involved in the transition process.

Among engagers, the proposal is likely to gain firm support. In a region where sub-state nationalism is frowned upon and rapid shifts from authoritarianism to democracy are by no means the first priority, there is every reason to believe the gradualist approach promoted here would be embraced. That is important, for China, India, Japan and leading members of the Association of Southeast Asian Nations (ASEAN) form the critical external context for political reform inside Myanmar. Working with and through the 14-nation Group of Friends assembled by UN Secretary-General Ban Ki-moon in December 2007, there are many levers they can pull to encourage major stakeholders to

---

[46] Compare South, "Political Transition in Myanmar."

commit to reform.[47] Most strategically placed is China, which is already a key political and economic player inside the country. With its extreme distaste for splittist tendencies and its concern to bring into being a stable and prosperous Myanmar as a means of opening up western parts of its own nation, Beijing could be expected to invest heavily in this proposal. Although the North Korea experience has given it little faith in multiparty talks, there remains a possibility that China would be prepared to join discussions among key regional powers designed to mirror and facilitate the process of political dialogue inside Myanmar.[48] India and ASEAN would also be supportive.

Among isolationists, there would be concern about strands in the proposal that engage the military, undercut ethnic nationality claims and delay elections. Indeed, ever since the late 1980s a staple of political commentary in North America and Europe has been the need for a swift return to democracy, and few look beyond elite-level talks to social underpinnings and nation-building projects. At the same time, however, there is a recognition that little has worked in Myanmar, and that policymakers must move beyond established positions. Hillary Clinton made this point early in her tenure as Secretary of State. The Obama administration endorsed it through a policy review announced in September 2009, and tentative contacts were established immediately thereafter. On these grounds alone there could be support for this proposal. Moreover, once it becomes clear that a global consensus was a real possibility, and that on this basis the international community could start to confront major humanitarian problems inside the country, the support would become more firm. In a context where sanctions policies led from the US have demonstrably failed, this proposal would offer a fresh start.[49]

[47] UN News Centre, "Secretary-General Convenes Meeting of 'Group of Friends' on Myanmar," December 19, 2007, http://www.un.org/apps/news/story.asp?NewsID=25140&Cr=myanmar&Cr1, accessed November 26, 2009.
[48] International Crisis Group, *China's Myanmar Dilemma*, Asia Report No. 177 (Brussels: International Crisis Group, 2009).
[49] Ian Holliday, "Rethinking the United States's Myanmar Policy," *Asian Survey* 45:4 (July/August 2005), pp. 603–21.

In practical terms, the contributions outsiders might make are legion. Among states, the possibility of multiparty talks has already been mentioned. While it would be useful if these could take place within a UN framework, that is not a necessity. To encourage reform efforts, supportive states could also gradually open up preferential trade policies. If times of difficulty were encountered, they might have to consider intervening to keep the peace while nation-building efforts got underway.[50] Among non-states, aid agencies from around the world could perform key tasks in responding to humanitarian disaster and building indigenous capacity.[51] The standard caveats about appropriateness and sensitivity always need to be borne in mind, but no more so in Myanmar than anywhere else. Also in the non-state sector, critical contributions could be made by corporations, particularly those that subscribe to an agenda of corporate social responsibility and are keen to work in settings where they really can make a difference.[52] Many reforms are of course required for Myanmar to become a viable place to do business.[53] The legal framework is inadequate, corruption is rife and skill levels are low. However, if the country's internal and external environments can be aligned through parallel dialogue processes, it should be possible to make a start in introducing necessary changes.

[50] Paul Collier, *The Bottom Billion: Why the Poorest Countries Are Failing and What Can Be Done about It* (Oxford: Oxford University Press, 2007).

[51] International Crisis Group, *Burma/Myanmar after Nargis: Time to Normalise Aid Relations*, Asia Report No. 161 (Brussels: International Crisis Group, 2008). South, "Political Transition in Myanmar," pp. 249–52. Karl Dorning, "Creating an Environment for Participation: International NGOs and the Growth of Civil Society in Burma/Myanmar," in *Myanmar's Long Road to National Reconciliation*, ed. Wilson, pp. 188–217.

[52] Ian Holliday, "Doing Business with Rights Violating Regimes: Corporate Social Responsibility and Myanmar's Military Junta," *Journal of Business Ethics* 61:4 (November 2005), pp. 329–42. Ian Holliday, "The Yadana Syndrome? Big Oil and Principles of Corporate Engagement in Myanmar," *Asian Journal of Political Science* 13:2 (December 2005), pp. 29–51.

[53] Sean Turnell, "Burma's Economy 2004: Crisis Masking Stagnation," in *Myanmar's Long Road to National Reconciliation*, ed. Wilson, pp. 77–97. Sean Turnell, "Burma's Insatiable State," *Asian Survey* 48:6 (November/December 2008), pp. 958–76.

Above all, external engagement in a full Myanmar transition needs to be targeted and sustained. While nation-building talks gather pace, it must do all it can to contain nationalist conflict and sponsor disarmament and demobilization. At the same time, it must work with local people and agencies to build a thick network of bonding civic institutions to function as a social safety net for democracy. It must keep the leading actors in a pacted full transition focused on the task at hand, while progressively expanding the incentives for citizens to keep faith with the project. If all this can be brought to pass, a real chance of fundamental change will open up.

Conclusion

Myanmar has tasted democracy in the past and many of its people yearn to do so again in the near future. Now that the military junta has scheduled a general election for 2010, the best route lies in working with the grain of the ruling generals' road map. While the political system formed in 2010 will fall far short of the demands made by opposition forces, it will generate a platform for the kind of gradualist change that comparative analysis shows is essential for divided societies. By expanding the sphere of political legitimacy beyond a very small elite, it will enable actors from across the political spectrum to come together and work on the single most important challenge facing the country: building a common sense of identity. To succeed, they will need initially to overlook the deficiencies of discipline-flourishing democracy, and focus on containing nationalist conflict and creating a participatory and inclusive nation. Only when some success has been registered here should they look beyond the limited 2010 legislature, and press for free and fair elections to a parliamentary system informed by principles of proportional representation and asymmetrical federalism.

Acknowledgments

Work on this chapter was supported by an award from the Research Grants Council of the Hong Kong Special Administrative Region, China [Project No. HKU 744407H]. The author is grateful for editorial guidance provided by Lowell Dittmer. The usual disclaimer applies.

Chapter 3

Ethnic Conflict in Burma: The Challenge of Unity in a Divided Country

Tom Kramer

Abstract

Burma has been afflicted by ethnic conflict and civil war since independence in 1948, exposing it to one of the longest-running armed conflicts in the world. Ethnic minorities have long felt marginalized and discriminated against. Minority rights were further curtailed after the 1962 coup. Ceasefires were negotiated with most of the ethnic armies after 1989, but the latter retained their arms and much of their autonomy. The SPDC has been keen to disarm the ethnics and incorporate their armies into border guard units, but the latter have resisted (with Chinese support) and the issue remains unresolved.

Keywords: Karen; Kachin; Wa; Shan; Rohingyas; Border Guard Force.

Burma/Myanmar[1] has been afflicted by ethnic conflict and civil war since independence in 1948, exposing it to one of the longest-running armed conflicts in the world. Ethnic minorities have long felt marginalized and discriminated against. The situation worsened after the military coup in 1962, when minority rights were further curtailed. The military government has as yet refused to take the political demands of ethnic minorities into account, for the most part treating ethnic issues as a military and security issue.

---

[1] In 1989 the military government changed the official name of the country from "Burma" to "Myanmar". Using either "Burma" or "Myanmar" has since become a highly politicized issue. The UN uses "Myanmar", but it is not commonly used elsewhere in material written in English about the country. Therefore "Burma" will be used throughout this chapter. This is not meant to be a political statement.

The civil war, which has lasted for 60 years, has caused great suffering for the peoples of Burma. The fighting has mainly taken place in ethnic minority areas, the population there suffering most. Decades of conflict have driven the civilian population into absolute poverty and despair. Military campaigns of the Burma Army (the *Tatmadaw*) against ethnic armed opposition groups have been accompanied by serious human rights violations against the civilian population. As a result, tens of thousands of lives have been lost, and hundreds of thousands of people have fled their villages to seek refuge in the forests or in neighboring countries. Fighting has also spilled across international borders, further creating regional instability.

International attention has been mostly focused on the plight of Aung San Suu Kyi and the democratic opposition in Rangoon, ignoring the crisis situation of the minorities. Ethnic conflict needs to be addressed in order to solve the political deadlock in Burma. Without doing so, the prospects for peace and democracy remain grim.

Ethnic Diversity

Burma is a diverse and divided country with many different ethnic groups, each with its own distinctive culture and traditions. There is a wide range of different languages and dialects. Ethnic minority groups make up some 30 to 40% of the population. One should note that there are no reliable population figures for Burma and all data should be treated with great caution, as the last serious attempt at an ethnic survey was carried out by the British colonial administration in 1931.

The State Peace and Development Council (SPDC) officially recognizes 135 different ethnic groups divided into eight major "national ethnic races": Burman, Mon, Karen, Kayah, Shan, Kachin, Chin and Rakhine.[2] However, ethnic opposition groups reject this classification.

---

[2] "Political Situation of Myanmar and its Role in the Region," Lt. Col. Hla Min, Office of Strategic Studies, Ministry of Defence, Union of Myanmar, October 2000, pp. 95–99.

They feel the military government is exaggerating the problem to argue that military force is needed to keep the country together.[3]

Most of the majority population, which is ethnically Burman[4] and predominantly Buddhist, lives in the central plains and valleys. In contrast, most ethnic minority groups live in the rugged hills and mountains surrounding the central lowlands. However, some minority groups such as the Shan, Mon and Rakhine are also Buddhist, residing in the valleys and plains where they once had powerful kingdoms.

Some of the ethnic minority groups living in the hills and mountains are also Buddhist, such as the eastern Karen, and the Pao and Palaung in Shan State. There are a large number of Christians among the Kachin, Kayah, Chin, and to a lesser extent within Karen ethnic groups. Furthermore there is a significant Muslim population, discriminated against not only by the government but also by the general population. The most abused is the Muslim community known as the Rohingya in northern Rakhine State.

The controversial 2008 Constitution divides the country into seven "regions", seven "ethnic states" and six new "self-administered areas". The regions are predominantly inhabited by the Burman majority population. The states are Mon, Karen, Kayah, Shan, Kachin, Chin and Rakhine, reflecting the main minority groups in the country. They comprise 57% of the land area. The self-administered areas are: the Naga Self-Administered Zone in Sagaing Division; the Danu Self-Administered Zone; the Pao Self-Administered Zone; the Palaung Self-Administered Zone; the Kokang Self-Administered Zone; and the Wa Self-Administered Division in Shan State. There are many other ethnic groups, such as the Akha, Lahu, Intha and others in Shan State. They have not been given special status under the new constitution.

Neither the regions nor the states are monoethnic, nor can they be seen to represent a whole ethnic group. There is a substantial non-Burman population in some of the regions, such as the Karen in the

---

[3] See, for instance, Harn Yawnghwe, "The Non-Burman Ethnic Peoples of Burma," Paper presented at Workshop on Burma in Oslo, December 8, 2001.
[4] I refer to "Burman" as a member of the ethnic group, and to "Burmese" as a citizen of the country.

Irrawaddy Region. Shan State has many other ethnic groups, such as the Akha, Lahu and Intha. At the same time there is a significant Shan population in Kachin State, and many Burmans live in the cities and larger towns of Kachin and Shan States.

Conflict Actors

At first glance, Burma's political conflict looks extremely complicated, as there are a large number of conflict actors. Apart from the military government, there is a myriad of armies and militias, some still fighting the military government, others having reached a ceasefire agreement. There is also a host of opposition groups based inside and outside the country. Furthermore, many of these groups and organizations have suffered from splits and factional infighting, often resulting in the formation of new organizations.

But if one takes a closer look, three main conflict actors can be identified: the military government, in power since 1962, currently called the SPDC; the democratic opposition, led by the National League for Democracy (NLD), which won a landslide victory in the 1990 elections; and ethnic minority groups, comprising a wide range of different organizations mostly formed along ethnic lines, including political parties, civil society organizations, and armed opposition groups, some of which have been fighting the central government since independence.

The UN General Assembly has since 1994 called for "tripartite dialogue" between the military, democratic opposition and ethnic minorities to solve the political problems in Burma. This notion has been supported by the latter two groups. Officially all conflict parties have stated publicly that they aim to work towards a democratic Burma. But until today the military government has refused to come to the negotiation table, and the political deadlock remains.

The conflict itself is about two main issues: the nature of the state of Burma and how state power (dominated today by the Burman majority) from the center relates to the periphery, inhabited by a wide range of different ethnic minority groups; and governance, as the military's control over all powers, executive, legislative and judicial, is contested by all other actors.

Independence and Civil War

The map of contemporary Burma was created under British colonial rule, its mountain borderlines — drawn with no consideration of the populations living there — today separating the country from Thailand, China and India. Hence various ethnic minority groups can now be found on both sides of the border. There are substantial Mon, Karen and Shan communities in Thailand, Naga and Chin also live in India, and ethnic Kachin (*Jingphaw*) can be found in India (*Singpho*) and in China (*Jingpho*). However, there have been no strong pan-ethnic movements among these groups.

During colonial rule the traditional leaders of central Burma were removed and replaced by British administrators. In contrast, local rulers of the hill areas were allowed to continue governing their areas relatively undisturbed, and were subordinate only to the governor. This dichotomy would have major consequences for future relations between the Burman majority and the ethnic minorities, planting seeds of resentment. The minorities got more political autonomy, but less development.

Burman nationalists were chagrined by the recruitment of mostly ethnic minority groups such as the Karen, Chin and Kachin rather than the Burman majority into the British colonial army. The success of British and American missionaries in converting large numbers of ethnic minorities to Christianity was also regarded with suspicion. During World War II these tensions increased. The Karen and Kachin were recruited to aid British and American Special Forces against Japanese troops behind enemy lines. Meanwhile, Burman nationalists led by Aung San, hoping to gain independence with the help of the Japanese, supported them in their campaign to push the British colonial government out of Burma.

Strong Burman resentment also grew against the Indians who took up important positions in the colonial administration. The immigration of many Indian and Chinese laborers, some of whom became successful businessmen, only added to these sentiments.

During the post-war negotiations, Burman nationalists advocated independence as soon as possible. For ethnic minority leaders, the key issues were self-determination and autonomy to safeguard their position in the future state. In 1947, the Panglong Agreement, intended as a basis for the new Union of Burma, was signed between Burman politicians and ethnic minority representatives from some of the hill areas. However, the agreement was inconsistent and not inclusive, with different groups obtaining different rights and some remaining unrepresented at the Panglong meeting. As a result, many issues were deferred for future resolution.

This situation was ripe for civil war, which erupted shortly after independence in January 1948. Within a year, the whole country was in turmoil. The Communist Party of Burma (CPB) went underground to fight the central government, which suffered mutinies in the army. Several newly formed ethnic minority nationalist movements, spearheaded by the Karen National Union (formed in 1947), took up arms to defend their communities in this chaotic period and to press their demands for more autonomy and equal rights in the Union.

The situation was further worsened in 1949 by the invasion of Kuomintang remnants, who were fleeing Mao Zedong's forces, into northeast Shan State. The ethnic minority regions have suffered the double curse of years of government neglect and the destruction wrought by the civil war, most of which has been waged there.

Military Rule

In 1962 General Ne Win staged a coup against the democratically elected government and created a one-party state led by the Burma Socialist Programme Party. The constitution was abrogated, opposition leaders put behind bars and any attempt to politically organize was severely repressed. All large industries and business enterprises were nationalized under the "Burmese Way to Socialism", the party's official doctrine. Burma was to become self-sufficient, and the generals isolated the country from the outside world. The country has been under military rule ever since.

By this time, the civil war had spread to Kachin and Shan States, where the Kachin Independence Organization (KIO) and Shan State Army also started armed uprisings. Fueled by growing dissatisfaction among the Kachin and Shan populations over the unequal position of ethnic minorities in the Union of Burma, they rapidly expanded their organizations and territories.

By the 1970s, two major opposition alliances had emerged. Along the Thai border, ethnic armed groups set up the National Democratic Front (NDF), which maintained a pro-West and anti-communist policy. During the Cold War, Thailand was seen by US policymakers as the "last domino" against communism in the region. While Burma was officially neutral, policymakers in Bangkok and Washington feared that it would not be able to withstand the "communist threat". Until the end of the 1980s, almost all territory along the Thai border was under the de-facto control of the NDF's Mon, Karen, Karenni and Shan armed opposition groups. They administered their own areas and were given tacit support by the Thai authorities. The Karen National Union (KNU) President General Bo Mya once described his organization as a kind of "foreign legion" for Thailand, guarding its borders against communism and preventing a link between the Thai and Burmese communist parties.[5]

The other major alliance, the Communist Party of Burma (CPB), was supported by China. Initially Chinese support for its Burmese sister party was limited, as China maintained official relations with the neutral Burmese government. However, relations with China changed after the military coup in 1962, and deteriorated rapidly following the 1967 anti-Chinese riots in Rangoon. The Chinese government felt that these were instigated, or at least tolerated, by Ne Win's military government. China subsequently put its full weight behind the CPB. In January 1968, thousands of CPB troops invaded northern Shan State from the neighboring Yunnan Province in China. Making alliances with local ethnic Kokang, Wa and Shan leaders, the CPB was soon able to overrun Burma Army outposts and establish a large liberated area encompassing nearly the entire Chinese border. The CPB succeeded in making alliances with some ethnic armed opposition groups, offering Chinese arms in return for political control.

---

[5] Martin Smith, *Burma, Insurgency and the Politics of Ethnicity* (London and New Jersey: Zed Books, 1999) p. 297.

By the end of the 1980s almost all border regions were controlled by armed opposition groups. These groups established liberated areas and set up their own administrations. The CPB, with Chinese support, was the largest military opposition group in the country, rivaled in strength by the pro-West NDF. Except for a brief accord reached in 1986, the two never established a military alliance. The gap between them was not only due to ideology (communism versus capitalism), but also reflected different geopolitical interests between China and Thailand (allied with the US). NDF parties were also angered by the Burman-led CPB support for left-wing movements within their ranks, which led to political factionalism and ethnic splits.

Ethnic Minority Organisations

Most of the many ethnic minority organisations in today's Burma are formed along ethnic lines. Over the last two decades the military position of the groups that took up arms to press for equal rights and self-determination has weakened. Since 1989, the majority of them have reached ceasefire agreements with the military government. Others have suffered military setbacks or defeats.

A wide range of ethnic minority political parties were formed to participate in the 1990 elections. Over a dozen of them won seats. Despite restrictions and many of them having been officially banned, these organizations try to function as well as they can. There are also a growing number of religious or community-based organizations in ethnic minority communities. The large number and variety of organizations reflects the strong sense of ethnic identity, and is a response to decades of repression of minority rights. Although these organizations have adopted different strategies, their goals are similar: greater autonomy; ethnic rights; and a federal state based on democratic principles.

Armed Groups

The principal groups still fighting the military government are the KNU, the Karenni National Progressive Party (KNPP) and Shan State

Army South (SSA-S) along the Thai border, and the Chin National Front along the Indian border. Most of these opposition armies no longer control significant territory, but operate as guerrilla forces from small, often mobile, bases. The most serious human rights abuses occur in these conflict areas, the vast majority committed by the Burma Army during counter-insurgency operations.

A host of other smaller armed groups can be identified, most of them based along the Thai border. There are also many splinter groups and breakaway factions from larger armed opposition groups, active in most conflict areas in the country. The last of the armed groups are local militias, which have no political objectives and are mainly involved in economic activities.

Since 1989, the military government has reached ceasefire agreements with over 15 armed opposition groups. They have had a deep impact on many ethnic minority communities, especially in the hills and mountains of northern Burma where the first truces were signed. Among the larger ceasefire groups are the United Wa State Party (UWSP), the Kachin Independence Organization (KIO), the New Mon State Party (NMSP), Shan State Army North, and the Pao National Organization. The ceasefire agreements have put an end to the bloodshed and curtailed the most serious human rights abuses. They have also facilitated easier travel and communication among communities in war-affected areas, and have led to some improvement in health and education services. Reconstruction in some of these former conflict areas has started.[6]

The truces, however, have not led to political agreements and have yet to transform into lasting peace. The uncertainty of the situation has also provided space for many illegal activities, including drug trafficking, illegal logging and other black market trading, gambling and human trafficking.[7] This has caused an influx of outsiders, including many from towns and cities from other States and Divisions,

---

[6] For more information, see Tom Kramer, "Neither War Nor Peace: The Future of the Cease-fire Agreements in Burma," TNI, Amsterdam, July 2009.

[7] See: Tom Kramer, Martin Jelsma and Tom Blickman, "Withdrawal Symptoms in the Golden Triangle: A Drugs Market in Disarray," TNI, Amsterdam, January 2009.

forcing local people out of their traditional way of life and generally damaging their livelihoods.

Some areas, such as Kayah and Shan States, have a patchwork of armies and different authorities. These include armies still fighting the central government, those with a ceasefire agreement and several breakaway groups with or without some kind of ceasefire agreement with the Burma Army. These chaotic situations have made life extremely difficult for local populations, often caught up in the cross-fire between conflict parties contending for control of areas and economic interests.

All armed opposition groups, including those with a ceasefire agreement, depend on the local population for finances (taxes), recruits (in some cases one boy per family), intelligence (service as guides and information about enemy movements) and food. There is also evidence of human rights violations by armed opposition groups, although to a lesser degree than that of the Burma Army. In some cases the civilian population face reprisals for providing support to the Burma Army or rival armed groups.

Armed opposition groups are unable to protect the communities they purport to represent from abuses by the Burma Army. And their continued armed resistance causes severe hardships for the people in the areas they operate. In some cases, local communities have, through the mediation of church leaders, asked armed groups to consider signing a ceasefire to relieve the burden on the population.[8] Despite this, most people still fear any armed group entering their villages.[9]

Some of the civilian population do support armed struggle, as is the case among the Karen, Shan and Kachin communities. They see armed resistance as protection against the Burma Army and as a strategy to press for their political demands. However, many people resent

---

[8] Interview with Kayah community worker, Mae Hong Son, January 2000.
[9] Human Rights Foundation of Monland, "Living Between Two Fires: Villager Opinions in Armed Insurgency," The Mon Forum, Issue No.1/2009, January 31, 2009.

the abuses by armed opposition groups. Popular support for the groups is also affected by the lack of consultation and communication with local communities. People are discontented with what they perceive as the leadership's weak capacity to lead. Some communities are unhappy with the armed groups' resistance to any independent community-based organizations. A war-weariness permeates local communities, who for decades have born the brunt of the effects of the civil war as well as the consequences of local splits and rivalries between different armed ethnic groups.

Armed groups have also been accused of involvement in the drug trade. Opium cultivation in Burma has declined in the last ten years, although the exact quantity is debated. At the same time, production of amphetamine-type stimulants (ATS) has increased significantly. The United Wa State Party (UWSP) has been singled out and demonized by the international community for all the drug problems in the region. In 2005 the US Department of Justice announced the indictment of eight UWSP leaders, including its chairman Bao You Chang, on heroin- and methamphetamine-trafficking charges. It calls the UWSP "one of the largest heroin-producing and trafficking groups in the world".[10]

Clearly the UWSP is not innocent of narcotics-related crimes. But to single them out for all the drug problems in the region and to blame everything on "drug kingpins" or "narco-armies" is too simplistic. History has long shown that there are very few conflict actors in Burma whose hands are clean on this issue. The involvement of Burma Army units and commanders in the drug trade has also been documented. In 2007, the US stated that Burma had "failed demonstrably" to meet international counter-narcotic obligations — failing, among other things, to "investigate and prosecute senior military officials for

---

[10] US Department of Justice, Press Release: "Eight Leaders of Southeast Asia's Largest Narcotics Trafficking Organisation Indicted by a Federal Grand Jury in Brooklyn, New York." United States Attorney, Eastern District of New York, January 24, 2005

drug-related corruption".[11] Furthermore, the drug trade is a hugely profitable business, and it is clear that corruption and the involvement of people in high-ranking offices in all countries in the region plays an important role.

Armed groups have also been involved in other business opportunities, including logging, mining, gambling and other black-marketeering, to finance their organizations. Other powerful non-political actors are benefiting (mostly economically) from the current political instability in the country, and the uncertain status of armed groups and the future of the ceasefire agreements. These include foreign actors such as Chinese and Thai logging companies and drug traders, who see no benefit in peace and reconciliation.

Political Parties

After the military government announced that elections would take place in May 1990, a large number of political parties registered. Many of them were formed along ethnic lines. Some ethnic minority politicians argued that it was better to join or support the NLD, presenting a united front rather than a divided opposition. However, most saw the election as an historic opportunity to form organizations to represent their own interests.

Among the political parties that won seats are the Shan Nationalities League for Democracy (23 seats), the Arakan League for Democracy (11 seats) and the Mon National Democratic Front (5 seats). The Chin National League for Democracy and the Zomi National Congress won 5 of the 13 available seats in Chin State. This national coalition of ethnic groups comprising the United Nationalities League for Democracy won 67 out of 485 seats.

---

[11] Other reasons included: unsatisfactory efforts by Burma to deal with the burgeoning ATS production and trafficking problem; failure to take action to bring members of the UWSP to justice following the unsealing of a US indictment against them in January 2005; and failure to expand demand reduction, prevention and drug-treatment programs to reduce drug-use and control the spread of HIV/AIDS. US Department of State, International Narcotics Control Strategy Report, 2007, Washington DC.

The main objective of these parties was to establish states in a federation or, in some cases, autonomous territories, with equal rights for ethnic minorities based on democratic principles. Some parties also had specific demands related to local issues. Initially these parties kept a low profile, prioritizing their survival as a legal entity. In 1998 the NLD with a number of ethnic minority politicians set up the Committee Representing the People's Parliament. It called upon the military government to convene the parliament. This led to a new wave of arrests.

In 2002 ethnic minority parties formed the United Nationalities Alliance, an informal discussion platform to prepare for an eventual tripartite dialogue. Its members are closely allied with the NLD. The SNLD and seven other political parties participate in the UNA.

The military government placed many restrictions upon political parties, and ethnic minority parties were no exception. With the exception of the SNLD and six other parties, all ethnic parties from the 1990 election were declared illegal during the 1990s. Since 1990, many leaders and MPs have been arrested and given long jail sentences. In February 2005, SNLD leader Hkun Htun Oo was arrested and subsequently sentenced to a 106-year prison term.

Civil Society Organizations

Following the 1962 coup, Burma was closed off from the outside world, and all large companies, media and institutions were nationalized. Civil society organizations were banned or placed under strict government control, and members of the political opposition were put behind bars. After 1988 the new military government, known as the State Law and Order Restoration Council (from 1997, the State Peace and Development Council), proceeded to create its own mass organizations, such as the Union Solidarity and Development Association. Its explicit mandate is to support the policies of the military. The military government claims that the organization has millions of members, but many of them were forced to join or face the loss of jobs or positions.[12]

Religious organizations, especially at the local level, whether Christian, Buddhist, Muslim or Hindu, have a history of instituting social welfare activities, in many cases beyond their own communities. Some of them, such as the Myanmar Council of Churches, the Myanmar Baptist Convention and the Catholic Bishops Conference, have long-standing nationwide networks. They have long been involved in community development activities, an essential part of their work. Generally speaking, the Christian minority organizations have established better contact with international organizations than the Burman Buddhist majority have accomplished.

The conclusion of the ceasefire agreements since 1989 further provided opportunities to create new local organizations and expand existing ones. This has been the case especially in Kachin and Mon States. In Kachin State a number of new community-based initiatives and local NGOs, such as the Metta Development Foundation and Shalom Foundation, work on social and economic development, mainly in regions where war was fought.

In Mon State, the main civil society actors to emerge after the ceasefire between the New Mon State Party (NMSP) and the military government in 1995 were religious and social welfare networks. The Mon Literature and Buddhist Culture Association and the Mon Literature and Culture Committee have provided teaching of the Mon language, culture and history. The NMSP has actively supported these initiatives.[13] In Shan State the Shan Literature and Cultural Committee have also been very active promoting and preserving Shan culture and literature. Other ethnic groups have established similar organizations.

However, not all armed groups have welcomed community-based initiatives. More than half a century of conflict and civil war have left a militarized society. Initiatives by civilians to organize themselves

[12] David I. Steinberg, *Burma: The State of Myanmar* (Washington DC: Georgetown University Press, 2001), pp. 110–115.
[13] Ashley South, *Mon Nationalism and Civil War in Burma: The Golden Sheldrake* (London and New York: Routledge, 2004) pp. 195–196.

have often been looked upon with suspicion. Despite some exceptions, the ceasefire groups are still very much top-down and authoritarian organizations, run in a military fashion. In areas controlled by
the UWSP, for instance, very little opportunity is allowed for local
people to organize themselves.[14]

Continued fighting in Shan and Karen States has made it very difficult for local organizations to operate. The military government is
suspicious of civil society organizing in such areas, seeing it as a political front for ethnic nationalists. According to a member of the Karen
Literature and Culture Committee: "They seem as much afraid of
literature and culture groups as they are of armed organizations."[15]

Although the religious organizations are essentially non-political,
their leaders have taken part in political events. A number of church
leaders have played an important role as go-betweens in the ceasefire
negotiations. Reverend Saboi Jum from the Kachin Baptist Convention
(KBC) was part of the mediation team in talks with the KIO. Catholic
Bishop Sotero from Loikaw, the capital of Kayah State, played an important role in some of the negotiations with groups in Kayah State.

From 1994, Christian Karen leaders from Rangoon mediated
between the KNU and the military government to explore possibili-
ties for a ceasefire and a peace agreement. They started as independent mediators, later forming the Karen Peace Mediator Group,
comprising five members based in Yangon. Their efforts facilitated
four rounds of talks between 1995 and1997, after which negotiations
finally broke down.

Buddhist and Christian religious leaders in Karen State set up the
Karen State Peace Committee to promote peace-building and networking with Karen civil society organizations. There had previously
been some resentment among Karen State leaders that the mediation
process was dominated by Christian Karens from Rangoon.[16]

---

[14] Tom Kramer, *The United Wa State Party: Narco-Army or Ethnic Nationalist Party?*,
Policy Studies 38 (Southeast Asia) (Washington, DC, East-West Center, 2007).
[15] Shah Paung and Lawi Weng, "Junta Clamps Down on Ethnic Culture Groups,"
The Irrawaddy, June 8, 2007.
[16] Interview with Karen NGO representative, November 2004.

The Karen Development Committee, a social organization working on cultural, educational and health issues, has also been involved in peace-building activities. In April 2002 it organized a Karen congress attended by 120 Karen delegates representing 28 Karen civil society organizations from different geographical areas, religious backgrounds, and organizations. The Karen Development Network, formed in January 2003, focuses on developing greater capacity in the education and communication sector.

In January 2004, the SPDC established a verbal truce with the KNU, both sides agreeing to continue talks to reach an official ceasefire agreement. It led to a temporary halt to most of the fighting.[17] This created new space for local initiatives, and was a great stimulus for civil society organizations in Karen State. According to one observer, "Because of these peace talks Karen organizations are less harassed, and Karen organizations really mushroomed. Now there are more then 30 of them."[18] These include Karen faith-based organizations (Christian churches and Buddhist monasteries), women's and youth groups, and various other local culture, literature and music groups.[19]

Alliances and United Fronts

There have been numerous attempts to forge united fronts among opposition groups, and a wide range of different alliances and united fronts have been formed. However, none of these have been nationwide and all-inclusive. This is partly due to repression from the military government. However, internal divisions, especially over strategy (armed struggle versus ceasefire versus political means), are an obstacle. There are also conflicts related to ideology, resources (including the drug trade), historic grievances and personal influence.

The first successful alliance consisting solely of ethnic minority organizations, the National Democratic Front (NDF), was set up in

---

[17] Interview with General Bo Mya, February 8, 2004.
[18] Interview with Karen NGO representative, November 2004.
[19] Keynote address at Intra-Karen Community Dialogue, Alan Saw U, March 19 & 20, 2004.

1976 and included the KNU, NMSP, KNPP and the SSA along the Thai border, the KIO in the north, and some smaller groups in Shan State. The anti-communist and pro-Western NDF was rivaled in strength by the Communist Party of Burma (CPB) and its allies. Attempts to form a united front between the CPB and the NDF failed. With the collapse of the CPB in 1989, most of its allies signed a ceasefire agreement with the military government, increasing the military pressure of the Burma Army on the NDF members.

After the military crackdown on the democracy movement in central Burma in 1988, about 10,000 students and political activists fled to the jungle bases in the areas liberated by the NDF, where they set up new organizations. In 1988 they formed a united front, the Democratic Alliance of Burma, consisting of most of the NDF members and Burman opposition groups. In 1992 a wider front, the National Council of the Union of Burma, was set up. Apart from DAB members, it included the National Coalition Government of the Union of Burma. The latter had been set up in exile by members of political parties and MPs-elect (mainly NLD) who had escaped a new wave of arrests after the 1990 elections.

Throughout history, alliances between ethnic minority and Burman opposition groups have suffered from mutual suspicion. According to one Karen leader, "We have tried many times to form a stable united front. The thing is whenever we talked about federalism, no Burmans agreed with us. They always say the ethnic groups are breaking up the country, that it is very dangerous. So we felt we had to form the united front with the ethnic groups only, with the common aim. My understanding is that the NDF is the only organization that will stand up for the ethnic groups. It will guarantee the establishment of a federal union. If there is no NDF, we will have to worry for all ethnic groups."[20]

On the Chinese border, a number of ex-CPB ceasefire groups formed the Peace and Democracy Front. In August 2009, the Burma Army attacked the Kokang army, one of the alliance members, after it refused government orders to reform. A statement was announced, detailing a new military alliance between four key

---

[20] Interview with KNU President Padoh Ba Thin, February 1999.

ceasefire groups along the Chinese border: the KIO, UWSA and the groups based in the Kokang and Mongla regions.[21] However, when the Burma army attacked, none of these groups came to the aid of the Kokang Army. This raises questions about the strength of the alliance should another member face attack by the Burma Army. Of the alliance members, only the KIO and UWSA have a significant number of troops.

Armed groups such as the KIO hope that social, humanitarian and economic development will lead ultimately to political development and reconciliation. They entered into a truce with the military government as a strategy to seek political change. In contrast, most other NDF members want to first reach a political settlement before signing a ceasefire agreement.

Grievances and Aspirations

The main grievances of ethnic minority groups in Burma are the lack of influence in the political decision-making processes; the absence of economic and social development in their areas; and what they see as the military government's Burmanization policy, which translates into repression of their cultural rights and religious freedom. Ethnic minorities in Burma feel marginalized and discriminated against and, in effect, the armed rebellions in Burma are their response.

Political Participation

Resentment, suspicion, and mistrust are rife among ethnic groups in Burma. They feel discriminated against by ethnic Burmans, who have until today dominated the national political arena. Ethnic minority organizations have been deeply suspicious of successive Burman-dominated governments, claiming that they have not made a sincere attempt to solve the ethnic minority crisis.

---

[21] "Declaration on the Kokang 8.8 Disturbances by the Myanmar Peace and Democratic Front," August 21, 2009.

These grievances increased after Ne Win came to power in 1962. Ethnic minority organizations feel that Ne Win's policies, officially aimed at national unity, have enlarged the gap, further increasing suspicion and misunderstanding between the ethnic minorities and Burmans. Since this time, the military government has argued that its rule is necessary to keep the country together and "to save the union". However, ethnic minority leaders say the military government is building a unitary state based on central Burman identity, and accuses it of chauvinism and a policy of "Burmanization".

Most ethnic minority organizations now reject separatism, preferring instead a federal state based on democratic principles that safeguard their political, economic and cultural rights. The key aspirations are self-determination and equality. The large majority of groups support the NLD's call for a tripartite dialogue between the military, the democratic opposition and ethnic groups to find a lasting solution to the political deadlock.

Recognition of Ethnic Conflict as the Key Political Issue

Ethnic minority leaders resent that the international community and Burman opposition perceive the resolution of the ethnic minority problem to be less important than the democratic cause. The 1988 uprising and the 1990 elections focused the international community's attention on events in Rangoon, where opposition leader Aung San Suu Kyi became an international icon in her peaceful campaign for democracy and human rights.

The dominant argument is that first a democratic government should be achieved and the military government removed, and only then can the issue of ethnic minority representation and rights be resolved. Political progress in the capital has to come first.

The ethnic minorities are often portrayed as victims. The Karen often simply feature as refugees, Shan as internally displaced persons (IDPs), and the Wa as poor opium farmers, with no mention of their political concerns and demands.

Ethnic opposition groups note that some international observers think that the ethnic minority issue is too complicated to understand, because there are so many different actors with various points of view, and therefore not worth engaging with. The ethnic groups point out that while the strategies of ethnic minority organizations may differ, their goals are quite similar.

The ethnic groups that signed a peace truce with the military government sense a lack of interest and understanding of the changes brought about by the ceasefire process. Similarly, they feel that the international community has shown little interest in ending a civil war that has had such a huge impact on ethnic minority communities.

In particular, the impact of the ceasefire agreements between the government and a wide range of ethnic minority armed groups has almost been ignored by the international community. Support for these groups to develop their regions has been minimal, creating great frustration and disappointment among ethnic minority community leaders.

These problems are exacerbated by the position of the democratic opposition in Burma, which has well-established relations with the international community, in particular with the West. Ethnic opposition groups appreciate the role of Aung San Suu Kyi, and believe they will be able to negotiate with her about the future of Burma. Nonetheless, some feel that her party does not consider the ethnic issue a central element in the political future of Burma, and has had no appropriate policy to address this fundamental cause of state failure and conflict since independence.[22]

Economic Rights and Development

Although Burma is rich in resources, the country is very poor. Decades of war and mismanagement have brought the country, once the world's largest rice exporter, to the brink of economic collapse. And the ethnic minority areas have suffered the worst.

Minority leaders complain that while the central government has been keen to extract natural resources from the ethnic states and sell them abroad, the money earned has not been invested to develop these isolated and war-torn areas.

---

[22] Interview with senior member of a ceasefire group, August 2008.

The military government has profited from the timber, precious stones (gold, jade and rubies) and gas and oil reserves sold to foreign companies without any consultation with local communities, which have suffered negative social and environmental consequences from these projects. They have lost economic resources, received no compensation for damages, and have never been offered a share in the profits.

Neighboring countries have also profited greatly from the political instability in Burma. Chinese and Thai companies have been able to play different conflict actors off against one another. Furthermore, the weakness of the Burmese state and the uncertainty of the situation encourage corruption at the local level by army and government authorities as well as the local commanders of ceasefire groups. As a result, natural resources are being extracted at low prices with large profits for the Chinese and Thai companies and authorities, with little or no return investment to develop the border regions.

In southern Burma two international consortia have been created to explore gas fields in the Gulf of Martaban and establish two pipelines to Thailand, for the Yadana and Yetagun gas projects.[23] The Burma Army manages the security for these projects and has been accused of committing human rights violations in doing so. A recent report claims that the military government has earned billions of dollars in revenue from the two projects but has not invested any of it to develop the country. In addition, the money has yet to be accounted for in the national budget.[24]

In southern Shan State the military government plans to build the Tasang Dam on the Salween River. The project has been strongly criticized by non-governmental organizations and the ethnic

---

[23] The Yadana consortium consists of Total (France), Chevron (US), the Petroleum Authority of Thailand (PTTEP) and the Myanmar Oil and Gas Enterprise (MOGE) and the Yetagun consortium of Petronas (Malaysia), Nippon Oil (Japan), PTTEP and MOGE. ERI, Total Impact, 2009.

[24] EarthRights International (ERI), "Total Impact: The Human Rights, Environmental and Financial Impacts of Total and Chevron's Yadana Gas project in Military Ruled-Burma (Myanmar)," September 2009.

opposition. In 2007 project oversight was awarded to a Chinese company.[25] In the same year, the military government and the state-owned China Power Investment Corporation signed an agreement to build seven hydropower projects in Kachin State to supply China with electricity. Preparations for construction of the controversial Myitsone Dam, opposed by local communities, began the same year.[26]

The scale of logging increased dramatically after 1988. The most serious damage has occurred in the ethnic minority areas along the borders with Thailand and China, which contained previously untouched forest reserves with various types of hardwood and important watershed areas. The situation is compounded by a dramatic increase in demand for natural resources by Thailand and especially China. According to a recent report, this illegal cross-border trade between Burma and China continues, although at a lower pace since 2005.[27]

Large-scale mining of the country's rich mineral resources by foreign companies, mostly Chinese, has replaced small-scale mining by villagers and local companies, leading to significant job losses for local communities. The Chinese companies often illegally purchase logging and mining concessions from whoever will sell them, be it the Regional Commanders of the Burma Army or from local ceasefire groups in areas where the government is not in control.

Social and Cultural Rights

Social and cultural rights of ethnic minorities in Burma deteriorated rapidly after the coup of 1962. Ethnic minority languages were

---

[25] Salween Watch, Southeast Asia Rivers Network, Center for Social Development Studies, "The Salween under Threat, Damming the Longest Free River in Southeast Asia," October 2004, and Kyaw Thu, "Kachin Hydropower Study Due in December," *The Myanmar Times*, March 24–30, 2008.

[26] Kyaw Thu, "Kachin Hydropower Study Due in December," *The Myanmar Times*, March 24–30, 2008, and Saw Yan Naing, "Irrawaddy Dam Construction Begins, Human Rights Abuses Begin," *The Irrawaddy*, January 29, 2008.

[27] Global Witness, "A Disharmonious Trade: China and the Continued Destruction of Burma's Northern Frontier Forests," London, 2009.

virtually banned in the education system under the BSPP. Publications in ethnic minority languages, including newspapers and books, suffered the same fate. After 1988 a number of state colleges in ethnic minority states were upgraded to university status, but ethnic minority leaders claim that any change is only in name.

The destruction of the traditional Shan palace in Kengtung by the army in November 1991 is seen by many Shan as part of a deliberate attempt to destroy their culture. Kengtung, located in the eastern Shan State, was the largest of the 33 Shan principalities, and the palace was the seat of one the Shan traditional rulers, the *sawbwa*. Hence its destruction created enormous resentment among the Shan population. The minority communities see this act, along with others, as part of the military government's effort to Burmanize them.

Many armed opposition groups have set up education departments to teach their own languages. In Mon State the NMSP extended adult-literacy and various capacity-building activities to areas in Mon State, including areas outside NMSP control. The NMSP has been able to promote Mon National Schools, teaching in the Mon language. The majority of the students come from government-controlled areas, where teaching in minority languages is not allowed beyond fourth grade. The Mon Literature and Buddhist Culture Association and the Mon Literature and Cultural Committee, which had been promoting Mon literacy and cultural training programmes, have been able to expand and systemize their activities after the ceasefire.[28] As is the case outside Mon State, cultural and literature committees are a clear testament to the aspirations of the minority groups.

Religious Rights

Religion remains a very sensitive issue in Burma. Many of Burma's ethnic minorities practice a different religion from the Burman

---

[28] Ashley South, *Ethnic Politics in Burma: States of Conflict* (London and New York: Routledge, 2008) pp. 195–196.

Buddhist majority. A significant number of the Karen, Kachin, Chin and Karenni population is Christian, mostly Baptists and Catholics. British and American missionaries converted them during the 19th century. Christianity is also practiced by many Lahu and Naga. State promotion of Buddhism and the perceived discrimination against other religions, including Islam and Christianity, is resented. The Burma Army's policy of erecting Buddhist temples in ethnic minority areas is seen by some as an attempt to destroy and assimilate ethnic minority cultures.

Although Buddhism is not the state religion, some Christian organizations complain that, despite a government of religious free-dom, there are severe restrictions. For example, in Chin State villagers have been reportedly, pressured to adopt Buddhism, and there have been reports of restrictions on building new churches.[29]

Burma's Muslim population has probably suffered the most from religious and ethnic discrimination. Anti-Muslim riots have taken place on numerous occasions in several towns in central Burma. In May 2001, shops, homes and mosques in Taungoo were attacked by over 1,000 people, leading to the death of at least nine Muslims. In October that same year, more serious violence broke out in Prome, where Buddhist crowds attacked Muslim property. Later that month, smaller-scale anti-Muslim unrest took place in Pegu, a town in lower Burma. Muslim community leaders claim that these attacks are insti-gated, or at least tolerated, by the military government.[30]

Tensions are particularly strong in Rakhine State, where the Rohingya, a Muslim minority, face ethnic and religious discrimination. During 1991 and 1992 about 250,000 Rohingya fled to Bangladesh following an army campaign. Most of them have been repatriated to Rakhine State by the UN High Commission for Refugees, but they face limited freedom of movement, forced labour and administrative barriers to marriage, and many are not recognized as Burmese citi-zens. Historic conflicts between ethnic minority groups, between the

---

[29] US State Department, "1999 Report on Religious Freedom," Washington DC, p. 99–112.
[30] Human Rights Watch — Asia, "Crackdown on Burmese Muslims," July 2002.

Rohingya and Rakhine population in Rakhine State, for instance, further complicate the religious landscape and tensions.[31]

The Humanitarian Dimension

Since the outbreak of the civil war in 1948, many people have died in or as a result of the fighting. The great majority of civilian casualties are from ethnic minority areas, where most of the fighting has taken place. However, reliable data on the number of conflict-related casualties are not available. In 1989 SLORC leader General Saw Maung stated that the death toll "would reach as high as millions". A more realistic estimate might be 10,000 casualties per year during the four decades prior to 1991.[32] What seems clear is that the number of deaths has decreased since the ceasefire agreements of 1989.

In its military campaigns against armed opposition groups, the Burma army has used the "Four Cuts" (*Pya Lay Pya*) strategy since the 1960s. This policy aimed at cutting off the four links between the insurgents and the civilian population (food, finance, intelligence and recruits). The military campaigns directly targeted the civilian population, resulting in the forced relocation of hundreds of thousands of people to special sites near Burma Army camps. The campaigns have, until today, often been accompanied by gross abuses of human rights, including extrajudicial and summary executions, torture, rape, the confiscation of land and property, and forced labor.[33]

The fighting and the military campaigns have forced large number of civilians to leave their homes. Over half a million people are displaced in conflict areas in the eastern part of the country along the Thai border. Today, an estimated 130,000 ethnic minority refugees are living in camps in Thailand and 35,000 Rohingya refugees in

---

[31] Amnesty International, "Myanmar: The Rohingya Minority: Fundamental Rights Denied," May 18, 2004.

[32] Martin Smith, *Burma, Insurgency and the Politics of Ethnicity.* (London and New Jersey: Zed Books, 1999) pp. 100–101.

[33] See, for instance, Amnesty International, "Myanmar: Crimes against Humanity in Eastern Myanmar," ASA 16/011/2008, June 5, 2008.

Bangladesh. Following the breakdown of the Kokang ceasefire in September 2009, some 37,000 refugees fled to China, although most of them have returned to Burma.[34]

Militarization

The military government has been trying to build a state based on Burman national identity. The current "Union of Myanmar" is presented as a logical continuation of the traditional Burman kingdoms of the valleys and plains of precolonial Burma. Ethnic minorities reject this argument, claiming that they were never under direct rule of any of these kings, and that they only became part of the Union of Burma by signing the Panglong agreement in 1947. To date, the military government refuses to broach any consideration of federalism with ethnic minority organizations.

The Burma army justifies its rule by referring to its role in the struggle for independence from the British. It claims that it saved the newly formed Union of Burma from collapse in its early years by pushing the insurgents out of the central plains and into the hills and mountains of the border regions.

The military government's leaders argue that only the military can maintain the country's national unity. They claim that it had to take "decisive action" on a number of "political crises", as was the case in 1962 and in 1988, or the country would have fallen apart. Hence any resistance or opposition to military rule is an act against the "union" and the national interest.

From a military perspective, the army has been quite successful in the last decade. The army has expanded significantly, from about 170,000 soldiers in 1988 to an estimated 400,000 troops.[35] At the

---

[34] Thai Burma Border Consortium, "Internal Displacement and International Law in Eastern Burma," October 2008; Tom Kramer, "Burma's Cease-fires at Risk," TNI, Amsterdam, 2009; and Médecins Sans Frontières (MSF), "Rohingya desperation in Bangladesh" June 23, 2009.

[35] Andrew Selth, *Burma's Armed Forces Power Without Glory* (Norwalk: Eastbridge, 2002) p. 296.

same time armed opposition groups have suffered setbacks or defeats. The Burma military has gained unprecedented access to border areas. Furthermore, since 1989 the military has signed ceasefire agreements with the large majority of the armed opposition groups, thereby neutralizing or marginalizing most of the armed opposition in the country.

The country is divided into 13 military regions under the control of Regional Commanders, who have a great deal of autonomy in their area. Burma is an army state, and army officers shadow or control all functions of the state. In some ethnic minority areas, the only representative of the government is the army, the only entity in the country with a nationwide presence.

Conflict Management

The military government has focused on "managing" conflict rather than solving it. The aim is not to eliminate armed opposition and insurgent groups, but rather to contain and divide them. The army has adopted and applied a "divide and rule" policy, multiplying the number of armed groups, further contributing to a high degree of militarization in the country. Inevitably, the civilian population is the victim of all of this, especially in areas with different armed groups present.

In August 2009, the Burma Army occupied the Kokang region after several days of fighting, ending two decades of ceasefire with the Kokang Army, the first of over 20 armed opposition groups to conclude a ceasefire agreement with the government. The resumption of fighting in northern Burma raises speculation about the other ceasefires. Tensions are rising and the ceasefire groups have put their armed forces on high alert. They are preparing for battle but say they will continue to seek political change through dialogue, and will not fire the first shot.

The Burma Army's strategy in the Kokang region follows a long and consistent pattern. Instead of a total offensive against all ceasefire groups, the Burma Army prefers to take them on one by one, focusing on weakening them by military, political and economic means, hence stimulating the fragmentation of groups. When internal divisions within opposition groups develop, the army subsequently allies itself with breakaway factions. An example of this is the creation of the Democratic Karen Buddhist Army (DKBA), which broke away from the armed opposition Karen National Union in 1995, following an internal conflict between Buddhist and Christian leaders.

The military government will also probably continue to strengthen various pro-government militias in border regions and in areas near ceasefire groups to provide a buffer. Some of the many other militias in the country date back to the 1970s, established to counter the threat posed by the Communist Party of Burma. Others in Shan State were formed by remnants of Khun Sa's Mong Tai Army, which agreed to a "surrender" ceasefire with the military government in early 1996. The military government has recently promoted the formation of new groups, such as the Rawang Rebellion Resistance Force (RRF) in the northern Kachin State, which challenges both the KIO and New Democratic Army–Kachin presence in the strategic N'mai Khu area. The RRF, led by a Kachin businessman, describes itself as a "people's militia".

Future Prospects

On 10 May 2008, just a few days after a powerful cyclone devastated the Irrawaddy Delta and Rangoon, leaving 130,000 dead and more missing, the military government held a referendum to approve the controversial new constitution. According to the military government, it was approved by over 90% of the voters. Opposition groups contest this and say the referendum was not free and fair, and that the constitution does not represent the will of the people.[36]

Under the new constitution the seven divisions (*taing*) have been renamed "regions", while the seven states (*pyi-neh*) retain their previous denominations. Six new self-administered areas have also been created. These are the Naga Self-Administered Zone in Sagaing Division; the Danu Self-Administered Zone; the Pao Self-Administered Zone; the Palaung Self-Administered Zone; the Kokang

---

[36] See, for instance, National League for Democracy (Liberated Area), "Constitutional Referendum in Burma," Referendum Campaign Committee, Thailand, June 2008.

Self-Administered Zone; and the Wa Self-Administered Division in Shan State. One of the main differences is that there will be a parliament and cabinet not only on the national level, but also on regional and state levels.[37]

The constitution, however, fails to address the main grievances and aspirations of the armed ethnic opposition groups. The ceasefire groups made several attempts to improve both the process and substance at the military government-appointed National Convention which drew up the new constitution. They submitted a number of proposals in 2004, calling for self-determination for their areas, but these were rejected by the military government. In February 2005 six ceasefire groups sent a letter to the National Convention Chairman, repeating their demands. They demanded removal of the provision that the military would continue to play a dominant role in politics. They also demanded communication between the delegates at the National Convention and their leaders, and immediate engagement in peace talks with armed groups that had not yet signed a ceasefire, to enable them to participate in the National Convention.[38] These demands were all refused by the military government.

The military government has been adamant that it wants the ceasefire groups to disarm, but they are unlikely to do so unless some of their basic political demands are met. This is the key issue today and may lead to further fragmentation among armed groups. The tension in northern Burma comes amid pressure by the military government to transform the ceasefire groups into the Border Guard Force (BGF) and efforts to organize a general election in 2010, the country's first since 1990.

Widespread opposition to the BGF proposal increases uncertainty about the future of the ceasefires and a peaceful transition to a lasting

---

[37] Ministry of Information of the Union of Myanmar, Constitution of the Republic of the Union of Myanmar, Printing & Publishing Enterprise, September 2008. These are the Naga, Danu, Pao, Palaung, Kokang and Wa Self-Administered Areas.
[38] Human Rights Foundation of Monland, "SPDC's National Convention: Silencing Down the Cease-fire Group's Voices," *The Mon Forum,* Issue No. 2/2005, February 2005.

political settlement. Accepting the proposal would effectively break up ceasefire groups into small separate units of 326 soldiers, divorced from their present ethnic administrations and military structures. Each BGF would include 35 members of the Burma Army, including one of the three commanding officers in each unit.[39]

Several ceasefire groups have rejected the SPDC's proposal. Exactly how this military and territorial transformation would be put into practice has yet to be worked out, and negotiations are ongoing. Some militias, such as the RRF, say that they have been told by the military government that they do not have to transform into a BGF and can continue to exist in their present form.[40]

The KIO has proposed that it become a Kachin Regional Guard Force, remaining a single organization under a central command. The KIO argues that the BGF proposal is too limited, only dealing with the transformation of its military wing. The KIO has a large administrative structure with many civilian departments, including health, education, culture and justice.[41]

Although the military government has announced elections for 2010, no date has been set, and the new election law detailing rules and regulations has yet to be promulgated. The government has already indicated to the ceasefire groups that they need to form new political parties formally separate from their present organizations. Those who join these political parties must take off their uniforms and resign from the armed groups.

Those armed groups still fighting the military government have outrightly rejected the 2008 constitution and the 2010 elections. They say these will "neither solve the political crisis faced by the entire people nor will it lead to national reconciliation and democracy".[42]

---

[39] Tom Kramer, "Burma's Cease-fires at Risk: Consequences of Kokang Crisis for Peace and Democracy," TNI Peace & Security Briefing No. 1, September 2009.
[40] Interview with source close to the RRF, September 2, 2009.
[41] Interview with KIO official, September 1, 2009.
[42] Central Executive Committee National Democratic Front (NDF), NDF Statement Expressly Rejecting the SPDC 2010 elections, October 5, 2009.

Armed groups with ceasefires are unhappy with the situation, but say they will participate in the elections because there is no alternative. In Kachin State, the KIO, in cooperation with two other Kachin ceasefire groups and representatives of Kachin civil society, have announced that they plan to register as the Kachin State Progressive Party to contest the 2010 election. In anticipation, six KIO leaders resigned from their KIO duties in September 2009.[43] In Mon State, four former central committee members of the New Mon State Party (NMSP) and several Mon community leaders have set up an "election working committee" to prepare a political party to participate in the 2010 elections. The NMSP will not run, but it will allow members to resign in order to join the party.[44]

Stressing the importance of resolving Burma's political and ethnic problems, the KIO is opposed to dealing with issues summarily, proposing they be negotiated after the 2010 elections. "It is not possible to make a transformation within a limited time frame," said a KIO leader. "We need more time and negotiation for such a transformation process, and will need to do this step by step."[45] The ceasefire groups maintain that they will not be the ones to resume hostilities.

The civilian population fears the future. "We are worried the fighting will break out again, and can't even sleep at night because of the situation," said a villager in a KIO area. "We have had the experience of war, of those difficult times, when our villages were burnt down. If the fighting will break out again, the civilians are the ones who will suffer most. If war starts, many people will flee to China."[46]

Burma has been under military rule since 1962, but civil war has been ongoing since independence, and has caused great suffering for its people. Ethnic conflict must be resolved in order to bring about a lasting political solution. If ethnic minority grievances and aspirations are not addressed, sustainable peace and democracy are extremely unlikely to be achieved. Burma's legacy of state failure will endure.

---

[43] Interview with Dr Tu Ja, September 2, 2009.

[44] Lawi Weng, "New Mon Party Forming for Election," *Irrawaddy*, September 8, 2009.

[45] Interview with senior KIO leader, September 1, 2009.

[46] Interview with 50-year-old woman in a village in a KIO area, August 31, 2009.

Chapter 4

Relieving Burma's Humanitarian Crisis

Christina Fink

Abstract

Burma's succession of military leaders has shared an indifference to the welfare of its people, whether the Burman majority or the minority ethnic groups, with the result that poverty, disease, and illiteracy have become part of a pervasive humanitarian crisis. Western human rights groups have attempted to alleviate the crisis but the SPDC has limited their efforts, suspecting them of turning the people against the regime.

Keywords: Cyclone Nargis; merit-making; NGOs; UNDP; FEC.

Burma was historically known as the golden land because of its plentiful natural resources and wealthy kingdoms. Yet today, over one-third of the children below the age of five are malnourished and poverty is endemic. This chapter analyzes the deepening of the humanitarian crisis in Burma over the past 20 years as well as the gradual development of the humanitarian aid sector. It considers the regime's position on humanitarian needs, the root causes of the various humanitarian crises, and the constraints on and accomplishments of the humanitarian sector.[1]

---

[1] Information for this chapter comes from interviews conducted between August and October 2009 with Burmese and expatriates involved in the field of humanitarian assistance, from interviews for earlier projects, and from confidential and public reports. Interviewees are not cited by name at their request.

The Regime's Perception of Humanitarian Needs

A report by the International Crisis Group in 2002 asserts that four values affect the top generals' attitudes toward humanitarian assistance: national ownership of aid and development, governmental control over the population, national pride and top-down development.[2] All of these factors have led the generals to be resistant to international assistance unless it is on their own terms. It is also important to stress that the regime has tended to see the humanitarian needs of various population groups as limited in scope and requiring little assistance from anyone. This view stems from the way the regime understands state–society relations.

Both Callahan and Duffield have argued that the regime's perspective reflects its inheritance of a colonial structure of governance which exerted control through coercion and paid little attention to the welfare of the colonized.[3] Duffield further asserts that the current military regime, like its colonial predecessor, has viewed the population under its control as self-reliant.[4] This model is fundamentally different from a modern welfare state which sees itself as having clear responsibilities to provide a social safety net for its citizens. I would add that the top generals and, in particular, Senior General Than Shwe, are equally influenced by pre-colonial structures of rule, in which coercion was the primary factor in relations between the ruler and the ruled.

Burmese kings viewed their subjects as a source of labor and resource provision in times of peace and war. The king's responsibility to his people was to provide protection through military might and generous support for the Buddhist religious establishment. While the fostering of Buddhism was understood as cosmologically important

---

[2] International Crisis Group, *Myanmar: The Politics of Humanitarian Aid*, April 2, 2002, p. 3.
[3] Mary Callahan, *Making Enemies: War and State Building in Burma* (Ithaca: Cornell University Press, 2003), pp. 42–43; Mark Duffield, *On the Edge of 'No Man's Land': Chronic Emergency in Myanmar* (Bristol: Center for Governance and International Affairs, University of Bristol, 2008), pp. 7–8.
[4] Duffield, p. 8.

for maintaining a peaceful and prosperous kingdom for all, the construction of permanent religious edifices also helped kings establish their legacies. Similarly, public works such as roads and large-scale irrigation systems were constructed both for the benefit of the population and to enhance the reputation of the king. Pre-modern rulers did not bother with the provision of education or health. These services were provided by monks and local healers.

The regime today demonstrates analogous behavior. The leaders focus their attention on Buddhist merit-making, which has continued to resonate with the Buddhist population to a certain degree, and infrastructure projects, including the building of a new capital, tellingly named Naypyidaw, or "Royal Abode". Far fewer resources are devoted to the development and support of services that are less visible and more temporal in nature. While schools and health centers have been built in many areas, little commitment has been made to the provision of human and material resources to make these institutions effective service providers. Even as the regime's revenues have increased over the past 20 years, the percentage of GDP invested in health and education has declined. In 2006, only 1.4% of GDP was spent on health and education, far less than in other countries in the region.[5] This is in contrast to the period of parliamentary rule from 1948 to 1962 when government investment in health and education increased relative to GDP and social indicators reflected a steady improvement in living standards.[6]

The regime's minimal provision of social welfare assistance to the population reflects the top generals' attitude that the people have always survived without much government support and will continue to do so. Likewise, in times of natural disaster, one-off provisions of charity assistance have been deemed sufficient. At the same time, most of the senior generals lack knowledge about the development of modern welfare states. Many of the leading generals, particularly

---

[5] United Nations Development Program, Human Development Report 2006, http://hdr.undp.org/hdr2006/, accessed on October 12, 2009.
[6] Anne Booth, "The Burma Development Disaster in Comparative Historical Perspective," *SOAS Bulletin of Burma Research* 1:1 (Spring 2003), pp. 3–4, 11.

Than Shwe, have little experience outside the country. Moreover, authorities at all levels tend not to report bad news and even falsify reports, leading the top leaders to believe that the humanitarian situation is far better than it really is.[7] Given that promotions are based on loyalty rather than problem identification and innovation, there is little dynamism in the bureaucracy or the military that might trigger significant policy changes or encourage a greater degree of state commitment to the provision of services. Moreover, because of the citizens' fear of the repercussions of criticizing the authorities, and their low expectations, there is virtually no pressure from below for the government to change its behavior.

The regime has primarily viewed the provision of humanitarian assistance both by international and domestic actors through the lens of its security. The work of humanitarian actors has been perceived as a possible threat to military rule, as they could potentially catalyze popular discontent with the authorities' policies and strengthen the capacity of local populations to oppose military rule. While UN agencies and international NGOs work hard to reduce the authorities' concerns, the working procedures and values which they seek to introduce differ greatly from those practiced by the authorities. Humanitarian aid workers have sought to introduce participatory needs assessments and decision-making structures, networking, transparency and accountability. If practiced effectively, all of these could enhance the communities' abilities to analyze their situations and to act independently from the state.

Root Causes and Manifestations of Burma's Humanitarian Crises

Over the past 20 years, people in Burma have suffered from policy-driven humanitarian crises, civil war and natural disasters. Because the generals in power since 1988 have been more ambitious in terms of their developmental and military objectives, the Burmese people have

---

[7] Charles Petrie, *End of Mission Report UN Resident and Humanitarian Coordinator, UNDP Resident Representative for Myanmar,* April 1, 2008, pp. 7–8.

suffered more than in the past. In the case of natural disasters, the regime has frequently disregarded or downplayed the humanitarian needs and, at times, impeded communities' access to aid.

Economic Policies

Although the regime opened up the economy to foreign investment and private enterprise in 1989, it still considers its control over the economy as closely linked to its own survival. Thus the regime has refrained from privatizing inefficient state-owned enterprises and allowed only a small number of businessmen to monopolize sectors of the economy. The relationship between the top businessmen and the senior generals is similar to the patron–client relations that characterized interaction between kings and nobles in the past. Businessmen are awarded licenses to engage in certain business activities in return for their loyalty to the regime. Licenses can be retracted at any time, thus compelling business-men to act in ways that will please the senior generals.

In keeping with the top generals' desire to closely control the eco-nomic sector, economic policies are made by senior military personnel rather than by trained economists. As Steinberg has noted, although the top generals and other high level authorities have received advice from numerous Burmese and international economic experts, this has generally not translated into improved policies for the population as a whole.[8] A clear example is the sudden removal of fuel subsidies in August 2007 to reduce the government deficit. Transportation and food prices skyrocketed with devastating effect, particularly for the urban poor: some people could literally no longer afford to go to work. Monks took to the streets with the hope that their peaceful chanting would awaken in the generals a sense of responsibility for the citizens' well-being. However once the demonstrations grew to include political groups, the regime responded with a brutal crackdown.

---

[8] David Steinberg, "Myanmar: The Roots of Economic Malaise," in *Myanmar: Beyond Politics to Societal Imperatives*, eds. Kyaw Yin Hlaing, Robert H. Taylor and Tin Maung Maung Than (Singapore: Institute of Southeast Asian Studies, 2005), p. 94.

Other government policies and practices have retarded the development of the urban economy. Major problems for businesspeople include difficulties in obtaining loans to start or expand businesses, the irregular supply of electricity, an unpredictable exchange rate affecting import and export prices, and the many uncertainties of doing business in the absence of the rule of law.[9] All of these factors have limited the development of the manufacturing and service sectors and thus minimized the number of workers they can employ.

As Turnell (Chapter 8) has demonstrated, the government has habitually spent far more than it earns through tax revenues and has managed the resultant deficit by printing money. This has led to average annual inflation rates of over 25% per year throughout the past two decades.[10] Inflation has eroded the purchasing power of consumers and has produced an extremely low savings rate. Although the regime's financial position has turned around due to revenue from the sale of natural gas, most of this money has not gone into the state budget but has been used for special projects, such as the building of the new capital.[11]

Misguided agricultural policies have gravely affected the well-being of farmers, who comprise roughly two-thirds of the labor force. First, farmers have difficulty obtaining sufficient credit at a reasonable price, because the government agricultural bank provides such small loans and farmers cannot use their land as collateral as all land is owned by the state. Private moneylenders offer larger loans, but at interest rates few can afford. As a result, few farmers can improve their yields. Second, the market price for rice in Burma is held artificially low through various restrictions on the sale, transport and export of rice. Third, farmers are often ordered to plant crops not of their

---

[9] See Sean Turnell, *Burma's Economy 2008: Current Situation and Prospects for Reform* (Sydney: Burma Economic Watch, Macquarie University, 2008); Steinberg, "Myanmar: The Roots of Economic Malaise," p. 93.

[10] Mya Than and Myat Thein, "Transitional Economy of Myanmar: Present Status, Developmental Divide, and Future Prospects," *ASEAN Economic Bulletin* 24:1 (April 2007), p. 99.

[11] See Turnell, this volume.

choosing, such as a second crop of rice in the dry season, when beans would be more profitable.[12] Land has become degraded in many areas, as farmers cannot rotate crops to restore the nutrients in the soil. Also, farmers may be reluctant to invest much in their land because it can be confiscated at any time.[13]

The nationwide campaign to plant 7 million acres of jatropha curcas between 2006 and 2008 also hurt farmers. Jatropha can be processed into biofuel and is meant to reduce costly fuel imports, but farmers were often forced to buy the seeds, use parts of their own limited farm land or kitchen gardens for cultivation and, in some cases, give up their farms and community grazing lands for jatropha plantations.[14] As of 2009, many of the plants had died because of lack of knowledge about how to care for them, while farmers still did not know whether or how much they would be paid for the seeds produced.

Farmers have increasingly borrowed money to make ends meet but are often unable to repay their debts. Growing rates of landlessness have resulted from farmers having to sell their land to pay off their debts.[15] The increase in landlessness is also due to the confiscation of land by the military, other state authorities and companies close to the regime. As detailed in the 2007 Center on Housing Rights and Evictions report on Burma, large and small plots of land throughout the country have been confiscated for development into military barracks and outposts, factory sites, rural plantations, commercial farming sites, mines, dams, gas pipelines and other infrastructure projects.[16] In northern Burma, armed ceasefire groups have also

---

[12] Interview.

[13] Turnell, 2008, p. 23.

[14] See Ethnic Community Development Forum, "Biofuel By Decree: Unmasking Burma's Bio-Energy Fiasco" Thailand, 2008, for more details on the campaign and its impacts. The report also notes that some Burmese suspect that jatropha was planted as a magical means to reduce the power of the democratic movement.

[15] See Food and Agriculture Organization, *Myanmar Agricultural Sector Review Investment Strategy*, 2004, p. 30.

[16] *Burma: Displacement and Dispossession: Forced Migration and Land Rights*, COHRE Country Report (Geneva, 2007), Chapter 6.

confiscated land in their areas of control for commercial purposes. In most cases, the dispossessed were not compensated for the loss of their land. Rural residents who are landless or have insufficient land depend on wage labor to earn enough money to buy rice however there are few opportunities for rural wage work.

The rural and urban poor are often unable to provide for their full nutritional needs, let alone other needs. According to Charles Petrie, a former UN Resident and Humanitarian Coordinator, following the gas price hikes in 2007, 73% of families' household expenditures on average was spent on food, while the figure was only 32% in Thailand and 52% in Bangladesh.[17] In addition, because of the costs associated with schooling and the need to have children help with family work or take care of younger children, many families are unable to send their children to school for more than a few years, and some children never attend. Health care is unaffordable for most. When treatment is necessary, families may resort to selling assets or going into debt to cover costs. Many have attempted to resolve this untenable situation by having one or more able-bodied members migrate internally or abroad in search of a job, so that they can send remittances back to the family.

Militarization

After 1988, the Burma Army increased the number of soldiers to approximately 300,000, and was able to penetrate more deeply into the ethnic states. Between 1989 and 1995, over a dozen ethnic nationalist armies made ceasefire agreements with the regime, while conflict continued in Karen, Karenni and Shan States of eastern Burma. Militarization is been carried out both to extend state sovereignty and to safeguard the regime's growing economic interests. The militarization of the ethnic states has taken a terrible toll on the civilian population, including a range of human rights abuses, increased poverty, malnutrition, exposure to disease and the breakup of families and communities.

---

[17] Charles Petrie, End of Mission Report, p. 5.

The particular counter-insurgency policies adopted by the Burma Army, the Burma Army's self-reliance policy, and inadequate salaries for military personnel have been the primary causes of the humanitarian crisis in conflict areas.[18] Rather than targeting the ethnic nationalist armies, the Burma Army focuses on removing civilians from areas where the ethnic nationalist armies operate. This is done through forced relocation orders, burning villages, destroying villagers' food stocks and laying mines around villages so villagers do not return. Between 1996 and 2007, more than 3,200 villages were destroyed, forcibly relocated or abandoned.[19] In addition, Burma Army soldiers view the local populations as supporters of the ethnic nationalist armies and therefore enemies of the state. Operating under orders or out of their own fear and anger, they often torture, rape and kill villagers with impunity, as has been documented by numerous local and international human rights groups.

Since the late 1990s, Burma Army battalions have no longer been provided with rations and instead have had to rely on themselves for food.[20] In practice, this has meant the theft or extortion of villagers' food, the confiscation of their land — with villagers sometimes having to work their own land for the battalion — and the sale of local resources and locally made products to generate income for the battalion. Villagers in conflict areas must also provide food to the ethnic nationalist armies and, although the demands tend to be less, the double burden makes it difficult for families to survive.

In and around the conflict areas, the use of forced labor is widespread on road extension projects and the building and maintainance of military compounds. Villagers must also porter supplies for the

---

[18] See Christina Fink, "Militarization in Burma's Ethnic States: Causes and Consequences," *Contemporary Politics* 14:4, 2008, pp. 447–462; and the Thailand Burma Border Consortium's annual reports on internal displacement.

[19] Information gathered by local humanitarian and human rights groups has been corroborated by high-resolution satellite images taken before and after villagers were displaced. See Thailand Burma Border Consortium, *Internal Displacement and International Law in Eastern Burma* (Bangkok, 2008), pp. 18–19.

[20] Andrew Selth, *Burma's Armed Forces: Looking Down the Barrel* (Brisbane: Griffith Asia Institute, 2009), p. 13.

army and act as human minesweepers. Soldiers and other authorities frequently extort cash from villagers, sometimes in return for not having to perform the above duties. Large swathes of land have also been confiscated in the ethnic states for the building of bases, the development of commercial plantations and the construction of energy-related projects.

As a result of all of these policies and practices, hundreds of thousands of villagers have fled or been displaced and are living in government relocation sites, other villages, the jungle or in neighboring countries. In the conflict areas, and particularly among internally displaced people in the jungle, rates of infant, child and maternal mortality are considerably higher than in government-controlled areas.[21]

Discriminatory Policies in Northern Arakan State

In northern Arakan State, the regime's discriminatory policies toward the local Muslim Rohingya population, which numbers ca. 800,000, combined with the problematic agricultural polices in force throughout the country, create enormous suffering. The regime does not recognize the Rohingya as a national race, and they were rendered stateless by the 1982 Citizenship Law. The regime's goal is to reduce and dilute the Rohingya population by applying military pressure, imposing highly restrictive policies and facilitating the movement of other population groups into the area. Persecution by the Burma Army led approximately 250,000 Rohingya to flee to Bangladesh in 1991–2. Many were eventually repatriated, but they were not given citizenship. The militarization of northern Arakan State has been accompanied by land confiscation for military use and for new settlers, the extensive use of forced labor, and arbitrary taxation by various authorities. Rohingya must obtain official permission to travel even from one village to another, and permission is often denied. This makes access to higher education, health centers and jobs particularly difficult. Rohingya must also receive official permission to marry, but

---

[21] Back Pack Health Worker Team, *Chronic Emergency: Health and Human Rights in Eastern Burma* (Thailand, 2006), pp. 32–33, 41.

long delays are common and high fees must generally be paid.[22] Since 2005, marriage licenses for Rohingya state that they can only have two children, while couples who marry illegally can be imprisoned for doing so. The impact of all these policies and practices is a severe reduction in the quality of life for most Rohingya villagers and the departure of many for Bangladesh and other countries.

Neglect of the Ceasefire Areas

The ceasefire agreements allowed the ethnic nationalist organizations to continue to administer their areas for a period of time, with the promise of development assistance from the regime. In fact, the government made only minimal effort to fulfill promises to help develop the ceasefire areas, and government restrictions on legal trade and exports have resulted in far less economic progress than the residents of ceasefire areas originally expected.[23]

Still, the humanitarian situation has improved in a number of the ceasefire areas because the cessation of hostilities allowed villagers to resume normal lives. In the larger ceasefire areas, the Burma Army has had minimal access and the government has generally not been able to impose its agricultural policies or collect taxes, so some of the ceasefire populations have faced fewer burdens than those in conflict areas and government-controlled areas. The smaller ceasefire groups however have lost control of their territory, and their populations face the same problems as others in militarized, government-controlled areas.

In the Kokang and Wa ceasefire areas of northern Burma, a humanitarian crisis has emerged primarily because of the ceasefire groups' policies. Although the regime ordered the ceasefire groups to eliminate poppy cultivation in their areas by 2015, the groups decided to implement the ban much earlier due to Chinese pressure and the expectation that they would receive substantial international

---

[22] Human Rights Watch, *Perilous Plight: Burma's Rohingya Take to the Seas*, 2009, p. 7.

[23] Tom Kramer, "Neither War Nor Peace: The Future of the Ceasefire Agreements in Burma," (Amsterdam: Transnational Institute, 2009), p. 24; see also chapter 3 of this volume.

support.[24] Little thought was given to how the villagers, who lived on steep mountainsides and relied on supplementary income from poppy production, would survive. The United Wa State Army forcibly moved large numbers of people to lower elevations where they could grow more rice, but many died from disease. In the mountains, the Wa leadership promoted the monocropping of rubber with Chinese capital, but this has provided little income for Wa day laborers to date. In the meantime, large numbers of villagers cannot grow or find enough food to meet their needs. While the regime is not responsible for this ongoing crisis, the authorities have done little to assist the Wa in humanely accomplishing a regime-imposed goal and have periodically made it difficult for humanitarian workers to access these areas.

In 2009, the Burma Army's push to assume sovereignty over the ceasefire areas put the well-being of several ceasefire populations at risk. In April 2009, all ceasefire armies were ordered to transform themselves into the Border Guard Force, which would be integrated into the Burma Army. Most ceasefire armies refused. In August 2009, the Burma Army attacked the Myanmar National Democratic Alliance Army in the Kokang region, leading over 30,000 people to seek temporary refuge in China. Similar military operations may be staged against other armed ceasefire groups. If they put up a fight, civilians will have to flee and risk losing their land and possessions.

Policies Regarding Natural Disasters

Regarding major natural disasters, the humanitarian crises that have resulted tend to be worsened by the fact that the authorities do not immediately respond with the level of assistance or access necessary to alleviate suffering. This is because of the regime's assumption that the people will manage by themselves, a lack of information about the severity of the problem, and security concerns about allowing humanitarian actors into affected areas.

When Cyclone Nargis struck in May 2008, the authorities did not expect the damage from the storm to be so severe and thus made few

---

[24] Ibid., p. 29.

preparations. Information regarding the extent of the destruction was hard to obtain because of difficulties accessing affected areas. In addition, suspicions about the intentions of some Western governments who wanted to provide assistance from their naval ships and a desire to go ahead with the planned referendum on the 2008 constitution without a substantial foreign presence led the regime initially to deny access to foreign aid workers. Instead, the regime said it would handle the crisis on its own although it simply did not have the capacity to do so. Ultimately, once the referendum was over and the Western naval ships had departed, a government mechanism was created to coordinate the international response and international aid workers were allowed to enter and work with few hindrances. By April 2009, however, access began to be restricted again. Shelter and livelihood needs were still great, but concerns about having too many foreigners in Burma in the lead-up to the elections became a more pressing concern.

In southern Chin State, a food crisis developed in 2007 following the flowering of a species of bamboo endemic in the state. The flowering happens every 50 years and leads to an infestation of rats which eat not only the bamboo flower but also all the crops. By 2008, as many as 100,000 people were reportedly in need of food aid, with the rats continuing to reproduce in large numbers and locust swarms also decimating crops.[25] Government officials did not provide any food assistance but said they would donate 1,000 bags of rat poison.[26] While humanitarian organizations inside the country were allowed to provide assistance once they realized the extent of the problem, high mountains and a lack of roads made access difficult. Chin and the closely-related Mizo groups had begun providing food aid cross-border from Mizoram, India, much earlier but in July 2009, the chairman of Chin State banned Chin villagers from receiving foreign assistance and asserted that recipients would be considered in

---

[25] Chin Human Rights Organization, "On the Edge of Survival: Conditions and Consequences of the Food Crisis in Chin State," *Burma* (Thailand, 2009), p. 1.
[26] Ibid., p. 13.

opposition to the government.[27] This order apparently stemmed from concerns that the Chin National Front, a small armed group that controls no territory but moves back and forth across the Burma–India border, would be involved in food distribution. Tens of thousands of able-bodied Chin had already left their villages in recent years because of the impact of militarization and land confiscation. With the ongoing food crisis, thousands more departed for India and Malaysia.[28]

The Impact of Sanctions on the Humanitarian Situation

Western governments have attempted to use an array of sanctions to compel the regime to rethink the way it deals with its political opposition. Broad-based sanctions, such as the US government's 1997 ban on American investment in Burma and its 2003 ban on imports from Burma, were meant to hurt the regime economically but they also affected small businesses and urban workers, including migrants from rural areas (see Kudo, this volume). Nevertheless, it is also notable that aside from the garment industry, businesspeople from countries with no sanctions on Burma have largely refrained from investing in manufacturing and service industries, suggesting that the difficulties of working in Burma account for much of the lack of investment.

The Development of the Humanitarian Sector: 1989–2009

The Growth of the International Humanitarian Sector

While the space for humanitarian assistance has opened up since 1989, there have been reversals as well, particularly during politically sensitive periods. As the International Crisis Group's 2006 report details, the 2004 sacking of General Khin Nyunt and his colleagues

---

[27] "Chairman of Chin State Bars Foreign Aid," *Khonumthung News* (India), July 30, 2009.
[28] Chin Human Rights Organization, *On the Edge of Survival*, pp. 11–12.

led to a period of greater difficulties for international aid organizations.[29] The new generals assigned to deal with foreign humanitarian aid workers initially took a tougher line, and organizations working in sensitive ethnic areas suffered. In 2005, the World Food Programme could not get permission to send rice to northern Arakan State for several months. In August 2005, the Global Fund to Fight AIDS, Tuberculosis and Malaria withdrew from Burma because of new government restrictions on travel to project sites and more cumbersome regulations regarding the procurement of medical supplies.[30] Because it was running the largest aid initiative in the country, the Global Fund had also been under greater international pressure to ensure that none of its program funds or supplies would end up in the hands of the regime or regime-affiliated organizations. In November 2005, Médecins Sans Frontières–France decided to pull out because they were no longer allowed to access project sites in Karen and Mon States and could not even share their malaria data with local health department officials.[31] The fact that some international organizations decided to withdraw while others remained reflected variations in the specific circumstances of different organizations as well as different points of view regarding when an organization's operating principles should be considered too constrained by the authorities' policies.

In 2006, the authorities closed down the five filed offices of the International Committee of the Red Cross, which had been providing assistance and protection to civilians in eastern Burma.[32] Also in 2006, highly restrictive guidelines for all international NGOs were announced, leading to increased surveillance and greater difficulties in obtaining permission to visit project sites. Over time, the situation became a bit more relaxed, particularly in central Burma, and most

[29] International Crisis Group, "Myanmar: New Threats to Humanitarian Aid," (Brussels, 2006), pp. 5–10.
[30] "The Global Fund Terminates Grants to Myanmar," *The Global Fund to Fight AIDS, Tuberculosis and Malaria*, August 18, 2005.
[31] "Why the French Section of MSF Has Ended Its Activities in Myanmar," *Medecins Sans Frontiers*, March 30, 2006.
[32] "Myanmar: ICRC Pressed to Close Field Offices," *International Committee of the Red Cross*, November 27, 2006.

international NGOs were able to continue working as before. Moreover, a number of the points in the guidelines, while cumbersome, were only half-heartedly applied.

Another low period followed the suppression of the monks' demonstrations in 2007. The UN Resident and Humanitarian Coordinator, Charles Petrie, issued a statement saying that the demonstrations resulted from a deteriorating humanitarian crisis in the country.[33] The top generals were incensed that the statement implicitly blamed the regime and was made public. Charles Petrie was ordered to leave the country. This was a big loss because he had made great efforts to expand the scope of humanitarian assistance in Burma and to attract funding.

In 2008, international aid workers were initially barred from entering the country to provide Nargis relief but later given very good access. This was facilitated by the creation of a new and highly effective mechanism, the Tripartite Core Group, composed of ASEAN, the UN and the Burmese government. Because of its access to high-level leaders, it could obtain quick authorizations from the government as needed. During this period, the number of international NGOs working in Burma increased from 40 to 80.[34] The new international humanitarian workers often pushed the authorities to grant permission for projects or activities that NGOs with a longer presence in the country felt were too sensitive to broach. In some cases, they were successful. However, they generally relied on Burmese staff in their organizations or partner organizations to make the demands. This was stressful for the Burmese staff, given that 21 Burmese cyclone relief volunteers and journalists were imprisoned for criticizing the regime's inadequate response or acting in other ways the regime disapproved of.[35] In 2009, many of the new organizations

---

[33] Thomas Fuller, "Myanmar Junta Expels Top UN Official," *The New York Times*, November 2, 2007.

[34] Refugees International, *Burma: Capitalizing on the Gains* (Washington DC, March 2009), p. 1.

[35] Assistance Association for Political Prisoners (Burma), "21 Cyclone Nargis Volunteers Still in Prison," (Mae Sot: Thailand, 2009).

sought to extend their mandate and expand their project areas outside the Delta but it was not clear if all would be able to continue to operate in the country and visas, for some, became much more difficult to obtain.

Despite the uncertainties of working in Burma, funding for humanitarian assistance has steadily increased as donors have become more aware of the humanitarian needs on the ground. Other motivations for Western donor governments include wanting to balance punitive measures against the regime with the provision of support for the general population, and wanting to engage the regime through the provision of humanitarian assistance. Some donors and aid providers have also viewed the provision of assistance through Burmese organizations as a means to decentralize governance at the local level and support the development of a more competent and dynamic civil society sector.[36] At the same time, donors and aid organizations have increasingly sought to address structural poverty to the extent they can by providing support for agricultural projects, microcredit, livelihoods development and community development. International donors have also tried to increase their leverage and impact by creating joint funds, such as the Three Diseases Fund which addresses TB, malaria and HIV/AIDS, and receives money from several governments.

The sanctions imposed by the US and the EU allow for the provision of humanitarian assistance but include restrictions on what kind of aid can be provided and how it is provided. Western donor governments do not provide large-scale development assistance or allow assistance to go through the Burmese government, although some newer programs allow coordination with the authorities up to the township level. Sanctions have prevented multilateral institutions from supporting infrastructure development in Burma because of concerns about corruption and strengthening the position of the SPDC. Similarly, the UN Development Program which normally works through governments is restricted from doing so in Burma. As

[36] See Ashley South, *Civil Society in Burma: The Development of Democracy Amidst Conflict* (Washington DC: East-West Center, 2008), for a fuller explanation.

a result, it has focused on community development despite having little previous experience in this area. The sanctions have also had the effect of holding humanitarian actors to a high standard of accountability, which is seen as burdensome by some but appropriate by others.

The Growth of the Domestic Humanitarian Sector

Between 1989 and 2009, the number of national and community-based organizations also increased dramatically in response to growing needs, greater humanitarian space and expanding international support. Brian Heidel, who surveyed NGOs in 2003, identified over 60 Rangoon-based independent NGOs addressing social welfare needs and suggested that the number countrywide may be up to 270.[37] In response to Nargis, numerous informal groups and community-based organizations formed to provide and distribute assistance. According to one report, $40 million of cyclone relief aid was channeled through more than 500 local NGOs and groups, some of which have since dissolved.[38]

Over the last 20 years, the scope of humanitarian assistance provided by religious establishments and related organizations has expanded significantly. For the Buddhist clergy, in keeping with their traditional roles of providing refuge, education and various forms of healing, assistance has primarily taken the form of setting up or expanding "orphanages" and free schools for needy children. In fact, many of the children in the orphanages have at least one parent, but the parent or parents cannot provide sufficient food or school fees. Some parents in conflict areas send their children to orphanages in government-controlled areas for their safety. The number of monastery schools for lay children at the elementary level has mushroomed

---

[37] Brian Heidel, *The Growth of Civil Society in Myanmar* (Bangalore: Books for Change, 2006), pp. 8, 16.
[38] Kerren Hedlund and Daw Myint Su, "Support to Local Initiatives in the Nargis Response: A Fringe versus Mainstream Approach," *Humanitarian Exchange* 41 (December 2008), pp. 19–20.

to over 1,000 in the past decade, but only a handful of high schools have been allowed by the authorities.[39] Some abbots have also permitted clinics and hospices for people suffering from HIV/AIDS to be established on the monastery grounds, although occasionally the authorities have denied or revoked permission. Respected abbots have, in certain cases, been able to protect the villagers around their monasteries from forced labor, and monasteries which receive more food donations than the monks need distribute extra food to the poor. After Nargis, well-known abbots, some with international followers, raised funds inside and outside the country to provide assistance through monasteries in the Delta.

The organization of humanitarian assistance among the Buddhist clergy has been almost exclusively at the level of individual abbots. Because Burmese monks have a history of involvement in political resistance movements, the regime seeks to closely regulate their activities. Abbots are linked into a national hierarchy overseen by a supreme council aligned with the regime, making it difficult for them to organize independent networks.

Christian denominations and affiliated groups make up a disproportionate number of the local organizations working on humanitarian assistance and development. While the Christian churches and organizations also come under regulation and scrutiny, their structures were independently formed. They have been able to quietly carry out relief, education, health, small-scale development and capacity-building programs for members of the Christian community in the ethnic states and other parts of the country. After Nargis, some secular international donors channeled assistance through Christian organizations because of their good organizational networks and access. With more international contacts and exposure, and a more developed organizational structure, they have received more international funding than the monk-run programs.

---

[39] See Jasmin Lorch, "The (Re)-Emergence of Civil Society in Areas of State Weakness: The Case of Education in Burma/Myanmar," in *Dictatorship, Disorder, and Decline in Myanmar*, eds. Monique Skidmore and Trevor Wilson (Canberra: ANU E Press, 2008), pp. 156–7.

Some democracy activists have entered into the humanitarian field, either because they feel that opposition politics is too risky or because they feel that the most useful thing they can do for the population in the short term is to focus on immediate needs. They have been involved in providing free funerals for the poor, food assistance to the needy, Nargis relief, free clinics and setting up HIV/AIDs self-help groups. However, they come under extra scrutiny because the authorities worry that activists will use the humanitarian space to publicly highlight the regime's shortcomings and to organize communities with the ultimate purpose of revitalizing the opposition movement.

In the conflict areas, a range of new community-based organizations were formed largely by young people from the areas to provide food, health care and education to villagers and internally displaced people. Traveling together with armed ethnic nationalist soldiers for their protection, they nevertheless expose themselves to great risk because of the proliferation of landmines and the likelihood of being treated very badly if caught by Burma Army soldiers.

Humanitarian organizations with close affiliations to the regime, otherwise known as government-organized NGOs, have also increased in number. There are two main types: some, such as the Myanmar Maternal and Child Welfare Association, were established by the regime while others started independently but became more closely aligned with the regime because of pressure from the authorities or a desire to work with less hindrance. Government-organized NGOs are expected to participate in mass rallies denouncing the democratic movement, but members at the local level are often sincere about the work they are doing. Many international organizations have refrained from working with government-affiliated organizations but some humanitarian actors feel it is important not to exclude them from discussions about international best practice and alternative development models. The Union Solidarity and Development Association (USDA), established by Than Shwe to serve as a civilian front organization, has been more problematic. The authorities have made efforts to compel foreign organizations to work with USDA members, and humanitarian aid workers' visits to program sites are monitored by USDA intelligence personnel.

After Nargis, a new type of humanitarian actor emerged: high-level businessmen. Assigned by the regime to manage the needs in hard-hit townships in coordination with the authorities, the businesspeople had to take action. Exactly what they were supposed to do and how was not specified, but the businessmen competed against each other for publicity for their projects to show the top leaders that they were doing good work. While some businessmen did want to help in the emergency phase, the needs were too great. Some effectively facilitated the work of civil society groups, and they all reduced their efforts after international organizations were allowed in. However, the regime called on businesspeople again a year after the cyclone to provide credit to farmers in the Delta in order to help revitalize rice production.

The formation of village committees after Nargis brought local level authorities and selected (sometimes elected) villagers together to distribute assistance from international NGOs. Perhaps because of the emergency nature of the relief effort, the committees were usually not asked what the villagers needed but simply told to distribute the aid provided according to the procedure advised by the international NGO. When village committees were asked to determine needs, they tended to make decisions by themselves without consulting the villagers and rarely provided full information to the villagers about the decision-making process or why particular distribution schemes were adopted. The committees' behavior reflected both the modus operandi of some of the international NGOs and the prevailing political culture in which those with power feel they have the right to decide for others without having to be fully transparent to the beneficiaries. Religious leaders and other community groups have also tended to run their projects in the same top-down way that the authorities operate. Thus, a major focus of some of the international NGOs and donors with a longer presence in Burma has been to try to introduce more participatory, grassroots approaches and greater accountability.

Assistance Provided in Burma and Neighboring Countries

UN agencies and international and local NGOs have sought to provide assistance to both the rural and urban poor to the extent allowed by the government and their budgets. In 2007, the World Food Programme was providing food to 500,000 people and in 2008–2009 gave food assistance to an additional 1 million Nargis survivors.[40] Much assistance has gone into the health sector with programs established to address malaria, TB and HIV/AIDs, to provide free vaccinations and to provide nutritional supplements to malnourished children and pregnant women. Educational needs have been partially addressed where possible through the provision of pre-primary education, cash for school supplies and other school-related fees, and food for children attending school, which encourages parents to send their children. The UNDP and various international and local NGOs have sought to assist rural families through the provision of water and sanitation, microcredit, livestock, rice banks and other community development projects. Other projects have addressed sustainable agriculture, environmental preservation and child protection. These projects have had significant impacts on families in a number of the project areas but, given the scale of the needs, the impact of the assistance at the macro level is still quite limited.

The people in the conflict areas have some of the greatest needs in terms of food security and health but they are the least accessible to humanitarian workers. While international NGOs have sought access from the authorities, few have been successful. Religious groups have found ways to get food and other supplies into a number of areas, but their reach is limited. Unregistered community-based groups, which receive financial and technical support through international organizations based in Thailand or further abroad, are the primary deliverers of relief and health assistance in civil war areas. Still, because of the nature of the conflict and the lack of sufficient funding, their assistance can only cover short-term needs. Demining programs are particularly needed for conflict and some former conflict areas, but as of 2009, no such programs had been approved.

---

[40] "World Food Programme Expands Activities in Myanmar," *United Nations Radio*, January 9, 2008; World Food Programme website, http://www.wfp.org/stories/year-after-cyclone-myanmar-recovery-needs-wfp, accessed on October 10, 2009.

In northern Arakan State, international NGOs and UN agencies have been able to provide critical food assistance and primary health care, and to introduce small-scale microcredit and agricultural development initiatives.[41] However, the government's policies have not changed and the majority of the Rohingya population continues to hover at the level of bare survival.

In the Kokang and Wa areas, the World Food Programme has provided food assistance, while the UN Office of Drug Control and other NGOs have introduced some health and alternative livelihoods projects. Not all the projects have been successful, and the reach has been limited. The Chinese government provided some rice but no development assistance.

The number of Burmese migrant workers and asylum seekers in Thailand, India and Malaysia has continued to grow dramatically over the past 20 years, despite the fact that the governments of these countries offer them little or no protection. Over 150,000 people from eastern Burma have fled to refugee camps in Thailand while perhaps close to two million people from both conflict and government-controlled areas have ended up as migrant workers in Thailand.[42] None of Burma's neighbors have signed the 1951 UN Convention on Refugees although most have allowed the UNHCR to play a limited role in screening asylum seekers and granting person of concern status to certain categories of people. In Thailand, refugees receive food, materials for building shelters, education through high school and basic medical services from international NGOs.

Approximately 30,000 Rohingya remain in two official refugee camps in Bangladesh while approximately 170,000 more Rohingya who arrived after 1992 live a hand-to-mouth existence in makeshift camps or Bangladeshi communities.[43] The government of Bangladesh

---

[41] Chris Lewa, "Northern Arakan/Rakhine State: A Chronic Emergency," Paper delivered at the Burma/Myanmar Forum (Brussels, 2006), p. 2.

[42] "Thailand: Migrant Workers Unprotected and Uninformed," *Plus News*, November 11, 2007.

[43] Human Rights Watch, "Perilous Plight: Burma's Rohingya Take to the Seas" 2009, p. 6.

allows the UNHCR and international NGOs to provide only limited assistance in the official camps, with education permitted only through fifth grade, although slightly more services and trainings have been allowed in recent years. Among those outside the camps, some have managed to access certain Bangladeshi programs and services but they cannot receive assistance or protection from the UNHCR.

By 2009, growing numbers of Rohingya males were making the dangerous boat journey from Bangladesh to Thailand and then traveling over land to Malaysia to acquire jobs as illegal migrant workers. Approximately 1,000 men who were caught by the Thai Navy were put back out to sea while others languished in detention centers, for neither the Burmese nor the Bangladeshi government would accept them back.

Illegal migrant workers in all the neighboring countries are generally underpaid and may be jailed and sent back across state borders. International NGOs and local organizations have sought to provide assistance to Burmese migrant workers in the form of health care, education for their children and legal aid, and they have advocated the legalization of migrant workers' status. While some migrant workers can obtain legal status, neighboring countries have been reluctant to legalize large numbers of migrant workers, and the military regime only began cooperating with Thailand on the process in 2009.

Obstacles to Meeting the Needs of Affected Populations

Inside Burma, foreign and domestic humanitarian actors have faced obstacles in meeting the needs of the affected populations in Burma because of the regime's lack of interest, suspicion toward humanitarian aid workers, and the working style of the authorities. Uncertainties riddle every aspect of the process with regulations and practices varying from time to time, from place to place and from person to person. A lack of sufficient funding has also hampered organizations' ability to expand their reach.

To date, the government has not conducted a national needs assessment, nor have the authorities given permission for international agencies to do so. However, the government has allowed individual organizations to gather data in some areas on specific topics, providing a partial picture of the needs, although organizations often refrain from sharing their data with other organizations.[44] It has not been possible to conduct government-approved assessments in the civil war areas but some valuable surveys have been carried out by community organizations there.[45] Without a nationwide needs assessment, it is difficult to compare levels of needs or be able to prioritize assistance.

Another major difficulty is access, including obtaining permission to enter the country and to visit project sites. The process of obtaining a visa is generally time-consuming and opaque. While the process was greatly speeded up when the Tripartite Core Group facilitated cyclone recovery work, after March 2009, the old procedures were reinstated. Since then, visas even for Tripartite Core Group staff have sometimes taken months to obtain and, in many cases, must be renewed monthly.

Memorandums of understanding must be negotiated annually with the line ministry to which the organization will be reporting and all the proposed activities of the organization in each location must be listed. Despite the needs, access to conflict areas and some other sensitive areas such as mining sites, where drug use and prostitution are rampant, has been almost impossible.[46] Much staff time is consumed by preparing and negotiating the agreements at the national level, and then explaining the proposed activities again to the authorities in each project area. Sometimes permission is denied by authorities at the divisional or township level even though permission has been granted

---

[44] Adaeze Igboemeka, "Aid Effectiveness in Burma/Myanmar: Study on Development Agency Perceptions" (London: UK Department for International Development — South East Asia, 2005), p. 3.

[45] See in particular the Thailand Border Consortium's annual Internal Displacement surveys, which are based on the research of a number of local relief organizations, and the Back Pack Health Worker Team, *Chronic Emergency*, 2006.

[46] Philip Humphris, "Nargis and Beyond: A Choice Between Sensationalism and Politicized Inaction?" *Humanitarian Exchange* 41 (December 2008) p. 12, describes how MSF Switzerland repeatedly applied for permission to provide services in areas of Karen State but was always denied.

at the national level. However, it is also true that some local authorities, especially at the village level, are quite supportive of projects which they believe will clearly benefit their communities.

International staff must request permission each time they travel to their project sites outside Rangoon. Permission generally takes two weeks for staff to obtain, and even longer for visiting donors. Sometimes international staff and donors are denied permission with no clear reason given. While international aid workers had easy access to the Delta after the Tripartite Core Group was established, access became more restricted in mid-2009.

In addition, international staff must usually be accompanied by a government official when visiting project sites outside Rangoon. While this is usually not a problem, the costs must be covered by the organization. In reality, officials assigned to accompany international staff often make little effort to monitor them, although occasionally overly zealous officials make things more difficult.

Another important limitation is the degree to which the authorities themselves work in an atmosphere of fear and insecurity. Military and civilian authorities alike are generally unwilling to bring up sensitive issues with their superiors or to make any decisions that might get themselves in trouble. They will only act on orders but the orders can be vague, leaving authorities to try to second guess what superiors want. The result is many inconsistencies in policy implementation and often overly cautious attitudes. Officials who are seen as too friendly with foreigners are also suspect.

Aid organizations also have to deal with government corruption, taxes and restrictions on imports and movements of goods. With regard to Nargis relief, some local officials engaged in corruption in the distribution of government aid and, early on, community workers often felt it was better to smooth the way at checkpoints by offering gifts to the security personnel. However, the most egregious abuse was the use of the dual exchange rate to profit from foreign aid. In 2008, the regime skimmed off at least $10 million of aid money for Nargis relief by compelling the UN to exchange dollars for Foreign Exchange Certificates (FEC) at government banks, which can then be converted into Burmese kyat.[47] In June 2008, the market rate for \$1 was about 1180 kyat but the UN was given only 880 kyat for 1 FEC, which is supposed to be equivalent to \$1. It is also notable that the UNDP had been losing money on all its exchanges previous to the cyclone as well, but the FEC to kyat exchange rate dropped significantly in the month of June, suggesting the regime saw a special opportunity to make money off the relief aid.

Meanwhile, imported vehicles for NGO use are taxed at 300%.[48] Also, the process of importing medicines and other related supplies requires approval and can take months.[49] The World Food Programme must obtain numerous permits and clearances before it can transport food supplies from food surplus areas to restricted areas such as northern Rakhine State, with permission occasionally delayed for weeks or months. In general, disbursing humanitarian assistance requires far more time and money than should be necessary.

Local NGOs that want to register face difficulties, particularly if they do not have connections with higher-level authorities. Although a number of organizations have managed to register in the past 20 years, the process is long and complicated and involves approvals at many levels.[50] International NGOs consider it safer to work with registered local organizations, so it is harder for unregistered local organizations to attract foreign funding and expand their work. Nevertheless, some local organizations choose not to register and attempt to operate "under the radar" so they will not have to report to the authorities and risk being denied permission or being co-opted. Similarly, some foreign donors do not make themselves known to officials but quietly support and monitor projects in the country.

---

[47] "Junta Siphoning Off Myanmar Cyclone Aid: UN Report," *Indo-Asian News Service*, July 30, 2008.

[48] Philip Humphris, "Nargis and Beyond," p. 12.

[49] Population Services International Myanmar, Save the Children and the UN Joint Team on AIDS in Myanmar, "HIV Programming in Myanmar," *Humanitarian Exchange* 41 (December 2008), p. 27.

[50] Ibid., p. 27.

While this allows them to maintain greater independence, they may be limited in the degree to which they can scale up their support.

The poorly developed transportation and communications infrastructure greatly hampers the provision of assistance as well. Roads in many areas are little more than pothole-filled dirt tracks. Hired drivers are reluctant to take these roads because of the toll on their vehicles and the difficulty of obtaining imported spare parts. Communications are challenging because of the low number of land lines, strict limits on the import of mobile phones which makes them expensive and scarce, and the fact that there is little internet access outside cities and some larger towns. The highly irregular electricity supply also affects offices and clinics and requires the purchase of generators and diesel.

Successes and Limitations

Aid has reached a wide range of people in Burma and has included life-saving assistance as well as livelihoods and community development assistance. As one interviewed Burmese aid worker put it, "from outside Burma the impact seems small, but it is a lot for the receiving communities." Flexible organizations have found creative ways to operate both inside the country and across borders into conflict areas, even though many communities in the country still remain unreached or insufficiently supported. In the case of Nargis, 80% of villages surveyed by the Tripartite Core Group received relief assistance within a month of the cyclone, although a year later, many villagers still lacked the physical capital necessary to farm or fish.[51]

Overall, political imperatives and the security agenda are still paramount, with the regime concerned to reduce the international presence before undertaking the planned 2010 elections. Spaces are likely to continue to open and close, depending on the current political situation, the perceived sensitivity of the geographical area, the proposed project and the humanitarian actors involved. As a result, some international NGOs try to minimize the number of

---

[51] Tripartite Core Group, "Post Nargis Social Impacts Monitoring: November 2008", (Yangon, 2009), p. vii.

international staff and cultivate close working relations with local organizations that could continue projects if access to sites is cut off or the international NGO is shut down.

Both international and registered domestic humanitarian organizations tend to see themselves as needing to remain as low profile as possible so they do not draw unwanted attention to themselves. They generally do not publicize their activities nor do they publicly comment on the regime's policies or the difficulties of working in the country. International organizations are not only concerned about attention from the regime but also from advocacy groups abroad who have been critical of various foreign aid organizations and their policies.

In the 1990s, Aung San Suu Kyi and the NLD asserted that foreign humanitarian assistance was acceptable if agencies consulted with the NLD about proposed projects, did not channel aid through the government and ensured that aid was distributed equally.[52] However, the regime has opposed NLD involvement in approving projects, and during periods when Aung San Suu Kyi has been under house arrest, it has been impossible to consult her. One of the factors that has made donors cautious about supporting projects in the country is their concern that the NLD's conditions regarding humanitarian aid conditions cannot be met.

Despite the politicized aid environment, increased interactions between humanitarian workers and the authorities at various levels within both the civil service and the military have had a discernable impact. Authorities are now more aware of international norms regarding human rights and humanitarian aid. Local authorities are sometimes more careful about how they treat local populations because of the presence of humanitarian actors and concerns about information reaching foreign and exile media. Humanitarian workers have observed that over time and particularly during the Nargis response, more authorities have come to understand the purpose and nature of humanitarian assistance and therefore have become more

---

[52] See International Crisis Group, "Myanmar: The Politics of Humanitarian Aid," (Brussels, April 2002), p. 5.

supportive. Being open with the authorities and devoting a great deal of time to explaining activities and developing relationships with them has helped ease fears and build trust. In addition, various authorities have broadened their ideas regarding the scope of humanitarian needs and the range of possible responses. Nevertheless, once an authority moves on, the process of building understanding and trust must start all over again with the new person.

Some government policies in the humanitarian sphere have been changed as a result of international advocacy efforts. While these have not resulted in the commitment of much new government funding, they have allowed humanitarian workers to establish their own programs. UN agencies are in the best position to effect change at the national policy level, as the regime does demonstrate some concern for its relationship with the UN as a whole. The extent to which this leverage is used has depended on the particular personalities involved. Donor agencies have also sought to have an impact, with the weight of their governments behind them, although the regime does not always respond positively. International and local NGOs are less able to engage in advocacy at this level because of concerns for their programs' survival and a lack of interest from the top decision-makers.

One success has been persuading the regime to move from a position of denying that HIV/AIDS was a problem in Burma to agreeing that it must be addressed. The regime has not put much money into HIV/AIDS prevention and treatment but the Ministry of Health now allows UN agencies, NGOs and representatives of affected communities to participate in the meetings for the development of strategic plans on HIV/AIDS as well as coordinating and technical group meetings.[53]

Another achievement is the government's recognition of child protection as a legitimate concern whereas before it could not be mentioned because of the regime's insistence that all Burmese children were well taken care of. Since the regime ratified the Convention on Child's Rights in 1989, the government has had to report regularly to the committee monitoring countries' compliance. As a result

---

[53] Population Services International Myanmar *et al.*, pp. 27–28.

of this requirement and constructive suggestions from UN agencies and others, some positive changes have been made. Because of trainings provided by humanitarian organizations, government-run orphanages have become somewhat more child-friendly, the problem of sexual abuse of children is more recognized in the community, and female police have been more regularly assigned to deal with cases involving children. Human trafficking has also been acknowledged as a problem and given more attention.

Policies regarding government abuses of civilians have been more difficult to address. Nevertheless, through the concerted efforts of the International Labor Organization, laws banning the use of forced labor were decreed and the use of forced labor has been reduced at least in central Burma, if not in the ethnic states. On the other hand, the ICRC made many efforts to talk to the regime in private about ending human rights abuses in ethnic states but they were not successful and their programs were stopped.[54]

The efforts of UN agencies and other humanitarian actors have been successful when the policymakers came under sufficient pressure to do something and the solutions proposed were relatively easy to implement. However, even when better policies have been adopted, a lack of funding and resources, inadequately trained service providers and poor pay mean that sometimes there is little impact. For instance, even though some elementary teachers have been taught child-centered teaching methodologies, their class sizes have not been reduced and many rely on fees from tuition classes after school, so there are few improvements in the classroom.

At lower levels, NGOs have sometimes been able to influence the way policies are implemented, particularly when they can give good reasons and the authorities trust them. Over time, they have also been able to expand the vocabulary that can be used to describe humanitarian work. Words associated with opposition politics such as democracy, reconciliation and networks are not allowed, but aid workers can usually find ways to introduce concepts and practices which they feel

---

[54] "Myanmar: ICRC Denounces Major and Repeated Violations of International Humanitarian Law," *ICRC Press Release*, June 29, 2007.

are fundamental to community development and empowerment by using alternative terminology.

There have also been improvements in the capacity and coordination of the humanitarian aid sector. For instance, after Cyclone Nargis hit, the Local Resource Center was founded to provide training in financial management, organizational development, and reporting, monitoring and evaluation, along with technical trainings for key sectors.[55] Other capacity building efforts have focused on tackling a culture of authoritarianism and mistrust and creating more participatory and dynamic local organizations. Increased, albeit uneven, internet access and greater opportunities for travel outside the country have also helped expose Burmese humanitarian workers and interested government staff to new approaches.

Until recently, contact both between local NGOs and between local and international humanitarian organizations was minimal and irregular. Relationships were generally dyadic, with an international organization working closely with selected local organizations but having little contact with other organizations. The massive destruction wrought by Cyclone Nargis catalyzed organizations to reach out to different communities and to coordinate their work with other humanitarian actors. The Myanmar NGO Network, which formed in 2007, became much more organized in response to Nargis, and the UN established cluster groups on particular topics which met regularly and brought together a wide range of humanitarian actors. For many local humanitarian actors, linking aid groups is now recognized as important not only for better coordination but also for increasing confidence and breaking down mistrust.

It is interesting to note that some fears have not been realized. Donors and humanitarian organizations previously operating along Burma's borders have been able to work inside the country or maintain a presence in both areas. In addition, the aid agencies of the governments which have taken the toughest positions on the military regime have been able to run successful programs in Burma, although nationals from these countries do tend to face greater scrutiny.

---

[55] Kerren Hedlund and Daw Myint Su, "Support to Local Initiatives," p. 19.

Conclusion

Compared to many other countries in Southeast Asia, the humanitarian space in Burma is still extraordinarily limited and uncertain. However, compared to 20 years ago in Burma, there is far more space for humanitarian activity today. The US government's 2009 shift in position on Burma and the planned 2010 elections may also facilitate some improvements in the coming years. While the US government stated that sanctions would not be revoked until there was demonstrable progress on political issues, the US also announced it would increase its funding for humanitarian programs in Burma and engage with high-level Burmese authorities on a range of issues. This slight relaxing of US policy may lead other donors to increase their assistance. However, as Tony Banbury, the World Food Programme's Regional Director for Asia, noted in 2007, "Even with greater funding for aid agencies, humanitarian assistance alone will not be enough to transform the lives of the millions of vulnerable persons in Myanmar who need help".[56]

Questions for the future include whether post-election governments will feel more responsibility to address humanitarian needs, whether they will implement economic policies that lead to a reduction in poverty, and whether more of the revenues from the sale of natural gas and other resources will be channeled into social and economic development. In any case, humanitarian organizations will continue to have an important role to play in addressing immediate needs, in introducing new approaches to communities and local aid workers, and in attempting to influence authorities regarding policy making and practice. Ultimately, finding ways to address governance and economic issues will be crucial to resolving the various humanitarian crises in the country.

---

[56] "Humanitarian Aid Not Enough for Myanmar's Poor — UN Official," *WFP News Release*, October 18, 2007.

Part B
Elite Politics

Chapter 5

Daw Aung San Suu Kyi: A Burmese Dissident Democrat

Kyaw Yin Hlaing

Abstract

Aung San Suu Kyi, the daughter of Burma's founding leader General Aung San and winner of the 1991 Nobel Peace Prize, is probably the most famous Burman in the world — yet for some 15 of the last 21 years she has been in jail or under house arrest. The iconic leader of the National League for Democracy, Burma's erstwhile democratic opposition party, she is a charismatic leader who has never held governmental office. This chapter seeks to analyze her leadership role dispassionately and to discuss her political future after the election.

Keywords: National League for Democracy (NLD); Depayin Incident; John Yettaw.

Daw Suu in Context

Daw Aung San Suu Kyi, to whom many Burmese refer as "the lady" or "Daw Suu", has been considered the leader of the Burmese pro-democracy movement, not just by locals but many people throughout the world. An Iraqi taxi driver in Gothenburg, Sweden, did not know where Burma was but he had heard of Aung San Suu Kyi. Likewise, a Nigerian taxi driver in Chicago had never heard of Burma's new name, "Myanmar", but he knew who Aung San Suu Kyi was. Since winning the Noble Peace Prize in 1991, she has been deemed the goddess of democracy. Many appear to believe that she is the answer to all of Burma's political problems. Some go so far as to say that the problems will persist until Daw Suu leads the country. However, from the point of view of the ruling junta, she is the source of all of Burma's political problems. A retired government officer even claimed that all political problems could have been resolved if Daw Suu were not "worshipped as the goddess of the Burmese democracy movement".[1] Not surprisingly, Daw Suu has been put under house arrest three times. In May 2009, the government transferred Daw Suu to the notorious Insein jail after she allowed an uninvited American guest, who swam across a lake to her residence, to stay in her house for two days. She was then charged with violation of the terms of her house arrest and sentenced to a three-year prison term including hard labor, which the government later commuted to an 18-month sentence under house arrest.

Because Burma is a predominantly Buddhist country, its society is often described as either passive or pacifist. In spite of this description, the existence of a dissident culture has always been a big part of Burmese society. In the prayer most Buddhist Burmese recite every day, the government is referred to as one of the five biggest enemies of the people alongside prayers for freedom from government harassment. Throughout the postcolonial period, anti-government groups have been very popular among the Burmese people, especially the educated. For instance, between 1948 and 1962 — a period commonly known as the parliamentary period in Burmese political history[2] — all student unions in the country were dominated by groups affiliated to opposition parties. As a former student leader noted, "for most university students in the parliamentary days, it was an honor to be a part of an opposition group."[3] After the parliamentary government was brought down by the military in 1962, a large majority of the public stayed away from anti-government

---

[1] Interview with a retired government official (July 12, 2003), Yangon.

[2] The post-colonial political history of Burma can be divided into three periods. The first period (1948–1962) was known as the parliamentary period when the country had a British-style parliamentary system. The second period (1962–1988) was known as the Socialist period when the country was ruled by the military-backed Socialist government. The downfall of the Socialist government in 1988 was followed by the State Law and Order Restoration Council (SLORC) regime that was renamed the State Peace and Development Council (SPDC) in 1997.

[3] Interview with a former student leader (May 21, 2004), Yangon.

movements as the cost of participating in them was significantly raised. However, as in most other authoritarian countries, books and groups that were banned by the government remained popular and people still viewed anti-government student leaders as heroes. Like many other traditional societies, Burmese people often yearned for saviors who would rescue them from the crisis they were in. Since the government was the cause of many of their problems, many people often looked for a savior from among dissidents. That is why dissident leaders often assumed names like "conqueror of the one-party system" (*ta-pa-ti-naing*) or the "conqueror of the king" (*min-ko-naing*) in an attempt to attract the support and attention of the public.

Amid the 1988 nationwide protest that brought down the Socialist government, the public looked up to Daw Suu as a leader who could get them out of the crisis they were facing. Daw Suu joined the movement, promising that she would work hard for democracy in the country. Even after she became a leader of the main opposition party, the National League for Democracy (NLD), in the wake of the military takeover of the country, Daw Suu continued to act more like a social movement leader than the leader of a political party. Portraying herself as a follower of the Gandhian approach, Daw Suu engaged in civil disobedience by breaking the restrictions she considered unfair. While highlighting the injustice done by the junta in various parts of the country, she tried to convince the public that her party, with the support of the people, could bring not only democracy but also prosperity to the country. Some veteran politicians at that time privately complained that her approach, though nonviolent, was too confrontational.[4] Disgruntled by the high-handed actions of some military officers, a large majority of the public welcomed Daw Suu's anti-regime discourses and supported her and her party in any way they could.

The military government, for its part, was dismayed by Daw Suu's and her party's refusal to play the game according to its rules. Military

---

[4] Private conversations with some veteran politicians (1993–2006), Yangon and Mandalay.

leaders put her under house arrest whenever they thought she was a danger to the order they wanted to maintain in the country. Although the military's detention of Daw Suu seriously undermined the NLD, it helped her to win sympathy both from the locals and the international community. A former member of the NLD opined that it was in part because of the junta's mishandling of her that Daw Su became both internationally and domestically popular and finally won the Nobel Peace Prize.[5] At the moment, most senior military officers do not appear to want to have anything to do with her. At the same time, they do not seem to know what they should do with her either. Daw Suu, for her part, has not been able to do much to resolve the political problems of the country as she has spent most of her time under house arrest. However, her presence in Burmese politics has kept the weakening Burmese pro-democracy movement in the international limelight.

The Emergence of Daw Suu as a Leader of the Pro-Democracy Movement

Daw Suu was born to Burma's national hero, General Aung San, and Daw Khin Kyi in 1945. She was educated mostly in foreign countries, obtaining an undergraduate degree in Politics, Philosophy and Economics from Oxford University. Thereafter, she worked for the United Nations for a few years. After marrying British academic Michael Aris, she, along with her husband, worked for the government of Bhutan. When her husband took up a job at Oxford University, she became a researcher and writer. She did not interact with Burmese governments much after the military, led by General Ne Win, took control of the country and established a military-dominated socialist government in 1962. When she was drawn into the Four Eights movement in 1988, she was working on a PhD dissertation on Burmese literature. Given her past experience, Daw Suu did not seem to have any political ambitions. Though still a citizen of Burma, she had made Oxford her home. However, at the

---

[5] Interview with a former member of the NLD (June 14, 2006).

time the movement coalesced, Daw Suu happened to be back in Yangon, attending to her ailing mother. She was merely a spectator of the movement until her father's colleagues requested that she do something for the sake of the country. Being a late participant in the movement, Daw Suu initially was not the most prominent activist. However, the people's reverence for her father and approval of her straightforward style soon elevated her to one of the big three of the movement, along with Brigadier. General Aung Gyi, whose critical letters to General Ne Win played a crucial role in the outbreak of the movement, and a well-respected former military commander, General Tin Oo. Daw Suu and her colleagues tried to work for an interim government that could oversee a free and fair multi-party election. However, before they could bring all major political actors together, the military took control of the country.

Daw Suu then tried to form a grand national front with two other prominent members of the movement and other veteran politicians.[6] Although the plan to form a grand national front faltered, the big three came together and formed the main opposition party, the National League for Democracy. This coalition of groups led by the big three did not function well since its inception. Brigadier General Aung Gyi's and Daw Aung San Suu Kyi's groups accused each other of undertaking some actions without getting the approval of other groups. Factional politics at the center spread to local areas and the party became ridden with power struggles before it could properly form local branches. A former leading member of the NLD noted: "General Aung Gyi traveled around the country and made promises to the people who supported him without discussing these with the central executive committee. People at the local level then vied for positions in local branches. Ma Suu had to solve the problems by personally visiting those places."[7] Brigadier General Aung Gyi's group also claimed that

---

[6] Copies of letters to prominent politicians by Daw Aung San Suu Kyi and U Htwe Myint, the author's personal collection.
[7] Interview with a former member of the NLD (January 3, 2006), Yangon.

communists from Daw Suu's group, which was commonly known as the intelligentsia group, of forming local branches with their own supporters.[8]

The coalition of the big three came to an end when Brigadier General Aung Gyi asked Daw Suu to expel left-leaning people from her group. After failing to reach an agreement, the central executive committee decided to solve the problem by voting for an agreement that the losing group would have to quit the party. As General Tin Oo's group sided with Daw Suu's group, U Aung Gyi and his group had to quit the party.[9] This incident was a blessing in disguise for Daw Suu and her group. As General Tin Oo and his group members were not as aggressive and eccentric as Brigadier General Aung Gyi's group, the departure of the latter allowed Daw Suu and her colleagues to dominate the party. Even though General Tin Oo became the chairman of the party in the wake of Aung Gyi's departure, Daw Aung San Suu Kyi, as Secretary General of the party, emerged as the most powerful figure in the party. People did not even pay attention to the position she held; all 280 participants of the survey I conducted in 2005 identified her, not General Tin Oo or any other, as the leader of the party.[10] Daw Suu's role in the party was so big that she became synonymous with the party and became an irreplaceable leader of the NLD and the movement. That is why the NLD won a landslide victory in the 1990 elections even though Daw Suu could not run in it.

Daw Suu's Dissident Politics

As a late participant in the movement, Daw Suu had to try to legitimize her position as a leader of the movement. Because she was not an experienced political activist who had lived her life in Burma, Daw

---

[8] The Union National Democracy Party, *phyi-pon-ka-de-lo-ba* (This is what happened!), (UNDP: Yangon, 1989), p. 12.
[9] Ibid., pp. 16–17.
[10] This opinion survey was conducted by the author with the assistance of five young Burmese scholars between March and May 2005.

Suu tried to establish her legitimacy by shedding light on her association with her national hero father, General Aung San. In her earlier speeches to the public, she repeatedly referred to her father. She noted that although she did not have any political experience, as the only daughter of Aung San, she understood the complex nature of Burmese politics. She also noted that she had stayed away from politics, for, like Aung San, she did not want to be part of the political games in which politicians vied for power in a malicious manner.[11] In trying to reach out to military officers, she said that as the daughter of the founder of the Burmese army, she had a great deal of affection for members of the armed forces. She recalled that she was brought up by soldiers working under her father.[12] In trying to reach out to the initiators or leaders of the movement, i.e. students, Daw Suu promised that even though she worked closely with politicians of earlier eras, she would not let any of them use her for their political interests. In trying to mobilize the public, Daw Suu portrayed herself as a straightforward and honest person who was prepared to sacrifice her life for the country. Defining democracy as a system where governments function according to public opinions, Daw Suu repeatedly noted in public speeches that democracy was the only solution to the ongoing political problems in the country and called for the socialist government to hand over power to an interim government before a free and fair multi-party democratic election could be held.[13] Daw Suu and her comrades then tried to form a public consultative committee to guide the movement towards a lasting solution.

After the military retook control of the country and established a new government under the name of the State Law and Order Restoration Council (SLORC) in September 1988, Daw Suu came to adopt a confrontational approach. Noting that she did not trust the military government's promise to hold a free and fair election, Daw Suu spent a lot of time attacking the restrictions the government had

---

[11] Daw Aung San Suu Kyi's speech to the general public on August 26, 1988, the author's personal collection, p. 2.

[12] Ibid., p. 4.

[13] Ibid., p. 6.

imposed on political parties and the general public. Although they supported her wholeheartedly, some of Daw Suu's colleagues considered some of her actions to be very un-Burmese. For instance, a late senior politician once said,

> "Ma Suu is a very nice person. She tried to do what she could for the country. However, she sometimes lost self-control and started doing things which she, as a Burmese woman, should not do. When we were having a meeting with the election commission, she saw U Ne Win's picture being hung in the meeting room. She became very upset and started saying loudly that the picture of a killer should not be present in public places. She suddenly jumped on to the table to take the picture down. Almost everybody there was much older than she. She should not have done that. We were awed by her action."[14]

A retired military officer who used to work closely with Daw Suu also noted that he and some of his colleagues had decided to quit the NLD after they learned that Daw Suu was very hard-headed and did not like to listen to the advice of veteran politicians and retired military officers. He said,

> "I was working for her [Daw Suu] and the party, risking my life. Some time in 1989, Ma Suu and I came back from a trip together. While riding a car together, I said to Ma Suu that she should listen to the advice of senior people as she did not understand Burmese society well. After we got back to Yangon, she told General Aung Shwe that she did not wish to work with me. After I learned about it, I was very disappointed. I did not have any prejudice against her. I just wanted to help her out. I was so disappointed with that whole incident that I quit the NLD and stayed away from politics."[15]

Some senior politicians explained Daw Suu's behavior by noting that whenever there was a disagreement between senior politicians and young people, she sided with the latter. As they did not like many senior politicians, she did not often take the advice of veteran politicians well.

Daw Suu, for her part, appeared to have had the opinion that the public need not respect evil governments. She therefore did not

---

[14] Interview with Thakin Chit Maung (July 12, 2005), Yangon.
[15] Interview with a retired military officer (January 4, 2005), Yangon.

hesitate to refer to military leaders as fascists and to criticize the activities of the government she thought hurt the public. Daw Suu also repeatedly said in her speeches that the public must have the courage to defy those orders of the government they did not support. Therefore, when ex-commanders from her party were reluctant to engage in open protests against the government for fear that it might cause bloodshed, she angrily asked them if they were followers of Aung San or followers of Ne Win. A former nationalist leader noted,

> "She was basically asking all these ex-military commanders if they were cowards. She should not have talked to older people like that. We could only conclude that she was very Westernized."[16]

Regardless of such remarks, Daw Suu's actions appear to have gone down well with a large majority of the people. 73% of the 280 survey participants said they liked the fact that Daw Suu had the courage to challenge the military government.[17] For a large number of people, democracy meant anti-military and a democratic government meant a government formed by Daw Suu. When asked if they would figuratively define Daw Suu as "democracy", 83 out of 280 survey participants answered yes, and 74 said they would define her as "a democratic leader".[18] It is therefore no exaggeration to say that Daw Suu and the democratic movement have become synonymous. As most veteran politicians did not express their unhappiness with Daw Suu, the public was largely unaware of the internal problems within the NLD. Although government newspapers regularly reported the problems among NLD leaders, the public often believed the opposite of what these newspapers said. In addition, influential Burmese programs on the BBC and VOA at that time portrayed Daw Suu as a democracy idol by highlighting how she challenged the evil, authoritarian government. Distraught by the high-handed actions of the military government, the public, for its part, was prepared to unquestionably support any criticism or challenge against the government. Of the 287 people I

---

[16] Interview (December 2, 2002), Yangon.
[17] Opinion survey (March–May, 2005).
[18] Ibid.

interviewed in the last ten years, 185 said they wholeheartedly supported the manner in which Daw Suu challenged the military government and the way she criticized politicians who lacked the courage to stand up against the junta in 1989 and 1990. They all also said that Daw Suu was a person with good character and that it was acceptable to strongly criticize those who had done evil. One of the interviewees noted:

> "Many people I know sided with Daw Suu when Brigadier General Aung Gyi broke away from the NLD mainly because General Aung Gyi did not challenge the junta as forcefully as Daw Suu. Although General Aung Gyi had done a lot to bring down the Socialist government, we did not believe that he would be strong enough to bring down the currently military government. I know many people who rightly or wrongly believe that Daw Suu can do no wrong."[19]

To be sure, 43 of the 287 people said although they wholeheartedly supported Daw Suu in the early 1990s, with the benefit of hindsight (in 2002–2005), they thought that she should have been less confrontational in dealing with military leaders. Only 8 of the 287 interviewees said that they did not support Daw Suu's confrontational approach to military leaders.[20]

There was no doubt that her straight-talking style helped her become a popular political leader among the general populace and in the international community. In other words, her anti-regime activities gave her the legitimacy she needed to be a leader of the democracy movement. At the same time, her confrontational approach undermined all prospects for future dialogue between the government and the NLD. By the middle of 1989, it was quite clear that the NLD would win a landslide victory if the elections were truly free and fair. However, both Daw Suu and her colleagues did not appear to have come up with any concrete strategy on how to deal with a stronger enemy before they won the elections. Partly because of this, Daw Su was placed under house arrest for about six years and was barred from participating in the 1990 elections.

---

[19] Interview with a school teacher (June 2, 2006), Yangon.
[20] The rest either refused to answer the question or said "don't know".

After she was released from house arrest in 1995, Daw Suu became less confrontational in dealing with the junta. While repeatedly calling for a dialogue between the NLD and the junta, Daw Suu continued to play the role of tribunal of the oppressed by holding daily public meetings in front of her house. At those meetings, Daw Suu answered questions submitted to her in advance by people from various parts of the country. Needless to say, the questions dealt with issues ranging from the problems facing the general public to the failures and mismanagement of the government. In answering the questions, Daw Suu became culturally more sensitive than she used to be. Likewise, her speeches also referred to Buddha's teachings more frequently than before.

Unlike in the past, Daw Suu did not blame the government unnecessarily and at times disagreed with the people who wanted her to discredit the government. For instance, in response to the question that tried to ridicule the introduction of the Thai-style greeting in public places, Daw Suu said, "…I like it. It is a polite manner and is better than shaking hands in tropical countries like ours…"[21] At the same time, Daw Suu did not reject the government's requirement for the general public to share or pay for the cost of the construction of roads and schools. While calling for the government to be more responsible and not to overburden the public, she asked the people to do what they could for the development of their neighborhood, town, city and country.

While urging the public to have the courage to tell the truth and to point out the mistakes of the government, Daw Suu also advised the public to try to resolve their problems by working through the system. Instead of asking the public to do what they thought was right even if the government did not permit it, she asked them to try to get permission from the government or to explain to the authorities concerned what their intentions were before doing anything that could arouse suspicion.[22] When asked to address problems in the education system, she urged them to try working with school administrators and other authorities concerned.

---

[21] Transcript of Daw Suu's interaction with the audience of the public assembly, October 14, 1995, the author's personal collection.

[22] Transcript of Daw Suu's interaction with the audience of the public assembly, October 15, 1995, the author's personal collection.

Another significant change in the way Daw Suu described the nature of the government was that she began to make a distinction between military leaders and other segments of the bureaucracy and avoided criticizing the entire government in a sweeping manner. Commenting on the occasion where a police sergeant apologized for the beating of a person by four police officers, Daw Suu remarked,

> "I want to make a balanced comment on this issue both from negative and positive perspectives. The brutal harassment of the public by government officers is very bad. However, if the responsible officials apologized to the victims and tried to solve the problems by taking punitive actions against the abusers, the problem would be resolved.... I have a lot of respect for people who like to correct their own mistakes."[23]

Along with the aforesaid changes, Daw Suu also endeavored to demystify her exalted position as the goddess of democracy. She repeatedly stated in public speeches and interviews with foreign journalists that she was just an ordinary person working hard for the cause she believed in and that she could not achieve anything without the support of the general public. In many of her public speeches, she also said that it was not she who could deliver what the public wanted; the public would have to achieve it themselves.

However, probably because many people wanted her to challenge the regime, Daw Suu continued to try to legitimize the NLD by way of delegitimizing the military government. Her speeches repeatedly alleged that the NLD and its leaders were better than their counterparts in the military government. However, unlike before, she was very careful about the words she used. She stopped referring to the military leaders as fascists and repeatedly said that the military and the NLD must work together in order to resolve the problems in the country. It is interesting to note that while trying to keep the movement alive, Daw Suu stopped instigating the public to engage in open protests against the government. She only called on the international

---

[23] Transcript of Daw Suu's interaction with the audience of the public assembly, December 23, 1995, the author's personal collection.

community to do whatever it could, including the imposition of economic sanctions on the country, to promote democracy.

Regardless of the changes in her strategy and tactics in dealing with the junta and reviving the movement, Daw Suu remained popular among Burmese people. Of 200 participants of a survey conducted in 1998, 72% said Daw Suu was an extraordinary political leader, 10% said she was a good leader and only 5% disapproved of her leadership. 85% of the survey participants were not even aware that Daw Suu had become less confrontational than she used to be.[24] Probably because of the way the BBC, VOA and RFA covered her activities, the public was more aware of her negative comments on the activities of the junta than the conciliatory ones. In the view of 81% of the survey participants, Daw Suu continued to be the mouthpiece of the oppressed people.[25] However, by the mid-1990s, many people had become more cautious than they used to be in expressing their support for Daw Suu and the NLD. Of the 200 survey participants, only 15% said they would shout "long live Daw Aung San Suu Kyi" whenever and wherever they ran into Daw Suu.[26] 30% said they might have done so if they had run into her in 1989 but by the mid-1990s, they would not if the place was very crowded or if others were not shouting the same thing.[27] This was partly due to the rising cost of being labeled anti-government activists and partly because of the mini-bubble caused by the inflow of some foreign investment and the liberalization of the export and import sector in the first half of the 1990s. Since the government would not issue business licenses to open supporters of the NLD, many people became very cautious in expressing their support for Daw Suu. Lengthy prison terms meted out to ardent supporters also weakened her support base. As a result, in one of her public speeches, Daw Suu requested the people who confined

---

[24] This opinion survey was conducted by the author with the assistance of nine young Burmese scholars in 1998.
[25] Ibid.
[26] Opinion survey (1998).
[27] Ibid.

themselves to economic activities to try to get richer only after the country had become democratic.[28]

However, Daw Suu's goodwill to the junta did not last very long. She started to make disgruntled statements when the government did not react to any of her requests for meetings and dialogues. In 1998, Daw Suu and her colleagues formed the Committee Representing the People's Parliament (CRPP) with 250 people who had won the 1990 elections as a challenge to the government's National Convention. The government responded by outlawing the group and arresting a large number of politicians who were involved in it. She then started making trips to outlying areas to meet the general public. When the government stopped her from making such trips, she traveled as far as she could and staged protests by refusing to go back to Yangon. In 2000, after a few attempts to get out of Yangon, Daw Suu was placed under house arrest again.

In late 2000, there emerged rumors that secret meetings between senior military leaders and Daw Suu were going on. After her release from house arrest in early 2002, Suu Kyi sought to avoid offending senior military leaders. She also declared that the necessary confidence between the junta and the NLD had been established. She then visited some major projects the government had undertaken. However, this thaw period was rather short-lived. When the junta failed to comply with her demands to resume dialogue, Daw Suu began to resort to a confrontational approach, calling on the government to release all political prisoners and to honor the 1990 election result. To the junta's dismay, the NLD also renewed its commitment to the outlawed Committee Representing the People's Parliament and refused to call for economic sanctions on the country to be lifted.

Daw Aung San Suu Kyi and other leading NLD members then toured the country while engaging in party organizational activities. Between June 2002 and May 2003, Daw Suu visited 95 townships, where local authorities discouraged people from helping her and the NLD. All the speeches she gave during these trips attacked the government in one

---

[28] Transcript of Daw Suu's interaction with the audience of the public assembly, March 2, 1996, the author's personal collection.

way or another, and the government appeared to have interpreted Daw Suu's trips as a show of force against it. Members of the government-backed Union Solidarity and Development Association (USDA) were deployed to distribute anti-NLD pamphlets and organize anti-Daw Suu protests. Despite the government's efforts, Daw Suu continued to tour the country amid great public support. However, when she visited their townships, the anti-NLD protests became so aggressive that, by early 2003, many predicted an inevitable bloody clash between the two if Daw Suu's tours and anti-NLD protests continued. Things came to a head on May 30, 2003, when a clash broke out between government supporters and NLD members while Daw Suu was near the town of Depayin in central Burma. According to government sources, only four people were killed and 40 injured. In contrast, opposition sources reported some 70 deaths and over 100 injured. Attributing the commotion to unruly NLD members and their supporters, the government placed Daw Suu under "protective custody." Once again, Daw Suu became one of the most famous political prisoners in the world.

Although the movement was in a deadlock, Daw Suu remained popular among the general public and was still revered as the goddess of democracy. However, many people also began to show their frustration with the NLD. 135 of 280 participants of the aforesaid survey noted that although they continued to support Daw Suu and the NLD, they had begun to lose confidence in the ability of the NLD to effect changes in the country.[29] There also emerged a small group of activists who openly questioned the status of Daw Suu as the goddess of democracy. They said they continued to support her but could not accept the fact that nothing could move forward without her. They suggested that when Daw Suu was not around, others must take over the active leadership of the movement and deal with the government. They seemed to be prepared to support dialogue between the opposition and the junta even if Daw Suu was not a part of it. Although these people are still in the minority, their number is gradually increasing. As discounting Daw Suu could cost one's political career, many political activists who were willing to accept any tangible positive change in the political system,

---

[29] Opinion survey (March–May, 2005).

even without Daw Suu, did not discuss it openly. A prominent writer angrily responded to a critic of Daw Suu, saying, "I love Daw Suu. I worship her. I would do whatever she asked me to do. I would go to hell if she asked me to go to hell".[30] The above survey of 280 people revealed that many people shared the views of the writer. Of the survey participants, 200 stated that they loved Daw Suu. The website and mailing lists run by activists fiercely attacked the critics of Daw Suu. Messages sent out through the "Democracy for Burma" mailing list indicated that many still believed that "Daw Suu can do no wrong".

All in all, Daw Suu's dissident politics has been shaped by many factors. While leading the movement, she had to try to mould public opinion and in doing so, she was also changed by the public. She understood that for many people, democracy meant the opposite of military government and they believed it would do away with their sufferings. She also understood that the public appeared to have more interest in her comments on its problems and on the activities of the government than on democracy per se. As a result of these developments, Daw Suu spent more time attacking the military government than preaching democracy. Political activists who had the courage to openly address the sufferings of ordinary people and to criticize the military government were deemed by the general public to be heroes. Although she owed her initial popularity to her father, Daw Suu emerged as the most popular political leader of the country mainly because she had the courage to challenge the government more openly and frequently than any other political activist. In other words, a dissident democrat must be an anti-military activist before he or she can talk about democracy, or at least such was the nature of public political perceptions within the country.

The Junta's Position on Daw Suu

The military junta has long claimed its wish to establish a disciplined democracy in Burma. But the military leaders only wanted Daw Suu and other political activists to play the game by their rules. When Daw Suu repeatedly challenged the junta, she was viewed by the regime as

---

[30] Personal conversations (October, 2004).

the biggest mischief maker in the country. When Daw Suu did not abide by the rules it tried to impose, it began to undertake smear campaigns against both Daw Suu and the NLD through the state media. Hundreds of anti-Daw Suu articles published in government newspapers referred to her as "a lackey of imperialists," "the one that does not care about the purity of her own race," "the one who married a man from the ethnic group of which those who masterminded the assassination of her father was a part," "the one who did not understand and appreciate the goodwill of military leaders," "the one who did not genuinely care about the interest of the country," etc. The junta amplified its anti-Daw Suu campaign when she and other NLD leaders started calling on Western governments to impose economic sanctions on the country and to exert harsh pressure on the government.

Military leaders also tried to undermine Daw Suu by arresting many of her advisors. The junta also pressured many other capable members of the party to quit a disassociate themselves from it. Many detained NLD leaders were released on condition that they would retire from party politics. Although it has occasionally released political prisoners, Daw Suu's closest advisors like U Win Tin were kept behind bars for several years. The junta's smear campaign against Daw Suu did not appear to have a serious impact on the way the general public perceived Daw Suu. Of 280 survey participants, only about 5% said they regularly read anti-Daw Suu articles, 35% said they read them occasionally, 42% said they had read them a few times and the rest said they never read them. Of those who had read the articles, only 9% said they took them seriously, 35% said there was some correct information in those articles, and the rest said they did not take these articles seriously.[31] 9% of the readers said the articles did not change their attitude toward Daw Suu.[32] On the other hand, however, the junta's detention of Daw Suu's advisors and the resignation of many capable members from the party seriously undermined the NLD, especially when Daw Suu was placed under house arrest as well. Since the departure of these able members from Daw Suu's group in

---

[31] Opinion survey (March–May, 2005).
[32] Ibid.

the party, it fell into the hands of the aging members of the ex-com-mander's group. At the present moment, the aging caretaker leaders focus mainly on keeping the party alive and have not done much to consolidate the party's position vis-à-vis the junta. Three veteran politicians who were close to Daw Suu noted that the absence of capable members in the intelligentsia group also vitiated Daw Suu's ability to deal with the junta and to administer the affairs of the party.[33] Another veteran politician even said that if the original mem-bers of the intelligentsia group had been with Daw Suu, the Depayin incident could have been avoided:

> "The original members of the intelligentsia group respected Daw Suu but they did not necessarily follow her orders. They would argue with her on the things they did not agree with. The current senior party members are not assertive. They just listen to her. Any of the members of the intelligen-tsia group would not have let Daw Suu proceed with the trip if they thought the time was not right. When she does not get the right advice, she cannot make the right judgment."[34]

The main problem with the NLD and the junta was that both parties thought that they had the power to set the rules of the game for any possible dialogue. Daw Suu and her colleagues appeared to believe that the public had given them the mandate to lead the dia-logue. Military leaders, on the other hand, seemed to think that since they controlled the government, they should set the rules. After she was released in 1995, Daw Suu directly and indirectly indicated that she and her colleagues would meet military leaders on equal terms. The junta, for its part, only wanted Daw Suu to help it out, especially in its attempt to improve its reputation in the international commu-nity. Military leaders, however, did not make clear what they would give Daw Suu in return, should she agree to render her assistance. Similarly, although she repeatedly said that she was prepared to work with the junta, she did not clarify what she would be willing to give up in order to work with military leaders. In other words, both parties

[33] Interviews with three veteran politicians (July 5, 2008), Yangon.
[34] Interview with Thakin Tin Mya (January 3, 2006), Yangon.

mainly identified what they expected of one another. They became disappointed with each other when they did not get what they expected. It was partly because of this disappointment that both parties took hardline positions against each other. If Daw Suu had called for the lifting of Western economic sanctions, the Depayin incident might not have taken place. Similarly, if military leaders had made some concessions to the NLD, Daw Suu and her colleagues might not have taken such a confrontational approach. In a movement to initiate change, both parties have not found a way to work with each other.

To make matters worse, in early May 2009, an American man, John Yettaw, who was supposedly mentally ill, swam across the Inya Lake to Daw Suu's residence. Because he claimed that he was too exhausted to swim back, Daw Suu allowed him to stay in her house for two days. When the government found out about the presence of a foreigner in her residence, Daw Suu and her two assistants were charged with violating the terms of her house arrest and were sent to the notorious Insein jail. Some government officials apparently considered this incident a blessing in disguise, for they were at that time trying to find an excuse to extend Daw Suu's house arrest which was to expire at the end of May 2009. If convicted, Daw Suu could be imprisoned up to five years. Daw Suu was given a three-year jail sentence on August 11, 2009. A few minutes after the verdict was delivered, Home Minister General Maung Oo came into the court and announced Senior General Than Shwe's decision to commute the sentence to 18 months of house arrest. The lawyers' appeal to the divisional court was rejected. At the time of writing this article, the lawyers were planning to take the case to the Supreme Court. However, a source close to the government noted that although the initial trial could be completed in about three months, the appeal process could take one to two years. He also noted that it was certain that Suu Kyi would in one way or another remain under detention at least for more than a year because senior government officials believed she would jeopardize their plan to institute disciplined democracy in the country. As a result, the junta has remained a regime that has kept the world's most famous dissident democrat under house arrest — a policy position that yields gains for neither party and certainly not for the country and its inhabitants.

Some senior military officers have been quoted as saying that she looks exactly like General Aung San and that they wanted to treat her like a sister.[35] The general just wished that she had married a Burmese and that she did not challenge the government the way she had done. Most senior officers do not appear to trust her.[36] Some family members of senior military officers have confirmed that their fathers or uncles do not like Daw Suu because they feel she has created so many problems for the government. Some senior officers appear to think that she has been used by leftist politicians.[37] A businessman who is very close to several generals said,

> "The generals I know did not trust Daw Suu. They thought she was naïve and did not understand much about the country's politics. Some politically shrewd and egoistic veteran politicians manipulated her from behind the scene. They just wanted her to stop attacking the government and start helping the government to develop the country."[38]

All 15 friends of some senior military officers I interviewed said that it would not be easy to mend the bad relations between Daw Suu and the generals. An interviewee noted that because the generals were so uncomfortable with her, they would not even talk about General Aung San.[39]

It is worth nothing that not the entire armed forces dislikes Daw Suu. Many ordinary soldiers and their family members support Daw Suu. This is discernible from the fact that in the 1990 elections, NLD candidates won in constituencies with several military bases such as

---

[35] Communications with three mid-level government officials (August–September, 2009), Yangon.

[36] Ibid.

[37] Interviews with family members of some government officials (July–August, 2009), Yangon.

[38] Interview with a businessman (September 13, 2009), Yangon.

[39] Interview with a businessman (August 3, 2009), Yangon.

Mingalardon, Mawbi and Pyinoolwin. The wife of a retired sergeant said,

> "Even though my husband was a soldier, I did not like the government's National Unity Party. My husband did not vote in the 1990 election. He said that he did not want to betray his leaders. At the same time, he did not want to betray General Aung San by not voting for his daughter. My children and I voted for the NLD. Many family members of other soldiers also voted for the NLD. Even many soldiers voted for it. I would continue to vote for the NLD if it ran in the elections in 2010."[40]

Twelve other family members of soldiers also expressed their support for Daw Suu in my conversations with them.[41] They also revealed that several other family members of soldiers thought that Daw Suu could do better than the generals in ruling the country.[42] They also said they would vote for Daw Suu or her party again if they could vote freely.[43]

However, five soldiers I talked to said that they would have to follow the orders of their superiors. Even though they wanted a better government, they did not think the NLD would be able to form a better one that would do more for the welfare of the soldiers.[44] They did not think they could rely on Daw Suu and the NLD,[45] and therefore would vote for the candidates of the parties affiliated to the government.[46] They did not think the NLD was prepared to overcome all the difficulties in the upcoming elections. However, they also said they would not order their family members to vote for the government's candidates. Although these five soldiers I interviewed were by no means representative of the entire armed forces, they indicated that their views about Daw Suu and the NLD were shared by many of their colleagues.

---

[40] Interview with the wife of a soldier (September 12, 2009), Yangon.
[41] Interviews with family members of 12 soldiers (June–September 2009), Yangon, Mandalay and Pyinoolwin.
[42] Ibid.
[43] Ibid.
[44] Interviews with five soldiers (September 2–29, 2009), Yangon, Mandalay and Naypyidaw.
[45] Ibid.
[46] Ibid.

They also noted that they would not disobey the orders of their superiors. All of them just smiled when I asked who they would choose between Than Shwe and Daw Suu. However, they noted that if they had to choose between the military government and any political parties, including the NLD, they would support the military government. All of them said that the 2010 elections were going to be different from that held in 1990. They said that in 1990, their superiors did not order them to vote for any political party. They thought that they would be, at least indirectly, encouraged to vote for candidates supported by the government.[47] All in all, one can safely say that some members of the armed forces are sympathetic to Daw Suu, but many of them seem to have decided to side with their institution in the upcoming elections.

In late September 2009, in a letter sent to Than Shwe, Daw Suu offered to work towards the lifting of sanctions. She also asked for permission to meet with EU and US envoys in order to persuade them of the negative effect of sanctions on ordinary people. Soon after the letter was sent to Naypyidaw, Minister Aung Kyi met with Daw Suu. Although the issues discussed in the meeting were not made public, the fact that she was allowed to meet EU and US envoys indicated that there might be a thaw in the relations between the government and Daw Suu. In November 2009, the junta allowed visiting US Assistant Secretary of State, Kurt Campbell, to meet her at the government guest house. In addition, at the request of Campbell, the government allowed the NLD's Central Executive Committee members to meet Daw Aung San Suu Kyi. However, Daw Suu cancelled when the government did not allow U Tin Oo to attend the meeting.[48] At the time of making final revisions to this chapter, She still has not disclosed how she plans to convince Western governments to lift sanctions on the country. Be that as it may, her offer to work towards the lifting of sanctions without asking for anything in return will make it hard for the government to ignore Daw Suu's role in the country's politics.

---

[47] Ibid.

[48] "Daw San Suu Kyi Did Not Meet NLD Central Executive Committee Members," *The Voice* (November 9–15, 2009), p. 3.

Aung San Suu Kyi and Ethnic Minority Groups

Daw Suu's position on the country's minority problems has been that she would work with ethnic minority leaders to find solutions. Some of these leaders would like her to have a clearer and more concrete strategy. The Kachin and Shan leaders I interviewed said that whenever they asked her how she would deal with the country's minority problems, she mainly suggested holding another Panglong conference[49] to discuss the issues in detail after the county's political deadlock had been resolved.[50] Some other ethnic minority leaders said they were not sure how Suu Kyi would deal with minority issues.[51] A Kachin leader said,

> "I knew her father. I loved him. I met her when she came to Myitkyina. She was not very clear about how she would deal with the minority issues. I think she is a sensible person. But I am not sure about the people around her. At the end of the day, they are all Bamar. In fact, many of them were involved in the government's crackdown on the ethnic insurgent activities. Many of them seemed to think that they were superior to minority people. These people could influence Daw Suu in dealing with the minority's problems."[52]

Two Mon elderly men, three Karen leaders, three Shan leaders and one Rakhine leader shared the views of the Kachin leader.[53] Although Daw Suu would be a better dialogue partner than military officers, they were not sure that Daw Suu and the NLD would be able to solve the decades-long ethnic problems quickly.[54]

---

[49] The Pinlon conference was held by Aung San to discuss the formation of the union with ethnic minority leaders in 1947. The conference was named after the name of the town where it took place.

[50] Interviews with two Kachin leaders and two Shan leaders (June 15, 2004, and July 2, 2004), Yangon.

[51] Interviews with two Kachin leaders, three Shan leaders and four Karen leaders (January 2004–October 2008), Yangon.

[52] Interview with Kachin leaders (December 27, 2004), Yangon.

[53] Interviews with two elderly Mon men, three Karen leaders, three Shan leaders and one Rakhine leader (2004–2008), Yangon.

[54] Ibid.

Some minority leaders went so far as to say that working with the junta might not be very different from working with Suu Kyi, for in both cases they would still have to deal with a government dominated by the ethnic majority Burmans. A Shan leader noted that Aung San had taken minority colleagues more seriously than Suu Kyi. He recalled his meeting with Aung San:

> "I met Bogyoke (General) Aung San several weeks before he was assassinated. Our Shan leader U Tin Aye and I went to his residence. He came down and talked to us. He did not act like a big shot. He was really down to earth. Around lunch time, he asked us to have lunch with him. He was the most important indigenous person in the country at that time but he lived like an ordinary person. The dishes he offered were just regular dishes you would see in most houses in the country. When I first had an appointment with Daw Aung San Suu Kyi, I had to wait. There was a curfew at that time. I needed to get back home before 6 pm. She did not come back until 5 pm, so I had to go home. Her father would not keep us waiting like that. When I visited her father, we were taken to the living room. When I was waiting for her, I was asked to sit on a chair placed outside the house. I was like a tenant farmer waiting to see his landlord."[55]

The same Shan leader also noted,

> "...In fact Daw Aung San Suu Kyi betrayed us. In early 1989, she promised me that her party would not run in constituencies in the Shan State. She said she would leave seats in minority areas to local parties like mine. Later, the NLD decided to run in Shan State. When I asked why she did not keep her promise, she did not give me a clear answer."[56]

Ethnic insurgent groups that had made ceasefire agreements with the government were careful about commenting on Daw Suu and the NLD. Although they privately expressed their respect for Daw Suu and their willingness to work with her, the leaders of the ceasefire groups did not want to jeopardize their relationship with the government.[57] Once, a Kachin Independence Organization (KIO) member

---

[55] Interview, U Shwe Ohn (March 21, 2007), Yangon.
[56] Ibid.
[57] Interviews with Kachin and Karen leaders (February 2004 and January 2008), Yangon and Chiang Mai.

wrote a letter to Daw Aung San Suu Kyi, stating that the KIO supported her and her party. As a result, the then Intelligence Chief Khin Nyunt summoned a leading member of KIO, Dr Tu Ja, to see him in Yangon. At the meeting, General Khin Nyunt passed the letter sent to Daw Aung San Suu Kyi to Dr Tu Ja and asked him what was going on. Of course, Dr Tu Ja had to tell General Khin Nyunt that it was the action of one member, which the leadership of the KIO was unaware of.[58] Because they are financially weak, smaller ceasefire groups have to depend more on the government and therefore make even greater efforts to be on good terms with the government and try to distance themselves from the NLD and Daw Suu.

Daw Suu, for her part, seemed to think she could easily work with ethnic minority leaders. She once said to a *Time* magazine correspondent,

"We have very good relations with the ethnic minorities, and I would like to point out that two of the ethnic nationality parties represented in the CRPP were second and third after the NLD in the [1990 elections]. ...So you could say that we have managed to reach an understanding with some of the most important ethnic nationality groups. If given half a chance we could establish perfectly good relations with the ceasefire groups. If the SPDC wants to test it, why don't they let us meet the ceasefire groups and see how we get on?"[59]

Daw Suu went on to say,

"We understand them (ethnic minority leaders who are a part of the CRPP). They want to represent their own states and that's no problem for us. We can still work together. We don't believe in a zero-sum situation. It doesn't mean that if we don't win (the elections in minority areas), the party that wins becomes the enemy. In fact, we look on them as our allies, and we are very happy that our allies are well represented in their states."[60]

---

[58] Interview with a Kachin leader (December 28, 2004), Myitkyina.
[59] Aung San Suu Kyi, "This government is not capable of running the economy", *Time Asia, http://www.time.com/time/asia/magazine/99/1115/burma.aungsansuukyi.html.* Accessed on October 1, 2009.
[60] Ibid.

In fact, Daw Suu tried to convince ethnic minority leaders when-ever she had a chance that she took the ethnic issue very seriously. In a statement she released through the UN special envoy, Mr Gambari, in 2007, Daw Suu noted,

> "In this time of vital need for democratic solidarity and national unity, it is my duty to give constant and serious consideration to the interests and opinions of as broad a range of political organizations and forces as possible, in particular those of our ethnic nationality races."[61]

Regardless of the reservations some ethnic minority leaders have had about her, Daw Suu has been very popular in many minority areas. In fact, the NLD won in many constituencies in the Kachin, Karen and Mon states in the 1990 elections. Even though her party did not win many seats in the Shan and Rakhine states, she was still popular in those two areas. Tens of thousands of minority people wholeheartedly welcomed her when she visited. Informal conversa-tions with about 50 Shan people and 25 Rakhine people during my visits to the two states confirmed that Daw Suu was quite popular there. Many of them said that although several candidates from her party did not win in their states, they were sure that Daw Suu would win if she contested in the elections representing any constituency in their respective state. When Daw Suu was on trial for the John Yettaw case, many exiled ethnic leaders, including Kachin, Shan and Karen leaders, expressed their concern for her. While criticizing the junta for mistreating Daw Suu at the trial, Duwa Mahkaw Hkunsa, General Secretary of the exiled Ethnic Nationalities Council (Union of Burma) (ENC), noted that she was one of the few Bamar leaders who had won the hearts and trust of the minority people and wanted to play a leading role in uniting all ethnic groups in Burma.[62]

[61] "Burma's Pro-Democracy Icon Aung San Suu Kyi Pay Constant and Serious Consideration on Ethnic Nationalities," *Chinland Guardian*, http://chinlandguardian.com/articles/740-burmas-pro-democracy-icon-aung-san-suu-kyi-pay-constant-and-serious-consideration-on-ethnic-nationalities.html#. Accessed on October 1, 2009.
[62] "Burma: Ethnic Minorities Draw Inspiration from Aung San Suu Kyi", *MIzzama*, http://www.unpo.org/content/view/9618/236/. Accessed on October 1, 2009.

Hkunsa also said, "We believe she can lead the process of national reconciliation and also build a federal union, which we, the ethnics, have been demanding".

All in all, Daw Suu is a popular political figure among ethnic minorities. Although some ethnic minority leaders were not happy that she did not have a clear ethnic policy, other minority leaders were satisfied with the fact that she would work with them to find solutions for the country's ethnic problems.

Daw Suu and the International Community

The fact that the Four Eights movement occurred when the Cold War was waning worked in favor of Daw Suu and the NLD. Unlike previous regimes, the current military regime was not anti-West. Military leaders seemed prepared to work with any foreign governments that would recognize them. It was due to the harsh policies adopted by the Western countries that the junta became anti-West and significantly more authoritarian. With structural changes in the international system, Daw Suu and the pro-democracy groups readily received Western support. Thanks to her aggressive performance as an opposition leader and the promotion of her as an irreplaceable leader of the democratic movement by overseas Burmese pro-democracy groups, Daw Suu was accepted by Western governments as the only viable alternative to the military government. Consequently, many Western countries came to base their policies on Daw Suu's policies towards the military government or what they thought Daw Suu would want of them. Although Western governments criticize the military government whenever it takes strong action against members of opposition groups, it was mainly when the military government took severe action against Daw Suu that they tried to undertake concrete, punitive actions against the military government. For instance, the US government imposed a wide-ranging economic embargo on Burma after the Depayin incident. A former American government official alleged that US policy towards Burma was controlled solely by Daw

Suu.[63] He also noted that although many US government officials were aware that economic sanctions were not working, they would not discuss lifting the sanctions on Burma until Daw Suu called for it. Similarly, a senior EU official noted that EU countries were troubled by the worsening social and economic problems in Burma, which were partly a function of Western economic sanctions.[64] However, he also said that the EU could not change its Burma policy until Daw Suu called for a reverse in the Western policy towards Burma.

Daw Suu, for her part, relies heavily on Western countries. Whenever she is able to contact the outside would, she asks Western governments "to use their liberty to promote the liberty of Burmese people".[65] And after she was released in 1995, Daw Suu came to rely more on Western countries than on the general public in trying to effect political changes in the country. As noted above, for fear of the junta's severe punitive actions against the general public, she called on Western countries to exert pressure on the Burmese government more frequently than before. Daw Suu, however, has had limited impact on the Burma policies of the junta's major allies, China, India and the ASEAN countries. The Indian government initially supported the Burmese pro-democracy movement wholeheartedly when it was led by the Bharatiya Janata Party (BJP). However, in order to prevent Chinese expansion in the Indian Ocean, it had to try to improve its relations with the Burmese junta and so began to stay away from the pro-democracy group since the mid-1990s. Because Burma was a member of ASEAN, other member governments did not openly support Daw Suu and other pro-democracy groups until the mid-2000s. Since the 2003 Depayin incident, some ASEAN governments have started to criticize the military junta openly and senior politicians from Thailand, the Philippines and Malaysia expressed their support for Daw Suu publicly. Taking advantage of the frustration of ASEAN

[63] Personal Communication with a former American diplomat (October 12, 2004), DeKalb, Illinois.
[64] Ibid.
[65] http://dassk.org/index.php/topic,8483.0.html.

governments with their Burmese counterpart, Daw Suu tried to reach out to ASEAN leaders by requesting assistance in helping the Burmese people to solve their political problems. Members of opposition parties from many ASEAN countries have recently formed the ASEAN Democracy Caucus for Burma to press their own governments into pressurizing their Burmese counterpart to speed up the democratization process. Several ASEAN diplomats were present at Daw Suu's recent trial in the Insein prison where they openly expressed their sympathy for her.

At the moment, Western countries continue to support Daw Suu and the NLD and have repeatedly called for her release and that of several other political prisoners. The Western economic sanctions have undermined the position of the junta. The US government has also tried to take the Burma issue to the UN Security Council. But although Western economic sanctions have undermined the position of the junta, with the help of China, India and to a certain extent, Russia, the junta has managed to defy all Western pressures and remain in power. In fact, it is arguable that the military junta has determined that there are no benefits to be derived from changing the status quo. Nor are there significant losses from resisting such change domestically or internationally. Consequently, the stalemate is poised to continue into the foreseeable future until new opportunities avail themselves.

After acknowledging the failure of sanctions, the Obama administration announced that it would consider engaging with the military regime.[66] In the middle of August 2009, Senator Jim Webb of Virginia paid a visit to Naypyidaw and had a meeting with Than Shwe. Webb managed to get permission to see Daw Suu and secured the release of John Yettaw on humanitarian grounds. The US government also allowed Foreign Minister Nyan Win to visit Washington DC for the first time in nine years in late September 2009. Secretary of State Hillary Clinton noted that the US continued to stand by Daw Suu and other pro-democracy forces. In addition, Clinton said that sanctions would not be lifted until substantial political reforms

---

[66] "Clinton on Burma", *The New Yorker*, (February 20, 2009), http://www.newyorker.com/online/blogs/georgepacker/2009/02/clinton-on-burm.html.

had taken place. A US diplomat also said that the congressmen and senators in the United States would not find the 2010 elections legitimate if the NLD did not participate in it.

In sum, although they have started to engage with the military government, Western governments do not plan to make very many fundamental changes to their policies towards Burma. However, the Obama administration does not seem likely to impose more sanctions on Burma. At the same time, Western governments have made it very clear that they will not do anything that would undermine Daw Suu and pro-democracy groups.

Daw Suu and the Future of Burma

For proponents of Daw Suu and the NLD, the future of Burma is precarious. Daw Suu cannot do much at the moment and the NLD under its aging caretaker leadership is barely functioning. NLD leaders have not done anything lately other than issuing occasional ultimatums to the government and asking the international community to pressure them. The old caretaker leaders cannot do anything when the junta ignores their demands. The momentum of the Burmese pro-democracy movement is not as strong as it was ten years ago. In fact, many leading members of the overseas Burmese pro-democracy groups have mentioned to me that the movement has been in a downward spiral since 1996. However, Daw Suu's detention has had some positive impact on the movement; it attracted the attention of the international community. Since she is deemed synonymous with the NLD and the democratic movement, Daw Suu has also become critical to the movement. This means the movement has gone awry whenever she was detained or kept incommunicado. In other words, whenever the fate of Daw Suu became precarious, the fate of the movement became equally so. This link between Daw Suu and the movement has to be realized for any accurate appraisal of the situation since it presents both opportunities and constraints.

The movement could have remained stronger if Daw Suu had managed to bring the different factions together. One of the major successes of Daw Suu's father, General Aung San, was to establish a comprehensive and inclusive organization, the Anti-Fascist People's Freedom League (AFPFL). In contrast, She has failed to bring various groups in the democracy movement together. While Daw Suu and her colleagues have also tried to establish a national front, the NLD is by no means a comprehensive one like the AFPFL. Although most pro-democracy activists have expressed their willingness to work under the leadership of Daw Suu, many activists and groups operating both inside and outside the country are quite disunited and have engaged in smear campaigns against each other. In some cases, they under-mined each other more seriously than the government. Although Daw Suu occasionally talked about the importance of unity and brought all parliamentarians-elect together under the supervision of the Committee Representing the People's Parliament, she, as the most well-respected leader of the movement, failed to unite different pro-democracy groups and stop the bickering among them. The fail-ure to deal with this fragmentation from within the movement has weakened it or, at the very least, not allowed it to achieve its potential. Daw Suu might have been able to do more if she had not been placed under house arrest for almost two decades. However, it must also be noted that she failed to do it even when she was free between 1995 and 2000.

On the other hand, Burmese military leaders do not seem worried about the future. They have their own plans for the future of the coun-try. The junta held the National Convention in 1992 to formulate principles to be considered in drafting a new constitution. Although it initially attended the National Convention, the NLD announced in 1996 that it would boycott the convention "until such time as a dia-logue is held on national reconciliation, the genuine multi-party democracy system and the drafting of a constitution which is supported and trusted by the people."[67] In 2003, not long after the Depayin inci-dent, the junta revived the long-stalled process of holding a National Convention, this time in the context of a seven-step road-map toward

---

[67] Aung San Suu Kyi, "Press Conference Statement: the Observation of the National League for Democracy on the National Convention," November 22, 1995.

"democracy" in Myanmar.[68] The SPDC invited NLD leaders to drop their boycott and rejoin the convention. The NLD agreed, then changed its mind and said it would take part only if the generals first released its detained leaders, Daw Suu and U Tin Oo.[69] When the government did not comply, NLD leaders resumed their boycott. Senior military leaders said the convention would go on without the NLD.

On September 3, 2007, Myanmar's ruling junta finally concluded the National Convention, 14 years after it had begun. The convention had adopted 104 principles for the new constitution. Although most opposition groups rejected the principles, senior military officers openly expressed their determination to go ahead with the road map. Some senior military officers reportedly stated in official meetings that the government did not need the support of the opposition groups in order to implement the road map. However, in the wake of the forceful crackdown on the monk-led protests in some major cities, the government announced that its leader Than Shwe would meet Aung San Suu Kyi if the latter stopped confronting the government and stopped calling for the international community to impose economic sanctions.[70] The junta even appointed a cabinet minister to deal with Aung San Suu Kyi directly.

---

[68] The seven-step road map announced by the SPEC includes: "(1) Reconvening of the National Convention that has been adjourned since 1996. (2) After the successful holding of the National Convention, step-by-step implementation of the process necessary for the emergence of a genuine and disciplined democratic system. (3) Drafting of a new constitution in accordance with basic principles and detailed basic principles laid down by the National Convention. (4) Adoption of the constitution through national referendum. (5) Holding of free and fair elections for *Pyithu Hluttaws* (Legislative bodies) according to the new constitution. (6) Convening of *Hluttaws* attended by *Hluttaw* members in accordance with the new constitution. (7) Building a modern, developed and democratic nation by the state leaders elected by the *Hluttaw*; and the government and other central organs formed by the *Hluttaw*." See also Kyaw Yin Hlaing, "Myanmar in 2003: Frustration and Despair?" *Asian Survey* 44: 1 (January/February 2004), 87–92.

[69] The National League for Democracy, Statement for National Convention, May 14, 2004, http://www.dassk.com/contents.php?id=757.

[70] See Sebastien Berger, "Aung San Suu Kyi: Leader Offered Meeting," October 10, 2007, http://www.telegraph.co.uk/news/main.jhtml?xml=/news/2007/10/05/wburma105.xml.

Since then, some meetings between Daw Suu and representatives of the junta have taken place, and she has also been allowed to see certain party members. This was mainly due to mounting international criticism of the junta's suppression of peaceful protests by Buddhist monks.

Despite these positive developments, the junta has made it very clear that it will not revise the 104 principles. On October 18, 2007, the junta formed a committee that included retired and serving government officers, businesspeople and representatives of government-organized non-governmental organizations (GONGOs) and ethnic groups to draft the new constitution. In February 2008, the junta announced that it would hold a referendum for the new constitution on May 10, 2008, and that the new elections would be held in 2010. The copies of the constitution were made available to the public in April 2007. Meanwhile, senior Burmese generals were reportedly unhappy with Daw Suu for releasing a statement to the international community through UN special envoy Mr Gambari without consulting with them.[71] The government has stated that it will work with opposition groups only so long as its rules are adhered to. For her part, Daw Suu seems unwilling to abide by the government's parameters. While the junta was preparing for the referendum, some senior military officers publicly confirmed that Daw Suu would not be allowed to run in the 2010 elections.[72] It also appears that the government will try to keep her under detention until after the elections. The referendum for the new constitution was held on May 10 in most townships in the country, and on May 24 in the 24 townships that had been seriously damaged by Cyclone Nargis earlier that month. On May 25, the government announced that the new constitution had been approved by 92.4% of the voters. By early 2009, many foreign countries, including some in the EU, concluded that the government could not be stopped from implementing its road map. Therefore, while pressuring the government to make the elections more inclusive, EU and US diplomats were

---

[71] Interview with a government official (April 28, 2008), Yangon.
[72] "Democrat banned from Myanmar elections," *The Manila Times*, February 21, 2008. http://www.manilatimes.net/national/2008/feb/21/yehey/world/20080221worl.html.

privately encouraging the NLD and other opposition parties to run in the 2010 elections. However, the new constitution has made it almost impossible for Daw Suu to participate. Clause 59/f precludes anyone whose family members are "entitled to enjoy the rights and privileges of a subject of a foreign government or citizens of a foreign country".[73] Daw Suu's two grown sons are British subjects. As a result, unless clause 59/f is amended, Daw Suu will not meet the requirements.

While the NLD does not seems to know what it should do to resolve the political impasse, the junta seems prepared to proceed with its own plan without Daw Suu and the NLD. Some recent editorials from government newspapers indicate that the junta has already written off the roles of Daw Suu and the NLD in Burma's political transition. At the moment, the NLD seems unable to do anything other than call for international pressure on the military government to undertake genuine political reforms and release all political prisoners.

The NLD could have been in a better position if Daw Suu and her colleagues had found a way to exploit the factional struggles between senior military officers. Although the junta hardly missed any opportunity to undermine the NLD, Daw Suu and her colleagues failed to reach out to the officers who accepted in principle that political reform had to be undertaken for the country's future. Some associates of former Prime Minister Khin Nyunt informed certain Western governments through go-betweens that there were those who understood the need for political change in the country. They in turn asked for more understanding and support in awaiting such change. Some reliable sources noted that there were those in the NLD who knew of the relatively liberal position of General Khin Nyunt but did not do anything as mutual trust was not forthcoming. Later, he was purged from the government, along with his entire intelligence apparatus. Not surprisingly, both Daw Suu and her colleagues treated the upper echelons of the military government as unitary and either challenged or tried to work with all of them at the

---

[73] http://rspas.anu.edu.au/rmap/newmandala/wp-content/uploads/2008/04/burma-constitution-2008.pdf.

same time. The result was that the NLD remained weak even though the junta was ridden with factional struggles and opportunities for selective collaboration presented themselves.

The NLD would also have been better prepared to deal with the junta if Daw Suu and her colleagues had managed to turn the NLD into a properly institutionalized party. Currently, the NLD looks more like the political following of a charismatic leader rather than a real political party. The group functions well only when the leader is around. The NLD is currently in a critical state and needs to undergo reform. Its old caretaker leadership has not been able to do much for the party beyond striving to keep it alive. They have not taken initiatives or formulated bold policy positions. However, bold initiatives are needed if the party is to reform and rearm itself with a clearer strategy. Whenever local party members make a request to the NLD leadership, the only response is that the matter will be considered. This means that they will only institute reforms after consulting with Daw Suu. The party defers to her in everything and needs to ascertain her views prior to any. Daw Suu's former close adviser Win Tin, upon his release from prison in September 2008, reportedly had tried to reform the party. However, according to a source close to the NLD, some senior members successfully blocked Win Tin's plan and so the way the party functioned did not change significantly even several months after he became engaged in the party's activities. These former military commanders are like incapable caretakers as they are unable to do much without Daw Suu. A prominent activist-cum-writer noted with frustration:

> "The NLD without Daw Suu was like a body without soul. It functioned more like a moribund organization. People always compared our country with South Africa. The ANC functioned well even when Nelson Mandela was not around. The NLD did function well without Daw Aung San Suu Kyi between 1989 and 1995. But since then, the NLD did not function like a credible organization whenever Daw Aung San Suu Kyi was not around. The future of the NLD is in serious doubt unless the government releases Daw Aung San Suu Kyi and lets her reform the party."[74]

---

[74] Interview (June 1, 2006), Yangon.

My intention is not to suggest that Daw Suu and the NLD have become history. As previously noted, Western countries and a large number of Burmese still hold the view that any political transition without Daw Suu is meaningless. A survey of 300 people conducted in June 2009 revealed that although only about 55% of the participants said they strongly supported the NLD, 82% said that still strongly supported Daw Suu.[75] At this point in time, nobody knows what will happen to Daw Suu, the junta or the country even in the near future. Equally, nobody at this point knows what Daw Suu would want to do about the political deadlock if she had a chance to do something about it. This vacuum in the political leadership of the NLD is a serious issue since the future of the party rests on it, especially if the stalemate continues. Leadership transition and succession are also important issues for the NLD, whether inside or outside the fold of the government. Failure to address this issue may well deal a mortal blow to the party in the long run. On the other hand, the military government may be able to proceed with its own plans, yet it cannot write Daw Suu out of modern Burmese political history. As long as they do not find a way to work with her, Daw Suu will remain a popular dissident democrat and the junta will continue to be referred to as an "outpost of tyranny" by some Western governments. Clearly, some compromise is required by both parties to serve the national interest that both parties claim to represent. Daw Aung San Suu Kyi's offer to work towards lifting sanctions could improve relations. However, the government seems determined to keep her under house arrest until the 2010 elections. Sources close to the government note that her recent gesture of goodwill will not help her win a role in the elections. But no one knows for sure what will happen to her in the near future. At the present moment, Daw Suu's future, along with the political future of the country, remains as precarious as ever.

---

[75] This opinion survey was conducted by me with the assistance of eight young Burmese scholars in June 2009.

Chapter 6

Looking Inside the Burmese Military*

Win Min

Abstract

This article examines the internal dynamics of the Burmese military, focusing on struggles at the top level. It will explore the nature of and reasons for the struggles and assess the implications, especially for the current political impasse and possible changes in the future.

Keywords: Burma; Myanmar; military; intra-military groupings.

Introduction

For almost half a century, multi-ethnic Burma has been ruled by two main Burman-dominated military regimes that came to power through coups in 1962 and 1988. In 1988 the State Law and Order Restoration Council (SLORC), which later changed its name to the State Peace and Development Council (SPDC), took power after crushing nationwide pro-democracy demonstrations. In 1990, the junta held a multi-party election but refused to transfer power to the winners when the National League for Democracy (NLD), led by Aung San Suu Kyi, won an overwhelming victory. Instead, in 1993,

* This is a revision of the article that appeared in *Asian Survey* (November/December 2008). The author would like to thank Christina Fink, two anonymous reviewers from *Asian Survey*, and participants at the workshop on "Political Development in Burma/Myanmar", organized by the Asian Political and International Studies Association and the Konrad-Adenauer-Stiftung in 2007, for their comments and assistance.

the regime convened the National Convention, which was mostly filled with handpicked members, to draft the principles for a pro-military constitution. NLD members walked out in 1995, and the constitution was only completed in 2007. After the 2007 monk-led demonstrations, the SPDC held a referendum on the constitution in 2008 (with numerous allegations of intimidation and pre-marked ballots) and announced it would hold elections in 2010, but the military is still determined to play the leading role in the new government.

This chapter examines the internal dynamics of the Burmese military, particularly with regard to internal struggles at the top level. These intra-military dynamics remain largely hidden from the public eye until senior officials are removed from power. This chapter will identify the nature of the struggles, explore reasons for the various groupings, and assess the implications of these conflicts, especially with regard to the current political impasse and possible changes in the future.

Intra-Military Groupings: Types and Reasons

As Samuel Huntington noted, unity is highly valued in all militaries. The Burmese military is no exception.[1] It may consider itself to be a cohesive institution because it has not suffered any mutinies along ideological or ethnic lines in more than 50 years. Huntington also noted that many military leaders have perceived party politics as dividing the people.[2] In Burma, generals point to the 1950s when the leading political parties fought each other and seemed unable to solve the country's problems (though as we shall see, the Tatmadaw's record in the 1950s was little better). The Burmese generals have followed what Huntington termed "community without politics, agreement by command", implying that the military has a right to rule because it is the only institution that can hold the country together

---

[1] Samuel Huntington, *The Soldiers and the State* (Cambridge: Harvard University Press, 1957), p. 63.
[2] Samuel Huntington, *Political Order in Changing Societies* (New Haven: Yale University Press, 1968), p. 137.

and govern effectively.[3] According to Andrew Selth, despite the tensions between leaders in the military, unity has been maintained because military leaders believe their institution has an important role in preserving national unity and because they fear that if the military were no longer in power they could lose their privileges and be punished for past abuses.[4]

Nevertheless, as Mary Callahan has argued, the Burmese army is not a totally united institution, despite the value placed on military unity.[5] Army concerns about disunity become obvious whenever officers threaten to punish anyone whose actions they believe could split the military. In fact, rival intra-military groupings have formed since the 1960s, although they are not based on ideology or ethnicity. Instead, they have been organized around personal and structural dynamics. As Selth states, the Burmese military is "a collection of finely balanced institutional and personal loyalties".[6] Similarly, David Steinberg has argued that the "entourages" within the military have been based on personal loyalties to top generals, although he does not explain how these entourages formed.[7] This chapter demonstrates that most of the groupings have emerged out of *saya–tapyit* relations, which can be translated loosely as patron–client relations. The literal translation of the Burmese terms *saya* and *tapyit* is "teacher" and "pupil", respectively, but in the context of the military hierarchy, *saya* refers to senior officers and *tapyit* to junior officers. Patron–client relations start when the *saya* are battalion, divisional, regional or headquarters commanders and the *tapyit* are their respective staff officers. Some senior officers also

---

[3] Huntington, *Political Order*, p. 138.

[4] Andrew Selth, *Burma's Armed Forces: Power Without Glory* (Norwalk, CT: Eastbridge, 2002), pp. 266–7.

[5] Mary Callahan, "Of *Kyay-Zu* and *Kyet-Su*: The Military in 2006," in *Myanmar: The State, Community and the Environment*, eds. Monique Skidmore and Trevor Wilson (Canberra: Australian National University Press, 2007), p. 36.

[6] Andrew Selth, *Burma's Armed Forces*, p. 267.

[7] David Steinberg, "Myanmar Reconciliation — Progress in the Process?" in *Southeast Asian Affairs 2003,* eds. Daljit Singh and Chin Kin Wah (Singapore: Institute of Southeast Asian Studies, 2003), pp. 177–189.

draw in their relatives or military personnel from their hometowns as followers.

In addition, as Maung Aung Myoe has argued, one of the main causes of intra-military tension in Burma appears to be the lack of formal institutional arrangements for succession to the top positions.[8] This has historical roots. In the past, when Burmese kings died without being able to appoint a successor, rival sons and their family members sometimes killed each other to secure the throne. In modern times, the senior generals have purged second-tier generals to clear away any threat to the top and pave the way for their favorite generals. As a result, groups form around strong leaders so the subordinates can ensure their own survival and career advancement. Strong leaders also seek to promote their followers to powerful positions to secure and consolidate their power bases. The relative power of the top generals is partly related to the number of loyal followers they have and the positions these followers occupy.

In terms of structural dynamics, the groupings are often based on links to different military structures such as infantry vs. intelligence or center vs. regions. Alfred Stepan argues that in many armies there is often tension between the military and intelligence services over how much independent power the latter should have.[9] In Burma, significant tension exists between the infantry (combat) and military intelligence as well. The latter has tried to assert itself based on the claim that gathering good intelligence on political and armed opposition groups is essential for the survival of the regime. However, tensions led to the purging of almost all military intelligence officers in 2004 and the subsequent restructuring of the entire military intelligence apparatus.

At the same time, the generals at military headquarters (i.e., the center) have worried about the independent power of regional (field)

---

[8] Maung Aung Myoe, *Building the Tatmadaw: The Organizational Development of the Armed Forces in Myanmar, 1948–98*, Working Paper No. 327 (Canberra: Strategic Defense Studies Center, Australian National University, 1998), p. 31.

[9] Alfred Stepan, *Rethinking Military Politics: Brazil and the Southern Cone* (Princeton: Princeton University Press, 1988), pp. 13–22.

commanders in their respective regions, some of whom they fear could join together to challenge the central authority. This has led to the purging of powerful senior regional commanders and the reduction of regional commanders' power. This tension often develops when the regional commanders have significant control over battlefields and resources in civil war situations and therefore can build up their power bases. Regional commanders also try to increase their influence by nurturing particular businesspeople who will later become their main cronies when the commanders reach the top. At the same time, as Callahan has pointed out, because the War Office has not provided enough uniforms, food or ammunition to the troops in the field, the field commanders feel dissatisfied with the generals at the War Office.[10] Other groupings have formed around graduates of the two military schools, the Defense Services Academy (DSA) and the Officers' Training School (OTS), although this factor appears to be less significant.

Internal Struggles Before 1988

Mutinies after Burma's Independence

The first internal military struggle occurred after Burma's independence from Britain in 1948. It was based on ideological and ethnic tensions. Three months after independence, thousands of communist-leaning troops and a number of senior officers mutinied and joined the communist struggle.[11] When the minority Karen insurgency to create an independent Karen state broke out in early 1949, Karen and Kachin battalions also mutinied.[12] Senior Karen officers remaining in the Burma Army were forced to resign and an ethnic Burman officer, General Ne Win, became chief of staff.

---

[10] Mary Callahan, *Making Enemies: War and State Building in Burma*, (Ithaca, NY: Cornell University Press, 2003) pp. 147, 152.

[11] Martin Smith, *Burma: Insurgency and the Politics of Ethnicity* (London: Zed Books, 1999), pp. 108–109.

[12] Ibid., pp. 138–139.

Purges in the 1960s

In the 1960s, internal struggles revolved around perceived threats to the top leader and tensions between the staff in the capital and the regional commanders. In 1961, Brigadier General Maung Maung, considered to be the second- or third-highest ranking officer, was sacked, reportedly for his close ties to the American Central Intelligence Agency (CIA) and for being perceived as a threat to Ne Win.[13] Meanwhile, many regional commanders were sacked for being too independent and powerful in their regions, which made Ne Win worry that they might come together against him. However, the official reason given for their dismissals was that they had disobeyed Ne Win's order not to meddle in the 1960 elections.[14] Two regional commands were reconfigured into five divisional commands, over which the war office staff had greater control. Afterwards, power was tightly concentrated around Ne Win, together with his followers from the Fourth Burma Rifles and the northern military command. (Ne Win was the former commander of both units; the Fourth Rifles was the only Burman section that did not break away from the Burma Army during the 1948–49 mutinies.

In 1962, while Prime Minister U Nu was engaged in discussions over the ethnic minorities' demands for greater autonomy, the military staged a coup, claiming that granting such autonomy would lead to the disintegration of the country. A year later, the second-highest ranking officer, Brigadier General Aung Gyi, considered by many as a likely successor to Ne Win, was sacked. Though no official reason for the sacking was given, Ne Win and Aung Gyi had disagreed over how to manage the Burmese economy.[15] Aung Gyi, whose reputation grew with his successful management of the army's businesses, opposed Ne Win's policy of

---

[13] Callahan, *Making Enemies,* p. 199.
[14] Ibid., p. 200.
[15] Bertil Lintner, *Burma in Revolt: Opium and Insurgency Since 1948* (Bangkok: White Lotus, 1994), p. 178.

nationalization. Subsequently, Burma's thriving economy went downhill. After clearing out the second-tier generals, Ne Win's favorite general, San Yu, was picked as chief of staff in 1972. San Yu became Ne Win's follower when the latter was northern regional commander in 1948.

Purges in the mid-1970s

A new constitution was adopted in 1974, instituting one-party rule. Ne Win became the chairman of the leading party, the Burma Socialist Program Party (BSPP), and of the State Council, the lead policymaking body. The new chief of staff served only at the ministerial level and was not a member of the State Council. In 1976, Ne Win sacked General Tin Oo (the current NLD vice chairman), who was both the chief of staff and the defense minister, and his group, regarding them as a threat to his power.[16] Tin Oo was considered to be a professional soldier. His reputation grew among the ranks; he became a hero to the rising young officers who regarded him as different from Ne Win and his close circle, who had ruined Burma's economy. Later, Tin Oo was officially accused of withholding knowledge of an assassination plot against Ne Win by a group of young officers from the same DSA class, and he was imprisoned.[17] Another of Ne Win's favorites, General Kyaw Htin, was picked as commander-in-chief. Kyaw Htin had been a follower of Ne Win since serving under him in the Fourth Burma Rifles.

Purges in the 1980s

In 1983, former Military Intelligence (MI) chief Brigadier General Tin Oo (a different Tin Oo from the one above), the joint General Secretary of the BSPP, and his MI group were purged. This is primarily because the MI was becoming more powerful and independent.

[16] Selth, *Burma's Armed Forces*, p. 122.
[17] Until 1988, fewer graduates from DSA than OTS were appointed to senior positions.

Many officers referred to the general as "Number one and a half" and expected him to succeed Ne Win. All the messages passed to Ne Win went through him, making him a gatekeeper to the top.[18] Reports from the intelligence units in the field came directly to Rangoon, bypassing regional army commanders. This created tension between the MI and the regional commanders. When Tin Oo's son went to Thailand on his honeymoon, Thailand gave him the red carpet treatment. That made Ne Win's favorite daughter, who didn't receive the same treatment, very envious, reportedly a contributing factor in Ne Win's decision to sack Tin Oo.[19]

Along with the home minister, almost all the MI officers who were considered loyal to Tin Oo were arrested, purged or transferred to inactive posts.[20] The official reason given to the public was the misuse of state funds and corruption by Tin Oo and his subordinates. Following the purge, the entire MI was restructured to reduce the organ's power. The new MI chief was no longer the head of the powerful National Intelligence Bureau, which coordinated all military and civilian intelligence agencies.[21] MI units in the field were no longer allowed to report to MI headquarters directly but had to send reports through regional commanders. The restructuring severely weakened MI's intelligence capabilities and it was unable to prevent the North Korean bomb attack against the South Korean president and his cabinet ministers during their visit to Rangoon the following year.[22]

Internal Struggle After 1988

Military Chief Purged in 1992

After the SLORC came to power in 1988, power was distributed among its members, although Ne Win still maintained some influence.

---

[18] Interview with a former senior intelligence officer, June 2007, Washington DC.
[19] Ibid.
[20] Selth, *Burma's Armed Forces,* p. 122.
[21] Ibid., p. 104.
[22] Ibid., p. 123.

The SLORC comprised 10 officers from the Defense Headquarters (War Office) and nine regional commanders, balancing the power of the headquarters and field commanders. Unlike in the past, the first purge targeted the highest-ranking officer, Senior General Saw Maung, who was both commander-in-chief and chairman of the SLORC. He came from the grouping around the BSPP's third-highest ranking official, Aye Ko.[23] Aye Ko, a retired major general, had become a follower of General Ne Win in the Fourth Burma Rifles. Saw Maung was a relatively professional soldier but he became delusional after the military-backed party lost the 1990 elections.[24] According to a retired military medical doctor, Saw Maung had been drugged. However, many other officers believe his illness was the result of stress.[25] At the same time, some generals were frustrated that he had assured the foreign media that he would transfer power to the winner of the 1990 elections. Others were frustrated with his order to wipe out the armed Karen National Union, which seemed unrealistic at the time.

The purge was the result of a coordinated effort by Vice-Senior General Than Shwe (deputy commander-in-chief and vice chairman), Major General Khin Nyunt (Secretary 1), and Major General Tin Oo (Secretary 2), who held the second, third and fourth positions in the SLORC respectively, together with the Rangoon Commander.[26] They asked Ne Win to order Saw Maung to retire.[27] Saw Maung's pictures were removed from government offices and his name was erased from the military's history books. The immediate, critical impact of this purge was to dash all hopes of a transfer of power to the elected NLD.

After the sacking, Senior General Than Shwe became commander -in-chief and chairman of the SLORC. He is considered to be another

---

[23] Interview with a family member of a former senior military officer, February 2006, Washington DC.

[24] Interview with Maj. Aung Lynn Htut, former military intelligence officer and former Charge d'Affaire at the Burmese Embassy in Washington, June 2008.

[25] Ibid.

[26] Interview with a family member of a former senior military officer, June 2006, Washington DC.

[27] Ibid.

follower of Aye Ko.[28] He has a background in psychological warfare and is considered a good tactician.[29] Than Shwe has regularly used divide-and-rule tactics to weaken the power of other top generals. Inspired by former Burmese kings who demonstrated great military might and held absolute power, he had huge statues of three prominent kings erected in the new capital, Naypyidaw, which means "royal capital" in Burmese, constructed in 2005. Than Shwe is known for being paranoid, xenophobic and influenced by astrology. He appears to hate Aung San Suu Kyi personally and does not even want to hear her name.[30] He also had pictures of her father, independence hero General Aung San, and Ne Win removed from all offices after becoming commander-in-chief.

Than Shwe picked General Maung Aye for the position of army chief in 1992. Maung Aye was a regional commander who appeared to be less personally ambitious than other regional commanders. Vice-Senior General Maung Aye became the deputy commander-in-chief in 1993 and the vice chairman of the SLORC in 1994. While Maung Aye has been considered a hardliner in fighting against ethnic armies, he may be more open-minded about dealing with the NLD than Than Shwe. He engaged in a serious conversation with Aung San Suu Kyi in one of their secret meetings, while Than Shwe remained aloof.[31] Maung Aye appears to believe that the military's institutional integrity is the most important factor in holding the country together.[32] He and his followers have been far less involved than Than Shwe and his followers in the activities of the pro-military mass organization, the Union Solidarity and Development Association (USDA). Than Shwe oversaw the establishment of this organization in 1993 and assigned ministers close to him as secretariat members and central executive members. Part of the USDA is

---

[28] Ibid.
[29] Ed Cropley, "Than Shwe, Myanmar Junta's Old Fox," Reuters, October 3, 2007.
[30] Larry Jagan, "Suu Kyi and Democracy Divide Junta's Generals," *Bangkok Post*, April 8, 2003.
[31] Interview with a former close aide of Aung San Suu Kyi, April 2006, Bangkok.
[32] Interview with Aung Lynn Htut, June 2008, Washington DC.

expected to be transformed into a political party before the 2010 elections.[33]

Purging Regional Commanders

As in 1961, tensions developed in the mid-1990s between many of the officers in the War Office and the regional commands. With the opening up of the economy and the establishment of several ceasefire agreements with ethnic armed groups in the late 1980s and early 1990s, regional commanders gained tremendous political and economic power and began operating like warlords.[34] Because they were among the founders of the SLORC and contemporaries of Than Shwe, their seniority challenged the center. Among first-generation regional commanders of the SLORC were three popular and ambitious commanders (Lientenant General Tun Kyi, Lientenant General Kyaw Ba, and Lientenant General Myint Aung) who were seen by staff officers in Rangoon as a challenge to their power.

The officers in the War Office made attempts to reassert central control over the regional commands.[35] In 1995, almost all first-generation regional commanders were kicked upstairs as ministers. Ministers have less power than regional commanders because they do not have any troops under their direct command. However, they did retain their positions in the SLORC, the highest policymaking body. For two years, the new second- and third-generation regional commanders were not included in the SLORC.[36] Each generation of regional commanders consists of men who are generally within a three- to six-year age range. In 1997, the first-generation regional commanders of the SLORC, who were in their 60s, were removed

---

[33] Smith, *Burma: Insurgency and the Politics of Ethnicity*, p. 429.

[34] Selth, *Burma's Armed Forces: Power*, p. 262.

[35] Ibid.

[36] The second-generation regional commanders included Win Myint, who became the SPDC's Secretary 3, and Tin Hla, who became deputy PM. The third-generation regional commanders included Shwe Mann, Soe Win, Thein Sein, Tin Aung Myint Oo, Khin Maung Than, Ye Myint, Maung Bo, Kyaw Win, Aung Htwe and Tin Aye.

from the body. Tun Kyi, Kyaw Ba and Myint Aung were charged with corruption and put under house arrest. This period saw the first release of Aung San Suu Kyi in 1995, but she could not travel outside of Rangoon and there were no serious negotiations between the regime and her party. Than Shwe continued to consolidate his power, together with his followers, who mostly came from Light Infantry Division 88 and Southwest Command, which he had previously led.[37]

. In 1997, the SLORC renamed itself the SPDC. The second-generation commanders, who were in their 50s, and third-generation commanders, who were in their 40s, became SPDC members. The 1997 purge appeared to be coordinated by Than Shwe and Khin Nyunt.[38] Maung Aye may not have been involved in orchestrating this purge, since his fellow first-generation regional commanders were hit. In the mid-1990s, two new regional commands (coastal and triangle) and more than a dozen new divisions (regional operation commands and military operation commands) were established to dilute the power of the regional commanders and to increase efficiency in administering the regions.

Fate of New Regional Commanders

After the first-generation regional commanders were purged, the second-generation regional commanders were next. Lientenant General Win Myint, the fourth-highest officer and Secretary 3 of the SPDC, and Lientenant General Tin Hla, the deputy prime minister and Military Affairs minister, were sacked in late 2001.[39] Win Myint and Tin Hla were accused of involvement in corruption and put under house arrest. These two positions were never filled again, probably so as not to upset the power alignment at the top.

Meanwhile, a major reshuffle occurred among the regional commanders, designed to reduce the power of the third- (outgoing) and

---

[37] Interview with Aung Lynn Htut, June 2008, Washington DC.

[38] Interview with a former military intelligence officer, January 2007, Bangkok.

[39] "Myanmar's military makes big cabinet changes," Reuters, November 11, 2001.

fourth- (incoming) generation regional commanders at the same time.[40] However, the outgoing third-generation regional commanders were kicked upstairs as SPDC members without troops under their direct command. Still, the commanders were given staff duties at the War Office and some were made chiefs in the newly established four Bureaus of Special Operations (BSO), each of which have nominal supervision over two or three regional commands. Under this new arrangement, the fourth-generation regional commanders no longer enjoyed SPDC membership and their power was confined to their respective regions. After the 2001 reshuffle, there was a total of 13 members in the SPDC and the fourth-generation regional commanders had less power than their predecessors. Most were followers of Than Shwe and Maung Aye, rather than their contemporaries.

These four BSO positions were the result of diversifying the power of the former fourth-highest ranking officer, SPDC Secretary 2 Tin Oo, the army chief of staff and also the chief of the BSO. Tin Oo, who was close to both Than Shwe and Maung Aye but a rival of Khin Nyunt's, died in a helicopter crash in early 2001.[41] The regime reported that the crash was a result of bad weather but a Thai intelligence source and some local people reported hearing gunfire, leading some military analysts to wonder if it was the result of an internal power struggle.[42] Tin Oo had escaped a previous assassination plot in 1996 and another in 1997, when a parcel bomb explosion killed his daughter instead.

Consolidation of Power at the War Office

In 2001, Than Shwe put his protégé, General Shwe Mann (former Southwest regional commander), in the newly created joint chief-of-staff position (the new fourth-highest ranking post) to coordinate the

---

[40] Fourth-generation commanders included Myint Swe, Myint Hlaing, Ye Myint, Maung Oo, Htay Oo, Thar Aye, Ko Ko, Ohn Myint, Thura Myint Aung and Min Aung Hlaing.

[41] Amit Baruah, "Speculation over Tin Oo Successor," *The Hindu* (New Delhi), February 24, 2001.

[42] Interview with a Thai military intelligence officer, August 2002, Chiang Mai.

army, navy and air force, and to check the power of Maung Aye. The position of Southwest regional commander is important since the commanders can rise up to the top. Both Saw Maung and Than Shwe served as heads of the Southwest Regional Command in Irrawaddy Division. Moreover, Shwe Mann was given another important position, Brigadier General, General Staff, as commander of the Light Infantry Division 11, responsible for the outer security of the military's headquarters in Rangoon before the capital was moved to Naypyidaw.[43] Than Shwe carefully selects loyalists for this position because all military orders would normally pass through the brigadier, who could use this position to bypass the chain of command to communicate directly with field commanders for military operations. According to Maung Aung Myoe, this position has the privilege of having close personal relations with the military leadership and gaining their personal trust.[44]

Shwe Mann is 10 years younger than Maung Aye and may become the top leader in the future. He had been awarded medals for his brave fighting against the Karen National Union, the insurgent group that posed the largest military threat in the early 1990s. He is also personally loyal to Than Shwe.[45] Shwe Mann's family had served Than Shwe and his family as de facto personal assistants. For example, Shwe Mann's wife was a babysitter for Than Shwe's favorite grandson. Although Than Shwe wanted to promote Shwe Mann to vice senior general, Maung Aye has resisted this move since it would challenge his own seniority.[46] Shwe Mann appears to be pragmatic. He listens to businesspeople and seems to be willing to interact with the international community.[47]

---

[43] The current Brigadier General, General Staff is the commander of Military Operation Command 6 which takes responsibility for the outer security of Naypyidaw.

[44] Maung Aung Myoe, "A Historical Overview of Political Transition in Myanmar Since 1988". Working Paper Series No. 95 (Singapore: Asia Research Institute, 2007), p. 26.

[45] Interview with Aung Lynn Htut, May 2008, Washington DC.

[46] Ibid.

[47] Interview with a businessman, August 2007, Bangkok.

In 2001, Khin Nyunt's MI was also upgraded to bureau status from directorate level, making his rank equivalent to the chiefs of BSO. The 2001 reorganization led to an increasing concentration of power among the top three generals at the center, Than Shwe, Maung Aye and Khin Nyunt. Since then, internal struggles have been more likely to erupt at the Central Command, rather than between the center and regions.

The 2001 military reorganization coincided with the assignment of UN Special Envoy Razali Ismail to facilitate a dialogue between the regime and the NLD. Aung San Suu Kyi had been put under house arrest again in 2000 but was released in 2002. This time, she could travel outside Rangoon and some talks took place between the NLD and the regime, led by Khin Nyunt's MI group. This raised hopes that actual negotiations might begin.

The Military Intelligence Purge in 2004

However, these hopes were dashed when Khin Nyunt, the third-highest ranking officer, was purged because of his growing personal and institutional power which worried the top two leaders. Khin Nyunt's ascent to power and survival at the top depended on the influence of Ne Win, who had retired from the position of BSPP chairman in 1988 but continued to pull strings from behind for some years afterwards. Unlike other leading generals, Khin Nyunt was promoted to the top without having seen combat experience or serving as a divisional or regional commander. As a result, Maung Aye and many regional commanders did not respect him. When Ne Win's health started to decline in 2001, as did his influence on the junta. He was put under house arrest after his daughter and grandsons were accused of plotting a coup attempt in 2002, and passed away in late 2002. Incredibly, after ruling the country for 26 years, he was not given a state funeral. After his protector died, Khin Nyunt's position became shaky. From the beginning, Than Shwe had never completely trusted Khin Nyunt, whom he considered to be Ne Win's follower. In 1992, Than Shwe made his former personal security officer, Colonel Kyaw Win, MI deputy chief to keep an eye on Khin Nyunt.

Tensions had existed between Khin Nyunt and Maung Aye for many years, and also to some extent between Khin Nyunt and Than Shwe, as the MI became extraordinarily powerful. Although the MI was technically under the army, it acted like a free agent or a fourth branch of the military. Khin Nyunt and his MI managed to gain control over all the intelligence agencies, including the civilian ones. His local MI officers also reported directly to headquarters, bypassing the regional commanders. Khin Nyunt gained a reputation for striking ceasefire deals with many ethnic armed groups and, in later years, for winning over China, the Association of Southeast Asian Nations (ASEAN), India and Japan to counter Western pressure. He was also praised as a moderate or pragmatist who might be willing to work with the opposition.[48] Khin Nyunt's rising popularity and the growing power of the MI made Than Shwe and Maung Aye uncomfortable.

In 1994, Khin Nyunt created the Office of Strategic Studies to serve as a think tank for the regime. In fact, he had been working like a prime minister, even before he was assigned the job in 2003. He was given the position to counter increasing international pressure after the Depayin attack against Aung San Suu Kyi and her party, in which dozens of NLD members were killed. He managed not just the government's day-to-day activities but also worked as a spymaster, keeping a record of corruption charges to be used as justification for purges. This worried Than Shwe and Maung Aye, who felt that Khin Nyunt might turn on them in the future. Than Shwe asked Khin Nyunt to give up his MI post in order to focus on serving as prime minister, but met with refusal.[49] Khin Nyunt reportedly told others that he wanted to leave the post but was worried that his MI officers would face trouble without his protection.[50]

In the final showdown, it was Maung Aye, together with Than Shwe, who used corruption charges against MI officers to justify

---

[48] Interview with a senior western diplomat, April 2007, Chiang Mai.
[49] Interview with Aung Lynn Htut, June 2008, Washington DC.
[50] Ibid.

sacking Khin Nyunt. Khin Nyunt sought to protect his MI officers by trying to prove that regional commanders were as corrupt as the MI officers.[51] Major General Myint Hlaing, Maung Aye's former personal security officer, who was serving as the northeastern commander, arrested local MI officers at Muse in Shan State in September 2004. Troops from the Rangoon regional command and Light Infantry Division 11 raided Khin Nyunt's MI headquarters. The Rangoon Regional Command, which was responsible for the inner security of the military's headquarters, was headed by Major General Myint Swe, a nephew of Than Shwe's wife.[52] Light Infantry Division 11, which took responsibility for the outer security of the military headquarters, was headed by Brigadier General, General Staff, Colonel. Hla Htay Win, who was previously close to Maung Aye but later had good relations with both Than Shwe and Maung Aye.

Under Than Shwe's order, Maung Aye and Myint Swe arrested Khin Nyunt in 2004.[53] The next ear he was sentenced to 44 years' imprisonment but was put under house arrest instead. Several ministers, including the foreign minister, home minister and labor minister, and a number of ambassadors close to Khin Nyunt were also dismissed.[54] Followers of Than Shwe and Maung Aye were assigned to these positions.[55] Many intelligence officers were given prison sentences ranging from 20 years to nearly 200 years, the longest ever in Burma's history. However, MI Deputy Chief Kyaw Win escaped punishment, perhaps because of protection from his mentor, Than Shwe.

After Khin Nyunt was sacked, the SPDC's Secretary 1, Lientenant General Soe Win, became prime minister. Like Khin Nyunt, he had to give up his powerful position as Secretary 1; this post was given to

---

[51] Ibid., March 2008.

[52] Ibid.

[53] Interview with a former military intelligence officer, January 2006, Bangkok.

[54] Both the foreign and labor ministers were former MI officers, and the home minister got along with the labor minister when they worked together for ceasefire talks in Kokant area.

[55] Priscilla Clapp, "Building Democracy in Burma." Working Paper-02 (Washington DC: United States Institute of Peace, 2007), pp. 7–8.

Than Shwe's protégé, Lientenant General Thein Sein, adjutant general at the headquarters. Thein Sein had served as a junior officer to Than Shwe, including Brigadier General, General Staff, at the headquarters for many years.[56]

After Khin Nyunt was dismissed, the whole MI structure was completely dismantled and the National Intelligence Bureau dissolved.[57] An institution known as the Military Affairs Security (MAS) was established in its place. It was headed first by Than Shwe's protégé, Lientenant General Myint Swe, and later by Maung Aye's protégé, Lientenant General Ye Myint.[58] Ye Myint also served as a loyal follower to Maung Aye when the latter was eastern regional commander.[59] Local MAS officers cannot submit their reports directly to the headquarters but must send them through the regional commanders. The MAS initially was not as effective as the former MI, and this made it easier for organizers to prepare for and initiate the September 2007 demonstrations.[60]

The purge of Khin Nyunt had a big impact on negotiations with Aung San Suu Kyi and the ethnic armed groups, as well as on the regime's international relations. This is because unlike most other senior generals, Khin Nyunt was considered a pragmatist and was willing to interact with the various opposition groups and the international community. Even after the Depayin attack in 2003, Khin Nyunt negotiated and made compromises for the return of the NLD to the National Convention. However, at the last minute, Than Shwe rejected the agreement Khin Nyunt and his home minister had made with the NLD.[61] The 2004 purge of Khin Nyunt dimmed the possibility of the release of Aung San Suu Kyi or negotiations between the

---

[56] Interview with Aung Lynn Htut, May 2008, Washington DC.

[57] Aung Hla Tun, "Myanmar to release nearly 4,000 prisoners," Reuters, November 18, 2004.

[58] Callahan, "Of *Kyay-Zu*", p. 38.

[59] Interview with a businessman, October 2006, Bangkok.

[60] Kyaw Yin Hlaing, "Challenging the Authoritarian State: Buddhist Monks and Peaceful Protest in Burma," *The Fletcher Forum of World Affairs* 32:1 (Winter 2008), pp. 137–138.

[61] Interview with a senior diplomat, April 2005, Bangkok.

regime and the NLD, which the UN special envoy, Razali Ismail, had worked so hard for from 2000 to 2003. Razali resigned in early 2006 because he was not allowed back into the country after the sacking of Khin Nyunt.

Since Khin Nyunt had been the architect of the ceasefire agreements between the military and many ethnic armed groups, serious negotiations on ethnic demands at the National Convention did not take place. Maung Aye was not in favor of the ceasefire agreements when they were initiated in 1989; he appeared to believe that he could wipe out all the armed ethnic groups.[62] After Khin Nyunt's purge, four smaller ethnic ceasefire groups were forced to disarm, and a number of ceasefire leaders, including the Shan leader, General Sao Ten, were imprisoned for many years. The ceasefire groups' business activities, which had been allowed by Khin Nyunt, were restricted.[63] In August 2009, the regime attacked one of the smaller ceasefires groups, the Myanmar National Democratic Alliance Army, based in the Kokang region along the China–Burma border, for resisting its demand to transform into a Border Guard Force that would be placed under the Burmese military's command before the 2010 elections. Although other smaller ceasefire groups had to agree to join form the Border Guard Force, larger groups like the United Wa State Army and the Kachin Independence Organization have refused to do so.

The purge of Khin Nyunt also led to reduced interaction between the SPDC and the international community. Khin Nyunt was the only figure in the regime who understood the importance of relations with the international community. Both Than Shwe and Maung Aye are xenophobic and tend to view international nongovernmental organizations (NGOs) as potential foreign spies or neocolonialists.[64] Frustrated with the lack of political improvement in Burma, ASEAN persuaded the SPDC to skip its turn as the association's chair in 2006. UN agencies and international NGOs were placed under new

---

[62] Interview with a former military intelligence officer, February 2006, Bangkok.
[63] Zaw Oo and Win Min, *Assessing Burma's Ceasefire Accords* (Washington DC: East-West Center, 2007), p. 55.
[64] Interview with a former military intelligence officer, March 2008, Chiang Mai.

restrictions. The SPDC insisted that members of the pro-regime USDA must accompany staff from the International Committee of the Red Cross (ICRC) on prison visits. The ICRC refused and had to stop making such visits.

Since Khin Nyunt was close to the Chinese, both Than Shwe and Maung Aye developed closer ties with India and Russia while maintaining formal relations with China. Than Shwe visited India just a few days after sacking Khin Nyunt, and Maung Aye visited Russia in 2006 and India in 2008. Than Shwe has never visited China in recent years, although Maung Aye visited China in 2006 and 2009, and the next two prime ministers, Soe Win and Thein Sein, made trips there. Shwe Mann also visited China in 2007 and met the prime minister, and made a secret trip to China and North Korea in late 2008. However, China was very frustrated with the Burmese army's attack on the Kokang ceasefire group at the Chinese border in August 2009, which led to over 30,000 refugees crossing into China and hurting many Chinese businesses in the Kokang region.

Than Shwe and Maung Aye's Competition for Power in the 2005–09 Reshuffles

After the sacking of Khin Nyunt's group, it became clear that a power struggle was under way between the groupings around the two top generals. Before, power struggles had centered around Khin Nyunt and Maung Aye, with Than Shwe seeming to assume a mediating role. In fact, he played Khin Nyunt and Maung Aye off against one another. He took advantage of the divide to remove some of Khin Nyunt's followers from important positions and replaced them with his own followers, rather than Maung Aye's.

Whereas Khin Nyunt lacked fighting forces under his control, certain Burmese regional and divisional commanders tip their loyalty toward either Than Shwe or Maung Aye or both. If one group purges the other, the process could get out of control or lead to bloodshed. So far, both sides appear to be acting cautiously as they try to out-maneuver each other. However, they recognize the importance of stacking key positions with loyalists during reshuffles in order to shore up their power bases. This internal struggle may cause more uncertainty regarding promotions and retirements, frustrating some mid-level officers who are waiting to be promoted. Consequently, many of these officers may feel compelled to join one group or another, or to maintain good relations with both groups for their survival and advancement. As Maung Aye came from the DSA, he has tried to get more DSA graduates promoted to top positions. Than Shwe, who came from the OTS, must recruit both OTS and DSA graduates because the latter has graduated more officers than the former since 1988.[65]

In the May 2005 reshuffle, Than Shwe sought to strengthen his position by promoting Myint Swe (a former Brigadier General, General Staff) to become the first lieutenant general among the fourth-generation regional commanders. However, Than Shwe promoted Myint Swe very quickly and in exception to the normal practice: he even became a lieutenant general without graduating from the National Defense Collage.[66] Meanwhile, Than Shwe rotated many other fourth-generation regional commanders rather than promoting them, to thwart their ability to concentrate their power. These regional commanders were appointed in 2001 and are past due for promotion. However, Than Shwe appears to want to maintain the status quo as long as he can in order to maintain his advantage in the SPDC power structure vis-à-vis Maung Aye.

In early 2006, not long after the move to the new capital, another reshuffle took place in which both Than Shwe and Maung Aye appeared to be engaging in a balancing act, although Than Shwe came out ahead. Than Shwe promoted Myint Swe to be chief of the newly established BSO 5, the bureau's unit responsible for overseeing Rangoon after the capital was moved to Naypyidaw. Maung Aye promoted his protégés, Myint Hlaing and Ye Myint, to the positions of air defense chief and MAS chief, respectively. However, Ye Myint's power is limited: he cannot control the civilian intelligence agencies, which fall under the authority of Home Minister Maung Oo,

---

[65] Interview with Aung Lynn Htut, June 2008, Washington DC.
[66] Ibid.

believed to be Than Shwe's protégé. At the same time, two regional commanders close to Maung Aye were kicked upstairs to less-powerful cabinet positions. Major General Maung Maung Swe (Maung Aye's brother-in-law) and Major General Khin Maung Myint (who previously served under Maung Aye) were removed as regional commanders.

Than Shwe and Maung Aye both sought to promote their trusted supporters as fifth-generation regional commanders.[67] These incoming commanders are in their 40s and there is a significant age gap between them and the top leadership. Than Shwe appointed Myint Swe's follower, Wai Lwin, as commander of Naypyidaw Command (the inner security command for the new capital where the new military headquarters is located).[68] In return, Maung Aye secured the Rangoon commander position for Brigadier General Hla Htay Win (a former Brigadier General, General Staff), who was close both to him and Than Shwe.[69] However, Than Shwe's protégé, Myint Swe, who oversees Rangoon, checked Hla Htay Win. Than Shwe assigned Shwe Mann's protégé, Col. Tin Ngwe, as the new Brigadier General, General Staff, and commander of Military Operation Command 6 in Pyinmana, to check Maung Aye's power over the army. When Shwe Mann was a battalion commander, Tin Ngwe served under him as an adjutant officer.

In the 2007 reshuffle, which happened after the monk-led demonstrations that year. Than Shwe got the upper hand over Maung Aye. During the demonstrations, Than Shwe's decision to order a brutal crackdown on the monks angered many generals, including Maung Aye, who worried about tarnishing the military's image by

[67] Fifth-generation regional commanders are Hla Htay Win, Maung Shein, Wai Lwin, Aung Than Htut, Thet Naing Win, Khin Zaw Oo and Thaung Aye.
[68] Wai Lwin served as the deputy regional commander for Rangoon when Myint Swe was the Rangoon regional commander.
[69] Brigadier General, General Staff is a very strategic position in the military. Responsibilities include securing the outer security of the capital and the overall coordination of military operations. The Brigadier General, General Staff can earn the personal trust of top leaders and proceed to the top step-by-step from this position.

using excessive force against monks. In fact, Maung Aye had also disagreed with Than Shwe's secret order to plan the Depayin attack against Aung San Suu Kyi in 2003.[70] Consequently, he was removed from his powerful position as chairman of the Trade Council which regulates permits for internal and external trade. QuarterMaster General Lt. Gen. Tin Aung Myint Oo, who was close to Maung Aye before but later was loyal to Than Shwe, became the chairman of the Trade Council. Since then, Tin Aung Myint Oo has met with Than Shwe regularly and his wife has been getting closer to Than Shwe's wife.[71] Tin Aung Myint Oo was also promoted to Secretary 1 of the SPDC when then Secretary 1, Thein Sein, was appointed prime minister after the death of former Prime Minister Soe Win in October 2007.

In the 2007 reshuffle, Major General Thar Aye (who came from Than Shwe's hometown, Kyaukse) and Major General Khin Zaw (the former Mandalay regional commander) were promoted to BSO chiefs after the creation of a new BSO 6 position. Both had been regional commanders with connections to Than Shwe. Lientenant General Thura Myint Aung, the former southwest commander and a neutral figure between Than Shwe and Maung Aye, was promoted to adjutant general, a senior military position. Brigadier General Kyaw Swe, the former principal of the Defense Services Academy, was handpicked by Than Shwe to become the southwest regional commander. Shwe Mann's protégé, Tin Ngwe, was promoted to central (Mandalay) regional commander.[72]

In the June 2008 reshuffle, Than Shwe apparently tried to reduce the power of Maung Aye. Many of the BSO chiefs and other chiefs from the military headquarters, most of whom were close to Than

---

[70] "Depayin Tikekhitehmu Than Shwe Kotaing Amaintpay, Myanmar Than Ayarshe Haung Pyaw," [Than Shwe himself ordered the Depayin attack, said a former Burmese diplomat], Voice of America/Burmese, May 31, 2008.

[71] Interview with Hla Min, a former military intelligence officer, August 2009, Bangkok.

[72] His Brigadier General, General Staff position was filled by a new generation officer, Col. Maung Maung Aye.

Shwe, were removed from their positions and put into the military reserve force. However, they were replaced with fourth-generation regional commanders who were closer to Than Shwe than to Maung Aye.[73] Major General Ohn Myint and Major General Ko Ko (a former Brigadier General, General Staff), who became the new BSO chiefs, are both closer to Than Shwe; the other new BSO chief, Major General Min Aung Hlaing, appears to be neutral. Among the fifth-generation regional commanders, Hla Htay Win, who has grown closer to Than Shwe, was promoted quickly to the headquarters as the new chief of military training, together with his DSA classmate Major General Maung Shein. Maung Aye's brother-in-law, Maung Maung Swe, also lost one his two ministerial posts, the immigration portfolio, the official reason being so he could focus more on cyclone relief efforts. After Cyclone Nargis killed 138,000 people in Burma, Maung Aye ordered the Burmese embassy in Bangkok to allow a US military flight (C-130) carrying cyclone assistance to Burma, but the order was postponed by Than Shwe through his close minister Aung Thaung, also a USDA secretariat member.[74]

The mid-2008 reshuffle also reduced the power of new headquarters (War Office) staff including new BSO chiefs. It should be noted that the new military headquarters officers, including the new BSO chiefs, who have been promoted since 2006, are not included in the SPDC. This seems to be another step in Than Shwe's plan to reduce the power of the headquarters staff after reducing the regional commanders' power in 2001 by not including them in the SPDC. This will make it easier for Than Shwe to retire most of the current headquarters staff than in the past, when they were SPDC members. Also, sixth-generation regional commanders replaced outgoing fourth-generation regional commanders between late 2007 and mid-2008.[75]

---

[73] Than Shwe's followers, Ye Myint (BSO 1), Khin Maung Than (BSO 3), Maung Bo (chief of military ordinance) and Aung Htwe (chief of armed forces training) were retired. Maung Aye's follower, Kyaw Win (BSO 2), was also retired.

[74] Interview with Aung Lynn Htut, July 2009, Washington DC.

[75] The sixth-generation regional commanders include Tin Ngwe, Kyaw Swe, Myint Soe, Soe Win, Kyaw Phyo, Yar Pyae, Win Myint and Hla Min.

In the early 2009 reshuffle, Than Shwe seemed to have the upper hand over Maung Aye and managed it in a way to prepare for the 2010 elections. Most of the former headquarters staff, including BSO chiefs (third-generation regional commanders and contemporaries of Shwe Mann), who were put into the reserve force in mid-2008 but continued to remain in the SPDC, were finally retired from the military and the SPDC. Today, only six members are left in the SPDC.[76] However, another contemporary of Shwe Mann, Lientenant General Tin Aung Myint Oo (Secretary 1 of the SPDC), was promoted to general in March 2009 and became an advisor to Than Shwe. Since General Tin Aung Myint Oo is a hardliner, Than Shwe is likely to play off Shwe Mann, who appears to be less so, against Tin Aung Myint Oo, just as he had played off Khin Nyunt and Maung Aye against each other. Tin Aung Myint Oo has been tasked to focus on business issues, while Shwe Mann has been assigned to concentrate on national security issues.

At the same time, Prime Minister Thein Sein was put into the army reserve force. Meanwhile, three BSO chiefs were rotated among themselves in the reshuffle just as the regional commanders were in 2005 to prevent them from concentrating power in a particular area.[77] In February 2009, Immigration Minister General Saw Lwin, who was close to Maung Aye was sacked together with the construction minister. Neither were USDA secretariat members. Deputy Foreign Minister, Kyaw Thu, who appears to be closer to Shwe Mann and Maung Aye than to Than Shwe, and who gained a good reputation in the international community for his flexibility in dealing with the donor community on cyclone assistance, was also transferred to the less powerful position of chairman of the Civil Service Selection Board.

As a result, Than Shwe's followers continue to dominate the SPDC, the military headquarters, the regional commands and the ministries. However, at the mid-level commands, Maung Aye seems to have some loyalists since Than Shwe focused more on higher-level

---

[76] The six current SPDC members are Than Shwe, Maung Aye, Shwe Mann, Thein Sein, Tin Aung Myint Oo and Tin Aye.

[77] The chiefs of BSO 1, 4 and 6 were rotated among themselves.

appointments and now faces a generation gap. Nevertheless, Than Shwe has been relying more and more on his shadow government, also known as his kitchen government, in which different generations of his close assistant officers that he brought along from LID 88 are included. The group includes his special military advisor, Major General Nay Win, his security officers, Major General Hla Aung Thein (the military headquarters security commander) and Colonel Soe Shein (his personal security officer), and his current Brigadier General, General Staff, Colonel Maung Maung Aye.[78] Former MI deputy chief, Kyaw Win, who was also Than Shwe's former personal security officer, was included in the group until the MI was dismantled.

Future Possibilities

In the coming years, a generational shift in power will take place. Although Than Shwe has managed to consolidate power around himself, he is now in his late 70s and in declining health. His power will wane with his health. In early 2007, he was in Singapore for medical treatment and missed the Independence Day ceremony for the first time. He has diabetes and hypertension and has already had two mild strokes in recent years. Prime Minister Thein Sein, who is in his early 60s, already has a pacemaker. Maung Aye is in his early 70s and has had prostate cancer, although there have been no recurrences in recent years.

Nevertheless, Than Shwe has been implementing a strategy to guarantee his influence over the military and the government until his death. Than Shwe wants to ensure that he himself does not end up in the same situation as Ne Win or Saw Maung. As a result, he had the pro-military constitution approved in 2008, and plans to hold elections in 2010. Than Shwe believes he can manage this

---

[78] Nay Win and Hla Aung Thein were both promoted from Brigadier General to Major General while Maung Aye was away from the military headquarters a few years ago since Maung Aye had opposed their promotions previously.

process in a way that will ensure his continuing role in governing the country.

The first likely scenario for the near future is that Than Shwe will hold the elections in 2010 as he said he would at the Myanmar War Veterans Organization conference in October 2009. However, the election date, party registration laws and election laws have yet to be announced.[79] After the elections, he is likely to retire from the military together with Maung Aye, as he told UN Secretary-General Ban Ki-moon in mid-2009.[80] However, Than Shwe would create a patronage position or a body that he could use to continue to influence the government and the military. He may serve as honorary commander-in-chief or set up a central military council Comprising most of the SPDC members, like the one in China. He could lead this council since the constitution allows the military to manage all of its affairs as it likes.[81] He may continue to wield military budgetary power as honorary commander-in-chief or through the council, as Ne Win did as the chairman of the BSPP party after retiring from the position of president. Than Shwe controls the budget through two SPDC members, Tin Aung Myint Oo and Tin Aye, who run two military conglomerates, the Union of Myanmar Economic Holdings and the Myanmar Economic Corporation. These are the largest business organizations in the country and are likely to be expanded in the future.

Than Shwe may prefer for his loyalists to serve in the two most powerful positions under the new constitution — president (who is both head of state and head of government) and commander-in-chief of the military. The latter can nominate three powerful security ministers (Defense, Home and Border Affairs), appoint 25% of the parliamentarians and declare a state of emergency through the National

---

[79] "Senior General Than Shwe Addresses Second-Day Session of MWVO Conference" *New Light of Myanmar* October 10, 2009.

[80] Haseenah Koyakutty, "UN gains leverage over Myanmar," *Asia Times Online,* July 15, 2009.

[81] Ministry of Information, *Constitution of the Republic of the Union of Myanmar (2008)* (Naypyitaw: Printing and Publishing Enterprise, September 2008), p. 6.

Defense and Security Council which includes active-duty military representatives.[82] He is likely to have Shwe Mann serve as president and engage in all the travel that is required, while he himself remains in Naypyidaw. Than Shwe may have Myint Swe, who can serve for one term after the elections, or a younger-generation officer, Hla Htay Win, who can serve for two terms after elections, become the commander-in-chief.

In the first scenario, part of the USDA, of which Than Shwe is the patron, is likely to be transformed into a pro-military political party. The association has already been acting like a party, with branch offices all over the country, regular conferences, meetings and training sessions. Most of the secretariat members and central executive members of the USDA launched campaigns in different parts of the country to support the pro-military constitution in the 2008 referendum.[83] They have also launched unofficial elections campaigns in various parts of the country since early 2009, although the party-registration law has not been announced yet. However, after the party-registration law is announced, they are likely to be retired from their government posts so they can serve in the pro-military party.

---

[82] Ibid., pp. 75, 165. Maung Aung Myoe, "A Historical Overview of Political Transition in Myanmar Since 1988" p. 30.

[83] The secretary-general of USDA is Htay Oo (agricultural minister) and its joint secretary-general is Zaw Min (electric power minister no. 1). Its secretariat members are U Thaung (science and technology minister), Aung Thaung (industrial minister no. 1), Tin Htut (cooperatives minister), Kyaw Hsan (information minister), Thein Zaw (post and telecommunications minister). Its central executive members are Tin Naing Thein (commerce minister), Thein Aung (forestry minister), Ohn Myint (mining minister), Maung Maung Thein (livestock and fisheries minister), Thein Swe (transport minister), Thein Nyunt (border affairs minister), Soe Tha (planning and economic development minister), Khin Maung Myint (electric power minister no. 2), Than Htay (energy minister), Aung Min (railway minister), Thura Myint Maung (religious affairs minister), Thura Aye Myint (sports minister), Chan Nyein (education minister), Phone Swe (deputy home minister), Nyan Htun Aung (deputy transport minister), Aung Thein Lin (mayor of Yangon) and Maung Pa (deputy mayor of Yangon).

The USDA has become a power base for Than Shwe, with a membership officially estimated at 24 million, although many people were in fact forced to join. After Khin Nyunt was sacked, the USDA set up its own internal secret intelligence networks. Meanwhile, many local army commanders have become upset over the USDA's increasingly influential role in development within their areas. However, it is possible that some generals might retire from the military and also serve as the central executive committee members of this pro-military party. Some cronies, former government officers who are technocrats and local influential figures, might be included in the local-level leadership of the party to broaden its representation and to increase its chances of winning the elections (50% of the seats in Parliament). Smaller parties led by the SPDC's cronies, local influential people, and some ceasefire leaders might also be set up, or could be asked to run as individual candidates to win another 25%: these could be part of a coalition government controlled by the military.

In the first scenario, as long as Than Shwe is in control, any political, economic and social changes are unlikely since he has resisted both domestic and international engagement and pressure, and he has a firm grip on the military. However, when Than Shwe's influence wanes as his health declines further, younger generals, including Shwe Mann, Myint Swe and Hla Htay Win, might have some independent decision-making power and might be more open to the idea of gradual change, starting with economic liberalization and, to a lesser degree, political liberalization.

Second, outside scenario is that Than Shwe is unable to implement his plan of holding the 2010 elections. He could die suddenly or be removed from power because of his declining health. In this scenario, Maung Aye is likely to take his position and put his protégés (Myint Hlaing and Ye Myint) into key positions, to first check and later to replace Than Shwe's protégés (Shwe Mann and Myint Swe). There is a slight chance for dialogue between the military and the opposition if Maung Aye takes over, if sufficient domestic and international pressure emerges. This is because Maung Aye will not have as firm a grip on the military as Than Shwe has had and will be more vulnerable to pressure.

Conclusion

The Burmese military has asserted that it is cohesive, noting that there have been no serious mutinies since the late 1940s. However, it is not as cohesive as the generals have claimed. Throughout the period of military rule, intra-military groupings have emerged based on personal and institutional ties and purges have been carried out. It appears that the military has focused so much attention on promoting unity precisely because of the existence of groups vying for power. As long as there is no institutional arrangement for succession to the top, factions will continue to emerge in the military.

At the same time, hardline military leaders have been unwilling to give up political power. However, if a reform-minded senior general or clique were to assume leadership, there might be more space to begin a process of national reconciliation and political reform. Still, the military will seek to be cohesive and strong enough to play an important role in Burmese politics at least in the near future. The military's role in politics is deeply entrenched and it is determined to hold onto its prerogatives. Equally important, the generals are worried about losing their political and economic privileges and facing trials for their past human rights abuses. As a result, it is likely that while groupings will continue to form and jockey for power within the military, the generals will remain strongly committed to maintaining the unity of the institution.

Chapter 7

Naypyidaw vs. Yangon: The Reasons Behind the Junta's Decision to Move the Burmese Capital

Daniel Gomà

Abstract

For reasons never clearly explained, in November 2005 Burma's SPDC suddenly moved the administrative capital from Rangoon to Pyinmana, a small city (ca. 100,000) in the jungle some 200 miles (320 km) to the north, near which they constructed a new capital named Naypyidaw (royal city). This chapter explains why they did so, with what likely political, cultural, and fiscal consequences for the country.

Keywords: Pyinmana; Summer of Democracy.

Introduction

More than four years have passed since the military junta that has ruled Burma for nearly half a century decided to move the nation's capital.[1] On Friday, November 4, 2005, hundreds of civil servants from Yangon (Rangoon), the Burmese capital since independence in

---

[1] Since the adoption of the Adaptation of Expressions Law by the junta in 1989, which changed the official name of the country from Burma to Myanmar, the country's name has caused many polemics among Burma's scholars. Because both terms mean the same (the land of Burmans), I will use Burma for the period before 1989 and both names indistinctively when referring to the period after 1989. In that sense, I will use mainly Yangon instead of the former Rangoon.

1948, were informed that they were to pack their things and move both office and home to a new city in three days' time. The new administrative center would be located in the town of Pyinmana, 320 km (200 mi) north of Yangon, in the southern part of the Mandalay Division. With just a weekend to pack and leave, these civil servants had to leave families behind temporarily because adequate housing, schools and hospitals had yet to be built in the new city. Officially, Yangon remained the national capital and the new place was only the administrative capital. No name was given to the new city in the months following the move and the secrecy of the State Peace and Development Council (SPDC), the official name of the Burmese military junta since 1997, added more confusion to this situation.

The junta's explanation for this relocation of the government departments was announced at a short press conference held on November 7 by Information Minister Major General Kyaw San. Officially, it was "to ensure more effective administration of nation-building activities".[2] Some days later, the minister said that history would vindicate the controversial decision to relocate the country's long-time capital from Yangon to a remote town in central Burma, saying the move was "in the interests of the nation and the people".[3]

In the months following this decision, architects from around the country converged in Pyinmana to design and build a large-scale planned city. Apartment blocks were built for bureaucrats and their families, who were forced to move to the new city, as well as ministries and a large military area.[4] The ministries and normal working of the government were to be in place for the most part by the end of February 2006. On March 26, 2006, the SPDC announced that the city's new name was to be Naypyidaw (also spelled Nay Pyi Taw and

---

[2] "Government's Decision," *The Myanmar Times*, November 14, 2005.
[3] Naing Pyi Chit, "Army's New Graveyard," *Burma Digest*, November 19, 2005. http://burmadigest.info/2005/11/19/armys-new-graveyard, accessed November 26, 2008.
[4] Civil servants, who received a sharp pay increase during the weekend, complained about the poor infrastructure during the first months after their deployment there.

Nay Pyi Daw), the "Royal City", and the Minister of Progress of Border Areas and National Races and Development Affairs, Colonel Thein Nyunt, was appointed Mayor.[5] The new city, belonging to the Pyinmana District, was territorially organized into three townships: Pyinmana, Lewe and Alar.[6] One day later, on Armed Forces Day, more than 12,000 troops took part in a parade in the city, in the first major political event held officially in Naypyidaw. This event marked the proclamation of the city as the new capital of the Union of Myanmar.[7]

But why did Burma's military government abruptly announce at the end of 2005 that the capital was moving from the old city of Rangoon on the coast to a little town in the middle of a malaria-infested area, in an arid, mountain-framed spot in central Burma more than 300 km inland? The secretive SPDC has never revealed what lay behind such a decision. Apart from the official explanation, it is quite clear that there was more than one reason and that these motivations were extremely important and serious for Myanmar's generals. If not, they would not have taken the trouble to move the machinery of government north into the heartland of the country.

Yangon, "Enemy" of the Junta

The two main reasons for the Burmese junta's decision to move its capital from Yangon to a new location in central Myanmar are clearly political in nature. The first is a growing fear of large cities by the SPDC, while the second is related to geopolitical interests. The fear of big cities has become, in fact, one of the main internal problems

---

[5] "Pyinmana Mayor," *The Myanmar Times*, March, 20–26, 2006.

[6] Alar is the site of Naypyidaw's airport. A very small airport until then, it was renovated to become a modern airport of the new nation's capital.

[7] Although no official declaration was made by the government at that time, the SPDC announced that Naypyidaw was going to become the future capital of Myanmar in accordance with the new Constitution to be adopted in the coming years. In fact, to everybody in Burma, it was clear from March 2006 that Naypyidaw had become the nation's capital.

for the current rulers. This is especially evident in the case of Yangon. As a university and cultural center, the biggest Myanmar city has been since independence in 1948 (and even before then) very non-conformist towards the incumbent regime. But the nearly five decades of government by the *Tatmadaw* (the Burmese Armed Forces) has made Yangon a rebel axis against army rule.

The relation between the military and the city since 1962 has been extremely difficult. With its huge student and middle-class population, Yangon has always been a center of dissidence and opposition against the military dictatorship. For instance, some months after Ne Win's *coup d'état* (March 2, 1962), the back-to-school period was marked by student protests against the new military regime on the Rangoon University campus. The government's response was to send troops into the university and suppress the protesters. We do not know how many people died, but the death toll is estimated to be over 100. Twelve years later, in December 1974, amid important strikes due to the economic crisis, the fervor surrounding the death of former United Nations Secretary-General U Thant and the disrespectful attitude of the government regarding his funeral brought on a new explosion of angry protests led by university students. The revolt was suppressed again with bullets and many fatalities.

More important and fundamental to understanding the perception of Yangon as an "enemy" by the SDPC are the events of 1988. The largest uprising in contemporary Burmese history took place in the capital (in addition to other cities) from March to September, forcibly ending Ne Win's regime. While enjoying unprecedented freedom, the citizenry waited for positive changes. Nevertheless, on September 18 a new junta called the State Law and Order Restoration Council (SLORC, the predecessor of the SPDC) seized power and violently suppressed Burma's "Summer of Democracy." Thousands of protesters were killed.

Another important aspect for the SPDC is the religious relevance of Yangon. The city is the site of two of the country's most famous pagodas, Sule and especially the imposing Shwedagon, the principal Buddhist holy site in Myanmar. Both have been centers of political activism for decades. In 1988 Shwedagon functioned as a public space for political activities and was the site of Aung San Suu Kyi's first public speech against Ne Win's junta. Within the opposition against the government, political leaders and students have had the support of a large part of the *sangha*, the Buddhist clergy.[8] Monks have been politically active in the opposition to the dictatorship since at least the 1960s.

The lack of support for the junta in Yangon was evident in May 1990, when democratic elections took place after three decades of dictatorship. The National League for Democracy (NLD), led among others by Aung San Suu Kyi, obtained an overwhelming victory, starting in the Yangon Division, where the NLD won all but two of the 61 parliamentary seats in dispute, the remaining going to other parties opposing the military government. Even in the military districts the pro-regime National Unity Party (NUP) was defeated.[9] Refusing to give up power until a new constitution was drafted, the SLORC declared that it would govern until then, thus prolonging indefinitely the military dictatorship in the country.

The events of 1988 forced a new generation of SLORC/SPDC military rulers to accept a new reality: the possibility of losing control over the situation should a large revolt take place in the capital. The massive popular demonstrations of 1988 led to the collapse of the system. Only by force could the *Tatmadaw* maintain its power. And more importantly, the events of 1988 completely alienated both military cadres and society at large, including the majority of Burmans, Myanmar's main ethnic group (around 65–70% of total population). As Donald M. Seekins clearly states, "The inhabitants of the Burman heartland were schooled to think of it [the *Tatmadaw*] as the defender of national unity... This largely positive image was shattered after the

---

[8] It is estimated that the *sangha* in Burma today numbers around 500,000 between ordained monks and novices.

[9] Yangon is only one example of the great victory of the opposition parties in the whole country: in total, the NLD took 59.9% of the popular vote and won 392 parliamentary seats as opposed to 10 by the NUP (21.2%). The total number of parliamentary seats was 492.

massive shootings of 1988."[10] The positive image of the regime was destroyed forever.

Since 1988–1990, the SPDC has tried to prevent a recurrence of the "Summer of Democracy" in Burmese cities, to avoid the events of 1988 when all power mechanisms were paralyzed for weeks because of popular demonstrations. Among its policies, the SPDC initiated a transformation of Yangon's landscape with three main objectives: the strategic redesign of the city, including large-scale relocation of its population away from the center; development of capitalism and sponsorship of Buddhism with the renovation of the main sites (like the Shwedagon); and the construction of new pagodas.[11]

However, urban social tensions have increased since 1988 because of the continued economic crisis and the adoption of new capitalist policies that have mainly benefited the ruling class. As a place of struggle between the state and the people over whom it rules, the resistance of Yangon's population against the government continues both actively and passively with demonstrations occasionally erupting, the latest being the so-called "Saffron Revolution" of September 2007 when monks took the leading role. Also, in the last decade, several bomb blasts have occurred in Yangon, as well as in other cities, killing mainly civilians. But members of the armed forces and their families have been targeted too. Six months before moving the capital, several bombs exploded in Yangon and Mandalay.[12] All these violent episodes shook the SPDC leaders to their core and transmitted the feeling that they were, in fact, not safe in Yangon, thus reinforcing the need to insulate themselves from these urban social tensions.

The suspicion towards Yangon also extended to the other big cities of Myanmar. Of course, in abandoning Yangon as the nation's capital, the SPDC could have opted for another big city like

---

[10] Donald M. Seekins, *The Disorder in Order: The Army-State in Burma since 1962* (Bangkok: Lotus Press, 2002), p. 273.

[11] Donald M. Seekins, "The State and the City: 1988 and the Transformation of Rangoon," *Pacific Affairs* 78:2 (March 2005), p. 265.

[12] Helen James, "Myanmar in 2005: In a Holding Pattern," *Asian Survey* 46:1 (January–February 2006), p. 164.

Mandalay, Burma's second largest. It was the capital before British colonization and had the infrastructure to host again the new capital of the country with no huge costs.[13] But Mandalay is a center of Burmese culture and religious life. Like Yangon, the city saw massive demonstrations against the junta in 1988. Being also a university city and major cultural center, it is not strange that the NLD won an striking victory in Mandalay Division, taking 55 of the 56 parliamentary seats up for grabs in the 1990 elections, with the remaining seat going to an independent candidate. Furthermore, Mandalay has more religious significance than Yangon because the city, along with neighboring Sagaing, has the largest number of monasteries and monks in Burma. Monks have been very active politically in Mandalay and have always adopted a very firm stance against the junta's.[14]

Conscious of the hostility of the urban population towards the regime, the SPDC decided to create a new capital out of a little town and its surrounding areas. Naypyidaw was founded and designed exclusively to protect the military leaders and their families, the privileged elite, and create a place where they would be (and feel) safe.[15] The city is a refuge for the Burmese generals where they stay together and feel they have better control over the country. From this secluded world, free from urban social tensions, they can better control the

---

[13] The current top military leaders being very superstitious, there may have been another reason for them to refuse Mandalay as the new political center: it was the last capital of Burma before British colonization and it could have been perceived as the last capital of the SPDC and a signal of its imminent downfall.

[14] The senior monks (abbots) of Mandalay monasteries were famous for promoting a boycott of *Tatmadaw* personnel and their families after the shooting of some monks by soldiers in the summer of 1990. Known as "Overturning the Offering Bowl", this boycott consisted of refusing offerings from soldiers and their families and not participating in ceremonies sponsored by the army. Considered a severe form of punishment in Buddhist culture, it spread to other parts of the country.

[15] An example of this is that among the new buildings constructed in Naypyidaw there is no university. It was rare that a nation's capital would not have its own university. Only in Yazin, very close to Naypyidaw, are there two faculties, one for agriculture and another one for forestry. There are some engineering and medical institutes in the area, too, but no official university.

situation in big cities and not be afraid of demonstrations against the government. Relocating military and administrative institutions away from any possible future trouble, the junta remains in control of its functions and can coordinate an appropriate response. An example of this is the September 2007 protests, which were quickly and violently suppressed but posed no real threat to the stability of the regime.

Another interesting aspect of Naypyidaw is the absence of tourist interest. There are no particular places to visit in the area and from a historical point of view, it is only relevant because Pyinmana was the base of the Burma Independence Army led by Aung San (later renamed and reorganized into the Burma National Army by the Japanese) for a large part of World War II. It was there that the army and its officers were trained before moving to the area of Yangon at the end of the war. This, combined with the fact that trains from Yangon and Mandalay take nearly 10 hours each to reach the new capital, makes Naypidaw an isolated political center from which to exert control over a nation.[16]

A Geopolitical Move: From Fear of Invasion to Regional Control

The junta's fear of big cities is linked to another one: the threat of foreign invasion. Some analysts have pointed to a certain degree of paranoia among senior military figures that they might come under attack, specifically from the United States, and that a location further from the coast is strategically safer. The origins of these fears also stem from the 1988 events. During the Summer of Democracy of 1988 there were rumors in Yangon that ships (an aircraft carrier and four warships) from the US Navy's Seventh Fleet had entered Burmese

---

[16] However, this may change in the future. A new highway was opened in February 2009, connecting Naypyidaw with Mandalay and Yangon via the capital. This makes the trip between these cities shorter. But security is still high. When buses reach the area of Naypyidaw, the passengers have to leave the buses and pass a police control before taking the buses again. The trip from Yangon to Mandalay and vice versa crosses Naypyidaw but buses do not stop there.

waters, violating the country's sovereignty, in an effort to help the democratic movement.[17] Although the US embassy in Yangon issued a staunch denial, the threat of foreign invasion was planted in the minds of the new leadership, the SLORC.

The source of this threat is the strategic weakness of Yangon. For years, the SPDC/SPDC had been aware of serious breaches in security and information leakage from all government departments, including the Ministry of Defense. In a city like Yangon, with its foreign residents and embassies, the *Tatmadaw* felt it was under the surveillance of the "enemy".[18] On the other hand, although the big city is not on the coast, it is connected directly to the Indian Ocean by the Yangon River. Also, as it is situated in the northern part of the Irrawaddy Delta and connected with the large river by the Twante Canal, the metropolis is linked again to the Indian Ocean. By sending a small navy up the Yangon River or landing military forces in the delta, foreign troops could reach Yangon in a short period of time and topple the regime. This is the worst-case scenario for the SPDC and even if there is no evidence of a planned US attack against Myanmar, international sanctions and critics against the junta since 1988 have generated a strong siege mentality among Commander-in-Chief Senior General Than Shwe, the current top leader of the military regime, and his colleagues. This siege mentality was reinforced after the SLORC refused to acknowledge the results of the 1990 elections and the transfer of power, as it had initially promised to do. Since 1988–1990 the military regime has been subjected to a growing number of sanctions and condemnations by the United Nations and a boycott by the majority of the international community, making the increasingly nervous junta more suspicious towards the outside world, especially the West.

---

[17] Seekins, *The Disorder in Order*, p. 173. The US fleet was detected in the Andaman Sea but it did not enter Burmese waters. It seems that the ships were in the area in case it was necessary to evacuate US embassy staff and citizens living in Burma.

[18] Maung Aung Myoe, *The Road to Naypyitaw: Making Sense of the Myanmar Government's Decision to Move Its Capital* (Singapore: National University of Singapore, Asia Research Institute, Working Paper No. 79, 2006), p. 5.

Washington has focused its policy towards Burma on promoting sanctions and condemning the regime in the international arena but has never threatened to invade the country militarily. In that sense, the SPDC's fears of an invasion from the US with the objective to re-introduce democratic rule in the country seem groundless but such suspicions have never been quelled among *Tatmadaw* senior leaders.[19] On the contrary, the consequences of September 11, 2001, has had a profound impact on the way Burma's military rulers view the world and especially the new international policy of the US.

Burma's generals had been conscious of Yangon's strategic weakness since 1988 but it was the invasion of Afghanistan that the consequences of September 11, 2001, has had a really troubled them. This was reinforced by criticisms from the Bush administration regarding the SPDC. It was not by happenstance that in early 2002, only some months after the offensive against the Taliban regime began, the junta decided to move the Western Command Headquarters from Sittway (Sittwe), the capital of Rakhine State and the most important harbor of west Myanmar, to Ann, a more inland location.[20] Nevertheless, it seems clear that it was the invasion of Iraq in 2003 that convinced the senior *Tatmadaw* leadership of the necessity of moving the capital further inwards. If the US could unilaterally overthrow governments whose policies were inimical to Washington, the risk and danger for the suspicious junta was obvious. In fact, the area of Pyinmana saw the construction of an airport with a large airstrip, a military hospital, mansions and apartments, and bunkers and tunnels even before November 2005.[21] (North Korea, renowned for tunnel construction beneath the DMZ, played an important advisory role here. Additionally, in the years prior to 2005, the government had projected to move key

---

[19] Andrew Selth, *Burma and the Threat of Invasion: Regime Fantasy or Strategic Reality.* (Brisbane: The Griffith Asia Institute, Regional Outlook Paper No. 17, 2008), p. 4.

[20] Aung Myoe, *The Road to Naypyitaw*, p. 6.

[21] Stephen McCarthy, *The Black Sheep of the Family: How Burma Defines Its Foreign Relations with ASEAN* (Brisbane: The Griffith Asia Institute, Regional Outlook Paper No. 7, 2006), p. 12.

ministries (Defense, Internal Affairs, Foreign Affairs) to Pyinmana with the objective of having an alternative capital in case of a foreign attack against Yangon.[22] It is not so strange, therefore, that the first organ of the SPDC to be established in Naypyidaw was a new military regional command.

Concerned about a possible US invasion, The SDPC considered it to be of strategic importance[23] to construct a new capital in the central part of the country, with mountain ranges in the east and west. It was closer to China, the main supporter of the regime, and being more than three hundred km from the coast ensured a possible defense in case of a foreign attack and time to prepare a response against it.

Refuting all theories related to the fears of invasion at the November 7, 2005, press conference, Information Minister Major General Kyaw San explained that "with the expansion of the government's national development policies to border regions and remote villages, it was necessary to move the government's administration to a location which is more centrally located and placed strategically on major transportation networks".[24] For the SPDC, the move would enable a more effective administration of the whole nation. It is true that Naypyidaw commands the major communication links between Upper and Lower Burma and between east and west, ensuring its control over the main rivers of the Irrawaddy and the Sittaung, and the major roads from north to south (including the Yangon–Mandalay highway). But behind this official reason lies another geopolitical interest: control over peripheral and sensitive regions.

Since independence, Burmese governments have had to confront the aspirations of national minorities, among them the Karen, Kachin, Mon, Shan and Rakhine, and until 1989 the ambitions of Communist Party of Burma (CPB), which had been very active militarily up to

---

[22] James, "Myanmar in 2005," p. 164.

[23] The isolation of Naypyidaw allows for better control of state secrets and other confidential information.

[24] "Government's Decision," *The Myanmar Times*, November 14, 2005.

that point. All these armed insurgent groups were a clear threat to the authority of the Yangon-based government between 1950 and the 1990s, especially in the eastern part of Burma, where most of these guerrillas were active. Since the 1990s, with its reinforcement of Chinese weapons, the Burmese army has obtained important victories against these groups. On the other hand, it has successfully negotiated ceasefires with more than 20 groups. At this point, no insurgent activity really threatens the authority of the SPDC. Nevertheless, insurgent organizations like the Karen National Union (KNU) are still active in Karen State and other eastern parts of Burma, where there is still the risk of new activity despite the ceasefire groups.

The centrality of Naypyidaw, closer to Kachin, Karen and Shan States than Yangon, permits the state to project its power into the periphery, an area traditionally populated by non-Burman minorities.[25] The fact that Colonel Thein Nyunt, the Minister of Progress of Border Areas, National Races and Development Affairs, was appointed the Mayor of Naypyidaw while retaining his position in the national government clearly demonstrates that keeping border areas under closer observation was one of the SPDC's objectives when they moved the capital. Having its military headquarters in Naypyidaw permits the junta's troops to respond easily to troubles in the frontier areas. By relocating the central authority close to these strategic regions (some of them very important in the economy because of their natural resources), this control over its population is not only political but also psychological, preventing minorities from acting on separatist temptations or the desire to confront the national government.

A Legacy for the Future Generations

Two other reasons, although not decisive, may have contributed to reinforcing the SPDC's decision to create a new capital in Pyinmana. One is the desire of Senior General Than Shwe to bequeath a new center, a new political referent, to future

---

[25] Aung Myoe, *The Road to Naypyitaw*, p. 8.

generations of Burmese. It would be his great political legacy and his most important achievement. This was what the kings of Burma had done for centuries. Anawrahta in the 11th century created a new imperial capital in Pagan (Bagan) and erected some of its most impressive buildings.[26] Other monarchs did the same or left imposing legacies in the form of pagodas, temples or other constructions. Most famously, King Mindon (r. 1853–1878) ordered the construction of a new royal capital in Mandalay, including its huge palace complex.

Than Shwe is known for his megalomanic behavior. He and his family have been accused both inside and outside of Burma of acting like royalty.[27] In founding Naypyidaw, he is behaving like the rulers of the past. He even surpasses the hated Ne Win, whose "Burmese Way to Socialism" policy impoverished the country. Than Shwe has gone further — he has granted his nation a new capital. In that sense, he is like Anawrahta, Bayinnaung and Alaungpaya, the three famous precolonial warrior kings, whose huge statues stand in Naypyidaw and whom the top SPDC leader sees as his role models.[28] It is thus not so strange that Naypyidaw, a term used in precolonial Burma to denote the royal site or the place where the royal palace was situated, was chosen as the name for the new capital. Literally meaning "Royal City", but also translated as "Abode of Kings", it is considered a personal creation of Than Shwe's. It is the place for the new "king" of Burma and his "court" (the generals and their families) to rule over

---

[26] Bagan existed as the capital of a Burmese kingdom from the 10th century but it was Anawrahta who made it a shining capital of his empire.

[27] A famous video was posted on the internet showing images of the ostentatious marriage of Than Shwe's daughter in 2006. Some semi-official sources said the newlyweds received 50 million dollars worth of wedding gifts, which included houses, cars and jewellery, a tasteless extravagance in an otherwise poverty-stricken nation.

[28] Bertil Lintner, "The Generals Who Would be Kings," *The Washington Post*, September 30, 2007. Anawrahta is the founder of the Pagan Kingdom (First Burmese Empire). Bayinnaung is considered along with his brother-in-law Tabinshwehti the co-founder of the Second Burmese Empire in the 16th century. And finally, Alaungpaya founded the Third Burmese Empire (18th century).

all of Myanmar.[29] This link with royalty has been recently made more obvious in Myanmar's controlled media. During the inauguration of a religion at the beginning of 2009, Than Shwe was described as "doing like a good *min* (a Burmese term for king) who supports [Buddhist] religion".[30]

At the same time, one can include the consolidation of the political regime as a reason for his decision. Rulers of Southeast Asia, including the Burmese, have long moved their capitals in order to regenerate their kingdoms. Originally, capitals were founded with the objective of establishing a new dynasty or consolidating the ruling one. By doing so, Than Shwe and his comrades are insisting on the durability of the current political regime, even after the death of the current top leaders. Naypyidaw is, in that sense, the new capital of the "kingdom" (the Union of Myanmar) where the ruling "dynasty" (the *Tatmadaw*) is destined to govern for a long time yet. The new capital could be interpreted as the inauguration of a new era for the Burmese nation but with power remaining in the same hands.

This is linked to another characteristic of Burmese politics, the role of occultism.[31] Some sources have said that the decision to move the capital is also in response to the advice of astrologers. In Burmese history, astrologers and soothsayers have played a very important role as advisors of political rulers. Kings in precolonial times built new towns and palaces based on the advice of fortune-tellers. This situation has persisted in Burma into contemporary politics. It was astrologers who recommended the hour and day of

[29] Although no personality cult has developed around Than Shwe, his presence in the local press has increased substantially in the last ten years. On the other hand, during the author's first trip to Burma at the end of the 1990s, he saw portraits of General Aung San, the hero of Burma's independence, in public buildings. But these images of Aung San disappeared later. On one trip in 2007, the author saw for the first time a portrait of Than Shwe in a public building and another in a restaurant. Both places were located in the Mandalay region.
[30] Personal observation, Rangoon, 2009.
[31] Occultism and superstition, such as the belief in astrology and numerology, play a strong role in the still very traditional Burmese society and are connected with local Buddhism.

the independence of the Union of Burma in 1948.[32] Prime Minister U Nu and other leaders of the democratic period (1948–1962) very often asked for their advice. More notable is the dictator Ne Win (1962–1988), who was famous for his belief in astrology as well as the other occult arts, like numerology. Among his decrees was one that cars must drive on the right rather than the left side of the road so he would be safe from a *coup d'état* from the right.[33] His devotion to the number 9, considered to be a lucky number, was reflected in his 1987 demonetization when he ordered the replacement of old kyat notes with denominations of 45 (4 + 5 = 9) and 90 (9 + 0 = 9) kyats.

This belief in astrology and numerology seems to be shared by the current SPDC, which seized power on September (the ninth month) 18 (1 + 8 = 9), 1988. Like their predecessor, the SPDC generals have a special attachment to *yedaya*, magical rituals or practices used in Burmese culture to avoid misfortune. It is closely associated with the practice of astrology and is normally done with an astrologer's advice. One of the most common examples of *yedaya* is building a pagoda. Ne Win, for example, ordered the construction of the Maha Wizaya Pagoda close to Shwedagon in 1980.[34]

Considered the main promoter of Naypyidaw, Than Shwe shares with his predecessor this love for superstitions and it is well known that he asks the opinion of a council of astrologers before deciding on big issues. Some local observers believe the decision to move the capital was based on the advice of astrologers who serve the notoriously superstitious generals. Among the rumors was one that

---

[32] The day and time of Burma's independence from Great Britain in 1948 was decided by the government of U Nu in accordance with astrologers, who chose 4:20 a.m. on 4 January as the propitious time and date. It is interesting to note that the original choice of 11.56 a.m. on 6 January was discarded by Yangon two months before because it was regarded as unfavorable for the future development of the independent Union of Burma.

[33] Christina Fink, *Living Silence: Burma under Military Rule* (London: Zed Books, 2001), p. 41.

[34] The other reason for Ne Win's construction of the Maha Wizaya Pagoda was to earn Buddhist religious merit (*kutho*) for the next life.

Senior General Than Shwe's trusted soothsayers had predicted blood-shed in Rangoon and thus the necessity of relocating the country's capital. Not only that, on November 6, the first truck convoy of civil servants sent to take up their posts in Pyinmana left Yangon at the astrologically auspicious time of 6:37 a.m. The SPDC does not forget *yedaya* either. In November 2006, they started the construction of the great pagoda of Naypyidaw, a replica of the revered Shwedagon but one foot shorter than the original. Named Uppatasanti ("peace pagoda"), it was officially inaugurated in March 2009 by Than Shwe.[35]

Return to the Cradle of the Burmese Civilization

One last theory explaining the move of the capital has been defended principally by Michael Aung-Thwin of the University of Hawai'i. It rejects the argument of the fear of an American attack, the idea of a monarchic legacy or hostility towards big cities, although it does accept the role of geopolitics as an important reason and links it to the author's hypothesis. For Aung-Thwin, the junta's decision "[is] simply a return to the location of the traditional, pre-colonial seat of power".[36] From such a point of view, this theory is nationalistic and is linked to the idea that the Bamans (or Burmans), the main ethnic group in Myanmar, are the only ones with the right to hold political power in the country.

It is true that in precolonial Burma, kings would move their capitals occasionally and these always remained in the upper or central

---

[35] *The New Light of Myanmar*, March 10, 2009.

[36] Michael Aung-Thwin, "From Rangoon to Pyinmana," *Bangkok Post*, November 25, 2005. However, it is important to mention that Dr Aung-Thwin's assessment of Yangon's role is highly controversial. The city is the site of the Shwedagon pagoda, which is the holiest Buddhist site in Burma. Constructed by the Mons, one the country's main ethnic groups, it is considered holier than any place by the Burmans, most of whom accept its Mon origin. But Dr Aung-Thwin is known to argue that the Mons are not an important factor in Burmese history for reasons that are not clear to most other Burma specialists. That is why his arguments concerning Yangon should be viewed with great caution.

part of the country. This was the case of Pagan (Bagan, 11th–13th-century) and its immediate successor, until the dynasty of Toungoo became the main power and moved the capital to Pegu (Bago) in Lower Burma in the 16th century. One century later, the capital went back to the north and there it remained until the British conquest in the 1880s, with Mandalay being the last capital in Upper Burma. For Aung-Thwin, Yangon has always been considered by part of the post-colonial local political elite, especially the most nationalistic (among them the military leadership), as a colonial city, a foreign capital. It is in fact an old city, a port town named Dagon founded by the Mon minority more than 1,000 years ago, but it became a large city only because of British colonization. Until then, it was only relevant as the site of the famous Shwedagon pagoda, and its Burmese relevance dates back only to the mid-18th century when King Alaungpaya conquered it and named it Yangon (the "End of Strife"). It was during colonial times that Yangon became the capital of Burma, to serve the political and economic interests of Britain, being the main export harbor of the country.[37]

This situation makes Yangon a special capital. According to this theory, it is not even a real Burmese center (although today it is mainly inhabited by Burmans) and it lacks religious, historical and cultural weight in the Burmese world. There was no reason for it to be the political center of independent Myanmar because, in Aung-Thwin's words, "[Yangon] has been a constant reminder of the country's colonial experience."[38]

In this context, it is natural that the ruling junta, nationalistic and even xenophobic, decided to find a new political center in the so-called *Dry Zone*, the area between central and Upper Burma where geographic conditions prevent the southwest monsoon. This Dry Zone is considered the heartland of the country, the place where

---

[37] The British had built a new Rangoon on a grid plan on delta land, bounded to the east by the Pazundaung Creek and to the south and west by the Yangon River. By the beginning of the 20th century, it had become the most populous city of Burma.
[38] Aung-Thwin, "From Rangoon to Pyinmana."

pre-Burmese cultures flourished and later perished, and where the Burmese civilization was born more than 1,000 years ago. Here, all precolonial capitals (except Bago) were built. In other words, the Dry Zone is the cradle of the Burmese people as a nation. For Aung-Thwin, this area is so "very much a part of the Burmese people's psyche" that no protests can be expected against the decision to move the capital north. By selecting Pyinmana, the SPDC has made a return to Burmese origins, to the land where Burmans really belong. In that sense, it can be considered a "foetal return".

If this hypothesis were true, in moving the capital the junta would be continuing its policy of breaking with the country's colonial legacy, intensifying its process of decolonization initiated in the 1960s with the banning of learning English and continued later, for example, by passing the Adaptation of Expressions Law in 1989. In that sense, the transfer of the capital to Pyinmana/Naypyidaw would be the last step by the ruling government to "Burmanize" Myanmar.

Nevertheless, it is hard to imagine this reason as relevant to the junta's decision. There is no evidence to sustain the thesis that the SPDC was ready to spend a huge amount of money on constructing a new capital just to satisfy a supposed historic desire to return to the geographical origins of the Burmese world. Aung-Thwin, does not explain why the SPDC did not choose one of the former capitals, for instance Mandalay, where the existing infrastructures could have been used to host new ministries. And, if the desire were to return to the Dry Zone, why did the junta not move to a place closer to the Irrawaddy, like one of the former capitals in the area (Bagan, Mandalay, Amarapura, Ava, etc.)? Naypyidaw is far from this river venerated by the Burmese for centuries, in a place where no Burman powers bothered settling over the past 2,000 years.

Conclusion

The birth of Naypyidaw has raised questions about the military's vision for Myanmar. The new generals' heavily fortified capital is the most extreme example of how isolated they are from the population. For the Burmese people, the change of capital is another reason for discontent. Although repression deters any public criticism, one hears of civil servants and their families' discontent with being forced to abandon Yangon and establish themselves in central Myanmar.[39] People accuse the junta of neglecting the rest of the country by absurdly moving the capital, which has only made the bad economic situation worse. The total cost of constructing Naypyidaw, expected to house one million people, is estimated at between four and five billion dollars, in a country where the annual income is only 280 dollars per person.[40] The money comes from the sale of the country's rich natural resources (oil, gas, teak, etc.) to willing countries (among them, its Chinese and Thai neighbors) who have not signed onto the sanctions from the international community (see Chapter 9).[41]

The SPDC declared that the relocation of Myanmar's capital would not change the status of Yangon as the country's main center, especially when it came to business. The former capital remains the nation's commercial hub with its busy port and its strategic position in the area of the Irrawaddy Delta. The city, with its six million people, is under the direct control of the central government. But changing the capital has affected Yangon, as it has lost the benefits of having government ministries (and thereby suffered a monetary loss).

---

[39] The author can verify this discomfort. During one of his recent trips to Myanmar, locals refused to mention the name of the capital, as if it were cursed. This is especially evident in Yangon, which since 2005 has been clearly neglected by the central government.

[40] "Built to Order: Myanmar's Capital Isolates and Insulates Junta," *The New York Times*, June 24, 2008.

[41] Some rumors point out that relatives of Than Shwe had benefited from the contracts for the development of the new capital. This links to reports since early 2009 that state properties in Yangon had been actually for lease or sale. A Yangon informant I spoke with affirmed that the junta knows that the state's land and buildings in the city are valuable and is considering to lease them to allies or has sold them for profit. He insisted that some entrepreneurs had been reported visiting these areas. Although this business theory cannot be demonstrated yet, the author noticed during his last trip that the façades of some buildings in downtown Yangon (the City Hall, the telegraph building and others) had been recently painted after decades of neglect. Personal interview and observation, Yangon, 2009.

The decision to move the capital has worsened the image of the junta, even among its allies. Foreign diplomats in Yangon were notified on November 7 that the capital had been moved to Pyinmana. Burma's military rulers did not even bother to inform their ASEAN partners.[42] Some of them openly expressed their disappointment with the Burmese generals. This underscores the junta's strong distrust of foreigners, including its own allies. This behavior, and the secrecy surrounding the construction and functioning of Naypyidaw, may explain why all the embassies have decided to remain in Yangon.[43]

The founding of Naypyidaw clearly shows the weakness of Burma's military elite. It is a relentless pursuit of the unattainable by a regime that has been unable to develop the country and satisfy the needs of its people. But, although the reasons for moving the capital are diverse, there is one important aspect we cannot forget. The leaders and policies may change but the main objective is always the same: to preserve the *Tatmadaw*'s control over society. The SPDC may be conscious that in the future it will have to share power with a democratic government. Even if the capital is again moved to Yangon, to have the army center at Naypyidaw will be a Sword of Damocles hanging over the heads of democratic governments and will ensure that the *Tatmadaw* continues to play an important political role.

The city was confirmed as the nation's capital in the constitutional referendum of May 2008. Judging by Burmese history, Naypyidaw may not remain the nation's capital forever. But there is no doubt that it will endure as a political center as long as the regime that built it remains in power.

---

[42] McCarthy, *The Black Sheep of the Family*, p. 12.

[43] China, the main supporter of the military regime, criticized the decision to move the capital to Pyinmana, expressing surprise that such a poor country would consider such an expensive move and not even tell Beijing. See "Chinese Diplomats Criticize Myanmar's New Capital," *International Herald Tribune*, May 23, 2007.

Part C

Political Economy

Chapter 8

Burma's Poverty of Riches: Natural Gas and the Voracious State

Sean Turnell*

Abstract

Burma's recent emergence as a significant regional exporter of natural gas brings with it the promise of transforming the country's finances. Redeeming this promise, however, will require wholesale reform of Burma's fiscal and financial arrangements. Such reforms are as yet not in prospect. This chapter explores the financial potential of Burma's gas exports, the danger that they could yield a "resource curse", and the extent to which the state's fiscal demands undermine the country's economic progress.

Keywords: Burma; economy; public finance; financial systems; resource revenues.

For the first time in nearly half a century, Burma's external finances are moving beyond the precarious existence that has been moving beyond its characteristic indigence, to a scenario in which the *means* exists for effective capital accumulation. Driving this potential is the country's emergence as a significant energy exporter via its large recoverable reserves of natural gas. The rapid economic growth of China and India, and a world everywhere hungry for energy, has resulted in something of a scramble for access to Burma's gas. The end result is

* Sean Turnell is Associate Professor in Economics at Macquarie University in Sydney, Australia. The author would like to thank Lowell Dittmer, Khin Ohmar, Dr Naing Aung, Ron Ripple, Wylie Bradford, Alison Vicary — as well as a number of anonymous sources who, in the context of Burma today, unfortunately cannot be named.

swelling foreign exchange coffers that could enhance the country's economic development — or which could be dissipated in a wasteful spending spree. Burma's has long been a political economy of extremes, and unfortunately it is the latter scenario that is the most likely.

The purpose of this chapter is to explore the implications of Burma's gas bounty in the context of the country's fiscal and monetary circumstances. It begins by first examining, using independent sources, the size and potential of Burma's gas reserves and their likely future impact on the country's external position. This potentially encouraging story is then juxtaposed with an analysis of the dysfunctional condition of Burma's fiscal situation. Despite recent improvements in tax collection in a number of areas, the state continues to spend vastly in excess of its revenues. Burma's resultant budget deficits, which continue to exceed the windfall additions to the country's foreign reserves from gas exports, are largely "financed" by the country's central bank simply "printing money" as required.

The destructive repercussions of this strategy are apparent in the next section of the chapter, which explores the lack of finance available to the private sector in Burma. Crowded out by the demands of the state, private-sector capital accumulation is also greatly inhibited by a largely inoperative financial system. This is especially true in the agricultural sector, still the primary location of employment in Burma and the largest source of its gross domestic product (GDP). Next, the chapter brings all of these themes together in an examination of the extent to which, via the gas bounty, a "resource curse" might be underway in Burma. Noting recent spending on the new capital of Naypyidaw, nuclear energy and some dramatic pay raises for the military and civil service, the chapter finds that Burma's rising gas revenues do indeed promise to deliver more vice than virtue. Finally, the chapter concludes with some ideas as to how such an outcome might be avoided.

Burma's Natural Gas Windfall

For half a century, genuinely positive news about Burma's economy has been conspicuously missing. But Burma's emergence as a major energy exporter, which comes courtesy of its possession of large, exploitable fields of natural gas, has appeared against this dismal trend. Cumulatively, Burma's gas fields have confirmed recoverable reserves of around 540 billion cubic meters (equivalent in size to those of significant producers such as Australia). This is enough, at current prices and rates of production, to bring in around $3–5 billion annually for the next 30 years.[1]

The presence of natural gas in Burma has been known since the colonial era, but it is the presence of natural gas in a number of large, newly accessible offshore fields that excites attention now. Two of these fields, the so-called Yadana (Jewel) fields off Mouttama, and the Yetagun (Valiant Banner) fields off the Tanintharyi coast, came onstream in 1988 and 2000 respectively; they are the overwhelming source of Burma's current gas deliveries.[2] Yadana was a joint venture of Burma's state-owned energy company, the Myanmar Oil and Gas Enterprise (MOGE), in partnership with Total Oil (France), Unocal (US) and PTT Exploration and Production (PTTE, Thailand). The Yetagun fields were developed by MOGE, Premier Oil (UK), and Nippon Oil (Japan).[3] In the face of the threat of consumer boycotts, Premier Oil withdrew from Burma in 2002, to be replaced by Petronas of Malaysia.[4]

---

[1] British Petroleum, *BP Statistical Review of World Energy, June 2009,* http:// www. bp.com/.../bp.../statistical...review.../statistical_review_of_world_energy_full_report_2009.pdf, accessed July 17, 2009.

[2] For more on the background to the development of these fields and, more generally, Burma's energy policies, see Tin Maung Maung Than, "Myanmar's Energy Sector: Banking on Natural Gas," in *Southeast Asian Affairs 2005,* eds. Chin Kin Wah and Daljit Singh (Singapore: Institute of Southeast Asian Studies, 2005), pp. 257–292.

[3] Ibid., p. 265.

[4] At present Burma is the target of formal economic sanctions imposed by a number of countries, most significantly the United States and the European Union. Enterprises engaged in Burma are also subject to consumer boycott calls in these and other countries. In the wake of the crackdown on protestors in September/October 2007, both Total and Chevron (which acquired Unocal and its interest in Burma in 2005) have come under increasing formal and informal pressure to divest. The "sanctions debate" surrounding Burma is highly contentious and rather beyond the scope of this paper. For more, however, see Sean Turnell, "Burma's Economic Prospects," US Senate Foreign Relations Committee, US–Burma Relations, 109th Congress, March 29, 2006, http://www.senate.gov/~foreign/hearings/2006/hrg060329p.html, accessed November 5, 2007.

The primary customer of the output from the Yadana and Yetagun fields is Thailand which, in contrast to the long-standing economic relationship between the two countries, now runs a substantial trade deficit with Burma — of just over $2 billion in 2008.[5] Approximately 45% of Burma's formal export earnings in 2008 came from gas sales to Thailand, with most of the remainder coming from sales to Thailand and other countries of timber, gems, copper and pulses. Almost without exception, Burma's significant exports derive from extractive industries of one form or another. Overall, Burma ran a trade surplus in the year to March 31, 2008, of $3.3 billion.[6] Subtracting its large deficit on invisible items (services, interest payments and profit remittances) yielded a resultant increase in the country's foreign reserves to $3.6 billion. This is sufficient for more than a year of average imports and is in stark contrast to the bare subsistence balances that have been typical hitherto (see Table 1 below).

As can be seen from Table 1, the increasing revenues accruing to Burma from its exports of natural gas have come from both increasing gas prices as well as increasing export volumes.[7] These will be greatly boosted when production commences (likely around 2012) from new fields off Burma's Arakan coast. These fields, the most lucrative of which are collectively known as the Shwe ("gold") fields, have roughly the same gas reserves present (an estimated 200–240 million cubic meters) as those discovered at the Yadana

---

[5] Trade data here is as recorded by the Bank of Thailand, http://www.bot.or.th/ English/Statistics/EconomicAndFinancial/ExternalSector/Pages/StatInternational Trade.aspx, accessed July 17, 2009.

[6] Economist Intelligence Unit (EIU), *Country Report, Myanmar (Burma), July 2009*, (London: EIU, 2009), p. 16.

[7] The prices listed in Table 1 are a composite of those applying to the delivery of natural gas to a number of countries and regions. Gas export prices are typically quoted in British thermal units (Btu), a measure that accounts for both volume and energy intensity. Though there are other complications that must be taken into account in particular contexts, 1 Btu is equivalent to approximately 28 million cubic meters of gas.

Table 1. Burma's gas bounty

Year*	Gas export volumes (million Btu)**	Gas price ($US per million Btu)	Burma's international reserves ($US million)***
2005	344,919,700	7.43	873
2006	331,758,216	7.31	1,026
2007	472,970,464	8.45	2,503
2008	530,129,320	9.41	3,638

*As at the end of the financial year, March 31. Source: **Myanmar Central Statistical Organization, *Selected Monthly Economic Statistics* http://www.csostat.gov.mm, accessed July 17, 2009. ***International Monetary Fund, *International Financial Statistics* (Washington DC International Monetary Fund, June 2009), pp. 892–895. Unit conversions and calculations undertaken by the author.

and Yetagun reservoirs.[8] The Shwe fields were explored and developed by a consortium that comprised MOGE together with South Korea's Daewoo Corporation, the Korean Gas Corporation, the Gas Authority of India Limited and India's Oil and Natural Gas Corporation.

The ultimate customer of the gas actually delivered from Burma's Shwe fields will be China, which in 2007 "won" a fiercely contested bidding war against India and South Korea. This result provoked consternation in South Korea and India at the time, not least because China's reported bid of $US4.28 per million Btu was below that of India's offer of $US4.76 (Anupama 2007). China's Yunnan Province will be the recipient of the gas, courtesy of a 2,000 km pipeline that will come ashore near the port of Sittwe (via a facility at nearby Ramree Island), and run up and across Burma to Kunming. With little in the way of labor or environmental considerations to get in the way, construction of the Shwe pipeline could be completed relatively

[8] Estimates of the size of the Shwe fields vary, but those here refer to *confirmed* gas reserves according to British Petroleum's *BP Statistical Review of World Energy*. See also the Economist Intelligence Unit (EIU), *Myanmar (Burma) Country Report, May 2007,* (London: EIU, 2007), p. 22.

quickly (two to three years). Whether this happens so rapidly will depend on a number of factors, not least the trajectory of the international economy with the energy needs of China as a corollary. In mid-2009 reliable reports emerged that construction had started, not just on the gas pipeline, but also on an accompanying oil conduit through which China will pump oil brought by ship to Sittwe from the Middle East and Africa.[9] Such a method of delivering oil has long been a strategic objective of China, allowing it to reduce its erstwhile dependence on shipping that must navigate the Malacca Strait.

Since the dramatic announcements of substantial gas reserves in the Shwe fields, scarcely a month passes without further announcements (not all of which are reliable) of gas discoveries within Burma or off its coasts. From these, and other extractive industry exports, Burma will, for the indefinite future, accumulate foreign exchange in volumes that can, and should, make a difference in the struggle to lift the country beyond its present least-developed status. Whether it will redeem this promise, however, or fritter this bounty away instead, is a question to which we shall return in the final section of this chapter.

Burma's Dismal Public Finances

The most enduring affliction of Burma's economy, present from the moment the country came under the control of the military in 1962, has been the excessive financial demands of the state. Burma's last fiscal surplus (not coincidentally) was in 1962, and since then the state's profligacy has become habitual. Burma's military regime has not published data on its overall fiscal position since 1999/2000. Tax data are published but data on government spending are not. Nevertheless, as detailed below, it would appear that state spending in Burma is nearly twice the magnitude of its tax collections.

---

[9] See, for instance, Yeni, "Oil and Politics Don't Mix," *The Irrawaddy* 17:4 (July 2009), pp. 12–13.

Table 2. Burma tax and customs revenues (kyat million)

Year*	Commodities and services taxes	Income tax	Customs duties	Total taxes and duties
2006	226,481	144,402	17,894	447,964
2007	319,213	260,080	32,206	676,742
2008	384,597	334,140	37,278	838,257
2009	428,937	425,529	84,110	987,807

* As at the end of the financial year, March 31. Source: Myanmar Central Statistical Organization, *Selected Monthly Economic Statistics* http://www.csostat.gov.mm, accessed July 20, 2009.

In very recent times, however, the SPDC has instigated a number of changes to Burma's tax and subsidy arrangements that have had a modest impact on the country's fiscal position (Table 2). Most of these have included increases in consumption taxes and import duties of various kinds. The former include the dramatic increases in fuel prices that sparked the so-called "Saffron Revolution" in 2007, while the latter were occasioned primarily by successive increases in the exchange rate used in customs duty assessments (and which accordingly recognized the growing unreality of Burma's formal fixed exchange rate arrangements — more on which later).[10] Meanwhile,

---

[10] For more on the role of fuel price increases in triggering the Saffron Revolution, and for an account of these events generally, see Richard Horsey, "The Dramatic Events of 2007 in Myanmar: Domestic and International Implications," in *Dictatorship, Disorder and Decline in Myanmar, eds.* Monique Skidmore and Trevor Wilson (Canberra: Australian National University E Press, 2008), pp. 13–28. For more on the changes to customs revenues, see Asian Development Bank, *Asian Development Outlook 2007* (Manila: Asian Development Bank, 2007), p. 220. The exchange rate employed to determine customs duties rose from K100:US$1 in 1996 to K450:US$1 in 2004, followed by successive jumps to K850:US$1 and then K1,200–1,250:US$1 in 2006 — an effective twelvefold increase in customs duty rates in kyat terms over these years. EIU, *Myanmar (Burma), Country Profile 2006,* p. 22.

efforts to implement the taxation of income in recent years have brought about a doubling in the tax rates applicable to private enterprises (and their employees) from 10% to 20%, and an increase in the profits tax on foreign-owned firms from 35% to 40%.[11] As is apparent in Table 2, these increasing rates, and reports of a crackdown on otherwise widespread tax evasion, delivered a near-threefold increase in income tax revenues between 2005 and 2009.

But the increases in tax collections revealed in Table 2, dramatic though they are, come off an extremely small base and have done little to dent Burma's chronic fiscal deficits. In 2008, tax revenues amounted to a mere 4.4% of GDP. By way of comparison, a representative sample of developing countries constructed by the International Monetary Fund (IMF) found an average tax collection to GDP ratio of about 18% (38% for industrial countries).[12]

Of course, against the small amount of formal tax collection in Burma is the state's spending which is anything but small. As noted above, official statistics on state spending have not been available since 2000. Nevertheless, given the increases in central bank financing of state activity (Table 3), as well as other proxy indicators, a reasonable presumption is that state spending in Burma is nearly double that of tax revenues.[13] What is the state spending on? Not surprisingly, much of it goes to the military, which according to US Central Intelligence Agency (CIA) estimates, absorbed 2.1% of Burma's GDP in 2008.[14] A substantial amount of government spending also makes its way to Burma's numerous inefficient state-owned enterprises (SOEs), which absorb an estimated two-thirds of total state spending.[15]

---

[11] Ardeth Maung Thawnghmung and Maung Aung Myoe, "Myanmar in 2006: Another Year of Housekeeping?" *Asian Survey* 47:1 (January/February 2007), pp. 194–199.

[12] Vito Tanzi and Howell Zee, *Tax Policy for Developing Countries* (Washington DC: IMF, 2001), p. 3.

[13] Such an estimate is likewise consistent with that of the Asian Development Bank, *Asian Development Outlook 2007*, p. 221.

[14] Central Intelligence Agency, *CIA World Factbook*, https://www.cia.gov/library/publications/the-world-factbook/geos/BM.html, accessed July 20, 2009.

[15] EIU, *Myanmar (Burma), Country Report, July 2009*, pp. 12–13.

Table 3: State share of Myanmar's financial Resources, selected indicators (kyat million)

Year	Central bank lending to government	Commercial bank lending to government	Commercial bank lending to private sector	Unofficial exchange rate ($US/Kyat)*
2001	675,040	40,985	416,176	650
2002	892,581	43,248	608,401	960
2003	1,262,588	35,546	341,547	900
2004	1,686,341	89,217	428,391	1,000
2005	2,165,154	100,358	570,924	1,300
2006	2,762,626	186,998	652,892	1,450
2007	3,534,687	389,398	795,227	1,300
2008**	3,880,765	620,875	907,177	1,250

Source: International Monetary Fund, *International Financial Statistics* (Washington DC IMF, June 2009), pp. 892–893. *Approximate annual average, author's estimates. **As at December.

In contrast to the vast sums absorbed by the military and SOEs, Burma spends a paltry amount on health and education, collectively amounting to about 1.6% of GDP (0.3% on health, 1.3% on education).[16] This is less than half of that of the next lowest spender, Indonesia, among the ASEAN countries, and lower still relative to ASEAN's other poorest members, Cambodia and Laos, which spend 3.5% and 3.1% of GDP, respectively.[17] Burma is unique among its peers for spending more on the military than on health and education combined.

"Printing Money" to Finance the State

In the absence of adequate tax revenue, Burma's state expenditure is financed by the simple and highly destructive expedient of mandating

---

[16] United Nation's Development Programme, *Human Development Report 2007/2008* (New York: UNDP, 2007), pp. 249, 267.
[17] Ibid., pp. 247–249, 265–268.

the central bank to print or issue money in whatever volume is required. As can be seen from the first column in Table 3 below, such monetary expansion dwarfs taxation revenues. Moreover, and notwithstanding the belated increases in tax, the necessity for such financing is growing. In 2007, the latest full year for which we have data, central bank funding of the government rose by K772.1 billion ($634.4 million), up an extraordinary 28% on the previous year. Meanwhile, in the nine months to December 2008, the central bank lent an additional K346.1 billion ($288.4 million), an increase of 9.8% on the full-year total for 2007, clearly illustrating Burma's dire public finances.

The monetization of Burma's fiscal deficits brings with it a number of negative consequences, not least an inflation rate that is officially in low double digits but which is currently around 30% per annum.[18] Such inflation undermines both trust and the purchasing power of Burma's currency, the most transparent measure of which is the kyat's declining unofficial exchange rate. The final column of Table 3 illustrates this slide against the US dollar. Of course, as shall be detailed, the waning confidence in Burma's currency has had severe repercussions on the stability and proper functioning of the country's financial system.

A Dearth of Private Finance

Burma's current export (gas) bounty does not extend to its besieged private sector. The most important reason for this is simply that Burma's booming exports are controlled by the state and its enterprises. In the year to March 31, 2009, SOEs accounted for 55% of Burma's trade and their dominance is even more pronounced with respect to exports — 63% of which passed through state entities. Indeed, some 35% of total exports were earned by MOGE alone, which brought in $3.1 billion in 2008–2009.[19]

---

[18] Central Intelligence Agency, *CIA World Factbook,* https://www.cia.gov/library/publications/the-world-factbook/geos/BM.html, accessed July 20, 2009.
[19] Author's calculations based on data from the Myanmar Central Statistical Organization, *Selected Monthly Economic Statistics,* http://www.csostat.gov.mm, accessed July 20, 2009.

Largely precluded from access to overseas funds, and in the absence of a functioning stock market, bond market or any of the usual financing vehicles available to firms in other countries, formal finance for private enterprise in Burma is limited to that made available by the country's commercial banks (state and private-owned). Even here, however, the circumstances are dire. Bank lending in Burma has recovered somewhat since the 2003 banking crisis (more on which below) but it remains meager. In 2007, total funds lent by the banks were less than a quarter of those provided by the central bank to the state. Of course, as can be seen from the data in Table 3, a substantial component of commercial bank lending itself (more than 49% of the funds they provide to the private sector) also made its way to the government. Burma's banking sector, in short, scarcely performs an intermediation function, for which the fault once more lies in excessive state interference — in this case, heavy-handed and inappropriate regulation. There are many examples of this, but representative are restrictions imposed on Burma's banks that cap the interest rates they can charge on loans and pay on deposits, at 17% and 12%, respectively.[20] Such rates, well below even the most optimistic estimates of Burma's inflation rate, reward neither saver nor lender. The low levels of voluntary saving in Burma, and the inadequate lending to the private sector, are predictable consequences.

Burma's Deficient Banking System

Crowding out by the state is the biggest problem afflicting private sector finance in Burma, but it is by no means the only one. Burma's financial system is dysfunctional in other ways, a situation that was spectacularly revealed in the country's 2003 banking crisis. An event that was little noticed elsewhere, the collapse of Burma's leading banks in 2003 brought about at least two years of negative economic

---

[20] For more on the regulations distorting the functions of banks in Burma, see Sean Turnell, *Fiery Dragons: Banks, Moneylenders and Microfinance in Burma* (Copenhagen: NIAS Press, 2009), pp. 267–270.

growth, notwithstanding the official GDP numbers, and reduced Burma for a time to a near-barter economy.[21]

Even before the 2003 events, however, Burma's banking system did little to provide the finance desperately needed by truly productive private enterprise, and loans to businesses unconnected either to the banks or to the government were both expensive and scarce. Surveys of Burmese business owners conducted by the author reveal that the private banks are generally wary of lending to new enterprises that can offer little in the way of collateral. Meanwhile, for those that can put up collateral, the requirements are steep. A rule of thumb adopted by many banks is a demand for fixed-asset collateral of around 200% of the value of a loan.[22] Such collateral can really only be offered by well-connected borrowers within larger business groups and/or parties with links to government and military enterprises. These same surveys reveal that unconnected borrowers are also typically asked to pay hefty establishment fees for loans. Such fees function as recompense for the capped interest rates charged by the banks, but they also greatly boost borrowers' credit costs. The fees are sometimes informal — simple bribes paid to individual loan officers — but often they are imposed with the full knowledge of the bank management.[23]

The high collateral requirements and other loan costs have created a situation in Burma where private banks lend predominantly to enterprises and individuals able to generate both high and quick returns. Such enterprises tend to be engaged in highly speculative activities, in particular, hotel and real estate speculation, gold trading, jade mining, fishing and logging concessions and, for a brief period,

---

[21] For a comprehensive analysis of Burma's 2003 financial crisis, see Sean Turnell, Fiery Dragons: Banks, Monelenders and Microfinance in Burma, pp. 297–318.

[22] The surveys from which these accounts derive were conducted by the author in 2006–2007, and again in early 2009, in the United States, Singapore, Thailand as well as in Burma itself (remotely, via various secure channels). See also May Thander Win, "Banks Claim a Solid Recovery," *Myanmar Times,* July 31–August 6, 2006, http://www.mmtimes.com.

[23] This assertion is based on the interviews (above) by the author with borrowers from the banks.

garment factories. It has also been the case that an extra "return" could be gained if the borrowers were so-called leaders of national races, many of whom enjoy extra privileges through special access to high-yielding natural resource sectors.[24] Of course, sometimes banks will partner especially well-connected individuals on no terms at all, writing off their contribution as political insurance.[25]

Burmese enterprises generating returns in the medium to long term, such as manufacturers, receive little bank finance. According to a Japanese survey of 167 small to medium manufacturing enterprises (SMEs) in 2006, most rely upon self-financing and on funds available from friends and family, rather than bank loans.[26] This is true even for working capital and trade (supplier) finance, which sets the experience in Burma apart from that commonly observed for SMEs in other developing countries. The Japanese survey also drew attention to the fact that most of Burma's new banks are at the center of conglomerates and, in this context, demonstrate a bias in their lending to related entities.[27]

---

[24] Many of these leaders were those who had made ceasefire agreements between the groups they represented and the SLORC/SPDC. For more, see Bertil Lintner and Michael Black, *Merchants of Madness* (Bangkok: Silkworm Books, 2009), pp. 113–132.

[25] One of the most damaging issues surrounding Burma's banks is the widespread accusations that they are engaged in laundering the substantial money generated through Burma's narcotics trade. For more on this, see Sean Turnell, "Burma's Economic Prospects," pp. 14–16.

[26] This survey was conducted by Fumiharu Mieno, "Determinants of Debt, Bank Loan and Trade Credit of Private Firms in the Transitional Period: The Case of Myanmar," in *Recovering Financial Systems: China and Asian Transition Economies*, ed. Mariko Watanabe (Basingstoke: Palgrave Macmillan, 2006), pp. 146–176. See also Myat Thein, *Economic Development of Myanmar* (Singapore: Institute of Southeast Asian Studies, 2004), p. 143.

[27] Famously, these conglomerates include the Union of Myanmar Economic Holdings Limited (UMEH) and the Myanmar Economic Corporation (MEC). Whilst technically not SOEs, both UMEH and MEC are military-controlled entities with interests in almost every sector of Burma's economy. Both also control banks — the rapidly expanding Myawaddy Bank in the case of UMEH, and the smaller-scale Innwa Bank in the case of MEC. For more on these conglomerates and their banks, see Sean Turnell, *Fiery Dragons: Banks, Moneylenders and Microfinance in Burma*, pp. 265–266.

Beyond self-financing, for many enterprises, informal moneylenders remain their only source of capital. The ubiquity of moneylenders in Burma is time-honored and the emergence of formal private banks in the 1990s did little to dent their importance. Especially dominant is *ne pyan toh* (one-day lending), usually provided to market traders by moneylenders (mostly women in Burma) according to a common formula of an 80 kyat loan in the morning, and a somewhat usurious 100 kyat repayment the same evening. Such moneylending activity is also a significant source of competition for bank deposits since, as one moneylender explained,

> "Most people with money keep it as far away from the banks as they can. With inflation running over 20 per cent (sic), you'll lose money in a regular savings account. And why settle for 10 per cent a year when you can get three or four times that, with probably the same amount of risk, in the private money market?"[28]

Finance for Agriculture

Of all the private sector activities repressed by Burma's dysfunctional financial system, no situation is more acute, or its repercussions so dire, as in agriculture. For reasons as unfathomable as they are destructive, Burma's commercial banks are forbidden to lend to farmers for cultivation. In their place, as formal credit providers, there is the state-owned Myanma Agricultural Development Bank (MADB). This institution is supposed to be the sole provider of rural credit in Burma, but its own modest objective of providing finance to meet just 30% of a cultivator's production costs is internal recognition of its severe limitations. In fact, in practice the MADB falls well short of meeting even this modest target. Maximum loans to paddy cultivators (80% of all MADB lending is to such farmers), as of 2009, is currently capped at K8,000 ($7.20) per acre of paddy, against cultivation costs of the same crop of between K130,000 to K180,000 ($118 to

[28] Stephen Brookes, "Black Market Banking in Burma," *Asia Times,* April 18, 2006, http://www.atimes.com/, accessed July 23, 2009.

$164).[29] The minimum 93% financing gap is met via recourse to the moneylender — and by simply going without.

A significant reason for the MADB's parsimony is that the bank itself is desperately short of funds. Indeed, it has been effectively decapitalizing over recent years. As its primary source of funds, the MADB claims to have two million depositors, but in fact it attracts little in the way of actual deposits — a mere K4.6 billion ($3.7 million) in 2004.[30] Deposits in the MADB are inhibited by many of the same restrictions imposed on other banks in Burma, including those on the interest rates the bank can pay. But in addition to this, and even more damaging, has been a policy in place since 2003 that greatly restricts the ability of depositors to withdraw their deposits.[31] In the wake of this, the only wonder is that the MADB attracts any deposits at all.

In 2004 (the latest year for which we have such data) the MADB's capital stood at just K1.2 billion (around $1 million), an extraordinarily small financial platform upon which to pursue the functions of a countrywide bank with over 200 branches and engaged in a form of lending with strong covariant risks.[32] The MADB desperately needs an injection of capital, but the only recent policy in this direction is a most destructive order that compels the bank to pay the government a dividend of 25% of its annual profits. Alas, such profits that might be claimed by the MADB are likely to be entirely fictitious. Since 1991 the bank has been forbidden from writing off bad and doubtful debts; as a consequence it claims a repayment rate of 100%.[33] This fanciful figure may be compared to an

---

[29] David Dapice, Tom Vallely and Ben Wilkinson, *Assessment of the Myanmar Agricultural Economy* (Cambridge, MA: Harvard Kennedy School, Asia Programs for International Development Enterprises, 2009), p. 13.
[30] Food and Agriculture Organization of the United Nations (FAO), "Myanmar: Agricultural Sector Review and Investment Strategy" Working Paper No. 9, Rural Finance (Rome: FAO, 2004), p. 25.
[31] Ibid., p. 2.
[32] Covariant risk in this context refers to the situation in which *all* borrowers face circumstances that may inhibit their ability to repay their loans. Agricultural lending is especially susceptible to covariant risk because seasonal factors tend to have an impact on all borrowers simultaneously. Ibid., p. 5.
[33] Ibid., p. 10.

annual provision against bad debts by Thailand's analogous Bank for Agriculture and Agricultural Cooperatives of around 15% of its portfolio.[34] Restating the MADB's "earnings" to include any reasonable estimate of loan losses would eliminate any supposed profits, diminishing the bank's capital even before the extraction of the government's dividend.

The lack of finance imposes heavy costs on Burmese agriculture in terms of productivity, and greatly constrains the ability of cultivators to move to more capital-intensive modes of production. Even fertilizer is beyond reach for most borrowers reliant on MADB loans. One consequence is that fertilizer is now seldom used in Burma, a phenomenon that has the effect of reducing agricultural yields and income all round.[35] Dapice, Vallely and Wilkinson paint a dire scenario in the wake of this, and as revealed in a series of surveys they conducted amongst Burmese farmers in 2009,

> "…it is our opinion that crop output will fall significantly unless much more credit becomes available and crop prices improve markedly. With the prospect of less intensive farming and fertilizer applications falling…a significant reduction in paddy production is all but certain…"

Combined with falling incomes in step with the increasingly dire economic circumstances of rural Burma in general, the same researchers warn of

> "…a slow motion humanitarian crisis that would become visible only if civil disorder rose as hungry parents stole food or money to feed themselves and their children."[36]

---

[34] Bank for Agriculture and Agricultural Cooperatives, http://www.baac.or.tha, accessed July 21, 2009.

[35] Myat Thein, *Economic Development of Myanmar* (Singapore: Institute of Southeast Asian Studies, 2004), p. 143.

[36] David Dapice, Tom Vallely and Ben Wilkinson, *Assessment of the Myanmar Agricultural Economy* (Cambridge, MA: Harvard Kennedy School, Asia Programs for International Development Enterprises, 2009), p. 9. The results of the Harvard team's survey are supported by those of the Food and Agriculture Organization of the United Nations, *FAO/WFP Crop and Food Security Assessment Mission to Myanmar*, Special Report, (Rome: FAO, January 22, 2009).

A "Resource Curse" in Burma?

Known for centuries under a myriad of labels, the notion of a "resource curse" refers to the seeming paradox of a country that holds abundant natural resources but nonetheless underperforms economically.[37] Initially, the idea derived from observing harmful effects on the manufacturing sector of real exchange-rate increases via booming commodity exports (the so-called Dutch disease). But in recent times, attention has turned to the possible ways that resource windfalls can undermine good governance, democracy, the rule of law and other attributes and institutions conducive to economic growth. Resource revenues, being easy to distribute to well-connected insiders and others, are said to promote corruption and underinvestment in human capital, and to allow governments the wherewithal to be unresponsive to the needs of their (often non-tax paying) citizenry.[38] The most obvious manifestation of a resource curse along these lines are grandiose national "prestige" projects that litter much of the developing world.

Of course, Burma has long been without the political and economic institutions and attributes conducive to development. Yet, and despite the brevity of time in which its gas revenues have accrued, a resource curse already seems to be in play. Bad decision making by Burma's governments has been chronic, but the SPDC's new-found spending power does seem to have manifested itself in regrettable ways. Some particularly egregious examples, unfortunately from an expanding set, are given below:

---

[37] The first example of a resource curse was probably the negative effects on 16th century Spain of the influx of precious metals from the New World. The modern label for the phenomenon seems to have its origins in Richard Auty's *Sustaining Development in Mineral Economies: The Resource Curse Thesis* (London: Routledge, 1993).

[38] In 2008, Burma was judged by Transparency International as the second most corrupt country in the world (bested only by Somalia). See http://www.transparency.org/ accessed July 20, 2009. As noted above, however, the notion of a resource curse extends beyond simple corruption to include the broader distortions wrought generally by windfall gains.

Naypyidaw

For reasons much speculated on but still obscure, on Sunday, November 6, 2005, Burma's government apparatus decamped en masse to the newly constructed capital of Naypyidaw. This widely reported move, the astrological details of which have been a particular fascination, is the latest in a long list of peculiar decisions made by Burma's various military governments down the years, but whose economic effects have proved both ill and long-lasting.[39]

It is impossible to determine any precise financial cost for Naypyidaw. The details of its construction remain a closely guarded secret (even by Burma's standards). Estimates would be clouded by the reported widescale use of forced labor as well as the concessions that private firms were said to have received for building the physical infrastructure of the new capital.[40]

The construction of new capital cities is not unusual in countries suddenly presented with commodity largesse and seeking to assert a new political identity.[41] Almost universally, however, these capitals have proved extraordinarily wasteful of resources as well as conducive to bureaucratic sclerosis. With requests for export and import permits already clogging the information arteries to and from Naypyidaw, this particular piece of profligacy seems already to be costly for Burma, whatever the direct impact on the government's budget.

---

[39] Consulting astrologers, soothsayers and numerologists before making major decisions is common amongst ordinary Burmese, but it has become a particular habit of the Chairman of the SPDC, Senior General Than Shwe. According to the rumor mill, it was Than Shwe's astrologer who was decisive in the move to Naypyidaw, advising the General that Rangoon faced natural disaster and would become a source of political unrest. For a comprehensive account of the creation of Naypyidaw, and the many and varied theories behind this, see Dulyapak Preecharushh, *Naypyidaw: The New Capital of Burma* (Bangkok: White Lotus Press, 2009).

[40] Ibid. The Asian Development Bank simply says that the expenditure on Naypyidaw will offset whatever advances are being made in Burma in raising more tax revenue. Asian Development Bank, *Asian Development Outlook 2007*, p. 220.

[41] Such "new" capitals include Brasília (Brazil), Canberra (Australia), Ottawa (Canada) and, perhaps most pertinently for Burma, Abuja (Nigeria).

Pay Raises

Related to the transplanting of the capital, and in an apparent effort to avoid mass resignations and retirements of those unwilling to leave Rangoon, was the announcement in April 2006 of dramatically increased salaries for about one million civil servants and military officers.[42] These wage increases ranged between 500–1,200%. Justifiable perhaps in Burma's high-inflation economy, though other segments of society did not see an increase in their salaries or payments, the pay raises only added to the impression of a regime willing to spend new-found revenues for political acquiescence, whatever the economic consequences. In fact, as it turned out, any economic benefits accruing to the recipients of the pay raises were probably ephemeral. In expectation that inflation would accelerate as a consequence of the pay hikes, traders in Rangoon and elsewhere preempted matters, boosting prices as soon as the increases were announced. There was also a flight from the kyat and hefty increases in the price of gold, foreign currencies, and other inflation hedges. Of course, once more, the real losers in all of this were those outside the civil service and the army, whose lot was only worsened by the rising prices.

A Nuclear Burma?

Perhaps the most egregious of all the sudden spending announcements made in the face of Burma's growing gas windfall was that the country agreed on terms with Russia in May 2007 to construct a nuclear reactor.[43] A deal that was first mooted in 2000, it seemed to have been abandoned in late 2002, apparently because of Burma's inability to pay the advance in foreign exchange demanded by Russia. In the wake of Burma's accumulating foreign reserves,

[42] Ardeth Maung Thawnghmung and Maung Aung Myoe, "Myanmar in 2006: Another Year of Housekeeping?" p. 197.
[43] The following is but a brief sketch of this controversial project, for which no better source exists than Andrew Selth's "Burma and Nuclear Proliferation: Policies and Perceptions," Griffith Regional Outlook Paper No.12, (Brisbane: Griffith University, June 2007).

however, such restraint no longer exists. According to reports from the Russian side of the deal, the reactor is a 10-megawatt device that is accompanied by laboratories to produce medical isotopes (Burma's paltry spending on health has already been noted) and facilities to store nuclear waste. The financial cost of the reactor has not been disclosed officially but Russian sources have put it at around $500 million.[44] Of course, it is highly likely that strategic considerations, and possible lessons from the world's response to North Korea, are the prime motivations for Burma's decision to go nuclear.[45]

Some Concluding Thoughts on Ways Forward

Bad governance, corruption, fiscal irresponsibility, conflict over natural resources — all these recognizable symptoms of a resources curse pre-date the discovery of commercial quantities of gas in Burma. However, as this chapter has sought to demonstrate, the accumulation of foreign reserves occasioned by Burma's gas exports has transformed the country's finances and its spending, thus far in ways that are hardly positive.

The widespread prevalence of resources curse problems around the world has prompted the creation of a number of devices aimed at mitigating their impact. Perhaps the most prominent of these are resource "stabilization funds", institutions legally independent of the

---

[44] The source was Atomstroieksport, the agency overseeing Russia's international nuclear energy deals. See William Boot, "Nuclear Center to Cost $540 Million, But Who Pays?," *The Irrawaddy*, June 1, 2007, http://www.irrawaddy.org, accessed July 15, 2009.

[45] According to long-time Burma analyst and chronicler of Burma's armed forces, Andrew Selth, "of all Southeast Asian countries Burma has the strongest strategic rationale to develop nuclear weapons". Andrew Selth, "Burma–North Korea: Rumour and Reality," *Lowy Institute Interpreter*, June 29, 2009, http://www.lowyinterpreter.org/post/2009/06/29/Burma-North-Korea-Rumour-and-reality.aspx, accessed July 21, 2009. Selth cautions, however (in a manner that could likewise speak more broadly for the motivations of Burma's leaders, that "Burma's nuclear ambitions have never been clear".

state and into which resource revenues are paid.[46] Their function is to insulate the government's finances from the unpredictability and volatility of resource revenues while providing a vehicle in which to save and invest these revenues in productive ways. Of course, by squirreling away revenues in this manner, these institutions are also meant to help discipline spending. Stabilization funds have been employed in many countries, most of them inspired by Norway's extraordinarily successful State Petroleum Fund created in 1990 to manage windfall gains from its exports of North Sea oil. Similar stabilization funds have subsequently been established in Azerbaijan, Kazakhstan, Papua New Guinea, Venezuela and, most recently, East Timor. Alas, except for the last case, for which the jury is still out, these funds have proved a severe disappointment. The reason for this is simple. It boils down to the lesson that to be successful, stabilization funds need more or less the same good governance as is generally required to avoid a resources curse in the first place. Whatever the legal safeguards, in practice stabilization funds have proved no less susceptible to manipulation, mismanagement and outright plundering by the government than national budgets. The sobering reality is that stabilization funds seem only to be viable in countries, such as Norway, that do not need them.

A particularly promising device for reducing the ill effects of resource curse phenomena, one that might be especially suited to Burma, is a revenue distribution fund (RDF). As the name implies, an RDF has a very simple role — to distribute resource earnings directly to a country's citizens in the form of dividend payments. Little in the way of institution building is necessary for an RDF and, as a result, they can be created relatively quickly. Corruption is also minimized as minimal funds are accessible to the government and its agents. But RDFs bring other developmental benefits too. The revenues they provide constitute an alternative income stream and reduce income volatility for people who otherwise are subject to the vagaries and

---

[46] For an excellent introduction to stabilization funds, see Jeffrey Davis, "Oil Funds: Problems Posing as Solutions," *Finance and Development* 38:4 (December 2001), http://www.imf.org/external/pubs/ft/fandd/2001/12/davis.htm.

hazards of the agricultural season. The payment of a flat dividend to every citizen can also reduce income inequality, giving everyone a stake in the country's progress as well as constituting a powerful incentive against fund mismanagement. Best of all for long-term development, such dividends can become the basis for the creation of new businesses and economic activity, directly via the dispersed funds as well as via their use as loan collateral. The best known of the RDFs has operated in Alaska since 1976, but their usefulness to developing countries has been the subject of strong advocacy in more recent years by economists (who often couple such devices with the idea that the state could "tax back" a portion of revenues to provide for its own financing, but in development-friendly ways) seeking innovative ways to establish sound fiscal institutions in developing countries, as well as to avoid resource curse ills.[47]

Would Burma's current rulers create an RDF to distribute gas revenues to the country's citizens? Alas, it must be doubted. Government control, the very thing implicitly undermined by an RDF, would appear to be precisely the objective most desired by the SPDC.[48] Accordingly, this chapter must end with the pessimistic conclusion that there is no reason yet to suggest that Burma's leaders will avoid what has become their habitual tendency to miss opportunities. Burma passed up the chance to join its peers and neighbors decades

---

[47] See, for instance, Thomas Palley, "Combating the Natural Resource Curse with Citizen Revenue Distribution Funds: Oil and the Case of Iraq," Foreign Policy in Focus, Discussion Papers (May 2002), http://www.fpif.org/papers/, accessed July 20, 2009; Martin Sandbu, "Taxable Resource Revenue Distributions: A Proposal for Alleviating the Natural Resource Curse," Center for Globalization and Sustainable Development, Working Paper 21 (August 2004), http://www.earthinstitute. columbia.edu/cgsd/documents/sandbu_distribution_000.pdf, accessed July 21, 2009. Details of the Alaskan scheme, the Alaska Permanent Fund Corporation, can be found at its official website, http://www.apfc.org/, accessed July 16, 2009.

[48] Democracy, the rule of law, transparency and accountability in government decision making — surrounded and stimulated by a free press — are other "institutions" with proven efficacy in inhibiting the ill effects of a resource curse. Their establishment in Burma is, alas, rather less likely at the moment than the creation of a device such as an RDF.

ago when the latter embraced openness; and it sought the alternative path of isolation and the economic policies of dirigisme. The world's unquenchable thirst for energy is set to provide Burma with a new opportunity to correct the mistakes of the past. For the sake of the people of this once promising country, it must not be passed up.

Chapter 9

Myanmar/Burma: International Trade and Domestic Power under an "Isolationist" Identity*

Jalal Alamgir

Abstract

Conventional wisdom has it that Myanmar is a pariah nation, isolated from globalization. But that is a considerable oversimplification. Aside from the fact that official figures fail to take into account the country's enormous underground trade, Rangoon has since 1990 taken significant steps to open its economy. But this has been a selective opening, limited to economically and strategically complementary trade partners.

Keywords: Stolper-Samuelson theorem; resource famine; foreign direct investment (FDI).

Most accounts deem Myanmar's economy an extension of its political system: illiberal, repressive and closed to the outside world. As Johan Norberg put it plainly, the worst violators of democratic norms and human rights, namely "Burma, Cuba, Iraq, Libya, North Korea, Saudi Arabia, Sudan, Syria, and Turkmenistan", are precisely "the countries least affected by globalization and least oriented in

---

*Some parts of this chapter draw from an earlier paper: Jalal Alamgir, "Myanmar's Foreign Trade and Its Political Consequences," *Asian Survey*, 48:6 (2008), pp. 977–996.

231

favor of the market economy and liberalism."[1] Myanmar's history
certainly corroborates this thesis. From the 1960s till the late 1980,
the socialist/isolationist path crafted by General Ne Win defined
the parameters of the Burmese economy. SLORC and SPDC, the
successor regimes, have striven to direct the economy to benefit
primarily the military and its allies, and in so doing, choked the
country's market institutions and private economic actors. As Sean
Turnell, a leading Burma analyst, reports: "There are no effective
property rights in Burma, contract enforcement is non-existent, and
macroeconomic policy-making is arbitrary, erratic and ill-informed".[2]
The industrial economy remains dominated by either state-owned
enterprises or state-backed conglomerates that enjoy virtual monopolies. Accordingly, out of the 179 countries ranked by the
2009 Index of Economic Freedom, Burma occupies the fourth
position from the bottom, just ahead of Cuba, Zimbabwe and
North Korea.[3]

Counterintuitively, however, foreign trade is crucial to the survival of all of these countries that are reportedly "least affected by
globalization". While the nationalist identity fashioned by these countries typically projects the capitalist international economy in antago-
nistic terms, each remains, not surprisingly, desperately dependent on
foreign transactions for essentials, relegating the pursuit of autarky
more to rhetoric than to reality. North Korea, for instance, challenges
China's wishes politically at times, but its economic survival remains
dependent on an intimate trading relationship with China which, by
one estimate, has allowed North Korea to run an annual bilateral
trade deficit of close to US$500 million, a substantial sum compared

---

[1] Johan Norberg, *In Defense of Global Capitalism* (Washington, DC: The Cato Institute, 2003).
[2] Sean Turnell, "Burma's Economy 2008: Current Situation and Prospects for Reform," Burma Economic Watch/Economics Department, Macquarie University, Sydney, Australia, May 2008 p. 3.
[3] The Heritage Foundation, *2009 Index of Economic Freedom*, http://www.heritage.org/Index/Ranking.aspx, accessed August 13, 2009.

to the size of the North Korean economy.[4] Furthermore, international trade, however protected, is an income-generating activity, and therefore has long-term consequences on political power. Growth of trade can create important centers of wealth outside the government. Conversely, careful control of trade, even with policy liberalization, can strengthen regimes by allowing them to expand their orbit of allies. Developmental authoritarianism in Latin America, for instance, thrived by extending selective control and distribution of trade benefits.[5] Foreign trade flourishes in China despite an authoritarianism that remains politically strong.

Moreover, long-term patterns of foreign trade and interactions affect identity: the labels "pariah" or "isolationist", which are conferred frequently on Myanmar, make sense only in a specific context of time and space. These labels are salient insofar as the "standard" current in international political economy comprises a steady and unquestioned increase in economic and political openness. Between 1980 and 2006, the number of "free" countries (as a proportion of all countries for that specific year) increased by 47%.[6] This increase in political freedom took place during a period of economic prosperity fueled strongly by international trade. Between 1980 and 2005, world GDP increased by 305%, but world trade increased by almost 422%. The increase is

---

[4] Marcus Noland, Sherman Robinson and Tao Wang, "Rigorous Speculation: The Collapse and Revival of the North Korean Economy," Working Paper 99–1 (Washington DC: Peterson Institute for International Economics, 1999). China, however, has been taking a stronger and less conciliatory stance with North Korea. See You Ji, "China and North Korea: A Fragile Relationship of Strategic Convenience," *Journal of Contemporary China* 10:28 (August 2001), pp. 387–398; Evan S. Medeiros and M. Taylor Fravel, "China's New Diplomacy," *Foreign Affairs* 82:6 (November/December 2003); Meng Liu, "China and the North Korean Crisis: Facing Test and Transition" *Pacific Affairs* 76:3 (Fall 2003), pp. 347–373.

[5] See, for instance, Peter Evans, *Dependent Development: The Alliance of Multinational, State and Local Capital in Brazil* (Princeton: Princeton University Press, 1979).

[6] Data calculated from dataset by Freedom House (www.freedomhouse.org). By Freedom House's definition, "A Free country is one where there is broad scope for open political competition, a climate of respect for civil liberties, significant independent civic life, and independent media."

starker in low- and middle-income countries, where trade/GDP ratio increased from 34% in 1980 to 65% in 2004.[7] The average applied tariff rate in developing countries fell more than threefold from 37.8% in 1983 to 10.9% in 2005.[8] With liberalization on both economic and political fronts, the capacity for influence from a distance has increased concomitantly.[9] A global civil society now sustains opposition against the Myanmar regime with continual scrutiny, helping to define the country's identity internationally, and the regime, wary of penetration by this civil society, continues to restrict the activities of NGOs and IGOs in the country.[10] The conventional understanding of Myanmar's identity as "isolationist" makes sense only in context of these-developments — political, economic, and social — that constructs the expansion and deepening of cross-border interactions as standard or natural or, at the extreme, as the end of history.

Although deserved by certain criteria, the assignment of such an identity obscures important nuances. Contrary to received wisdom, Myanmar by some indicators has shown more hospitality toward foreign trade than other authoritarian regimes like North Korea or

---

[7] Calculated from World Bank, *World Development Indicators Online*, http://ddp-ext.worldbank.org, accessed March 9, 2007.

[8] World Bank, "Data on Trade and Import Barriers," http://econ.worldbank.org/wbsite/external/extdec/extresearch/0,,contentMDK:21051044~pagePK:64214825~piPK:64214943~theSitePK:469382,00.html, accessed August 3, 2007.

[9] For this type of conceptualization of globalization, see Anthony Giddens, *The Consequences of Modernity* (Cambridge, UK: Polity Press, 1990); Anthony Giddens, *Runaway World: How Globalization is Reshaping Our Lives* (London: Routledge, 2000); Robert Keohane and Joseph Nye, Jr., "Globalization: What's New? What's Not? (And So What?)," *Foreign Policy* 118 (2000), pp. 104–119.

[10] On globalization and its effect on social movements, see Kathleen C. Schwartzman, "Globalization and Democracy," *Annual Review of Sociology* 24 (1998), pp. 159–181; Hilary Wainwright, "Civil Society, Democracy and Power: Global Connections," in *Global Civil Society 2004/5* eds. Helmut K. Anheier, Marlies Glasius and Mary Kaldor (London: Sage, 2004); Sanjeev Khagram, James V. Riker and Kathryn Sikkink, eds., *Restructuring World Politics: Transnational Social Movements, Networks, and Norms* (Minneapolis: University of Minnesota Press, 2002). Michael Walzer, ed., *Toward a Global Civil Society* (New York: Berghahn Books, 1995); Steven Levitsky and Lucan A. Way, "International Linkage and Democratization," *Journal of Democracy* 16:3 (2005), pp. 20–34.

Zimbabwe have. It has been a member of the World Trade Organization (WTO) since 1995, committing itself to progressively liberalizing its foreign trade regime. Its tariff barrier, on paper, is lower than that of most other developing countries in the world. The political consequences of its pattern of trade are, similarly, more disaggregated than what would be suggested by assuming simple isolationism, supported by a key international patron. An isolationist identity highlights blunt political strategies, such as blanket repression, as the regime's basis for survival against expected or prevalent domestic and international currents. It would also suggest blunt counter-policies, such as wide sanctions and blanket condemnation that are supposed to push the regime further into supposed isolationism.

This chapter questions the assumption and utility of the conventional interpretation of Myanmar's regime as isolationist. I do so by proposing a better understanding of the regime's foreign trade, and by considering its political consequences on broad structural groupings, such as land, labor and capital. The chapter argues that the regime, in fact, has not been simply isolationist with regard to foreign trade. While its trade exposure has been declining, the regime welcomes trade under its terms, and has promoted trade in a strategic manner to strengthen its political power vis-à-vis competing socio-economic groupings. The chapter draws from the Stolper–Samuelson theorem to argue that declining trade exposure combined with an increased concentration in both trading partners and capital-intensive tradables have stifled the emergence of significant sources of power outside the state. International efforts to weaken the regime, therefore, will be mistaken to hope that politically strong alternatives will rush in to fill the void. Efforts to influence the regime need to be designed in a more disaggregated manner to weaken those sectors of foreign trade that sustain the regime and support those sectors that can potentially empower the domestic society, which remains brutally repressed.

Since Myanmar's external economic transactions are difficult to estimate reliably, I use the pragmatic approach of triangulating international sources for quantitative data: I draw from regional development banks and international financial organizations, whose versions of national statistics are somewhat cleaned up, and then, where possible, corroborate data against different reports to use either midpoint estimates or those data that have been cited in multiple analyses.

This approach, of course, is not unique to this study; it underlies most major analyses — from national developmental planning to poverty reduction strategy papers prepared by donor organizations. Moreover, Myanmar's foreign trade statistics are usually understated, for three components of its external transactions are excluded from officially reported data: the black market, which at times has been estimated to be close to the size of the official economy; arms imports, which are sizeable as a proportion of export earnings; and narcotics trade, which remains an important, though declining, source of foreign exchange. Analytically, this underestimation may be a "good problem" to have, since these sectors represent additional areas of international interaction which would help question Myanmar's isolationism. Nonetheless, we will include, to the extent possible, estimates of these three sectors to inform the main argument. My overall objective is to present and analyze data to ascertain key patterns in Myanmar's foreign trade; and then, based on what is observed empirically, offer some interpretations, comments and conjectures about its implications on the structural distribution of political power and political strategy. The study examines trade, not investment; foreign investment is only considered to the extent that it is related to foreign trade.

Untouched by Globalization? High Growth of Trade

The first assumption fueled by the narrative that poses Myanmar as a pariah is that the country remains largely untouched by the trade-driven globalization evident worldwide since the end of the Cold War. In fact, Myanmar's record on trade volume and growth has been impressively positive in the post-1990 era (see Fig. 1). In 1990, Myanmar's exports and imports amounted to $472 million and $880 million respectively. In 2006, they stood at $5.1 billion and $2.9 billion respectively. By 2002 the country had reversed a chronic trade deficit and begun running a trade surplus, and in 2006 its surplus amounted to almost $2.3 billion.[11]

---

[11] Calculated from Asian Development Bank, "Key Indicators 2008," http://www.adb. org/Documents/Books/Key_Indicators/2008/Country.asp, accessed August 8, 2009.

US$ Million

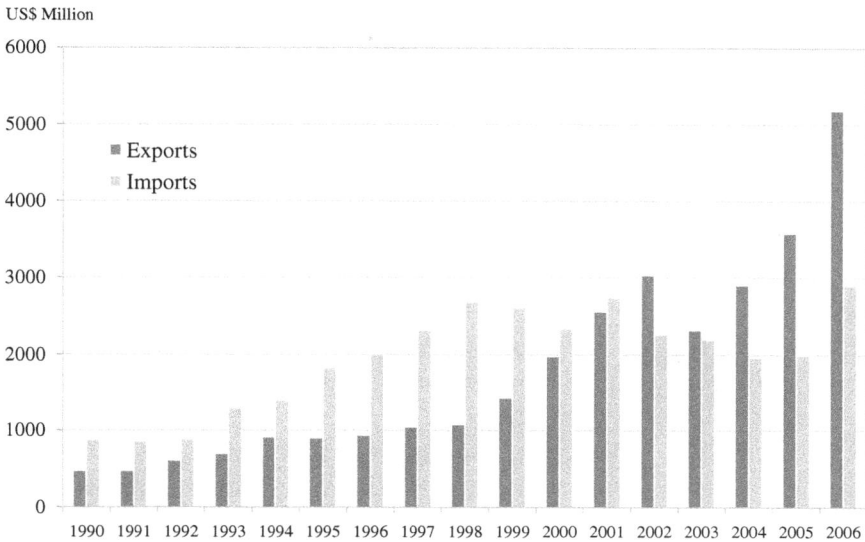

Figure 1. Myanmar's trade volume, 1990–2006

Note: US$ figures reflect conversion at the official exchange rate. The volume would be much lower if converted at the semi-official or the unofficial rates.

Source: Calculated from Asian Development Bank, "Key Indicators 2006," http://www.adb.org/statistics, accessed 8 August 2009.

This reversal of fortune has been driven primarily by energy exports, mainly gas. The first year that Myanmar exported gas was 1998, the value of which stood at less than US$1 million. By 2002, it exported over $800 million worth of gas, which contributed to its first ever trade surplus.[12] Natural gas exports amounted by 2005 to $1.4 billion, accounting for more than 87% of its trade surplus. A vigorous competitive interest by both China and India has provided a convenient trading line for the country, resulting in considerable

---

[12] "Myanmar Achieves First-Ever Foreign Trade Surplus," *People's Daily Online* (China), April 28, 2003, http://english.peopledaily.com.cn/200304/28/eng20030428_115932.shtml, accessed September 6, 2007. For more on Burma's gas exports, see Sean Turnell, "Burma's Insatiable State," *Asian Survey* 48:6 (December 2008) pp. 958–976.

financial and diplomatic resources for State Peace and Development Council (SPDC), the junta in power. Overall, SPDC has ascended to the advantageous position of acting as a referee between competing countries, a key illustration of which occurred in May 2007 when, offered a pipeline by both China and India, it decided in favor of China, arguably to obtain China's ongoing support in international forums, including the UN Security Council.[13]

On average, Myanmar's formal trade between 1990 and 2007 grew at the rate of nearly 13% per annum. This rate is impressive: it is higher than the 11% growth per year attained by Myanmar's high-trading Southeast Asian neighbors during the same period.[14]

Figure 2 shows the composition of Myanmar's official trade since the 1990s, comparing the relative shares (as a percentage of total exports or imports) of Myanmar's four top trading sectors. Historically, foodstuff, consisting primarily of pulses and rice, and non-fuel crude materials, consisting primarily of teak and other hardwood, used to be Burma's main export earners. The most significant shift in Myanmar's exports, as noted before, is the spectacular rise of mineral fuels since 2000 as the largest export-earning sector. This shift has significant implications on the relative political power of economic actors, as we will see later in the chapter. The composition of imports has been relatively stable, with manufactures, machinery, and transport equipment accounting for the bulk of imports.

The composition of official trade, as intimated earlier, excludes three large items: arms, narcotics and black market or underground trade. Inclusion of these sectors would increase Myanmar's trade volume substantially. However, we can only make intelligent guesstimates here, since comprehensive time-series analyses of Myanmar's unofficial trade are not available. In the 1980s, the size of the black market trade

---

[13] "Myanmar's Pipeline Politics," *The Economist Intelligence Unit ViewsWire*, May 23, 2007, http://www.economist.com/agenda/displaystory.cfm?story_id=8908775, accessed September 6, 2007.

[14] Calculated from Asian Development Bank, "Key Indicators," various years http://www.adb.org/statistics, accessed August 8, 2009.

	1990-1994	1995-1999	2000-2004
Key Export Sections*			

Food and Live Animals	38%	38%	20%
Crude Materials (excl. fuels)	36%	23%	13%
Mineral Fuels	0%	0%	26%

Key Import Sections*

Machines, Transport Equipment	32%	33%	26%
Basic Manufactures	15%	24%	26%
Chemicals	9%	12%	11%

Figure 2. Composition of official exports and imports, 1990–2004

Note: *Average proportion of each section to total exports or imports for the period specified. Only the three largest sections (as of 2000–2004) are shown in the table.
Source: Calculated from Asian Development Bank, "Key Indicators," various years, http://www.adb.org/statistics, accessed June 16, 2007.

was estimated to be between 50% and 85% of official trade.[15] This level can be assumed to have continued through most of the 1990s, since the basic structure of Myanmar's external economy, as reviewed above, remained by and large unchanged. Since 2000, the boom in energy trade, along with peace treaties that allowed more border trade to take place officially, are likely to have reduced the proportion of illegal trade to legal trade toward the lower end of the range. We also need to add $2.3 billion worth of arms imports between 1990 and 2005. Partly because of various embargos, arms imports have swung dramatically across the years, between a high of $299 million in 1993 to a low of $3 million in 2000. Narcotics trade reached a high in 2000, bringing in an estimated $200 million, but has decreased steadily since then, primarily due to a fall in production. Between 1996 and 2006, there has been an 87% decrease in the area under opium poppy

---

[15] Myat Thein, *Economic Development of Myanmar* (Singapore: Institute of Southeast Asian Studies, 2004), p. 80.

cultivation.[16] Taken together, the three elements — arms, narcotics and the black market — represented an estimated 105% of Myanmar's official trade in 1990. By my estimate, this proportion fell to an average of about 70% in the second half of the 1990s, and then to about 50% by 2005.[17]

Autarky Questioned: Estimate of Openness Ratio

The openness ratio, that is, the ratio of trade (exports and imports) to gross domestic product (GDP), is a useful estimator of how open the economy is to foreign trade. The ratio also indicates the importance of the external sector in the economy.[18] Not surprisingly, Myanmar's openness ratio has been significantly lower than any other country in Southeast Asia: Brunei, Cambodia, Indonesia, Laos, Malaysia, Philippines, Singapore, Thailand, and Vietnam. Calculated by official trade data and official exchange rates, Myanmar's trade/GDP ratio in 1990 was 5.6%, while for its geographic peer group (i.e., the nine Southeast Asian countries listed above) it was 90.6% on average. Myanmar's figure almost doubles if we take its unofficial trade into account, but it is still marginal compared to other countries of the region, and still much lower than the 70% average for the three least developed countries (LDCs) of Southeast Asia, Cambodia, Laos and Vietnam, which may offer a better benchmark in terms of the level of

---

[16] United Nations Office of Drugs and Crime (UNODC), *World Drug Report 2007* (Vienna and New York: UNODC, 2007), pp. 212–217.

[17] Arms trade statistics are taken from Swedish International Peace Research Institute (SIPRI), "TIV of Arms Imports to Myanmar (Burma), 1950–2006," SIPRI Arms Transfers Database, http://www.sipri.org/contents/armstrad/output_types_TIV. html, accessed on June 14, 2007. The narcotics trade is estimated from production and price statistics reported by the United Nation's *World Drug Report* of various years, assuming that 80% of production is eventually trafficked internationally. The black market trade is estimated by applying a constant decreasing arithmetic progression from 85% of total trade in 1990 to 50% by 2000 and thereafter. The combined value expressed in current dollars is taken to be the estimate for unofficial trade.

[18] See, among others, Alberto Alesina and Romain Wacziarg, "Openness, Country Size and Government," *Journal of Public Economics* 69:3 (September 1998), pp. 305–321.

economic development. In spite of comparable growth, foreign trade, in sum, played a smaller role in Myanmar. What is more, the openness ratio in Myanmar has declined steadily since 1990, while that of both benchmark groups exceeded 100% by 2003. By official exchange rate, Myanmar's openness ratio was less than 1% by 2003.

Judging by the burst in exports and the overall poor health of Myanmar's domestic economy, Myanmar's actual openness ratio must be much higher than the paltry figure suggested by official exchange rates. In fact, both the numerator (trade volume) and denominator (GDP) of Myanmar's openness ratio are suspect in official statistics: the first is usually understated and the second overstated. First of all, the country's official exchange rate greatly overvalues the kyat. The official exchange rate, for instance, puts Myanmar's substantial gas earnings at only 0.6% of budget receipts. At the market rate, the same earnings would not only exceed receipts but eliminate Myanmar's fiscal deficit. Termed "missing" gas earnings, these show up partly in Myanmar's foreign exchange reserves and partly go towards supporting the military and its various pet projects outside public accounting and tracking.[19] On the denominator side, the country's official GDP data tends to be inflated, which has been admitted by even Myanmar's government officials. In fact, if we convert Myanmar's officially reported GDP to US dollars using the official exchange rate, its national production, at $1.6 trillion, exceeds that of entire Southeast Asia! Mysteriously, the government itself reports the country's trade/GDP figure to be around 20%, a figure that does not match the official rate.[20]

Now, if we calculate trade statistics purely at the unofficial rate, Myanmar's openness ratio would approach 80–90%, which, while more comparable to that of its neighbors, is unrealistic by all observable qualitative accounts. The actual value of the currency, of course, lies in between. If not controlled through a messy three-tier system, it would be substantially higher than the official rate and lower than

---

[19] Turnell, "Burma's Economy 2008," p. 6.

[20] Peter Warr, "Trade, Growth and Equity in Myanmar," in *Trade, Growth and Inequality in the Era of Globalization*, eds. Kishor Sharma and Oliver Morrissey (London: Routledge, 2006), p. 148.

the black market rate. Taking the midpoint between the two values as a realistic guide, we can estimate Myanmar's openness ratio to be around 40–50%, indicating a moderate, though significant, importance of foreign trade to the country's economy. To triangulate, if we apply GDP and trade data reported by the IMF, the World Bank and the Asian Development Bank, we arrive at a fairly steady openness ratio of 55–59%, generally consistent with our estimate. While calculations from official data would imply a decrease in the ratio over the last 15 years, we cannot confirm it — but we can be fairly sure that there has been no substantial increase in this ratio since 1990, a point that will be important in the final section of this chapter.

The openness ratio is only an overall indicator. It does not mean that 55% of economic activity is related to foreign trade, nor does it imply that foreign trade activity is dispersed. The same ratio can be obtained in a situation where a single sector, dominated by a state-owned corporation, is responsible for the bulk of foreign trade. We will therefore look separately at the concentration of trade. We also do not know readily if Myanmar's comparatively low ratio is due to the country's unwillingness to trade or whether the reverse is true, that the world may not be as interested in trading with Myanmar. The question can be answered by analyzing bilateral and multilateral trade policies, which is not the task of this paper. Within the pool of quantitative data, however, a proxy indicator can be found in the average applied tariff rate (AATR). This is the average of applied tariffs across all tariff line items or categories. From an already low 6% in the mid-1990s, Myanmar's AATR fell further to about 4.5% in 2005. This connotes a much more open policy stance toward foreign trade than what is found in most developing countries. In 2005, the average AATR for the 142 developing countries of the world was more than twice, almost 11%.[21] It can be surmised that the Burmese regime has been applying low tariff rates in an effort to encourage trade, especially imports. In spite of low tariffs, the country's openness ratio

---

[21] World Bank, "Data on Trade and Import Barriers," http://econ.worldbank.org/wbsite/external/extdec/extresearch/0,,contentMDK:21051044~pagePK:64214825~piPK:64214943~theSitePK:469382,00.html, accessed August 3, 2007.

remains lower than the benchmark. There are multiple reasons. The West is reluctant to trade with Myanmar. But, in addition, there may be pure investment decisions, such as potential market size and purchasing power in Myanmar for imports, and cost-related reasons, such as labor or corruption-related costs for exports or unpredictable costs to enforce private property rights, as well as corporate moral/social responsibility, consumer activism, and the externalities from outright sanctions.

Isolationism Qualified: Trading Partners

The low-to-moderate openness ratio is consistent with the observable pattern in Burma's trade concentration, which shows that fewer countries are willing to engage with the junta extensively. Figure 3 summarizes the concentration of Myanmar's trading partners. Concentration or dispersion of trade can be estimated simply by taking

	1990-1995	1996-2000	2001-2005
Imports			
Top 10 Partners	81%	86%	89%
Top 5 Partners	76%	74%	76%
Exports			
Top 10 Partners	62%	67%	77%
Top 5 Partners	54%	52%	64%

Figure 3.   Concentration in trading partners, 1990–2005

Note: Percentage shown are yearly average for the period specified, for exports to and imports from the top ten trading partners, as a proportion of total exports or imports.
Source: Calculated from Asian Development Bank, "Key Indicators," various years, http://www.adb.org/statistics, accessed June 16, 2007.

a country's total imports and exports, and calculating the proportion that is contributed by its top ten (or five, or one) trading partners.

As the figure shows, between 1990 and 1995, on average 81% of Myanmar's official imports came from ten countries. China, Singapore, Japan, Malaysia and Korea, the top five countries, supplied 76% of its imports. By 2001–2005, the value of imports supplied by Myanmar's top ten sources had increased slightly to 89%, the bulk of which were still supplied by the top five countries: China, Thailand, Singapore, Korea and Malaysia.

A high concentration of trade partners is also visible in Myanmar's official exports data. During 1990–1995, the top ten destinations bought 62% of its exports, as measured in dollar value. By 2000–2005, the share of the top ten had increased to 77% of Myanmar's exports. The share of the top five also increased during that period. Thailand was the most important export destination for Myanmar, accounting for 44% of exports alone. Thailand was the top destination in 1990 as well but Myanmar's exports were more dispersed at that time, and Thailand accounted for only 10% of total exports.

Prior to 2003, the United States was one of the most important trading partners of Myanmar. Although the US had banned new investments in Myanmar in 1997, it had been purchasing a large share of Myanmar's products, and became in 1999–2000 its largest export destination. In 2000 and 2001, almost $500 million worth of Myanmar's goods and services went to the United States. In 2003, the US levied additional sanctions on Myanmar, banning Burmese financial transactions and exports to the US. But the potentially major effect on Myanmar's economy was somewhat offset by the willingness of other trading partners, especially in Asia, with whom Myanmar's SPDC regime has cultivated closer ties since 2000. Consequently, the regime was able to increase — despite the sanctions — Myanmar's total exports by 18% in 2004 and 24% in 2005. The share of Asian trading partners in Myanmar's total trade rose from 67% in 2000 to 82% in 2005.[22]

---

[22] Calculated from Asian Development Bank, "Key Indicators 2006," http://www.adb.org/statistics, accessed June 29, 2007.

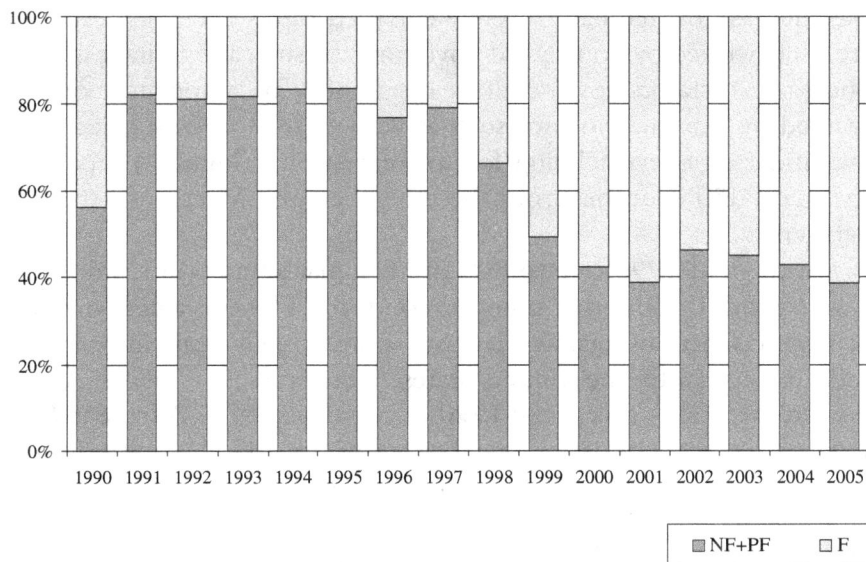

Figure 4. Top trading partners by regime type, 1990–2005

Note: NF+PF stands for 'Not Free' and 'Partly Free', which are Freedom House designators for democracies and semi-democracies. F stands for 'Free'. Percentage share of Myanmar's total trade is shown for each group.

Source: Trade data calculated from Asian Development Bank, "Key Indicators," various years, http://www.adb.org/statistics, accessed June 16, 2007; NF/PF/F data come from Freedom House, "Freedom in the World Country Ratings 1972–2007," http://www.freedomhouse.org, accessed August 31, 2007.

It is not surprising that, geographically, Asia will account for the bulk of the trade of a developing Asian country. But has Myanmar traded mostly with like-minded regimes? This question is analyzed in Fig. 4. In this analysis, the top trading partners, who account for the bulk of Myanmar's trade, are classified for each year between 1990 and 2005 according to the three main categories employed by Freedom House: free, partly free, or not Free. free countries are electoral democracies with a high degree of protection for political rights and civil liberties. In partly free countries, core political rights and civil liberties exist partially, weakened by actual discrimination, violence, corruption and foreign or military influence, etc. Countries classified as not free have severely curtailed rights and liberties; they are usually ruled by nonelected governments, such as "military juntas, one-party dictatorships, religious hierarchies, or autocrats", or are marked by extreme violence such as war, thereby forcing citizens to live under an overwhelming fear of repression.[23] Figure 4 separates the free ("F") countries from the others, among Myanmar's trading partners.

In the mid-1990s, up to 80% of Myanmar's trade (in US dollars) was conducted with other non-free countries. This was a period when economic sanctions against Myanmar were at their peak, imposed to various degrees by the United States, Japan and EU, following the regime's refusal to accept the 1990 electoral victory by Aung San Suu Kyi's party, the National League for Democracy (NLD). It was during this time that the regime increased economic ties with other authoritarian governments. The regime took active steps in particular to improve economic relations with China, bestowing on it the affectionate term "*paukphaw*" ("sibling"), an honor not given to any other country.[24] Western economic pressure on Myanmar, with the exception of the United States, was eased somewhat since the late 1990s. Since then, Burma's trading pattern also became relatively more indistinct with respect to regime type. The 2009 trial of Aung San Suu Kyi and the extension of her house arrest may result in tighter sanctions on Myanmar by other democracies, leading to another shift toward a greater concentration of non-democratic trading partners.

If we look further at the data, we detect an important distinction between exports and imports. On average, between 1990 and 2005, democracies within Myanmar's top ten partners bought 41% of its exports while non-democracies and semi-democracies accounted for 27% (the rest is attributed to countries outside the top ten trading

---

[23] See Freedom House's website, http://www.FreedomHouse.org, for details on the definitions.

[24] Toshihiro Kudo, "Myanmar's Economic Relations with China: Can China Support the Myanmar Economy?" Discussion Paper No. 66, Chiba-Shi, Japan: Institute Of Developing Economies, July 2006.

partners). The ratio is reversed with regard to imports. Democracies supplied 22% of Myanmar's imports and non-democracies (and semi-democracies) supplied 63%. Since 2001, China has become its single largest supplier, and by 2004 accounted for almost a third of Myanmar's official imports.

As in the general trade growth of the post-1990s era, Myanmar's trade growth with China is a relatively recent phenomenon. Prior to 1988, trade with China was much smaller, as Myanmar's borders were generally closed. In the first 15 years since the opening of the borders, based on data by China Customs, Myanmar's exports to China increased by 1.3 times. But its imports from China, comprising both consumer goods and raw materials, increased by over sevenfold, accounting for the bulk of Myanmar's trade deficit prior to its reversal due to energy exports, much of which in turn is destined for China. China provided economic and business cooperation, including foreign aid, to Myanmar at a time when its aid supplies dwindled due to sanctions and related externalities. China was also the supplier of raw materials and technical expertise behind a large expansion in the public sector through the creation of at least 480 public enterprises between 1990 and 2002.[25]

China's actual trade-related influence is higher than these figures suggest, owing to its tremendous importance as a supplier of arms, data on which is excluded from official import statistics. Between 1990 and 2005, China supplied 74% — $1.7 billion out of the total $2.3 billion — of Myanmar's arms imports. Russia was the second most important supplier, accounting for 17 percent of the total during that period. During 2000–2005, however, Russia displaced China as the main supplier, accounting for almost 59 percent of Myanmar's arms imports. While supplies from Russia and other countries have been sporadic — Russia, for instance, has not supplied any arms since 2002 — China has exported arms to Myanmar every year since 1990 and has been joined more recently by democracies such as India.[26]

---

[25] Kudo, "Myanmar's Economic Relations with China," p. 7 and p. 15.
[26] SIPRI, "TIV of Arms Imports to Myanmar (Burma), 1950–2006."

The Implications of Isolationist Trade on Political Power

In the context of the empirical analysis done so far, this section draws on macro-political theory to make general predictions about shifts in Myanmar's political structure that have arisen from its trade patterns. The main argument is that Myanmar's pattern of selective but high-growth trade, along with isolationist policies pressed on it by the West, has strengthened the regime and weakened the domestic basis of independent political power. It is important to recognize at the outset that the political benefits or costs of trade, while inevitable, are nonetheless accumulated over time; as such, to understand the effects of trade on macro-political change, such as democratization or the continuity of authoritarianism, we need to examine political structures with a broad brush, and we will begin by ascertaining theoretically which political actors stand to gain/lose from shifts in trade.

The Political Power of Land

The Stolper–Samuelson theorem remains central to understanding the broad political consequences of shifts in trade. It posits that trade protection favors owners of those factors of production in which society is poorly endowed and, conversely, that trade liberalization benefits owners of those factors of production that are abundant in society.[27] Recent work corroborates the theorem. Ronald Rogowski, for example, applied the theorem systematically to predict alliances among sectors that gain from trade and political conflict between gainers and losers.[28]

Land, labor and capital are the factors of production that appliers of the theorem consider at the broadest level. Myanmar is evidently abundant in land and poor in capital and labor. In 1990, agriculture accounted for 57% of Myanmar's GDP, and industry about 10%. By

---

[27] Wolfgang F. Stolper and Paul A. Samuelson, "Protection and Real Wages," *Review of Economic Studies* 9:1 (November 1941), pp. 58–73.

[28] Ronald Rogowski, *Commerce and Coalitions: How Trade Affects Domestic Political Alignments* (Princeton: Princeton University Press, 1989).

2005, the proportions had changed only marginally, to 51% and 14% of national output respectively. In 1998, the last year for which employment statistics are available, 82% of the workforce was employed in agriculture and only 7% in industry.[29] In this situation, following both Stolper-Samuelson and Rogowski, the prediction would be that increasing exposure to trade would make landowners politically more assertive — and thereby able to challenge the regime — and capital politically more defensive. Decreasing exposure to trade would have the opposite effect, with capital assertive and landowners defensive.

The review of Myanmar's trade data suggests that its overall exposure to foreign trade has been stable at low-to-moderate levels, even though trade volume has been increasing and trade exposure across the region has been increasing as well. Calculations based on official data suggest a steadily declining openness ratio. In this situation, we can posit that the power of those involved with land as a factor of production — landowners, farmers, sharecroppers and agricultural workers — has not increased in the past two decades or so. A deeper dive reveals evidence of a weakening sector. Since its colonial days Myanmar has been an exporter of agricultural products. By 1968, it had replaced Bengal as the leading exporter of rice in the world, and kept that position for more than a century.[30] In 1941, Burma's exports of rice amounted to more than 3 million tons, which by 1989 had fallen to a historic low of 49,000 tons.[31] Not only has low exposure to international trade kept the political power of rice farmers (and landowners) at bay, the state has reduced it even further by reserving the trade of "rice and rice products" solely for the state.[32]

---

[29] Asian Development Bank, "Key Indicators 2006," http://www.adb.org/statistics, accessed June 29, 2007.
[30] A. J. H. Latham and Larry Neal, "The International Market in Rice and Wheat, 1868–1914," *The Economic History Review*, New Series, 36:2 (May 1983), pp. 260–280.
[31] *Far East and Australasia 1996* (London: Europa Publications, 1996), p. 644.
[32] Ministry of Commerce, "Import and Export Procedures," http://www.commerce.gov.mm/import_export_procedures/index.html#an2, accessed April 3, 2007.

In the mid-1980s, teak, another land-based product, replaced rice as Burma's major export. But since then, not only has the exposure to foreign trade not increased in the country, the share of all land-based products, including rice, teak and pulses, has fallen in general. Because of state control of trade, a sizeable proportion of land-based products were traded illegally in the black market. Black market trade has fallen by almost half since the early 1980s, partly due to various peace treaties that the regime has signed with insurgent groups, bringing their economic activities under closer monitor. The other crucial land-based product is opium poppy, the mainstay of Myanmar's narcotics trade. The area under poppy cultivation has declined dramatically, from 163,000 hectares in 1996 to about 21,500 hectares in 2006. During this time, Afghanistan has overtaken Myanmar as the world's primary supplier. Benefits aside, the local economic impact of this shift in trade is significant. As the UN's *Global Drug Report 2007* notes, "The decline in cultivation poses serious challenges for the rural population ... who do not have viable alternative income strategies."[33] And what is now replacing teak as the last primary tradable is energy: the oil and gas sector will certainly surpass all previous export records in other sectors. These trends together imply that land-based groups, comprising the majority of Myanmar's populace, will find it more difficult, due to material circumstances, to sustain challenges to the regime. All else equal, their immiserization will instead enable capital, which is Myanmar's scarcer factor, to be politically more assertive.

Resource Famine and the Control of Capital

As a factor of production, capital may pose a political challenge by virtue of its independent commercial strength. Such a material challenge to the political status quo assumes, crucially, that capital is first of all private and, second, dispersed sufficiently to allow the growth of political independence. It is here that we need to appreciate the controls imposed intelligently by Myanmar's military rulers in order to thwart the rise of commercial power independent of the regime. This has two

---

[33] UNODC, *World Drug Report 2007*, p. 213.

complementary aspects. The first comprises orchestrating a resource starvation — we may even term it a "resource famine" — among the populace that is not directly connected to the state. The regime spends only 1.4% of GDP on health and education, which is less than 50% of what the next poorest member of ASEAN spends. Rural illiteracy in the country is now twice as common as it was during the British colonial period, and Burma's health system has been described by UNICEF as the second worst in the world, after war-ravaged Sierra Leone's.[34] Combined with the emasculation of land, there is little scope for capital accumulation in the countryside under these conditions.

The second, and complementary, aspect is that while capital is being accumulated in Myanmar, state policies are designed such that capital accumulation either takes place within the state's existing support base or is channeled specifically to increase the state's network of allies. Myanmar is the only country in Southeast Asia where the defense budget is larger than the budget allocated for health and education combined. The *Tatmadaw*, Myanmar's military, is the largest armed force in Southeast Asia by personnel. Their maintenance, together with the maintenance of state-owned enterprises, drains almost 80 percent of total state spending.[35] The web of state-owned enterprises ensures that capital accumulation remains concentrated within the state, which has been a major goal of Myanmar's economic policies. The State-Owned Economic Enterprises Law, enacted in March 1989, aims to create a strong convergence between state and capital, especially capital pertinent to trade. It made the key tradable sectors of the economy the sole preserve of SPDC-controlled entities: teak, petroleum and natural gas, pearls, jade and precious stones, fish and prawns, and metals, among others. Exceptions are granted to foreign investors, as long as they form alliances with state-owned enterprises (SOEs).[36] The state's recent privatization program also has

---

[34] Turnell, "Burma's Economy 2008," p. 3.

[35] Ibid. See also Turnell, "Burma's Insatiable State."

[36] US Department of Commerce, "Myanmar 2005 Investment Climate Statement," http://web.ita.doc.gov/ticwebsite/apweb.nsf/795c3ca6e24078cd85256bb1006b 330e/c35dec820c9ca5248525707c005d6367?OpenDocument, August 10, 2007.

been undertaken to widen the regime's network of allegiance by drawing in incipient local private capital, offering it minority equity stakes in SOEs, while retaining the state's controlling ownership. Capital remains the state's ally.

State monopolies, in association with foreign capital, directly control the highly capital-intensive oil and gas sector. The main player in this field is the state-owned Myanma Oil and Gas Enterprise (MOGE), which has partnered with foreign companies, especially Indian, Korean, Chinese and Malaysian entities. The flagship project is the Shwe Gas Project, Myanmar's largest energy venture, with direct interests in buying and trading expressed by China, India and Thailand. Aside from energy trading, much foreign investment has been going toward exploration, drilling and the development of infrastructure (such as pipelines and ports) to facilitate energy trading. In late 2005, a trading agreement was signed with PetroChina, centered on building a proposed pipeline to China's Yunnan Province. In 2006, Myanmar also signed a trading agreement with India and, later, Thailand joined the bidding for Shwe reserves.[37] The only local partner in the entire project, from extraction to trading, is MOGE. Similarly, petroleum refining is monopolized by Myanma Petrochemical Enterprise, which is fully owned by the state.

The key players in other major sectors of foreign trade are the Union of Myanmar Economic Holdings Ltd (UMEH) and the Myanmar Economic Corporation (MEC). Equity in UMEH is limited to the military establishment and family members of the military.[38] With its privileged position, UMEH finds it easy to form joint ventures with foreign investors, and controls a substantial share of gems, minerals and seafood trade. MEC, also set up by the military, is authorized to conduct business in virtually any sector, without the type of restrictions that normally apply to other private-sector businesses. Many other large contracts, from telecommunications to retail

---

[37] Matthew Smith and Naing Htoo, "Gas Politics: Shwe Gas Development in Myanmar," *Watershed* 11:2 (2005–2006), pp. 9–11.

[38] The Myanmar Campaign UK, *The European Union and Myanmar: The Case for Targeted Sanctions* (London: The Myanmar Campaign, 2004), p. 11.

to infrastructure development are provided to private businesses primarily on the basis of their loyalty and connections to the regime.[39]

Trade Sanctions and Political Structure

Trade policies and patterns in Myanmar have ensured that the structural distribution of political power remains conducive to the current regime's survival. The regime's trade policy has reduced the space for the majority of Myanmar's populace, who remain land-based, to evolve economic clout and, by extension, pose a political threat to the military regime. Simultaneously, the government's careful control over private capital in the tradable sectors, both agrarian and industrial, precludes their emergence as challengers of the political status quo. Outside these, finance capital, especially in the context of globalization, can be another potential source of pro-democracy pressure if it helps to increase the bargaining power of an entrepreneurial community.[40] The regime, however, controls international financial flows through a triple-tier exchange rate and a prohibition on foreign banks to handle foreign exchange. There is no independent capital market, and most formal equity in business entities belongs either to state-owned enterprises or conglomerates created and controlled by the military.

The material basis for sustained political opposition in Myanmar is therefore feeble. Given this situation, trade embargos and economic sanctions on Myanmar are unlikely to help create economic conditions favorable for democracy. Comprehensive US trade sanctions on Myanmar were responsible for curtailing, within a year, Myanmar's

[39] See, among others, US Commercial Service, "Doing Business in Myanmar: A Country Guide for US Companies," http://www.export.gov/docs/x_8663899.pdf, accessed August 12, 2007; Aung Zaw, "Can a Young Tycoon Save the Generals," *The Irrawaddy* (Chiang Mai Thailand), February 23, 2007; Amy Kazmin, "Burmese Get Glimpse of Superhighway," *Financial Times,* April 25, 2002.
[40] Sylvia Maxfield, "Capital Mobility and Democratic Stability," *Journal of Democracy* 11:4 (April 2000), pp. 95–106.

expanding ready-made garments (RMG) sector, since most of Myanmar's exports to the US consisted of garments. RMG, however, is a labor-intensive sector; it does not require a large capital infusion, does not face high barriers to entry, does not need direct state patronage, and does not provide opportunities for hefty kickbacks to the extent that capital-intensive sectors like power or petroleum can offer. If allowed to grow over time, it could have emerged into a proto-capitalist sector characterized by competition among dispersed private actors, increasing chances for the evolution of both an independent entrepreneurial class and a stronger working class. As the overseas Burmese lobby cheered the sanctions, many investors, including Japanese and Korean firms, quit their projects in Myanmar. 40% of South Korean textile firms that had set up operations in Myanmar are reported to have left the country by 2006. Others transferred their interests to more capital-intensive sectors, such as oil and gas.[41] This trend has likely strengthened the authoritarian state rather than pro-democracy political forces. Subsequent to the sanctions, the regime accelerated the development of the energy sector as an earner of foreign exchange. A few very large investors, working in alliance with the state, emerged as a result, concentrating commercial power.

The democratizing impact of Western sanctions therefore needs to be evaluated carefully. Blanket sanctions are likely to have been a setback, preventing the spread of commercial activity and also encouraging the concentration of economic power in capital-intensive sectors, thus strengthening the regime vis-à-vis its potential opponents. The sanctions, of course, accorded a moral victory for the political opponents of the regime — but they have probably reduced the chances for additional economic opposition to emerge. The regime's material position, as a result, has become more consolidated. Based on Myanmar's trade patterns, we can also surmise that sanctions have pushed the country closer toward Asia and toward avoiding ties with other Western democracies that are more susceptible to consumer and human rights activism. Authoritarian powers in the region, especially

---

[41] Michael Shuan *et al.*, "Going Nowhere," *Time International* (Asian Edition), January 30, 2006.

China, have provided political and military support to the regime. The consequent economic ties are not surprising. For example, one of the key reasons that Myanmar chose China, and not India, as the destination of its main gas pipeline has to do with the political shield China can provide as a permanent member of the UN Security Council. In January 2007, China vetoed a UN Security Council resolution that criticized Myanmar. It is also establishing commercial shipping and transit facilities in Myanmar, especially to gain maritime access to the Indian Ocean.[42] In addition, China is the major weapons supplier to Myanmar. The international economic-political nexus here is consistent with the expectations of existing research that free trade is more likely to occur within political-military alliances than across them.[43] Interestingly, Thai investment in Myanmar increased substantially after Thailand underwent a military takeover. Similarly, Bangladesh and Myanmar re-opened talks about creating overland direct trade routes and energy deals after a military takeover in Bangladesh in early 2007.

As we saw earlier in Fig. 4, there was a correlation between the height of sanctions and Myanmar's economic closeness to non-democratic and semi-democratic regimes. In fact, the West has lost its leverage over the regime by imposing trade sanctions that forced it to find supportive allies elsewhere. International pressure on an authoritarian regime is more likely in countries that have a high degree of penetration by Western media and non-government organizations (NGOs). As Levitsky and Way argue, in Peru and Slovakia, high penetration brought stronger and quicker pressure toward respecting human rights while more widespread abuses in countries with low penetration, like Belarus or Georgia, did not result in correspondingly strong pressure.[44] The overseas Burmese lobby remains active and strong but China's increasing domination of Burma's trade and

[42] "Myanmar's Pipeline Politics."

[43] Joanne Gowa, *Allies, Adversaries, and International Trade* (Princeton: Princeton University Press, 1994).

[44] Steven Levitsky and Lucan A. Way, "International Linkage and Democratization," *Journal of Democracy* 16:3 (July 2005), pp. 20–34.

foreign policy has dampened much of the pressure. In other words, trade ties between the West and Myanmar could have increased the West's political influence over the country at a macro level and also at a micro level through the workings of agencies. Hence, Myanmar has kept strict control over aid agencies after the 2008 Cyclone Nargis.

Over the past two decades, the economic identity of the country has certainly shifted away from "Burma" and its subtexts and contexts to "Myanmar". In the absence of universal acceptance, the West's imposition of isolationism as both normative and material strategies, however morally defensible, has resulted in a stronger, more controllable, material base for the regime. While the collective wisdom of macro-political theory points to the importance of independent sources of economic power outside the state in sustaining democracies, Myanmar's trade pattern and policies since the 1990s suggest that the regime has been a step ahead, in the sense that it has utilized external trade intelligently to bolster its economic resources, create fewer trusted foreign partners, and marginalize the local material bases that may have benefited from a secular rise in trade and possibly created pro-democracy pressures.[45] Its international trade now is isolated from the West, perhaps to the West's relief, but it is also *free* of the West, a fact that the regime is using increasingly as a symbol of an independent or defiant identity against the conformist currents of capitalism. In emphasizing his country's resolve to export energy, for instance, the Managing Director of MOGE asserted, "We don't care about the US sanctions. No matter what [George W.] Bush says, we will find a way."[46]

In a situation in which the domestic economy remains under a stranglehold and international trade is bolstering capital accumulation within the state, it is unrealistic to assume that a strong opposition will evolve out of the population at large at some point to wash the

---

[45] For an analysis of the structural bases of Burmese authoritarianism prior to the 1990s, see Jalal Alamgir, "Against the Current: The Survival of Authoritarianism in Burma," *Pacific Affairs* 70:3 (Fall 1997), pp. 333–350.

[46] Wang Ying, "Myanmar Will Export Gas 'No Matter What Bush Says'", *Bloomberg News*, http://www.bloomberg.com/apps/news?pid=20601013&sid=aei6gogFC3.s& refer=emergingmarkets, accessed September 10, 2007.

regime away. Unless the *Tatmadaw* itself rebels, the material bases of power to sustain such a movement do not exist. Even if such a movement arose from those who have nothing to lose but their chains, the repression unleashed on them will be conditioned by the stance of Myanmar's key trading and strategic partner, China, depending in particular on whether China would exhibit restraint, as Gorbachev did in the face of pro-democracy uprisings in Eastern Europe in the late 1980s. What is more likely is a slow liberalization from within the regime, if demanded consistently by its growing network of economic allies, such that a greater proportion of decision-making power is distributed internally, even though inaccessible to the majority of the people. In other words, as far as trade patterns suggest political effects, Myanmar is likely to follow the political path of Indonesia, but not that of the Philippines.

Part D
Foreign Policy

Chapter 10

China–Burma Relations: China's Risk, Burma's Dilemma

Min Zin

Abstract

The question of whether Burma is becoming a "client state" of China is frequently raised in media and scholarly writings. Although Sinophobic military top brass in Burma have never trusted China's overpowering influence, and in recent years have tried to diversify and reduce dependence on its northeastern neighbor, China's political and diplomatic protection remains indispensable for the regime's survival. Burma may fancy indirectly balancing against China by reaching out to the new US administration. However, this would be difficult unless the U.S. abandons its long-standing demand for political reform in Burma. This paper explains a possible new trend in China's foreign policy toward Burma, which attempts to resolve tension between China's rising role with increasing international responsibilities and multiple interests and its irrelevant non- interference foreign policy. This newly modified policy is now put to the test as China has to respond to the military regime's harsh handling of ethnic minority groups along Sino-Burma border.

Keywords: China; Burma; foreign policy; ethnic conflicts.

Introduction

This chapter will argue two key views. First, the Burmese military regime finds itself lacking the capacity to steer the country away from China's orbit, given the imbalanced relation between the two countries. The military junta perceives Burma as being caught in a triangular rivalry between China, India and the United States. The generals are highly aware of China's overwhelming strategic weight over Burma, and have appeared eager since the mid-1990s to diversify and reduce its dependence on China. Naypyidaw may manage to reduce its military and economic over-reliance on China, but China's political and diplomatic protection remains indispensable to the regime's survival. Unless Burma enjoys political and economic support from the West and its allies, the country will find it hard to restore the previous status of strategic neutrality. However, in order to achieve the removal of Western sanctions and the flow of developmental assistance, investment and technology transfer, the military must introduce inclusive and sensible political and economic reform, and improve its human rights record. Although the United States recently declared in its Burma policy review that it would focus on direct engagement with the junta, the prospect of resuming normalized relations with Burma remains unlikely so long as the current leadership in Burma refuses to undertake an inclusive reform process before the planned 2010 elections.[1] Burma's pariah status will then extend even beyond 2010. Therefore, the regime has no choice but to rely on China for political and diplomatic protection. In other words, Burma's dependency on China is more the consequence of the junta's struggle for survival amid difficult political realities than its own intentions. More importantly, China seems to be more and more determined not to accept any attempts to limit its economic and geopolitical influence in Burma, no matter where such an attempt comes from — the United States or even the military junta in Burma. The dilemma for the Burmese junta is how to break China's asymmetric influence without risking its own survival or provoking China's anger and damaging the cordial (and indeed vital) relationship.

Second, this chapter argues that China's strategy toward Burma is not a risk-free stance. China has recently appeared to pay more attention to the connection between the national reconciliation or nation-building process in Burma and its long-term strategic interests. In other words, China has modified its opportunistic foreign policy

---

[1] Kurt M. Campbell, Assistant Secretary, Bureau of East Asian and Pacific Affairs, "U.S. Policy Toward Burma: Statement Before the Subcommittee on East Asian and Pacific Affairs Senate Foreign Relations Committee", Washington, DC, US Department of State, September 30, 2009, http://www.state.gov/p/eap/rls/rm/2009/09/130064.htm.

toward Burma (i.e. maintaining relations with any government that remains friendly with China and supports its economic and security interests) to one that could resolve tension between China's emerging role as a global actor with increasing international responsibilities and multiple interests and its strictly defined and indiscriminate non-interference foreign policy. But Beijing does not yet have a coherent, clearly formulated policy in that new direction. Moreover, the different priorities and interests between Beijing and Yunnan Province (which is located along the Sino–Burmese border) in dealing with Burma tends to complicate Beijing's Burma policy. Thus this changing orientation is now put to the test as China must respond to the SPDC's handling of ethnic minority groups along the Sino–Burmese border. So long as the Burmese military fails to negotiate an acceptable political resolution with no less than 15 ethnic ceasefire groups whose strength reaches over 40,000 armed troops, the situation of "contained Balkanization" in Burma could lead to a resumption of localized armed conflict between certain ethnic ceasefire groups and the Burmese army. Since the most volatile areas are around the Sino–Burmese border, where formidable Wa and Kachin ethnic ceasefire groups are based, China is likely to face increasing instability in its southwestern neighbor, and consequential disruptions of its economic and strategic interests. The Burmese junta's recent military offensive against the Kokang ethnic ceasefire group based along the border, resulting in a massive flow of refugees into China, indicates that Burma may have serious security spillover effects for China. In short, China will more actively promote the goal of national reconciliation in Burma but it will not likely take the lead in pressing Burma to make it happen. Rather, Beijing will facilitate such a goal within the UN framework. However, if it is not achievable, China will not push hard on the junta and will prefer to maintain the current status quo (including maintaining ethnic ceasefire groups along the border as a buffer and lever against Naypyidaw) as a fallback policy choice.

Outlining Sino–Burmese Relations

Chinese President Jiang Zemin assured his Burmese counterpart, Senior General Than Shwe, during the latter's high-profile visit to

China in 2003, that new leaders of China would continue to "strengthen Myanmar–China *paukphaw* (fraternal) friendship with tradition and cooperation".[2] In June 2009, when the junta's deputy strongman Vice-Senior General Maung Aye visited China, Maung Aye repeatedly emphasized the importance of "*paukphaw* relations" between the two countries[3] which share a 1,384-mile border. In Burma, successive governments have described the relationship with China as "blood relatives" (*swemyo paukphaw*) since the 1950s.[4] In the sibling hierarchy, China enjoys the role of the older brother and Burma the younger. However, the relationship has had its problems.

This chapter will review a brief history of Sino–Burmese relations since 1949 when Burma, as the first non-Communist country, recognized the People's Republic of China (PRC). The review of chronological events will be done in the light of perceptions and strategies both countries have pursued since 1949. However, the paper will mainly focus on the post-1988 Sino–Burmese relationship which has profoundly and perhaps irreversibly deepened political, economic and military cooperation between the two neighbors, with regional and international ramifications. The paper will interrogate some of the key issues in Sino–Burmese relations, such as trade and economic cooperation, energy sector investments, security, and political and diplomatic relations. It will examine the risk China faces in Sino–Burmese relations. The structure of this chapter is organized to provide a

---

[2] *New Light of Myanmar* (January 12, 2003), available at http://www.myanmar.gov. mm/NLM-2003/enlm/jan12_ir1.html.

[3] The Ministry of Foreign Affairs, Myanmar, "Vice-Senior General Maung Aye meets Chinese Vice-President Mr Xi Jinping" (June 20, 2009), http://www.mofa.gov. mm/news/Vice-Senior%20General%20Maung%20Aye%20meets%20Chinese%20 Vice-President%20Mr.%20Xi%20Jinping.htm. The Ministry of Foreign Affairs, Myanmar, "Vice-Senior General Maung Aye meets Chinese Premier Mr Wen Jiabao" (June 21, 2009), http://www.mofa.gov.mm/news/Vice-Senior%20General%20 Maung%20Aye%20meets%20Chinese%20Premier%20Mr.%20Wen%20Jiabao.htm.

[4] According to a Burmese dictionary, the word "*paukphaw*" means "1. Sibling, 2. Intimate, and is an affectionate term conferred upon the Chinese by Myanmar people". *Myanmar–English Dictionary* (Department of the Myanmar Language Commission, Ministry of Education, Union of Myanmar, 1994), p. 266.

coherent understanding of Sino–Burmese relations in support of the two key arguments made in the introduction.

Strategic Foreign Policy Perceptions of China and Burma

China's strategic approach to Burma in the early decades until Mao Zedong's death was predominantly a dual-track or two-pronged policy that distinguished between "party to party" and "government to government" relations.[5] Chinese Prime Minister Zhou Enlai made the public statement during his visit to Burma in June 1954 as a reassurance to his host and the wider audience in the rest of Southeast Asia that a "revolution cannot be exported, and any attempt to export revolution must suffer defeat".[6] A joint communiqué issued by the prime ministers of Burma and China at the end of Zhou's visit affirmed the "Five Principles of Peaceful Coexistence" which have since become the theoretical foundation of Sino–Burmese relations.[7] Despite Zhou's assurance, the principles of peaceful coexistence and subsequent settlement of border disputes between the two neighbors in 1960, China supported underground and above ground Burmese

---

[5] Martin Smith, *Burma: Insurgency and the politics of Ethnicity* (Bangkok: White Lotus, 1999), p. 156; also see Tin Maung Maung Than, "Myanmar and China: A Special Relationship?" In: *Southeast Asian Affairs 2003*, eds. Daljit Singh and Chin Kin Wah (Singapore: Institute of Southeast Asian Studies, 2003), pp. 191–192.

[6] Xiaolin Guo, "Towards Resolution: China in the Myanmar Issue" (Central Asia-Caucasus Institute & Silk Road Studies Program, 2007), p. 33.

[7] The five principles are (1) mutual respect for sovereignty and territorial integrity, (2) mutual non-aggression, (3) non-interference in each other's internal affairs, (4) equality and mutual benefit, and (5) peaceful coexistence in developing diplomatic relations and economic and cultural exchanges. One day prior to signing this agreement with Burma, Chinese Premier Zhou Enlai signed the "Agreement between the People's Republic of China and the Republic of India on Trade and Intercourse between Tibet Region of China and India", in which the Five Principles of Peaceful Coexistence were first introduced. See EarthRights International, "China in Burma: The Increasing Investment of Chinese Multinational Corporations in Burma's Hydropower, Oil and Natural Gas, and Mining Sectors" (ERI, 2008), p. 3.

communists, in addition to cordial government-to-government relations.[8]

In the first decade of Sino–Burmese relations, one of the most threatening issues was the incursion of the defeated Chinese Nationalist (Kuomintang or KMT) troops into Burma's Shan State in December 1949. The number of troops reached 12,000 in February 1952, gearing up their attempt to retake China from the Communists.[9] The Burmese parliamentary government of U Nu feared that the continuation on Burmese soil of US-backed preparations for KMT invasion into China would provoke the Chinese Communists into eliminating KMT remnants and perhaps simply annexing all of Burma. With the start of the Korean War, Burmese observers worried that the United States might be setting up a second front in northeastern Burma.[10] As a result, Burma allowed Chinese Communist troops to enter Shan State, where they launched a joint military operation against KMT forces in 1960. The campaign began in November 1960 and ended in February 1961, followed by the CIA evacuation of 4,200 KMT "Anti-Communist National Salvation Army" men to Taiwan, and a further 6,000 to Laos.[11] Since the joint campaign contradicted the Burmese military's pride in its guardianship of sovereignty and territorial integrity, proclaiming that the *Tatmadaw* (the armed forces) never allows foreign troops to land on Burmese soil, official Burmese history never disclosed this Sino–Burmese joint military operation in 1960–1961.

In 1962, the military staged a coup and Ne Win's junta adjusted itself to accommodate China's dual-track policy while minding the demographic, military and economic superiority of China, and

[8] Ironically, at the onset of the Cultural Revolution (Summer 1966), the Burmese Communist Party elite members that had received training in China were summoned to Beijing and had an audience in the Great Hall of People with the Premier Zhou Enlai, who announced that it was time for them to go home and start a revolution in Burma. See Xiaolin Guo, "Towards Resolution", p. 39.
[9] Robert Taylor, "Foreign and Domestic Consequences of the KMT Intervention in Burma Data paper", (Cornell University, 1973), pp. 11–13.
[10] Mary P. Callahan, *Making Enemies: War and State Building in Burma* (Ithaca, NY: Cornell University Press, 2003), p. 156.
[11] Xiaolin Guo, "Towards Resolution", p. 36.

maintaining friendly state-to-state relations. However, Sino–Burmese relations hit rock bottom in the late 1960s during the Cultural Revolution, when China pursued a foreign policy guided by Maoist ideology rather than national interest and the Five Principles. The overseas Chinese community in Burma echoed the enthusiasm of the Cultural Revolution, wearing Mao badges, arm bands, and distributing thousands of copies of Mao's "Little Red Book". That led to the detention of hundreds of Chinese residents and anti-Chinese riots in the capital, killing many including embassy officials and destroying Chinese property. Many observers believed that the anti-Chinese riots were fomented by Ne Win's regime, who wanted to distract attention from a serious rice crisis in 1967 and deflect angry public protests from further escalation.[12] These violent riots triggered massive counter-demonstrations in dozens of cities across China, protesting against Ne Win's regime. The CCP provided full military and logistic support for the Communist Party of Burma (CPB). Beijing even later attacked Ne Win as a "Burmese Chiang Kai-shek" and "reactionary", and denounced his regime for "fascism", "sham socialism", "looting" and "massacres" over Radio Beijing in 1967.[13]

When Deng Xiaoping ascended to power in the post-Mao era, China's foreign policy changed virtually overnight. The shift was from a geostrategic to a geoeconomic policy, with a more cooperative strategy based on national interest rather than ideology.[14] China sought extended trade and economic relations with all countries in Southeast Asia, except Vietnam. Burma was no exception. Both countries resumed high-level official visits. China's opportunistic foreign policy of maintaining relations with any government that would remain friendly with China and support its economic and security interests[15] served as a guiding principle in Sino–Burmese relations.

---

[12] Martin Smith, *Burma*, p. 225, and Bertil Lintner, *Burma in Revolt: Opium and Insurgency Since 1948* (Thailand: Silkuorm Books, 1999), p. 242.

[13] Bertil Lintner, *Burma in Revolt*, p. 242, and Martin Smith, *Burma*, p. 226.

[14] Niklas Swanstrom, *Foreign Devils, Dictatorship, or Institutional Control: China's Foreign Policy Towards Southeast Asia* (Uppsala Universitet, 2001), p. 103.

[15] Wayne Bert, "Chinese Policy Toward Democratization Movements: Burma and the Philippines", *Asian Survey* 30:11 (November 1990), p. 1068.

However, when the 1988 democracy uprising broke out in Burma, the Chinese were faced with a dilemma. They wanted to stick with the old regime as long as it appeared able to co-opt, stifle or thwart the reform movement and maintain its hold on power. China obviously had an interest in the continuation of the status quo. On the other hand, China wanted to be ready to switch its loyalty to the opposition or prospective government if and when the existing government appeared vulnerable to defeat. During the peak of the 1988 uprising, *the People's Daily* of China even advocated peaceful demonstrations and called for a compromise solution, adding that if the army imposed martial law, another round of bloody conflicts would be unavoidable.[16] However, a month after Burmese military seized power again by launching a massive crackdown, China changed its coverage and refocused on normal relations with its southwestern neighbor. The fall of the CPB due to the mutinies within the party's ethnic rank in 1989 paved the way for China to remove this remaining obstacle to good Sino–Burmese relations. Beijing was believed to have facilitated cease-fire talks between the junta and ex-CPB ethnic mutineer groups.[17]

Since 1988–1989, relations between Burma and China have profoundly and perhaps irreversibly deepened in terms of political, economic and military cooperation, with regional and international ramifications. Burma has become of key importance to China in terms of natural resources and security. On March 27, 2009, China and Burma signed an agreement for the construction of fuel pipelines that will transport Middle East and African crude oil from Burma's Arakan coast to China's southwestern Yunnan Province — avoiding the strategically vulnerable Malacca Strait — while also drawing on Burma's own gas reserves.[18] By the year 2050, China is expected to achieve world-class blue-water navy status. Burma's geographical location offers a "land bridge" for the People's Liberation Army Navy (PLAN) to reach the Indian Ocean, reducing five to six days' voyage and

---

[16] Ibid. pp. 1068–1069 and 1074.

[17] Bertil Lintner, *The Rise and Fall of the Communist Party of Burma (CPB)* (Ithaca, NY: Cornell Unversity Sontheast Asia Program Publications, 1990), p. 54.

[18] Sudha Ramachandran, "China Secures Myanmar Energy Route", *Asia Times*, April 3, 2009.

avoiding the Strait of Malacca.[19] Burma also serves as a land bridge connecting the poor economies in the southwestern part of inland China with the growing economies of Southeast Asia, India and even with African and European markets. Thus, Burma is part and parcel of China's grand strategic design to achieve its overall goal of becoming a great power in the 21st century.[20]

On the part of Burma, its successive governments have been highly aware of its geographical position between China and India. Back in the 1950s, Prime Minister U Nu used to describe Burma as "hemmed in like a tender gourd among the cacti".[21] General Ne Win, who seized power from the civilian government of U Nu in March 1962, adhered to U Nu's policy of strict neutrality and non-alignment but added another foreign policy theme: isolation from the outside world.[22] In fact, Burma's foreign policy has been summarized by the current military regime as "independent" and "non-aligned" (in the Cold War context) up to 1971 and as "independent" and "active" thereafter.[23] When the State Law and Order Restoration Council (SLORC)[24] seized power in a stage-managed *coup d'état*, the junta put aside its principles of long-held neutrality in search of external economic, military and political support.

However, Burmese generals are highly mindful of the foreign policy dilemma they face due to the lack of alternative substantive powers they can rely on for the regime's survival. In 2004, when Bo

---

[19] Poon Kim Shee, "The Political Economy of China-Myanmar Relations: Strategic and Economic Dimensions", (The International Studies Association of Ritsumeikan University, 2002), p. 38.

[20] Ibid. p. 37, and Chenyang Li, "Myanmar/Burma's Political Development and China–Myanmar Relations in the Aftermath of the "Saffron Revolution", in *Myanmar/Burma: Challenges and Perspectives,* ed. Xiaolin Guo (Stockholm: Institute for Security and Development Policy, 2008), p. 117.

[21] Renaud Egreteau and Larry Jagan, "Back to the Old Habits: Isolationism or the Self-Preservation of Burma's Military Regime". (IRASEC, December 2008), p. 61.

[22] Donald M. Seekins, "Burma–China Relations: Playing with Fire", *Asian Survey* 37: (6 June 1997), p. 525.

[23] Tin Maung Maung Than, "Myanmar and China", p. 190.

[24] Later renamed the State Peace and Development Council (SPDC) on November 15, 1997.

Mya, Chairman of the armed ethnic Karen National Union, visited Rangoon for peace talks, General Khin Nyunt, who was then prime minister and the third-strongest man in the junta, said that the regime had to rely on China because the United States and others had sanctions against them.[25] In October 2005, when Major General Ohn Myint, then commander of the Northern Regional Command or Kachin State, held a meeting with provincial commanders and administrative officials to give a briefing of the SPDC leadership's instructions and analyses, he highlighted Burma's geopolitical reality:

> "Our country has now become a key location from which the United States could control the rising and stronger China. This is according to containment policy. We are now caught up in the triangular — relations of China, India and America".[26]

He used the English phrase "containment policy" in his Burmese-language briefing. Where the SPDC's Home Minister Major General. Maung Oo gave a speech to senior officers of the ministry in July 2008, the general also said,

> "[when] we look around at our neighbors, all that we see are American followers. When we see the ASEAN group, Singapore, Malaysia, Indonesia and Thailand are pro-American while Myanmar, Laos, Cambodia and Vietnam are exceptions. Only these countries of exception are in line with Myanmar. That's why we have to move closer to China. You might think that we are embracing China, and the minister backs up and advocates China because China favors and allies with the current government. No, it is not true. We can't stand alone in the world... According to the China-containment policy, the US/CIA intends to control China economically as well as politically. Burma is the only country that is a loop in their containment policy".[27]

---

[25] A video document of the meeting between Khin Nyunt and Bo Mya, that was leaked to the exiled community in late 2004.

[26] Second Quarterly Meeting, held on October 24 and 25, 2005, at Myitkyina City Hall, attended by Commander Major General Ohn Myint and Chairman of Provincial and Township SPDC. Confidential meeting minutes acquired by author from inside military source.

[27] Home Minister's Speech at Ministry's Organization Committee Meeting (No. 6/2008), held on July 6, 2008, at Home Ministry. Confidential meeting minutes acquired by author from inside military source.

Again, the Minister used the English phrase "containment policy" in his Burmese-language speech, indicating their "understanding" of geopolitics.

Burma, which has an acute awareness of the asymmetric differences in power, size and population, perhaps compounded by past Chinese invasions in the 13th, 18th and early mid-20th centuries, is always uneasy and suspicious of China. No matter how the official rhetoric goes — for instance, Senior General Than Shwe once referred to China as "the Myanmar people's most trusted friend"[28] — the xenophobic and Sinophobic Burmese military has never trusted the Chinese. While the military needs China's support, many officers are reportedly unhappy about the reliance on a historic enemy, which runs contrary to nationalist ideals about total sovereignty, though they are of course reluctant to say so publicly.[29] Aung Lynn Htut, an ex-deputy chief of a Burmese mission to the US who sought political asylum in Washington in 2005, said to this author,

> "When I was in the War Office in Rangoon, Than Shwe, Maung Aye and Khin Nyunt frequently discussed China–Burma relations. They know that China is not a good friend but they have to accept it as an inevitable reality. Particularly, Than Shwe and Maung Aye fought against CPB troops, which then received massive Chinese support, when they were in the infantry units. Than Shwe has refused to sign an agreement on the Irrawaddy Transportation Project, which has been in the process of negotiation since the late 1990s. The project includes building a container port near Bhamo, upgrading the road from Bhamo to the China border town of Lweje [then to Zhangfeng], and dredging the waterway of the Irrawaddy River so that it could be used for transporting up to two million containers per year in the future. The reason for Than Shwe's refusal was simple: he does not want to see Chinese flags on the Irrawaddy River".[30]

One of the recent reports said that Maung Aye, who had spent much of his military career fighting Beijing-backed communists,

---

[28] Chi-shad Liang, "Burma's Relations with the People's Republic of China: From Delicate Friendship to Genuine Cooperation", in *Burma: The Challenge of Change in a Divided Society,* ed. Peter Carey (Houndsmills: Macmillan Press, 1997), p. 80.
[29] International Crisis Group (ICG), "Myanmar: The Military Regime's View of the World" ICG Asia Report No. 28 (Bangkok/Brussels, December 7, 2001), p. 22.
[30] Author's interview with Aung Lynn Htut, April 26, 2009.

ordered shop signs to be taken down if Chinese lettering appeared above the Burmese.[31] During his military coordination meeting held on October 20, 2005, Major General Ohn Myint, then commander of Northern Regional Command or Kachin State which shares a border with China, also warned, "Since there is no eternal friend nor eternal enemy, we must understand foreigners are working for their own interest. [As the Burmese saying goes,] we have to understand that the extinction of a race will occur only when it is being swallowed by an alien race, not swallowed by the earth".[32] Major-General Ohn Myint's warning was a clear reference to Chinese immigration and their illegal businesses such as logging. The saying he cited is a typical warning that Burmese use with regard to the demographic threat of incoming Chinese and, to a lesser extent, Indians.

In brief, Burma is highly cautious and wary of China's overwhelming influence. The junta also views Burma as one of the few strategic nations that the US can not use in its containment policy against China. This perception largely defines the regime's strategic calculations and attempts at playing the regional security and diplomatic game in its favor. However, the dilemma for the junta is how to break China's dominating influence without risking its own survival. For its part, China increasingly views Burma as part and parcel of a grand strategic design to achieve its overall goal of becoming a great power in the 21st century.

Trade and Economic Cooperation

Military takeover and the attendant massive crackdown in 1988 led to the curtailment of international aid and development assistance to Burma, with the result that in early 1989 foreign currency reserves

---

[31] Ed Cropley, "Chinese Influx Stirs Age-Old Hatred in Myanmar", Reuters Mar 12, 2008.

[32] Second Quarterly Meeting on Military Coordination, held on October 20, 2005, at the Military Operation Hall of Northern Regional Command HQ. Confidential meeting minutes acquired by author from inside military source.

were reported to be down to US$9 million.[33] The junta had to resort to border trade with China as a lifeline for the Burmese economy. There was a remarkable increase in the volume of bilateral trade. In 1988, for example, the total trade between China and Burma was US$9.51 million. In 1989, it jumped to US$76.03 million, eight times that of the previous year.[34]

Although trade with China is very important for Burma, it has been seriously imbalanced at least since 1958. According to Chinese official statistics, China–Myanmar bilateral trade amounted to US$2.626 billion in 2008. China enjoyed a trade surplus of US$1.33 billion.[35] Some observers have speculated that much of the trade surplus could have flowed back into Burma in the form of investment in property and other assets or through the illegal drug trade.[36] Bilateral trade with China now accounts for 24% of Burma's total trade, making China its second-largest trading partner after Thailand (Table 1).[37]

China's developmental assistance has been critical to Burma, as the country suffers from Western-led economic sanctions and block-ades of loans and aid from international financial institutions. Chinese assistance usually comes in the form of grants, interest-free loans, or concessional loans and debt relief. In 1991, when SLORC for the first time since the September 1988 military coup faced a deep foreign reserve shortage, the Chinese government committed a grant of 50 million yuan (equivalent to US$15 million). In 1993, the Burmese

---

[33] David Arnott, *Challenges to Democratization in Burma: Perspectives on Multilateral and Bilateral Responses*, (International IDEA, 2003), p. 69.

[34] Poon Kim Shee, "The Political Economy of China–Myanmar Relations", p. 43.

[35] "Myanmar PM Meets New Chinese Ambassador *Xinhua*", February 20, 2009, http://news.xinhuanet.com/english/2009-02/20/content_10859234.htm.

[36] Maung Aung Myoe, "Sino–Myanmar Economic Relations Since 1988" Asia Research Institute Working Paper Series, No. 86 (April 2007), p. 5.

[37] "Sino–Myanmar Bilateral Trade Up 60 percent *The China Post*", November 4, 2008. http://www.chinapost.com.tw/business/asia/asian-market/2008/11/04/181677/Sino–Myanmar-bilateral.htm. Burma is also Yunnan's largest trading partner among the ASEAN countries, almost half of Sino–Burmese total trade. See International Crisis Group (ICG), "China's Myanmar Dilemma", Asia Report No. 177 (September 14, 2009), p. 19.

Table 1. Ranking of top four countries & Burma's trade volumes with them (US$ Million)

Country	2004–2005	2005–2006	2006–2007	2007–2008
Thailand	$1,451.48 (29.51%)	$1,621.91 (28.75%)	$2,681.25 (32.61%)	$3,094.85 (32.84%)
China	$785.57 (15.97%)	$849.33 (15.05%)	$1,353.71 (16.47%)	$1,632.47 (17.32%)
Singapore	$750.66 (15.26%)	$837.35 (14.84%)	$1,223.84 (14.89%)	$1,175.43 (12.47%)
India	$427.44 (8.69%)	$578.56 (10.25%)	$900.65 (10.96%)	$870.40 (9.24%)

Note: Figures within parentheses are corresponding shares as a percentage of total trade volume of Burma.
Sources: Ministry of Commerce; Central Statistical Organization; Directorate of Trade.[38]

junta received another interest-free loan of 50 million yuan from China.[39] Without the Chinese assistance and loans with no or low interest, the regime would not be able to run its state-owned enterprises and undertake the construction of new factories such as textile and sugar mills. In fact, the Chinese aid flow appears to support not just the regime's survival but its hard-line repressive policies as well. During his state visit to China in January 2003, Than Shwe secured China's agreement to offer Burma a RMB 50 million grant and a preferential loan amounting to US$200 million, the largest loan ever made by China to the Burmese junta.[40] Of course it may be coincidental, but just four months after China's commitment, Than Shwe

---

[38] Burmese trade data and statistics are notoriously unreliable and often the figures are completely distorted. For instance, the currency conversion is done at official rate $1 = 5.7 Kyat, while the market rate is $1 = 1,200 Kyat.

[39] Maung Aung Myoe, "Sino–Myanmar Economic Relations Since 1988", p. 19.

[40] According to the Burmese government, between 1989 and 2006, the PRC government provided over 2.15 billion Yuan and US$400 million in various forms of loans. There were also 10 million Yuan in debt relief and 200 million Yuan in grant aid. Moreover, the Chinese government also helped the Burmese junta secure private financial loans from Chinese banks and business firms. See Maung Aung Myoe, "Sino–Myanmar Economic Relations Since 1988", p. 19.

gave the order to stage a brutal attack against democracy leader Aung San Suu Kyi and her entourage traveling in central Burma in May 2003. The so-called "Depayin massacre" (Depayin being the town where the attack took place), which left at least 50 people dead,[41] led to the end of political talks between the junta and Suu Kyi, and to the house arrest of the latter until now.

Chinese investment in Burma is driven by both geopolitical and economic factors.[42] Official Chinese FDI in Burma is rather small but it is widely believed that there are a large number of hidden Chinese investments and business ventures, most of which are under the names of Burmese citizens to avoid going through the rigorous procedures stipulated by the national-level Myanmar Investment Commission (MIC). According to official statistics, however, total foreign investment in the military-ruled nation increased from US$172.72 million in the 2007–2008 fiscal year to US$985 million in 2008–2009, with China pouring the bulk of it into the mining industry. Official Burmese government statistics report that China accounted for US$856 million, or 87%, of the foreign investment in 2008–2009.[43] According to an EarthRights International report, there are a minimum of 69 Chinese multinational corporations (MNCs) involved in at least 90 hydropower, mining, oil and natural gas projects in Burma.[44]

If Burma wants to curtail China's economic domination, it also has to reduce its reliance on the resource-extraction economy and attract more foreign investment and technology transfer in order to export value-added products and so increase the value of its exports. However, the Western-led economic sanctions are one of the major obstacles preventing the junta, in addition to its own mismanagement and corruptions, from achieving broad-based industrial development. In order to achieve the removal of Western sanctions and the flow of

---

[41] Saw Yan Naing, "The Depayin Massacre, Five Years Later", *The Irrawaddy Magazine Online*, May 30, 2008, http://www.irrawaddy.org/article.php?art_id=12393.
[42] Maung Aung Myoe, "Sino–Myanmar Economic Relations Since 1988", p. 14.
[43] "China Cash Boosts Myanmar Investment: Ministry", *AFP*, July 17, 2009.
[44] EarthRights International, "China in Burma", pp. 1–8.

developmental assistance, foreign investment and technology transfer, the military must introduce inclusive and sensible political and economic reform and improve its human rights record. Since the prospect of inclusive reform is highly unlikely under the current leadership in Burma, the regime has no choice (whatever its intentions) but to depend heavily on China for foreign currency, cheap consumer goods and developmental assistance. This scenario is most obvious in Burma–China energy ties, which this chapter will now address.

Energy Sector

Burma has the world's tenth-largest natural gas reserves, estimated at over 90 trillion cubic feet (tcf) in 19 onshore and 3 major offshore fields. Recent discoveries of gas reserves have triggered intense competition between India, China, South Korea, Thailand, Japan and Singapore.[45]

In August 2007, the Burmese junta confirmed the sale of natural gas from the lucrative Shwe gas reserves to Chinese state-controlled oil company China National Petroleum Corporation (CNPC), and at a lower price than other competitors. It is widely believed that the regime had rewarded China as it, along with Russia, had vetoed the US-led resolution in January 2007 calling for inclusive political dialogue and democratization in Burma — the first time since 1973 that Beijing has vetoed any matter not related to Taiwan.[46]

Construction of the US$1.5 billion oil pipeline and the US$1 billion gas pipeline reportedly started in the first half of 2009, and is expected to be completed by 2013. The pipeline, roughly 2,800 km/ long, will cut through the heart of Burma, beginning near Kyaukphyu on the Arakan coast and running through Mandalay, Lashio and Muse before crossing into China at the border town of Ruili. The pipelines will terminate at Kunming in Yunnan Province. A gas

---

[45] Sudha Ramachandran, "China Secures Myanmar Energy Route", *Asia Times*, April 3, 2009.

[46] Stephanie Kleine-Ahlbrandt and Andrew Small, "China's New Dictatorship Diplomacy: Is Beijing Parting With Pariahs?" *Foreign Affairs* 87:1 (January/ February 2008), pp. 38–56.

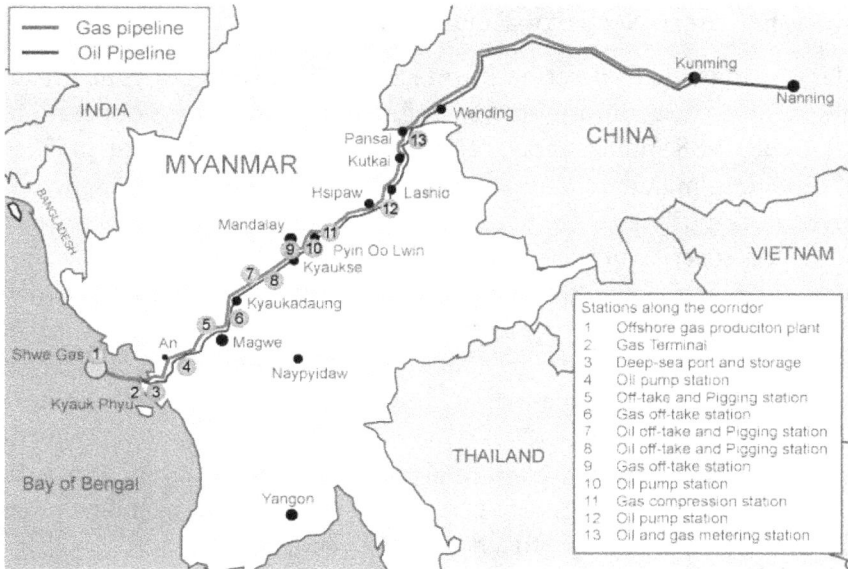

Figure 1.   Route of the oil and gas pipelines from western Burma to China's Yunnan Province

Source: Reuters

collection terminal and a port for oil tankers will be constructed on an island near Kyaukphyu (see Fig. 1). The entire cost of constructing the pipelines will be borne by China.[47] The gas pipeline may speed up efforts by China to tap gas reserves in Burma to meet strong economic demand. The oil pipeline will boost China's imports from the Middle East and Africa by reducing at least one-third the country's sole reliance on the Malacca Strait which currently delivers 80% of China's oil import but which runs the risk of falling into the hands of "hostile powers", pirates or terrorists. Moreover, pipelines are more economical than sea transport in the long term.[48]

---

[47] Sudha Ramachandran, "China Secures Myanmar Energy Route".

[48] Maung Aung Myoe, "Sino–Myanmar Economic Relations Since 1988", p. 17 and Pak K. Lee, Gerald Chan and Lai-Ha Chan, "China's 'Realpolitik' Engagement with Myanmar", *China Security* 5:1 (Winter 2009), p. 103.

Sino–Burmese Security Relations

Many analysts, who describe Burma as "a client state" of China, usually refer to the Sino–Burmese military and security cooperation. After the 1988 military coup, Burma departed from its past practice of obtaining military aid and arms imports, meaning that it eschewed large arms purchases from the superpowers in order to observe a policy of strict neutrality.[49] Burma then found China as its major source of arms supplies, which made arms shipments to pariah Rangoon at "friendship prices" in the wake of massive killings of pro-democracy protesters in 1988. The most significant move was the 1990 deal with China involving weapons and military equipment worth an estimated value of US$1.2 billion. Another agreement with Beijing to supply additional weapons and equipment worth US$400 million was reported in 1994.[50] The Chinese military has also trained of Burmese officers both in China and Burma.

Another important factor in Sino–Burmese security relations is China's strategic effort to use Burma as a springboard to secure direct access to the Indian Ocean. According to Shee Poon Kim, China is expected to achieve world-class blue-water navy status by the year 2050. Burma therefore would be potentially important for China to achieve its strategic presence in the Indian Ocean and its long-term two-ocean objective (direct access to the Pacific and Indian Oceans).[51] However, some analysts contend that rumors of Chinese military bases in Burma are not substantiated.[52] A Chinese scholar, while acknowledging the presence of Chinese military in Burma, noted, "The presence of China's military agency in these islands only reflects

---

[49] Toshihiro Kudo, "Myanmar's Economic Relations with China: Can China Support the Myanmar Economy?" Institute of Development Economics, Discussion Paper No. 66 (July 2006), p. 6.

[50] Tin Maung Maung Than, "Myanmar and China", p. 197.

[51] Poon Kim Shee, "The Political Economy of China–Myanmar Relations", p. 36.

[52] Andrew Selth, "Chinese Military Bases in Burma: The Explosion of a Myth", Griffith Asia Institute, Regional Outlook Paper No. 10 (2007), p. 1, and Jurgen Haacke, "Myanmar's Foreign Policy: Domestic Influences and International Implications", IISS, Adelphi Paper 381 (June 2006), p. 26.

China's intentions to provide logistic services and operational instruction to Myanmar's military forces rather than permanent residence in these areas".[53]

Observers detect that the Burmese junta has reduced its military dependence on China by reaching out to India, Russia, Pakistan and North Korea since the mid-1990s for defense purchases and training. In 2002, Burma purchased 10 MiG-29 jet fighters from Russia, to Chinese displeasure. According to reports, over 1,000 Burmese technicians have been trained in Russia since 2001 and hundreds of Burmese soldiers have undertaken courses on military science in Russia from 2003–04. Burma also attempted to make a deal worth US$5 million with Russia for the construction of a 10 megawatt nuclear reactor in Burma. Its has been military relationship with North Korea publicly noted since the early 2000s. Recent reports, photos and footage confirm that North Koreans have helped build the military defense system in Naypyidaw, providing tunneling expertise.[54]

However, China does not idly watch Burma's attempt to escape its influence. China responds by twisting the generals' arms. For instance, it insisted that Myanmar pay interest on loans that had originally been granted interest-free when the junta sought closer defense ties with other countries in the region.[55] China thus remains a key supplier of Burmese defense, especially low-level equipment such as trucks and ammunition. As Donald Seekins argues, China's military support makes it easy for Burmese military hardliners to use their instrument of preference — brute force — to govern.[56]

Chinese military support, together with its economic domination, has fueled age-old anti-Chinese sentiments in Burma, especially after

---

[53] Chenyang Li, "Myanmar/Burma's Political Development", pp. 123–124.
[54] Bertil Lintner, "Tunnels, Guns and Kimchi: North Korea's Quest for Dollars — Part I", *YaleGlobal* (June 9, 2009) and Aung Zaw, "Asia's 'Axis of Evil' Flexes its Muscles", *The Irrawaddy*, June 23, 2009.
[55] Sudha Ramachandran, "Yangon Still Under Beijing's Thumb", *Asia Time*, February 11, 2005.
[56] Donald M. Seekins, "Burma–China Relations", p. 539.

the regime's crackdown on protests in September 2007.[57] China is
aware that its involvement in the SPDC's repression and its exploitation of Burmese natural resources could spark communal violence
similar to the anti-Chinese riots of 1967. Chinese leaders frequently
request the Burmese military to take care of overseas Chinese in
Burma.[58] However, so long as it relies on the junta for the protection
of overseas residents in Burma, China's strategy toward Burma will
remain risky.

Political and Diplomatic Protections

Since the 1988 military coup in Burma, China's political and diplomatic protections have been vital for the regime's survival. China
adopted an opportunistic foreign policy of maintaining relations with
any government that would remain friendly and serve China's security
and economic interests, irrespective of that government's propensity
for reform.[59] A Chinese scholar confirmed this pragmatic trait in
China's Burma policy in more direct language: "The Chinese government will develop friendly relations with Myanmar whatever the ideology of its government as long as it does not become a strategic
pawn of other countries or organizations to contain China's
development".[60]

However, this policy of self-serving pragmatism appears to be
more and more untenable for at least two reasons. First, it puts China
in a difficult dilemma whenever the Rangoon regime faces serious
vulnerability in domestic power shifts. Much as China had an awkward time readjusting its policy of tacit support for reform during the
1988 democracy movement back to a pro-SLORC stance, Beijing
also found itself in policy confusion when Aung San Suu Kyi's, opposition party, the National League for Democracy, won a landslide

[57] Ed Cropley, "Chinese Influx Stirs Age-Old Hatred in Myanmar", Mar 12, 2008.
[58] "Chinese Premier Expects Myanmar to Care About Overseas Chinese", Xinhua,
February 1, 2006.
[59] Wayne Bert, "Chinese Policy Toward Democratization Movements".
[60] Chenyang Li, "Myanmar/Burma's Political Development", p. 127.

victory in the 1990 multi-party elections. After the elections, Cheng Ruisheng, the Chinese ambassador in Rangoon, visited the NLD office and personally congratulated the NLD on its victory. The ambassador subsequently also called for the release of Suu Kyi, saying Beijing wished to see "national reconciliation in Burma".[61] The Burmese junta was very disappointed with China's shifting loyalty.[62] Again during the September 2007 protests, China faced an uneasy situation. The 2007 protests revealed how China's opportunistic foreign policy toward Burma was challenged in the international arena. This is the second reason why an opportunistic policy is increasingly unsustainable. As China wants to be seen as "a responsible stakeholder" in international politics, it would like to avoid being associated with the brutal dictators in Burma. In the wake of the 2007 crackdown, Burma has become not only a source of embarrassment for China especially inasmuch as the international community increasingly delegates China to resolve the Burma problem. After the "Saffron Revolution" erupted in September 2007, Chinese Premier Wen Jiabao contacted US President George W. Bush, Japanese Prime Minister Fukuda Yasuo and British Prime Minister Tony Blair by phone to discuss the situation and the measures to take.[63] China eventually agreed to the issuance of UNSC Presidential Statement in October 2007 and the usage of the expression "strongly deplores the use of violence against peaceful demonstrations in Myanmar".[64] China facilitated UN Envoy for Burma Ibrahim Gambari's first visit to

---

[61] Martin Smith, *Burma*, p. 414.
[62] Powerful SLORC Secretary 1 and Intelligence Chief Khin Nyunt even asked the NLD why the party mentioned only the Chinese ambassador's visit when it has met with many Western ambassadors. "No foreigner will love our country... We do not pay attention to their pressure on us...we do not pay the slightest attention to their pressure". *Working People's Daily*, July 14, 1990.
[63] Li Chenyang and Lye Liang Fook, "China's Policies towards Myanmar: A Successful Model for Dealing with the Myanmar Issue?", *China: An International Journal* 7:2 (Sep 2009), p. 270.
[64] Statement by the President of the Security Council, 11 October, 2007. http://daccessdds.un.org/doc/UNDOC/GEN/N07/538/30/PDF/N0753830.pdf?OpenElement.

Rangoon (from September 29 to October 3, 2007) since November 2006.[65] In short, China's new role in the international system obliges the country to re-examine its purely opportunistic foreign policy. China's policy toward Burma will not be an exception in the long run, though some unique situations such as geographical proximity should be acknowledged.

However, China neither wants nor really can ask the Burmese regime to "commit suicide", no matter how much Beijing would like to improve its public image regarding Burma.[66] It has a huge stake in the country, as in the construction of fuel pipelines. The junta can still count on China for a UNSC veto. For the generals, to have China as a permanent member of UNSC is of great significance. The top generals perceive that the US is pushing for its sanction regime (economic sanctions as well as travel ban) to become a UNSC resolution. They even expressed their concerns about the possible consequences of the UNSC Presidential Statements on Burma. Major-General Maung Oo said,

"There have been two Presidential Statements on Burma. When the UNSC issues its third Presidential Statement, it will lead to a resolution. Then all 192 members must follow it. If it was a US instruction, countries can refuse to follow. But if it is done by UN bodies such as UNSC, the ILO must follow. There are three areas of punishment: first, economic sanctions blocking Burma's export/import, second, arms embargo and the last is dispatching UN Peacekeeping Forces to Burma. What they are now doing is not that harsh yet but they intend to designate Burma as a black sheep and punish it in the UN forum... Therefore, the State has a crisis in international relations. We will continue to play "ad hoc" strategy.... We want to make friends with all, not to make enemies. We play a triangular game".[67]

[65] Renaud Egreteau and Larry Jagan, "Back to the Old Habits", p. 66.
[66] Stephanie Kleine-Ahlbrandt and Andrew Small, "China's New Dictatorship Diplomacy".
[67] Home Minister's Speech at Ministry's Organization Committee Meeting (No. 6/2008). When the Burmese military uses the triangular or trio relations of China, India and America, they implicitly or often explicitly refer to Thailand and Bangladesh as America's proxies.

The general continued to explain how the US-led West has used the concept of "crimes against humanity" and "responsibility to protect" via UN mechanisms against Burma, and how China as a permanent UNSC member can shield Burma from these interventions. In short, so long as the Burmese generals perceive UNSC as a threat and China's protective role as indispensible, Burma will find it hard to steer itself away from China's influence.[68]

With their obsessive perception of the critical role they play in the US's "China containment policy,"[69] the Burmese military may wish to resort to indirect balancing against China by engaging, if possible, with the new US administration. However, unless the US abandons its long-standing demands, including the release of Suu Kyi and other political prisoners and undertakings of political dialogue with the democratic forces and ethnic groups, this strategy appears unfeasible. The current junta under Than Shwe wants good relations with the US only if it does not compromise its grip on power.

---

[68] China played a facilitating role between Russia and Burma at the time of the 2007 veto. Russia also used its veto to block a Western-led resolution. But Russia does not have direct strategic interest in Burma. The military regime has attempted to intensify its relation with Russia by sending a senior delegation (the junta's deputy head visited Russia in 2006 he could not meet the Russian president), buying military equipment, a nuclear reactor has (which not yet materialized) and receiving Russian training for its military officials. However, the generals in Naypyidaw still feel they cannot rely on Russia to defend them in the UNSC. Author's telephone interview with a Burmese diplomat, June 2009.

[69] During his meeting with Than Shwe and senior leaders of the regime, US Senator Jim Webb — who feels China's influence in Burma furthers "a dangerous strategic imbalance in the region" warns that "if Chinese commercial influence in Myanmar continues to grow, a military presence could easily follow" (Jim Webb, "We Can't Afford to Ignore Myanmar", *New York Times*, August 25, 2009), may have reinforced the Burmese junta's perception of its self-designated role in China's containment. During his conversation with Suu Kyi, the US senator apparently referred to Beijing's involvement in Burma as a "fearful influence". However, Suu Kyi told Webb that she rejects such terminology with regard to China and wants Burma to be on good terms with all its neighboring countries as well as the international community at large. "She said China is Burma's neighbor and wants to be a good friend of Burma. She said she did not see China as a fearful influence." Wai Moe, "Suu Kyi Clarifies Her Sanctions Policy," *The Irrawaddy*, August 18, 2009.

More importantly, China also seems to be more and more determined not to accept any attempt aiming to undermine its economic and geopolitical influence in Burma, no matter where it comes from — the United States or even the military junta in Burma. After the Obama administration signaled that it was reviewing its Burma policy and Stephen Blake, director of the State Department's Mainland Southeast Asia Office, made a visit to Naypyidaw in the last week of March 2009 and met the junta's foreign minister in direct talks, China appeared to be worried about possible US involvement and subsequent influence in Burma. Dr Jian Junbo, an assistant professor at the influential Institute of International Studies at Fudan University, Shanghai, wrote a very strong op-ed article in *Asia Times*, warning that the US's attempt to resume its influence in Burma could pose a challenge to China that would reduce or even end the Middle Kingdom's influence there. "Geopolitical competition by big powers seems a very possible future for Southeast Asia, which is not good news for the countries in the region. Whatever happens, China is unlikely to withdraw from Myanmar because it has already developed very deep economic relations with it. China needs Myanmar's raw materials, and more importantly needs its ports to transport goods to other countries in Africa and Middle East."[70] The Chinese scholar warned that "the US should recognize the fact that China is an important actor in Southeast Asia when it plans its engagement policy in Myanmar, and the US would face great difficulty if it tried to exclude China from its new Myanmar policy."[71] He also laid out dos and don'ts for the US with regard to its Burma policy, opining that Beijing would be happy if the US could engage with Myanmar purely as a business partner.

However, Beijing appeared to lean toward reconciliation in Burma and to encourage the junta to undertake an inclusive political settlement along the UN's demands following the fall of Khin Nyunt, whom China had backed as a reformer. Instead of continuing unilateral military rule, China wants the junta to make a settlement

---

[70] Jian Junbo, "China Wary of US–Myanmar 'detente'", *Asia Times*, April 17, 2009.
[71] Ibid.

from a position of strength, as it has come to believe that the Burmese opposition has become less radical in its political demands. China, particularly officials in Yunnan Province, has increased its outreach to the opposition movement in exile. More remarkably, they have allowed conferences and seminars on Burmese issues to take place in China. This is something the Chinese have learned from watching exiled Burmese civil society groups operating in Thailand.[72] According to Aung Lynn Htut, in an official meeting in Washington DC in 2003, a Chinese intelligence officer said with regard to China's Burma policy that Beijing would even accept Daw Aung Sun Suu Kyi if she took power.[73]

China in fact does need a political settlement in Burma for two reasons. First, a negotiated settlement could provide stability in both the political landscape of Burma in general and the Sino–Burmese border area in particular. Political stability in Burma will allow institutionalized economic cooperation between the two countries, given that the Chinese have expressed frustrations about the unpredictable decision-making process of the Burmese military.[74] Stability in the Sino–Burmese border region will help both countries to deal effectively with cross-border issues such as drug production and trafficking, crime and pandemic disease. Second, a political settlement, consolidating the China–Burma status quo, would lift the burden of Burma off Chinese shoulders since Beijing has received increasing criticism and blame for Burma's failures in the diplomatic arena and international media. China wants Burma to woo more international acceptability. It even brokered talks between US Deputy Assistant Secretary of State for East Asian and Pacific Affairs and two Burmese ministers in Beijing in June 2007.[75]

---

[72] Aung Zaw, "China's Troublesome Little Brother", *The Irrawaddy* 17:6 (September 2009).

[73] Author's interview with Aung Lynn Htut, April 26, 2009.

[74] Ibid.

[75] "Myanmar, US hold rare talks in China over Aung San Suu Kyi" Channel NewsAsia, June 29, 2007.

All in all, China appears willing to modify its purely opportunistic policy towords Burma. However, it doesn't mean that China wants radical change in Burma. If political change comes to Burma, a country of real strategic significance to China, Beijing would want to shape when and how that happens.[76] At the same time, China is still not certain how to make this new approach work without damaging its economic and security stake in Burma.[77] This newly modified policy is now put to the test as China responds to the regime's handling of ethnic minority groups along the Sino–Burmese border.

China's Risk

The Burmese military has initiated ceasefire agreements with no less than 17 ethnic rebel groups since 1989 and has allowed these groups to retain their arms and control extensive blocks of territory over the past 20 years. The regime constantly points to the ethnic ceasefire groups as the defining feature of its "national reconsolidation" policy and as evidence of its claims to legitimacy.

However, the success of the military's ceasefire strategy is now seriously challenged as the junta needs to bring the ceasefire groups under the command of the Burmese military,[78] reclaim territory from

---

[76] Stephanie Kleine-Ahlbrandt and Andrew Small, "China's New Dictatorship Diplomacy".

[77] However, China has recently expressed interest in co-funding a major crude oil transshipping and processing terminal on the west coast of Malaysia. That terminal also offers Beijing an alternative route for its Middle East imports should relations with Burma sour or a change of regime occur there. The China National Petroleum Corporation (CNPC) is also reportedly about to sign an agreement with Bangladesh's government-controlled PetroBangla to search for oil and gas both on and offshore. William Boot, "China Hedges Its Energy Bet with Move into Bangladesh." *The Irrawaddy Online*, September 2, 2009.

[78] According to the military's 2008 constitution, "All the armed forces in the Union shall be under the command of the Defense Services." Constitution of the Republic of the Union of Myanmar (2008), Chapter VII, Clause 338, Ministry of Information, September 2008.

them, and push them to transform into political parties ready to contest the 2010 elections. This will be a major test of the military's "contained Balkanization" of the ethnic areas; failure to achieve these goals could trigger an outright conflict and, in a worst-case scenario, initiate another era of regional instability.[79]

On April 28, 2009, the senior officials of the Burmese junta met with the leaders of some ethnic ceasefire groups including Wa and Kachin, based along the China–Burma border, and instructed them to reduce their troop levels and transfer them to the control of the junta no later than October 2009. The military junta would then reform these remaining troops as the Border Guard Force (BGF) to be commanded by the junta's commander-in-chief through his regional commanders and assigned to their respective areas.[80]

All ethnic groups are well aware that minority rights and their aspiration for a federal union are not guaranteed under the military's constitution. The indications so far suggest that major ethnic groups such as Kachin, Wa and Mon are not likely to give in to the junta's demands. Even though the ceasefire groups are pressured by the neighboring China and Thailand to compromise their positions and negotiate with the regime, the end result is not likely to be what the regime envisions — a Burman-dominated central state control over the periphery and an end to armed insurrections. At best, the ceasefire groups will face inter-group divisions, with some groups giving in and others resisting disarmament, as well as intra-group splits, with one part of a group surrendering and another part resuming fighting. But ethnic conflict will not fade away soon.

However, in August 2009, the Burmese army ended its two-decade ceasefire with the Kokang ethnic group (known as the Myanmar National Democratic Alliance Army — MNDAA) by attacking and occupying the Kokang region. Despite China's repeated

---

[79] Min Zin, "Ethnic Minorities Hold the Key to Burma's Future" *The Irrawaddy Online*, January 23, 2009.
[80] Official instruction document in Burmese language given by Lt. General Ye Myint and other generals to ethnic leaders during the April 28, 2009, meeting. Author acquired the document from ethnic ceasefire groups.

warnings to the Burmese leadership not to use violence against ethnic ceasefire groups along the Sino–Burmese border, the Burmese generals decided to ignore them and launch a surprise offensive to crush the MNDAA, forcing 37,000 refugees to flee into China's Yunnan Province. China issued an uncharacteristically stern warning that Burma should "properly solve its domestic issue to safeguard regional stability in its border area with China". The Chinese Foreign Ministry also urged Burma "to protect the safety and legal rights of Chinese citizens in Myanmar".[81] The statement, posted on the Chinese Foreign Ministry's website in late September, said military conflict in the Kokang region bordering China "harmed the rights and interests of Chinese citizens living there". A Chinese ministry official urged the Burmese side "to thoroughly investigate the case as soon as possible, severely punish the law-breakers, and inform China of the results... [and] to take concrete steps to avoid recurrence of similar incidents."[82] Local authorities in Lincang, a region in southwestern China bordering Burma, have demanded 280 million yuan (US$41 million) in compensation from the Burmese regime for loss of property incurred during a junta offensive in Kokang in late August.[83]

In fact, Yunnan Province has close historical ties with these ethnic groups and a strong interest in maintaining the status quo.[84] China maintains its closest relationship with the United Wa State Army

[81] "China Urges Myanmar to Safeguard Border Stability", *Xinhua*, August 28, 2009.
[82] "Myanmar Urged to Safeguard Lawful Rights of Chinese Citizens", *Xinhua*, September 26, 2009.
[83] Ko Htwe, "Chinese Authorities Seek Damages from Junta", *The Irrawaddy*, October 1, 2009.
[84] The ICG report even argues that Yunnan authorities expressed satisfaction with the UNSC initiative against Burma because they prefer a weak central government in Burma that allows them to engage local actors with fewer constraints. See International Conflict Group, "China's Myanmar Dilemma", September 2009. However, a well-connected observer in Kunming insists that Beijing and Yunnan generally have the same policy approach despite some differences in priority and emphasis, as Yunnan is more sensitive to the ground situation in Burma. Author's phone interview with a former Burmese Communist Party rebel in Kunming, October 28, 2009.

(UWSA). In the wake of the Kokang conflict, a Chinese delegation comprising of various government agencies including military, police, border security, cross-border trade and agriculture, among others, visited the UWSA headquarters and discussed the volatile situation in the region.[85] Independent analysts believe that the military build-up of the UWSA has been supported by China.[86] China knows that the ethnic insurgency in Burma has shown resilience in the past six decades. Many of them were often defeated or co-opted by successive central governments in Burma, but they resumed their resistance to the central government by relying on China (via the Communist Party of Burma) and illegal businesses (such as drug trafficking and logging). Moreover, China no longer trusts the junta. Thus, it prefers to maintain the ceasefire groups as a buffer and lever against Naypyidaw's unpredictability until a more reliable government is set up in Burma after the 2010 elections.[87]

China's major concern is that if the Burmese military attacks the other ceasefire groups along its border — particularly Wa and Kachin — it would upset stability in the region. While the strength of

---

[85] "Chinese officials Visit Panghsang", *Shan Herald*, September 11, 2009.

[86] Tony Davis and Edo Asif, "UWSA Prepares for Confrontation", *Jane's Defense Weekly*, October 25, 2006, and Tony Davis, "Lord of War: Running the Arms Trafficking Industry", *Jane's Intelligence Review*, April 18, 2008. Even after the fighting in Kokang region, some well-connected sources in the border area have detected an increased flow of weapon sales from China to the Wa region. Author's interview with a military analyst in Yunnan Province, November 8, 2009.

[87] Author's phone interview with an observer in Kunming, September, 2009. In December 2008, Chinese officials are said to have encouraged Wa and Kachin cease-fire groups to write a letter to President Hu Jintao and Premier Wen Jiabao. In the letter, the ethnic groups highlighted their ancestral roots in China, emphasizing that "Wa and Kachin people's hearts are forever devoted to China." They also asked China to mediate and help resolve the ethnic conflict and civil war in Burma. "Letter to Chinese President Hu Jintao and Premier Wen Jiabao", signed by Pauk Yu. Chan, Chairman, United Wa State Party Central Committee, Government of Wa State, and Lanyaw Zawng Hra, Chairman, Kachin Independence Organization, December 11, 2008. A document acquired by the author. Some local analysts on the Sino–Burmese border believe China's solicitation of such a letter may indicate that Beijing wants to use it as a lever against Naypyidaw should it prove necessary.

the Kokang ceasefire group is estimated at 1,000–1,500 troops, the strength of the Kachin Independence Organization (5,000–6,000) and the United Wa State Army (15,000–20,000) are significantly greater. Both organizations have clear political goals and nationalistic agendas, with considerable popular support. The regime also has logistic constraints because its army does not have a presence inside the Kachin or Wa ceasefire areas, as it does in Kokang.[88]

With their overwhelming military might, the Burmese army might be able to conquer the headquarters of the UWSA and KIO ceasefire groups in a few weeks or months, but it would be almost impossible to suppress the subsequent guerrilla insurgency and restore stability in northeastern Burma.If the military decides to wage war against the Wa and Kachin, the border area will be severely destabilized due to massive refugee flows, the disruption of trade and potential obstruction of the pipeline project. Then the fighting and the consequent humanitarian fallout could be the issue raised in the UNSC as Western governments push for action. The military's uncooperative stand and the use of violence against ethnic ceasefire groups could prompt China to reconsider its alliance with Burma and impose both pressure and inducements. If the junta continues to disregard China's warnings, the latter may converge with the West in dealing with the Burma problem and comply with the use of UN mechanisms to move against the Burmese generals.[89]

Andrew Selth, however, argues that "while it suits Burma to develop its relationship with China now, it will always retain the option of drawing back from China's close embrace".[90] Selth cites Vietnam and North Korea as precedents in either detaching from China's influence or even resisting China's invasion (Vietnam) or refusing to

---

[88] Tom Kramer, "Burma's Cease-Fire at Risk: Consequences of the Kokang Crisis for Peace and Democracy", TNI, September 2009.

[89] China has exercised such a policy shift in its relations with North Korea and agreed to stricter UNSC sanctions after Pyongyang conducted nuclear tests in October 2006 and May 2009. Jayshree Bajoria, "The China–North Korea Relationship", Council of Foreign Relation, July 21, 2009.

[90] Andrew Selth, "Chinese Military Bases in Burma", p. 21.

surrender sovereignty (North Korea).[91] However, these examples may not fit the Burma case. Unlike Vietnam, Burma, which is facing serious popular opposition in terms of urban unrest and ethnic resistance, does not enjoy the luxury of alienating its reliable powerful neighbor. Unlike North Korea, Burma does not possess nuclear weapons as a bargaining chip and cannot afford to stand alone in playing the destabilizing game of an outlaw state. More importantly, the current international consensus on Burma (as in the UNSC demand for political reform) will prevent other powers (ASEAN, India, Russia) from supporting the junta unconditionally, or from playing a game of power balancing or Cold War-type hedging against China. In fact, these countries and regional groupings view their relations with China to be more important than that with Burma. Thus, it is hard for the Burmese generals to find reliable alternative supporters to ensure their survival.

In any case, China's role is now about to be put to the test, as Beijing must respond to the regime's handling of ethnic minority groups along the Sino–Burmese border. So long as the Burmese military fails to negotiate an acceptable political resolution with these 17 ethnic ceasefire groups (whose strength exceeds 40,000 armed troops), the situation of "contained Balkanization" in Burma could lead to a resumption of localized arm conflicts between certain ethnic ceasefire groups and the Burmese army. Since the most volatile areas are around the Sino–Burmese border, where formidable Wa and Kachin ethnic ceasefire groups are based, China is likely to witness an era of instability along its southwestern border and consequential disruptions of its strategic and economic interests, possibly including the fuel pipelines that will run through ethnic minority areas.

Conclusion

Whether Burma is becoming a "client state" of China is a matter of degree and terminology.[92] The Sinophobic military top brass have

---

[91] Ibid. p. 21.
[92] International Crisis Group (ICG), "Myanmar: The Military Regime's View of the World", p. 22.

never trusted China's overpowering influence in Burma, and in recent years have tried to diversify and reduce its dependence on China. With its perception of America's strategy of containment against China and its perceived role in this geopolitical equation, Burma may fancy indirectly balancing against China by reaching out to the new US administration. However, this would be difficult unless the US abandons its long-standing demands, including the release of Suu Kyi and other political prisoners and that the regime engage in political dialogue with the democratic forces and ethnic groups. In the conclusion to its policy review, the US also stated that it alone cannot promote change in Burma and has stepped up dialogue and interactions with China.[93] Naypyidaw may manage to reduce its military and economic over-reliance on China, but China's political and diplomatic protection remains indispensable to the regime's survival. Unless Burma enjoys political and economic support from the West and its allies, the country will find it hard to restore its previous strategic neutrality. Burma's dependency on China is more of an unintended consequence of the junta's survival struggle than its intentions, given its marked nationalism and Sinophobia. More importantly, China seems to be increasingly determined not to accept any attempt to undermine its economic and geopolitical influence in Burma, no matter where such an attempt may arise.

On the other hand, China is increasingly aware of the risk of its purly opportunistic policy toward Burma, and has appeared to pay more attention to the connection between its long-term strategic interest and genuine national reconciliation and the nation-building process in Burma. In other words, Beijing appears willing to modify its opportunistic foreign policy toward Burma, but does not yet have a clear and coherent policy. Beijing has been gradually changing its Burma policy but the shift cannot be expected to be quick or

---

[93] Kurt M. Campbell, "US Policy Toward Burma: Statement Before the Subcommittee on East Asian and Pacific Affairs Senate Foreign Relations Committee", Washington, DC, September 30, 2009. http://www.state.gov/p/eap/rls/rm/2009/09/130064.htm.

dramatic. It will be slow and well-calculated.[94] A possible direction is that China will more actively promote the goal of national reconciliation in Burma but without taking the lead in pressing Burma to make this happen. Beijing is after all beset by its own dissident problems, especially among minority nationalities. Beijing will, if anything, facilitate reconciliation within the UN framework. However, if that is not achievable, China will not push the Burmese junta. They will prefer to maintain the current status quo, including having ethnic ceasefire groups along the border as a buffer and lever against Naypyidaw, as the fallback policy choice. But this newly modified policy is now about to be put to the test much faster than Beijing wishes, as China must respond to the regime's troublesome handling of ethnic minority groups along the Sino–Burmese border.

---

[94] Min Zin, "The China Factor", *Bangkok Post*, Sunday Perspective, January 27, 2008.

Chapter 11

India's Unquenched Ambitions in Burma

Renaud Egreteau

Abstract

Though India and Burma shared a colonial identity, they have since independence had a more complicated and divergent relationship. Burma looks to India to counterbalance China's overweening influence, an interest India shares and has been happy to abet. But India has been less successful in its quest for cooperation in boundary pacification and counterinsurgency measures or in fully satisfying India's burgeoning resource needs.

Keywords: Look East Policy; PLA; ULFA; kala.

Introduction

"In recent years, we have made great strides in our bilateral relations that have truly become multifaceted". (M. Hamid Ansari, Vice President of India, Yangon, February 5, 2009).[1]

After several years of opposition to the Burmese military junta that took power in September 1988, the Indian government's approach toward Burma[2] underwent a significant shift in the early 1990s. Indeed, the March 1993 visit to Rangoon by the late Jyotindra Nath Dixit, then India's foreign secretary and top diplomat, marked

---

[1] Speech available online at http://vicepresidentofindia.nic.in/content.asp?id=202.
[2] In this article, I use the English terms "Burma" and "Rangoon" instead of the vernacular terms of "Myanmar" and "Yangon" for linguistic simplicity, and without any political connotation or judgment.

a turning point in the Indo–Burmese relationship, as India softened its criticism of the ruling Burmese junta and began to engage it cautiously. With the regional geopolitical framework quickly evolving, New Delhi intended to re-establish the toehold it previously held in Burma during the colonial period, when the Burmese province was vitally linked to the rest of British India. Demonstrating new interest in a country that has long lived in isolation, New Delhi's policymakers have indeed many reasons to focus on the strategic and economic benefits that the Burmese geopolitical field can offer to an emerging India. As a part of New Delhi's "extended neighborhood", Burma has consequently been included in India's new regional strategic vision that was redefined in the early 1990s.

This chapter seeks to assess the effectiveness of India's new approach to Burma, 15 years after it opted for a concrete policy shift. While bilateral cooperation has been strengthened, as the above quotation from the Indian vice president indicates, we argue that India still has not fulfilled its main objectives there. Rather, we claim that India has faced significant resistance from both the Burmese regime and the socio-economic environment in achieving its foreign policy goals there. After a brief analysis of India's historical perceptions of Burma, this chapter will analyze India's emerging interests and critically assess New Delhi's performance against those objectives. These objectives include coordinating effective counter-insurgency measures along Indo–Burmese borders, improving bilateral economic relations, making forays into a still underexploited Burmese energy market, and countering China's growing influence in the region. We will subsequently examine some of the continuing obstacles India faces in its foreign policymaking as far as Burma is concerned. In essence, this chapter argues that India has derived more frustration than success from its new "velvet policy" toward Burma.

India's Historical Perception of Burma: A Fundamental Misreading

India has always had a peculiar relationship with its Burmese neighbor. One ancient legacy that Indian civilization gave to Burma was Buddhism, and it is often recalled when bilateral cultural exchanges are promoted today. But more recently, Burma was deeply influenced by India during its colonial period (1826–1948) when the British annexed the Burmese province and brought in members of various Indian communities to run its administration and economy. Indians of Tamil, Bengali, Punjabi, Gujarati and Gurkha origin quickly began dominating trade, land property and the financial lending system in British Burma as well as the civil administration, educational system and police and military forces; this continued from the end of the 19th century until Burma's separation from India in 1937.[3] In 1931, the number of people of Indian descent was estimated to be over one million out of Burma's total population of 14 million, with half of Rangoon's population being Indian.[4] Therefore, the predominance of Indians in the province's colonial demographic and economic configuration as well as their role in militarily suppressing Burmese indigenous rebellions[5] created strong resentment within the "Burman" (*Bama'r*) ethnic group, which still constitutes the majority of Burma's population. This resentment sparked several waves of anti-Indian and anti-Muslim riots during the 1920s and 1930s as well as nationalist (i.e., anti-minority) policies in the 1940s and 1960s. Since then, the Burmese frequently have been bitterly suspicious of India and Indians, mostly referred to by the Burmese by the derogatory term of "*kala*" (from "ku-la" or "foreigner" in Burmese, and "kala" or "black" in Hindi/Urdu languages).

On the other hand, Indians have generally had a rather positive image of Burma which has traditionally been perceived as a part of India's wider sphere of influence. For many Indians, Burma is still *Suvarna Bhumi* (the "Golden Land" in Sanskrit) where minorities of Indian origin took advantage of the British colonial system to get rich and, in return, contributed to the economic development of

---

[3] For a detailed analysis, see Nalini Ranjan Chakravarti, *The Indian Minority in Burma: The Rise and Decline of an Immigrant Community* (London: Oxford University Press, 1971).

[4] Bertie Reginald Pearn, *A History of Rangoon* (Rangoon: American Baptist Mission Press, 1939), p. 290; and Walter Sadgun Desai, *India and Burma: A Study* (Calcutta: Orient Longsman, 1952), p. 28.

[5] Such as the Saya San Revolt in 1930–1931.

the province.[6] Indian academics, in fact, have often ignored the anti-Indian feelings prevalent in Burmese society and instead focused on the mutual friendship between Indians and Burmese, and Burma's golden economic age fostered by Chettiar, Marwari or Sindhi communities.[7]

World War II and Burma's independence in 1948 triggered the first tide of emigration of Burmese Indians, forced back to India because of their loyalty to the British in the face of the Japanese invasion and then by post-1948 nationalistic property and citizenship laws. In 1962, the advent of an openly xenophobic military rule in Rangoon put the finishing touches on the "Burmanization" of the country.[8] By nationalizing and "Burmanizing" the economy and society, General Ne Win's regime encouraged the flight of more than 200,000 Indians who had stayed in Burma after 1948. From this point on, India and Burma maintained minimal official relations, mainly on cross-border matters but also including personal meetings between Indira Gandhi and Ne Win. But India did not develop any strong threat perception from Burma, largely because of the latter's economic autarky, self-imposed political isolation and absence of regional military ambitions. The Indian public, in fact, continued to hold a generally positive view of Burma. An idealized approach suited Indian policymakers perfectly well when Burma began to be torn apart by the 1987–1988 pro-democracy uprising. In response to this crisis, New Delhi took an openly sympathetic stance toward Burmese students and activists led by the charismatic

---

[6] This overall assessment is based on many personal discussions with Indian academics, politicians and diplomats as well as with Burmese Indians who fled Burma in the 1960s to settle back in India. Interviews were conducted in India from 2002 to 2009.

[7] See, for instance, as the author omits the fact that Burmese nationalism first grew upon anti-Indian sentiments, as the motivation for the separation from India in 1937 proves: Rajshekhar, *Myanmar's Nationalist Movement and India*, 1906–1948 (Delhi: South Asian Publishers, 2006). See also the well-researched book of the Australian economist Sean Turnell, who underestimates too, we would argue, the strong Burman resentment against the Chettiars: Sean Turnell, *Fiery Dragons, Banks, Moneylenders and Microfinance in Burma* (Copenhagen: NIAS Press, 2009).

[8] Robert A. Holmes, "Burmese Domestic Policy: The Politics of Burmanization", *Asian Survey* 7:3 (March 1967), pp. 188–197.

Aung San Suu Kyi, whose close links with the Nehru–Gandhi family were well-known in India since the 1960s.[9] However, as the regional strategic order began to change in Asia in the early 1990s, India launched a new "Look East" policy under the Congress-led Narasimha Rao government, a strategy clearly aimed at creating closer ties with the booming Asian economies to its east. At the same time, China began gaining a foothold in Burma, benefiting from the vacuum left by the international community — including India which joined in ostracizing the new military regime that took over in Rangoon after the September 1988 coup.[10] Since Burma was a potential continental gateway to mainland Southeast Asia for both India and China, officials in New Delhi began wondering whether it was best to ignore or oppose Burma's new military junta. Thus, New Delhi had to reassess and redefine its Burma policy in order to protect and enhance its emerging geopolitical interests on its eastern flank from 1993.

India's Emerging Strategic Interests in Burma

Many reasons can be brought to light to explain the shift in India's Burma policy and its courting of the Burmese military regime from the early 1990s. Three of them are crucial: the search for stability in India's troubled Northeast region, the economic opportunities tendered by Burma, and the attempt to counterbalance China's growing regional presence.

Instability in India's Northeast: The Burmese Connection

In the early 1990s, India's most concrete and immediate regional interest was fostering stability in the seven states of its troubled

---

[9] Pramod K. Mishra, "India's Burma Policy", *Strategic Analysis* 12:10 (January 1989), pp. 1183–1200.

[10] The new Burmese junta (SLORC) dropped the socialist and autarchic policy inspired by General Ne Win since 1962 to opt for a more liberal economic and diplomatic opening-up. Only China responded positively to the SLORC's new geopolitical mantra in 1988.

Northeast.[11] Since India's independence in 1947, the region has experienced continual political instability caused by numerous reccurring ethnic-based insurgencies, sovereignty clashes with China and chronic underdevelopment.[12] The various insurgent outfits developed a strong separatist credo against New Delhi and have used violence as their main political tool to this end. They have ignored official borders, finding the remote hills of western Burma, Bangladesh and Bhutan to be opportune areas to obtain shelter, support and financing, while China long stood as their main patron. The Naga, Assamese, Tripuri and Manipuri (Meithei) armed groups established clandestine networks of jungle bases, training camps, arms and drug trafficking routes, and extortion, fake currency and smuggling systems in the neighboring Burmese Sagaing Division and Kachin State.[13] For decades, Burmese authorities turned a blind eye to the presence of anti-India groups operating out of the remote Naga, Patkai and Lushai hills. Both unable and unwilling to flush them out, Rangoon has found the presence of these insurgent groups to be potentially effective bargaining chips vis-à-vis New Delhi, for getting more military assistance as well as more economic opportunities from the Indian side. For this reason, *Tatmadaw* (Burmese Army) local officials have tacitly allowed the groups to build up extensive underground connections in remote regions only marginally under the Burmese central government's political control. Aware of this unstated policy, which generates a substantial financial (licit or not) cross-border flows at the local level, India established direct links with some of Burma's own rebel ethnic groups in the 1980s to counteract Rangoon's implicit support of anti-India groups. For example, Indian

---

[11] India's Northeast region is currently comprised of seven federated states: Arunachal Pradesh, Assam, Manipur, Meghalaya, Mizoram, Nagaland and Tripura. Arunachal Pradesh and parts of Assam are territories still claimed by China which does not recognize the delineation of the Sino–Indian border defined in 1914.

[12] Renaud Egreteau, *Instability at the Gate: India's Troubled North East and its External Connections* (New Delhi: CSH Occasional Paper, No. 16, 2006).

[13] Since 1974, Burma comprises seven administrative States which have an ethnic base (Kachin, Chin, Rakhine, Mon, Karen/Kayin, Karenni/Kayah and Shan) and seven Divisions dominated by Burman populations.

intelligence agencies offered to help train Kachin rebels in order to craft an informal buffer between Northeast insurgent groups and the Burmese Army along the Indo–Burmese border.[14]

The Burmese government knew of these linkages, as well as the moral and financial support India openly gave to Burman pro-democracy groups in Rangoon, especially during the 1988 urban uprisings. During the late 1980s and early 1990s, pro-democracy Burmese students, as well as Kachin and Chin leaders, were welcomed in India's Northeast states — and even in New Delhi — often after dramatic treks through the jungle.[15] In response to India's expanded support for pro-democracy activists and ethnic rebels, the *Tatmadaw* increased its support for anti-Indian insurgents such as the People's Liberation Army of Manipur (PLA) and the United Liberation Front of Assam (ULFA).[16] Thus, mutual mistrust further fueled insurgencies in their respective border regions in the early 1990s.

However, New Delhi lost one of its strongest allies when the Kachin rebels negotiated a ceasefire agreement with the SLORC in 1993. This prompted New Delhi to review its strategy options in Burma. Pushed by military priorities, India decided to begin engaging the Burmese regime to gain its cooperation in helping to promote stability in the Northeast. J.N. Dixit's March 1993 visit to Rangoon presented both countries with an important opportunity to discuss the issue of military collaboration in relation to their respective frontier unrest. Indo–Burmese military cooperation took concrete shape in April 1995 when both armies conducted a joint counter-insurgency operation (*"Golden Bird"*) against various ethnic rebel outfits.

This joint operation was aimed at dismantling the remote base camps of ULFA, PLA, both the Khaplang and Muivah factions of the

---

[14] Bertil Lintner, *Burma in Revolt — Opium and Insurgency Since* 1948 (Chiang Mai: Silkworm Books, 1999), p. 395.

[15] Personal interviews with pro-democracy Burman/*Bama'r* activists (New Delhi, 2002–2007), as well as former leaders of the Kachin Independence Organization (New Delhi, April 28, 2003) and the Chin National Front (CNF) (New Delhi, March 29, 2006).

[16] Subhir Bhaumik, *Insurgencies in India's Northeast: Conflict, Co-option & Change* (Washington: East-West Centre, Working Paper No. 10, July 2007), p. 32.

National Socialist Council of Nagaland (NSCN-K and NSCN-M, respectively) and the Chin National Front (CNF). The expedition considerably weakened these rebel groups, but Rangoon withdrew before the operation could bring more success when India granted the Nehru Prize for International Understanding to Aung San Suu Kyi, leader of the Burmese democratic opposition, in May 1995.[17] Thus, one of the main components of improving Indo–Burmese relations — military cooperation in confronting the various ethnic insurgencies along their frontier — appeared to have faltered in the 1990s. Cooperating to confront these insurgencies was actually more crucial to India's national security than to Burma's. After all, with the notable exception of the Naga rebels, none of the anti-Indian insurgent groups presented a concrete and immediate threat to Burma's national unity and territorial integrity, as they did to India's.

India's "Look East" Policy: The Burmese Economic Gateway

India has also found engaging Burma to be increasingly attractive because of the trade and economic opportunities this emerging relationship potentially offers. Fascinated by the rise of Southeast Asian economies, India launched a "Look East" Policy in 1991 to help gain increased economic and strategic influence in the region. Southeast Asia begins with Burma and for this reason Indian policymakers had to include their eastern neighbor in their emerging economic strategy. This became even more important when Burma entered the Association of Southeast Asian Nations (ASEAN) in 1997. As a part of this "Look East" policy, two institutional projects were initiated by India, Burma being their primary geographical node: the Bangladesh–India–Myanmar–Sri Lanka–Thailand Economic Cooperation (BIMST-EC) Agreement[18] in 1997 and the Mekong–Ganga Cooperation (MGC)

---

[17] "More Importance Has Been Attached to the Prize to Suu Kyi Than Bilateral Relations", *Outlook India*, December 27, 1995.

[18] The acronym BIMSTEC became the Bay of Bengal Initiative for Multi-Sectoral Technical and Economic Cooperation when Bhutan and Nepal joined the club in 2004.

Agreement in 2000. From the other side, China launched the Kunming Initiative or Bangladesh–China–India–Myanmar (BCIM) in 1999. These technical multilateral projects were welcomed by the Burmese regime because they enabled it to re-enter the regional diplomatic and commercial scene — beyond ASEAN — after decades of isolation. This new regionalism was aimed at enhancing trade and investment opportunities in and around Burma, especially through infrastructure construction programs like the Trans-Asia Highway project. These efforts paved the way for greater regional cooperation with New Delhi at its forefront. At the same time, regionalism offered India in the late 1990s an opportunity to balance institutionally the rising Chinese presence and initiative in the Mekong subregion.[19]

India also wanted to benefit from a direct bilateral commercial relationship with Burma — once an important supplier of rice for India and a source of great pride for the Tamil and Bengali expatriates who controlled the lion's share of Burma's colonial economy. After the 1994 Indo–Burmese border trade agreement allowing 22 items to be traded, the first official border crossing was opened in April 1995 between Tamu in the Sagaing Division of Burma and Moreh in the Indian state of Manipur. Remarkably, bilateral trade increased from an insignificant $62.15 million during the 1988–1989 fiscal year to $328.53 million in 1997–1998.[20] These trade figures rose despite the numerous difficulties Indian investors and traders faced in a still inward-looking and state-controlled Burmese economy. In 2001, the then Indian foreign minister, Jaswant Singh, inaugurated a 160-kilometer road linking the border town of Tamu to Kalemyo and Kalewa, two Burmese commercial towns further south. This India–Myanmar Friendship Road, which cost $2.58 million to construct, was aimed at facilitating trade links between India's

---

[19] Renaud Egreteau, *Wooing the Generals — India's New Burma Policy* (Delhi: CSH-Authorspress, 2003), pp. 102–112. Since 1992, China has largely extended its influence through cooperation with the Asian Bank of Development in the Greater Mekong Subregion (GMS) comprising its own Yunnan Province, Burma, Laos, Vietnam, Cambodia and Thailand.

[20] Embassy of India (Yangon), *India–Myanmar Cooperation: New and Innovative Opportunities (on the occasion of the Made in India Show in Myanmar, 19–22 February 2004)*, (Yangon: L.B. Associates, 2004), p. 15.

Northeast and Mandalay, the second most dynamic city in Burma after Rangoon, and beyond to the rest of Southeast Asia.[21]

India also planned other economic projects with the Burmese in the 1990s. These included construction of port facilities in western Burma near the city of Sittwe, railway upgrading, hydropower projects, as well as exploitation of Burma's natural resources such as oil, gas, timber, agricultural products and precious stones. Even though energy cooperation was planned as early as 1993, it did not materialize until 2002, when two state-controlled Indian firms, Oil & Natural Gas Corporation Limited (ONGC Videsh for its foreign arm) and Gas Authority of India Limited (GAIL), attempted to help exploit natural gas resources in the Arakan (Rakhine) fields. In January 2002, these firms joined a consortium with Korea Gas, Daewoo International and the Burmese state-owned Myanmar Oil & Gas Enterprise (MOGE) to exploit the A-1 gas block near the port of Sittwe. Three years later, the same consortium gained access to another Arakanese block (A-3), while a private Indian company (Essar Oil) invested in two other Arakanese fields (A-2 and L blocks).[22] With new ambitions in the Burmese energy sector in the early 2000s, India chose to compete in a regional market from which most Western oil companies are barred from competing by international sanctions against the Burmese military junta.

India's Attempt to Counter China's Growing Influence: Threat Perceptions in the Burmese Region

Since the end of the 1980s, India has developed its foreign policy and military doctrine largely around the challenge of countering China's growing influence in Asia and the implications of a "rising

---

[21] "India Opens Burmese Road as Link to ASEAN", *The Bangkok Post*, February 16, 2001.

[22] For details, see Tin Maung Maung Than, "Myanmar Energy Sector: Banking on Natural Gas", *Southeast Asian Affairs* (2005), pp. 257–289; and Marie-Carine Lall, "Indo–Myanmar Relations in the Era of Pipeline Diplomacy", *Contemporary Southeast Asia* 28:3 (December 2006), pp. 424–446.

China" for India's own economic, political and military emergence. The Sino-Indian War of 1962 left deep scars within India's military and political elite and a strong anti-China lobby remains lodged in New Delhi even today. Still perceiving China as a "threat" despite high-level diplomatic visits and a number of bilateral agreements signed in the 1990s and 2000s, a large section of India's military establishment continues to fear India's strategic encirclement by China and its allies in the region. For example, both Pakistan and Bangladesh have established strong economic and military partnerships with China, and Burma appears to be moving closer to the rising Asian giant as well.[23]

Bilateral relations between China and Burma have improved greatly since the late 1970s, largely as a result of the "open-door strategy" initiated by Chinese leader Deng Xiaoping after his 1978 visit to Rangoon. The main purpose of the open-door strategy was to open up China's southwestern provinces of Yunnan and Sichuan to the Indian Ocean through the Irrawaddy River corridor running southward from the Sino–Burmese border.[24] By promoting new ties with Burma and offering to rebuild its derelict continental and maritime infrastructure, China hoped for convenient access to this new economic gateway. Sino–Burmese rapprochement was made concrete in 1988 as Beijing took advantage of the post-coup political and economic vacuum left by the international community's sanctions against Burma. As a result, China gained a secure foothold in Burma within just a few years, much to India's chagrin.

India became aware of the viability of the Sino–Burmese partnership as early as 1989, when cheap Chinese goods began flooding markets in Northeast India. But it was rumors about China's military involvement with the SLORC that spurred New Delhi to retool its Burma strategy around the "China factor". First, China's assistance

---

[23]John W. Garver, "Asymmetrical Indian and Chinese Threat Perceptions", in Sumit Ganguly (ed.), *India as an Emerging Power* (London: Frank Cass, 2003), pp. 109–134.
[24]Pan Qi, "Opening the Southwest: An Expert Opinion", *Beijing Review* 28:35 (September 2, 1985), pp. 22–23.

in rebuilding crumbling roads, bridges and other infrastructure throughout Burma was perceived by Indian strategists as a potential threat, for they feared this could give China direct access to India's Northeast. Second, India worried that China could establish a maritime bridgehead on the Indian Ocean near vital sea lanes of communication (SLOCs) in the Andaman Sea by upgrading port facilities and naval bases along the Burmese coastline. This could potentially threaten India's maritime security. Third, China gave the Burmese military an opportunity to increase its strength and modernize its equipment at very low cost by signing a $1 billion deal in 1989 and a $400 million agreement in 1994. As a result, *Tatmadaw* troops acquired new weaponry and increased their manpower to about 400,000 soldiers in the early 1990s.[25] Finally, India was prompted to change its policy toward Burma after suspicions arose in 1992 about Chinese plans to set up a surveillance network along the Burmese coast, with a special focus on Great Coco Island, north of the Andaman archipelago. The alleged plans indeed included the construction of sensitive monitoring facilities there, only a few nautical miles from Indian territory.[26]

Thus, from 1993 onward, India tried to deal directly with Burma's ruling junta to prevent Burma from becoming a Chinese military "pawn" or satellite against Indian interests.[27] According to Indian strategists and think tanks, befriending the Burmese generals with a policy of "constructive engagement" — like the one initiated by

---

[25] Bertil Lintner, "Myanmar's Chinese Connection", *International Defence Review* 27:11 (November 1994), p. 24. Before the SLORC's coup, the *Tatmadaw* could only count on about 185,000 men. Now, figures are around 350,000 Burmese soldiers: see Andrew Selth, "Known Knowns and Known Unknowns: Measuring Myanmar's Military Capabilities", *Contemporary Southeast Asia* 31:2 (August 2009), pp. 272–295.

[26] "Smoke Signals", *Far Eastern Economic Review*, November 12, 1992; and "Sino-Myanmar Ties Irk Delhi", *Times of India*, November 20, 1992.

[27] See Mohan J. Malik, "Sino–Indian Rivalry in Myanmar: Implications for Regional Security", *Contemporary Southeast Asia* 16:2 (September 1994), pp. 137–156; and Andrew Selth, "Burma and the Strategic Competition Between China and India", *The Journal of Strategic Studies* 19:2 (June 1996), pp. 213–230.

ASEAN — and trying to gain a strategic foothold in Burma would enable India to deal with the potential threat posed by a rising China on its eastern flank and somehow counter China's thrust in other neighboring countries as well.[28] Thus, the "China factor" weighed heavily in India's revised Burma policy.

An Assessment of India's New Approach Toward Burma

Fifteen years after it was first initiated, India's new approach toward Burma has met with mixed results. Specifically, India continues to face immense frustration in Burma's lack of effective cooperation in confronting ethnic insurgencies in India's Northeast, and Indo–Burmese economic relations remain grossly underdeveloped, with India losing ground in the very competitive Burmese energy market. In contrast, New Delhi has been much more confident in its dealing with the "Chinese threat" through Burma, downplaying the prospect of Burma sliding into China's strategic orbit entirely or in any hostile way.

India's Frustration Over Cooperative Counter-insurgency in the Northeast

Since India's decision to award the Nehru Prize for International Understanding to Burmese dissident Aung San Suu Kyi in 1995, both India and Burma have tried to improve their strained bilateral relations. Two official visits by Burmese Chief of Army Staff General Maung Aye to India in January and November 2000 were particularly important in this process of confidence building.[29]

---

[28] As recommended by a few works published by the *Institute of Defence Studies and Analysis* (IDSA, New Delhi) and by former Indian military officers: Phunchok Stobdan, "China's Forays into Burma — Implication for India", *Strategic Analysis* 16:1 (April 1993), pp. 21–38 ; Baladas Ghoshal, "Trends in China–Burma Relations", *China Report* 30:2 (April–June 1994), pp. 187–202 ; Udai Bhanu Singh, "Recent Trends in Relations between Myanmar and China", *Strategic Analysis* 18:1 (April 1995), pp. 61–72.

[29] "India and Myanmar Look to Bury Years of Distrust", *Jane's Defense Weekly*, January 18, 2000.

Military-to-military contacts increased after these visits and both armies began conducting new parallel offensives against insurgent outfits along the Indo–Burmese border, especially targeting the Naga rebels of the NSCN-K in 2001 and 2002.[30] In October 2004, during General Than Shwe's landmark visit to New Delhi, India presented the head of the Burmese junta with a model of effective counter-insurgency collaboration it had formulated in December 2003 with Bhutan in confronting ULFA rebels during "Operation All Clear".[31] General Than Shwe publicly reassured India of his country's cooperation on the issue, and since then, the Burmese authorities have kept promising that Burma's territory will not shelter any external armed outfits.[32] Subsequently, localized operations against insurgent groups based in the Burmese Kabaw Valley (Naga Hills) have been conducted by Burmese security forces each winter, with India's intelligence and material support.[33]

India indeed began sending arms shipments to Burma in 2002, after years of staunch refusal to sell weapons to the latter's ruling

---

[30] The National Socialist Council of Nagaland (Khaplang) — NSCN-K gathers mainly Naga rebels from Burma.

[31] A large-scale week-long military operation jointly launched by the Royal Bhutan Army and the Indian Army on December 15, 2003, dislocated 30-odd rebels camps: Arijit Mazumdar, "Bhutan's Military Action against Indian Insurgents", *Asian Survey* 45:4, (July–August 2005), pp. 566–580.

[32] Ministry of External Affairs (India), *Joint Statement Issued on the Occasion of the State Visit of H.E. Senior-General Than Shwe, Chairman of the State Peace and Development Council of the Union of Myanmar to India (25–29 October, 2004)*, (New Delhi: October 29, 2004). More recently: "Myanmar Assures Its Soil Won't Be Used By N-E Insurgents", *Press Trust of India*, February 7, 2009.

[33] See for each winter operations since 2000: "Myanmar Army Launches Offensive Against Naga Rebels", *The Times of India*, December 1, 2000; "Myanmar Junta Cracks on Indian Ultras", *The Hindustan Times*, November 7, 2001; "Guerrilla Bases in Myanmar Intact, Claims Naga Rebel Leader", *The Hindustan Times*, January 8, 2004; "Myanmar Launches Crackdown on Indian Militant Camps", AFP, December 3, 2004; "Burma Army Attacks Indian Rebels Fighting from Its Territory", *AP*, December 6, 2005; "Naga Rebels Brace Up to Face Myanmar Army", *The Indian Express*, October 4, 2006; "NSCN(K) HQ Raided in Myanmar", *The Indian Express*, February 16, 2007.

military junta.[34] These shipments were at first limited primarily to counter-insurgency weaponry but they soon expanded to include a wide range of equipment such as radar produced by India's state-owned Bharat Electronics, 105-mm light artillery guns and airborne surveillance radios.[35] These arms and equipment sales were intended to make the Burmese junta more sympathetic to India's national security interests in the Northeast and to boost the *tatmadaw's* over-all operational capabilities, including that against anti-Burma insur-gent groups. However they — and other planned arms sales that included various types of aircraft — prompted an adverse reaction from the international media, worldwide activist groups and Western chancelleries, making the overall policy value of the sales debatable for India.[36]

Despite India's military assistance to Burma, the counter-insurgency operations launched every winter against Naga and Manipuri rebels by the Burmese armed forces have not fulfilled New Delhi's expecta-tions. Even the Indian defense ministry has regularly admitted the lack of clear progress on the Northeastern front.[37] Only a few concrete results have recently been obtained by India via Burmese counter-insurgency operations against anti-India groups. For example, a few remote training camps of the NSCN-K were destroyed by the *tatmadaw* in 2005, 2006 and 2007, as well as a few other PLA or ULFA home bases.[38] Some drug and arms trafficking routes along

---

[34] In 2002, an Indian official from the Ministry of External Affairs' Burma Desk claimed that India was sending only "non-lethal" military equipment to Burma (telephone interview by author, New Delhi, July 22, 2002).

[35] "India Swaps Arms for Co-operation with Myanmar", *Jane's Defense Weekly*, October 11, 2006.

[36] For details and discussion, see Rahul Bedi, "Indian Transfers More Defenders to Myanmar", *Jane's Defense Weekly*, May 16, 2007; and Amnesty International, *Indian Helicopters for Burma: Making a Mockery of Embargoes*, ASA 20/014/2007, July 16, 2007, report available online at: http://www.amnesty.org/en/library/asset/ASA20/014/2007/en/dom-ASA200142007en.pdf.

[37] For details, see Ministry of Defense (India), *Annual Report 2003–04*, (New Delhi: Government of India, 2004), p. 12.

[38] "NSCN(K) HQ raided in Myanmar", *The Indian Express*, February 16, 2007.

the Indo–Burmese border have also been disrupted, in addition to illegal arms caches and heroin refineries broken up in both Chin and Kachin States of Burma as well as in the Sagaing Division.[39]

Yet, Burmese counter-insurgency operations against anti-India rebel groups have not produced the overall results that were initially expected when the bilateral understandings between India and Burma were forged in 1993.[40] Most of the anti-India rebel groups, such as the Nagas (the NSCN-K and NSCN-IM), the Assamese (ULFA) and the Manipuris (the PLA, the United National Liberation Front-Meghen or UNLF, and the Kanglei Yawol Kanna Lup or KYKL), are still operating from the remote hills of western Burma.[41] Their camps — which consist of small huts in the jungle — are exceptionally mobile and their information networks remain very reliable, thus facilitating their continued resistance. In fact, it is not only the inability or incapacity of the Burmese armed forces to successfully engage the anti-India rebels but also the reluctance of local and military Burmese authorities to allow the armed forces to do so that irks Indian policy-makers.[42] For example, local police forces and Burmese Army officers have established close links with all of the insurgent and criminalized outfits, whether they come from India or Burma. Bribes, rewarded tipoffs, bartering, money laundering, drug dealing and illegal sales of light military equipment are commonplace along the Indo–Burmese border because of the region's flourishing underground economy and the poor living conditions of *Tatmadaw* soldiers and low-ranking Burmese officers.[43]

---

[39] Interview, Embassy of India in Burma, Rangoon, March 10, 2006.

[40] For a closer academic analysis, see Dominic J. Nardi, "Cross-Border Chaos: A Critique of India's Attempts to Secure its Northeast Tribal Areas through Cooperation with Myanmar", *SAIS Review* 28:1 (2008), pp. 161–171.

[41] "Junta Allows Indian Rebels to Set Up Base: GOC Indian Army", *Mizzima News*, October 19, 2009.

[42] Renaud Egreteau, "Militant Mire: Battling Insurgency in Northeast India", *Jane's Intelligence Review* 20:2 (February 2008), pp. 18–23.

[43] Interviews with Burmese activists exiled in Imphal (Manipur), and with Meithei and Naga scholars and students working along the Indo–Burmese border, Manipur University, Imphal, Manipur, India, March 2005.

Indian officials are perfectly aware of this situation and have tried to get a firmer commitment from the Burmese armed forces to assist more actively in counter-insurgency operations against anti-India groups.[44] This constant but gentle pressure on the Burmese junta has been exemplified by the numerous diplomatic visits made by Indian political and military leaders (including the Indian Army Chief in October 2009) since General Than Shwe's trip to India in 2004, in which counter-insurgency was a central point of discussion.[45]

New Delhi has few options at hand in light of Burma's inability or reluctance to effectively confront anti-India rebels operating from its territory. Yet Indian security officials remain reluctant to press Rangoon too aggressively on this issue because they know how ethnic insurgencies in the Northeast could escalate precipitously if the Burmese junta — if not China — decided to actively aid the rebels. As a proof of this potential, Burma had no qualms in January 2002 about releasing 200-odd PLA and UNLF-M activists previously arrested on Burmese soil, much to New Delhi's displeasure.[46] Consequently, India can expect only limited results emanating from Burma's assistance in coordinated counter-insurgency operations. Burma's cooperation has so far been only half-hearted and, in fact, its government may have cleverly used this issue as a bargaining chip with New Delhi, showing India that it can — and will — keep the upper hand in cross-border interactions. While India is not in a position to completely fulfill its objectives regarding coordinated

---

[44] Interviews, Embassy of India, Rangoon, March 21, 2007, and November 9, 2007.

[45] Off the record, many Indian intelligence officers have expressed their frustration at the lack of successful achievements in the area of coordinated counter-insurgency. Personal discussions with various Indian intelligence officers (both active or retired) in Delhi, Rangoon, and Bangkok between 2005 and 2009.

[46] Those released included the UNLF-M leader himself, Rajkumar Meghen. Personal discussion with Subir Bhaumik (BBC correspondent), Guwahati, India, September 11, 2004. Bhaumik recalled an interview he had with the then Indian ambassador to Burma, Vivek Katju, who publicly expressed its disappointment in face of the Burmese volte-face.

counter-insurgency, neither can it disengage with Burma on this issue, with looming perceived threats emanating from China.[47]

Indo–Burmese Trade Still Lagging

India has tried to rapidly expand its commercial ambitions in Burma, knowing full well the potential economic benefits the country has to offer after decades of self-imposed autarky and the underexploitation of its natural resources. Burma is also a potential trade conduit to Southeast Asia and southwestern China, as Yunnanese investors and traders have since the late 1980s established a viable North–South corridor along the Irrawaddy River. Yet, official statements aside, extensive Indo–Burmese trade has been slow to materialize even 15 years after the first steps toward bilateral economic cooperation were undertaken. Both governments had proudly announced during the diplomatic trip to Rangoon by then Indian Vice President A.P.J. Abdul Kalam in November 2003 that bilateral trade would reach $1 billion by 2006, but this was then delayed until late 2008.[48] In 1988, bilateral trade worth $62 billion was recorded. Then, there was a frustrating stagnation in trade ranging between $320 million and $420 million during the period from 1997 to 2005 in spite of the 1994 border trade agreement. More recently, although figures are annually reviewed and differ from Indian and Burmese sources as well as within Indian ministries (External Affairs regularly gives different figures from the Ministry of Commerce), exchanges rose to about $600 million in the 2005–2006 fiscal year[49] and $920 million in

[47] "Eye on China, Army Chief on Myanmar Visit", *The Times of India*, October 10, 2009.

[48] Embassy of India (Yangon), *Joint Statement On the Visit to Myanmar by HE Bhairon Singh Shekhawat, Vice-President of the Republic of India*, Yangon, November 4, 2003.

[49] $636.66 million according to the Indian Department of Commerce (http://commerce.nic.in/eidb/iecnt.asp) and $569 million according to the Rangoon-based Embassy of India in Burma, (http://www.indiaembassy.net.mm/commercial/commercial_relations_1.asp), both accessed on October 20, 2009.

2006–2007.[50] Only in 2007–2008 did it reach about $995.37 million, still falling slightly short of the predicted mark of $1 billion.[51]

Numerous obstacles have prevented bilateral trade from growing as quickly as both countries had originally predicted. For example, New Delhi has insisted since 2001 that responsibility for constructing the Kalewa–Mandalay part of the Tamu–Kalewa–Mandalay road lies with Burma, not India. Lacking the finance and political will to open up to an Indian region which remains very unstable, the Burmese authorities drag it on, still favoring their North–South Chinese economic connection. This issue is emblematic of the lack of viable continental infrastructure since the colonial era that links India to Burma's main trade corridor, which runs southwards from Yunnan Province to Rangoon. Due to these shortages and hesitancies, Indo–Burmese trade cannot be expected to flow beyond the border areas as both countries had originally hoped, much to the despair of local business communities. In October 2008, the initiative taken by the Indian Minister of Commerce and Power, Jairam Ramesh, to extend the list of authorized items of goods to be legally traded between the two countries (from 22 to 40) did not much change the pace of the border trade, with only two to three crucial goods traded in currency only (mostly agriculture products).[52] Moreover, many Indian investors and traders have reconsidered their economic involvement in Burma because of the country's inadequate banking system and its lack of economic stability. Investing in Burma, in short, requires a high dose of motivation for businesspersons unfamiliar with the country, whose society and economy have been under tight military control for decades. Informal trade, corruption, bribes and the absence of a credible legal system to protect commercial agreements have put off many Indians (and others) despite their eagerness to invest in

---

[50] Ibid. $921.87 million according to the Department of Commerce, $926.54 million according to the External Affairs.

[51] Ibid.

[52] Barter system remains highly favored by local traders: "Indo–Myanmar Border Trade Still Remains a Distant Dream", *The Hindustan Times*, July 24, 2009.

Burma.[53] Burmese Indians who left the country in the 1960s and 1970s but still have a few connections there are often helpful to investors wanting to do business in Burma. But such informal networks are grossly insufficient to increase the volume of trade in any significant way, especially without official and institutional channels of transaction.[54] Many Indian businesspersons who settled in Rangoon also prefer to represent more lucrative Singaporean or Malaysian companies, thus enhancing Burma's trade with Southeast Asia at the expense of India — Singapore being Burma's main banking and trade hub after China. In short, Burma's state-controlled economic system, irrespective of so-called liberalization policies initiated by the SLORC in the late 1980s, remains a formidable obstacle to increased business activity there.

As a consequence, commercial relations between India and Burma have been limited for the most part to a few specific sectors. For example, India imports two-thirds of Burma's beans and pulse production, as well as many timber and wood products.[55] On the other side, Burma imports less than $200 million worth of goods from India,[56] starting with pharmaceutical products, a sector which is almost entirely dominated by Indian companies such as Dr Reddy's Laboratories and Ranbaxy.[57] Indian products are sparse in local Burmese markets because they are unable to compete with cheap Chinese and Thai goods. Indian investment in Burma has thus focused more on larger and state-sponsored infrastructure projects such as railways, port facilities, hydropower plants and energy development.

---

[53] Personal discussion with Naresh Kumar Dinodiya, President of the Indians of Myanmar Association, Rangoon, January 25, 2005.
[54] Interview with Mak Patel (consultant for the Indian Ministry of Energy in Rangoon), Rangoon, Burma, March 6, 2006. Mr Patel was born in Burma into a Gujarati family. He fled the country in 1970 but has been an important actor in establishing increased bilateral energy cooperation between India and Burma.
[55] Interview with the Commercial Counsellor, Embassy of India, Rangoon, January 28, 2005.
[56] This inevitably leads to a severe unbalanced bilateral trade in favor of Burma.
[57] Interview with C. Murali, President of the India–Myanmar Business Club, Rangoon, Burma, January 27, 2005.

Yet, even in energy cooperation, India's newly asserted ambitions have seen little success.[58] The Indian thrust into this sector has encountered increasing disappointment since 2005, including harsh negotiations over forming the Indo–Korean–Burmese consortium— led by the South Korean firm Daewoo — to conduct offshore natural gas exploration.[59] In addition, the construction of a pipeline to distribute natural gas from the A-1 and A-3 blocks' reserves sparked fierce debate in India, affecting its relations with both Burma and Bangladesh, while leaving the door open to China and other competitors. In January 2005, New Delhi sought to secure a deal with Burmese authorities on the right to acquire all natural gas extracted from the Arakan fields and bring it back to India. But the burdensome decision-making process in New Delhi, the numerous conditions delineated by Bangladesh to allow the Indian pipeline to cross its territory, the security risks inherent in India's Northeast (the second proposed route for the Indo–Arakenese pipeline), and a much more concrete and advantageous offer forwarded by China in 2006 prompted the Burmese authorities to reconsider the Indian project.[60]

Despite recent negotiations encouraged by then Indian president A.P.J. Abdul Kalam during his official visit to Burma in March 2006 and then Indian Minister of Petroleum and Natural Gas Murli Deora in September 2007 (at the crux of the Burmese monks' demonstrations), India lost the multi-billion dollar deal to China in June 2009.[61] Indeed, after three years of bilateral talks, China National Petroleum Corporation (CNPC) signed with the Burmese authorities (represented by the No. 2 of the SPDC, General Maung Aye) a memorandum of understanding on the construction of the $2 billion pipeline purported to bring crude oil into Yunnan, but above all the natural

---

[58] Marie-Carine Lall, "Indo-Myanmar Relations in the Era of Pipeline Diplomacy", *Contemporary Southeast Asia* 28:3 (December 2006), pp. 424–446.

[59] Interview with a Korean diplomat, Embassy of South Korea, Rangoon, January 27, 2005.

[60] "PetroChina Seeks Myanmar Gas Deal", *Myanmar Times*, January 16–22, 2006.

[61] Sudha Ramachandra, "China Secures Myanmar Energy Route", *Asia Times*, April 3, 2009.

gas extracted by the Ind–Korean Shwe Gas consortium in the Arakan fields.[62] This 1,100 km pipeline (including around 870 km on Burmese soil) would give Beijing — which has constantly maintained a loyal attitude toward the ruling Burmese junta since 1988 — a lion's share of the Arakan offshore gas fields without directly exploiting them.[63] At the same time, the Gas Authority of India Limited (GAIL) secured shares in the A-7 Block in December 2006, but cut short its participation six months later when it realized the financial difficulties about to be faced.[64]

Despite severe setbacks for India, its policymakers and business circles have not dropped their tentative thrust into the Burmese energy market irrespective of the Chinese presence. For instance, ONGC Videsh acquired three other gas assets off the Arakan coast (AD-2, AD-3 and AD-9) in September 2007, and Essar Oil started test drilling in 2009 for the onshore L Block and offshore A-2 Block it has owned since 2005.[65] These latest agreements were sealed during a period of intense global condemnation of the Burmese regime (the "Saffron Revolution" in 2007, the reaction to Cyclone Nargis in 2008), and were believed to earn billions of US dollars yearly through energy deals.[66] This state-driven policy clearly illustrates that India still intends to get an energy toehold in Burma before the Chinese or Western companies get it all.[67]

---

[62] CNPC Press News Release, June 19, 2009, available online at http://www.cnpc.com.cn/en/press/newsreleases.

[63] China crucially vetoed a US-sponsored UN Security Council resolution condemning Burma on its human rights record in January 2007. Many other examples of Chinese support to Naypyidaw in past years can be given, and Burma's decision to grant China a larger portion of its still under-exploited energy market can be interpreted as a reward for Beijing's diplomatic support of Burma on the international stage amidst pressures to democratize.

[64] "GAIL to pull out of Myanmar Block", *The Financial Express* [New Delhi], July 18, 2007.

[65] "ONGC-Videsh Wins 3 Blocks in Myanmar", *Business Line* [New Delhi], September 23, 2007 and "Myanmar Strengthens Co-op with Foreign Countries on Energy", *Xinhua*, July 28, 2009.

[66] Sean Turnell, "Burma Isn't Broke", *Wall Street Journal*, August 6, 2009.

[67] "Myanmar Burning, MEA Told Deora: We Need to Visit But Keep It Low-Key", *Indian Express* [New Delhi], September 27, 2007.

In a nutshell, India has not only failed to get a substantial commercial foothold in Burma a decade after the two countries signed the border trade agreement (after all, a $1 billion annual trade with a direct neighbour is not much, and is even less than the India–Poland bilateral trade in 2009), it also faces continuing difficulties in establishing a clearly defined economic partnership with the Burmese regime. Given the logics of geography and historical legacies, a viable east–west trade corridor aimed at linking India's Northeast region to Thailand and southwest China via Mandalay and Rangoon has yet to materialize. It is uncertain how much further, and at what rate, Indo–Burmese commercial ties will deepen in the future, but the prospects are evidently not as promising as Indian authorities had initially hoped when including Burma in their 1990s Look East policy.

Coping with a Rising China in Burma and the Indian Ocean

Strangely enough, the issue with which India may have gained the most traction with its revised Burma policy is probably in countering the threat of a rising China, at least militarily.[68] Since 1989, India has kept a close eye on China's suspected direct military involvement with the SLORC and the potential threat to India's national security, whether along the Indo–Burmese frontiers or on the Indian Ocean. Rumors from international security and journalistic communities about the construction of a surveillance network ranging from the Burmese islands of Zadetkyi (in the Tenasserim Division) and Man-Aung (off Arakan State), to suspected naval bases at Kyaikkami (south of the city of Moulmein) and Hainggyi Island (Irrawaddy Delta), including Monkey Point (in Rangoon), Great Coco Island off the Andaman Sea, and the ports of Kyaukphyu (on Ramree Island), have always been taken seriously by Indian officials. But it appears that these rumors of China's alleged military involvement in Burma may have been grossly overestimated, if not simply incorrect, in past years.

---

[68] Renaud Egreteau, "India and China Vying for Influence in Burma: A New Assessment", *India Review* 7:1 (2008), pp. 38–72.

In fact, many of these rumors were just that — rumors. Even the Indian embassy in Rangoon admitted the triviality of such conjectures surrounding, for instance, the Coco Islands (definitely the most easily remembered alleged spearhead of the Chinese in Burma), a decade after these suspicions first arose.[69]

Recent analyses by Andrew Selth, who first academically criticized the credibility of Chinese military involvement in the Coco and Hainggyi islands in the mid-1990s, has subsequently debunked this suspicion which however had played a crucial role in defining India's new Burma strategy in the early 1990s.[70] Personal observations made during my own fieldwork in the region also seem to verify the conclusion that concerns about Chinese military involvement with the SLORC in Burma were overestimated, if not simply incorrect, especially regarding the possible existence of huge, modern naval bases and military infrastructure built by China on Burmese territory.[71] Not only were sites named by intelligence or news reports merely fishing harbors (such as Kyaikkami) or tiny naval bases (Monkey Point at the end of Rangoon's Strand Road), but these rumors wrongly dismissed the strong aversion of the Burmese military to see foreign forces or bases operating directly and at will on Burma's own soil. In gradually essaying a more accurate evaluation of the Chinese presence in Burma, the Indian intelligence and military establishments have, in fact, admitted the non-immediacy of the "China threat" there. But still,

[69] Personal discussion with H.E. Rajiv K. Bhatia, Ambassador of India to Burma (2002–2005), Rangoon, Burma, May 10, 2004. Also see "India Says No China Defence Posts on Myanmar Island", *Reuters*, August 24, 2005.

[70] For details on this issue, see William Ashton, "Chinese Naval Base: Many Rumours, Few Facts", *Asia-Pacific Defense Reporter* (June-July 1993), p. 25; William Ashton, "Chinese Bases in Burma: Fact or Fiction?" *Jane's Intelligence Review* 7:2 (February 1995), pp. 84–87; Andrew Selth, *Chinese Military Bases in Burma: The Explosion of a Myth*, Griffith Asia Institute Regional Outlook, Volume 10 (Griffith University, 2007); and Andrew Selth, "Known Knowns and Known Unknowns: Measuring Myanmar's Military Capabilities", *Contemporary Southeast Asia* 31:2 (August 2009), pp. 272–295.

[71] Personal fieldwork in Rangoon, Kyaikkami (Mon State), Sittwe and Kyaukphyu (Arakan State) (October 2005 and March 2007).

the trauma remains and they have not ruled out the possibility that China will edge closer to India's borders on other fronts, such as Tibet or the Indian Ocean.

The realization that Chinese military involvement was not as extensive as originally feared subsequently increased India's level of comfort and trust with the Burmese military regime. High-ranking bilateral visits by military officials from 1999 onward contributed to a better understanding between the Indian and Burmese armed forces, especially between both navies. For the Indian Navy, three main goals were pursued in getting closer to its Burmese counterpart: gaining rights to berth and refuel in Burmese ports, conducting joint naval operations, and acquiring intelligence on the Chinese presence in Burma. For the Burmese Navy, drawing closer to the Indian Navy was also a desirable goal because India's fleet clearly dominates the Bay of Bengal and appears willing to train Burmese naval officers. In December 2002, an Indian Navy flotilla was allowed to berth for the first time in Thilawa, the port built by Singaporean and Chinese companies near Rangoon.[72] In May 2003, two vessels of the Indian Coast Guard followed suit and later that year the first Indo–Burmese joint naval exercises were conducted in the Andaman Sea.[73] Indo–Burmese naval cooperation continued when two Indian warships made a port call at Rangoon's harbor in May 2004 and two other rounds of joint exercises were held in December 2005 and January 2006.[74]

Thus, Indo–Burmese naval cooperation is apparently developing at a significantly faster pace than Sino–Burmese maritime and intelligence collaboration. Moreover, India enjoys one of the most

---

[72] "Indian Fleet Calling Myanmar Port", *Xinhua*, December 21, 2002. Incidentally, the Chinese Navy has never berthed there, in spite of China having played a key role in building the harbor facilities near Rangoon.

[73] For details, see Ministry of Defense (India), *Annual Report 2003–04*, (New Delhi: MOD Publications, 2004), p. 69; and Renaud Egreteau, "India Courts a Junta", *Asia Times*, September 20, 2003.

[74] For a discussion, see Ministry of Defense (India), *Annual Report 2004–05*, (New Delhi: MOD Publications, 2005), p. 47; and "Fleet Expansion in Mind, Myanmar Looks to India for Expertise", *Indian Express* [New Delhi], January 13, 2006.

advanced and well-equipped naval bases in the region in the Far
Eastern Naval Command based at Port Blair in the Andaman Islands,
a few nautical miles from Burma's Coco Islands.[75] Indian security
analysts have surmised, and gotten assurances from the Burmese
authorities that the military equipment Burma received from China
during the 1990s is insufficient to pose a serious threat to India's
security. Furthermore, when the Burmese Army gradually opted for
a diversification of its global arms supplies to balance its dependency
on China, it approached India in a very logical way in addition to
Russia, Ukraine, Pakistan, Singapore and Yugoslavia. Indian military
academies are now welcoming Burmese officers and the Indian Air
Force has set up a bilateral program to train Burmese pilots.[76] In all,
it appears that India has gained more certitude in dealing with the
"China factor" in Burma than in its other stated goals such as
improving counter-insurgency in the Northeast and drastically
improving commercial relations.

Geopolitical Obstacles to Furthering India's Interests in Burma

Nevertheless, New Delhi's policy shift toward the junta has not produced the desired economic and strategic foothold in Burma. India
faces many geopolitical obstacles that hinder further enhancement of
its strategic and economic interests in Burma in the mid-term.
Unless the obstacles are overcome or somehow transformed, India's
ability to further advance its interest in Burma will remain a daunting
challenge.

First, China's political and economic influence in Burma remains
a considerable obstacle for India. China is rightly perceived as the
Burmese junta's closest ally, although the partnership has known its
ups and downs since 1988. China's economic weight and political
influence in Burma has grown markedly over the past two decades,

---

[75] David Scott, "India's 'Grand Strategy' for the Indian Ocean: Mahanian Visions",
Asia Pacific Review 13:2 (November 2006), pp. 97–129.
[76] "India to Firm Up Military Ties with Myanmar", *The Hindu*, June 24, 2007.

but its influence is not absolute or all-encompassing.[77] For example, the turmoil sparked by the street protests in Burma in September 2007 demonstrated China's potential influence with the ruling military junta in comparison to other countries, but it also showed the limits of China's leverage. The Burmese authorities' violent crackdown on protestors provoked widespread and vocal condemnation worldwide, and the international community logically turned to China for assistance in trying to convince the junta to avoid further bloodshed. Beijing played a key role during the crisis, tempering international calls for further condemnation of the junta or even immediate institutionalization of democracy in the country, while pressuring the Burmese regime to take a less confrontational approach.[78] India, in contrast, was never asked to play this type of crucial diplomatic role in relation to Burma.[79] The same situation prevailed after the passage of Cyclone Nargis (May 2008) and after the international outcry caused by Aung San Suu Kyi's trial orchestrated by the regime (May–August 2009). Nonetheless, even if China has been extremely frustrated with the lack of progress in the internal Burmese political situation as well as the Sino–Burmese border volatilities throughout 2009,[80] its high degree of political and economic influence in Burma continues to present a strong obstacle for India to more effectively push for its own economic and strategic goals there.

Second, India cannot offer on the international scene the economic weight and diplomatic leverage the Burmese regime expects from a friendly global power. China and Russia both enjoy crucial veto power in the United Nations Security Council, whereas India is not in a position to fully support any resolution condemning the Burmese government at the New York assembly. Enduring tensions

---

[77] For an analysis, see Tin Maung Maung Than, "Myanmar and China: A Special Relationship?" *Southeast Asian Affairs* (2003), pp. 189–210.
[78] Interview, Chinese Embassy in Burma, Rangoon, February 26, 2008.
[79] Interviews with various foreign diplomats based in Rangoon, Burma, November 2007 and February 2008.
[80] Larry Jagan, "Beijing and Burma No Longer Best Friends", *Asia Times*, October 4, 2009.

within the China–India dyad also deter Burma from getting too involved in contentious Sino–Indian issues. Neither U Nu (1948–1958 and 1960–1962), nor General Ne Win (1962–1988) ever took position in the China–India border dispute or the Tibetan issue (or even during the 1962 India–China war), and the current Burmese military leadership appears to follow that policy precedent, trying to avoid embarking on a global Sino–Indian rivalry beyond Burma.

Third, the political use of xenophobia and nationalism has been an effective tool for successive Burmese military regimes, including the current one, in defining external threats to the country's sense of national sovereignty and security.[81] Both India and China have had to confront expressions of this anti-foreigner sentiment, despite cordial high-level partnerships between them and Burma's rulers. There is little doubt that lingering "Sinophobia" and "Indophobia" in contemporary Burma still constitutes a strong sociocultural constraint on deepening relations between these two countries and Burma, one that Indian policymakers have not fully taken into account. More specifically, anti-Indian sentiments, born out of the colonial period when Indian minorities were perceived as second-rank colonizers and economic exploiters, continue to be a powerful hedge impeding India's ambitious economic or strategic push into Burma. Most of Burma's economy was rapidly "Burmanized" after independence in 1948, first with nationalistic laws, and then with the expulsion of foreign business communities in the 1960s, illustrating the strong resentment of the Burmese psyche against a wide Chinese or Indian domination like that built up during the colonial era. The same configuration could still prevail today and for this reason, Indian officials in Burma have been consciously trying to shape a better image of their country and people (still called "*kalas*" by the Burmese) since the early 1990s.[82]

---

[81] For an analytic discussion, see Mya Maung, "The Burma Road to the Past", *Asian Survey* 39:2 (March–April 1999), pp. 265–286; and Mikael Gravers, *Nationalism as Political Paranoia in Burma: An Essay on the Historical Practice of Power* (Richmond, Curzon, 1999).

[82] Interview with the Consul General of India, Mandalay, Burma, March 6, 2007.

Nonetheless, India continues to be perceived in a questionable, if not negative, light within Burma's dominant political culture, notwithstanding the cultural events, Bollywood movies, educational exchange programs and Buddhist pilgrimages New Delhi has promoted there.[83] Distrust and suspicion of India's long-term ambitions in the region also remain entrenched within the Burmese intellectual elite, including various exiled pro-democracy communities. Many pro-democracy Burmese activists, in fact, cannot come to terms with New Delhi's new "velvet policy" toward the ruling junta.[84] The image of a greedy (yet democratic) India wooing the Burmese military junta for its own national interests has angered many exiled pro-democracy activists who are upset about India's apparent neglect of the Burmese democratic struggle.[85] India faces both overt xenophobia and more subtle perceptions of opportunism throughout multiple layers of Burmese society.

Fourth, the geographical configuration of the still-unsecured border poses another powerful obstacle to India's economic and strategic ambitions in Burma. Historically, Burma has always been organized along its north–south corridor following the Irrawaddy fluvial plain. In spite of the existence of trade routes dating back to the ancient Silk Road and traditional migration routes, crossing the country from east to west is much more challenging because of the rugged hills and mountains — mostly ethnic-dominated — that encircle the heart of "Burman Burma" and separate it from the Brahmaputra Valley of India. The continuing political instability in India's Northeast also hinders the possibility of Indian policymakers using the area as an immediate gateway to Burma and the rest of Southeast Asia. As long as the political turmoil lingers in the Northeast, New Delhi cannot expect to use its

---

[83] After the passage of Cyclone Nargis, India gave a $200,000 donation to restore Rangoon's prestigious Shwedagon pagoda; see *New Light of Myanmar*, June 25, 2008, p. 7.

[84] Discussion with Dr Tint Swe, Minister of the Burmese government in exile, New Delhi, India, October 16, 2009.

[85] This is the outcome of many personal interactions with leaders of the Burmese exile community living in India or in Thailand, conducted between 2002 and 2009.

eastern frontier to benefit from any economic opening up with Burma without significant security concerns and challenges. This, despite strong debates in Northeastern intellectual and security circles.[86]

Finally, internal divisions within Indian society, whether about the role of the Northeast within the global India–Burma dyad or India's desired and appropriate relationship with a military-ruled Burma, continue to impede a more aggressive and effective foreign policy for New Delhi. The issue of democracy remains sensitive in India, where many intellectual, activist and political circles keep slamming India's "soft engagement" of the Burmese military regime. These critics remain, however, entrenched pressure groups, with few members of parliament, far-left political parties, engaged academics or lawyers trying to influence the formulation of India's policy options, and their concrete leverage appears more and more marginal today, despite a fair media publicity.[87]

Conclusion

More than a decade and half of strategic engagement with and courting of the Burmese military junta in Rangoon has not succeeded in fulfilling India's foreign policy objectives in the region. In particular, India's ambitions in Burma have been frustrated by New Delhi's inability to coordinate effective counter-insurgency in the Northeast and its inability to increase bilateral trade, which lags far behind Sino–Burmese and Thai–Burmese economic cooperation. In contrast, India's primary satisfaction gained from its new Burma policy has been effectively "managing" the perceived military threat posed by a "rising China" in Burma. In wider geopolitical terms, India's setbacks in Burma may actually have helped stymie an open and threatening strategic rivalry between India and China — a potential "Great Game" — from taking shape in the region. After all, it takes two to

---

[86] Sanjib Baruah, *Postfrontier Blues: Toward a New Policy Framework for Northeast India* (Washington: East-West Center, 2007).
[87] Various interviews with pro-democracy Indian and Burmese activists, New Delhi, October 16, 2009.

tango, and Beijing and New Delhi do not compete in the same economic sectors (except the energy market), or for the same goals and objectives, in Burma. This makes direct and threatening encounters between them less probable. Thus, the triangular relationship among India, Burma and China is better understood in terms of respective spheres of influence rather than direct confrontation.

New Delhi's exceptionally cautious and reactive approach toward Burma's military junta is largely predicated on the fear of losing what little was gained through its new "velvet policy" since 1993. But to be in a better strategic position, India needs to decide, once and for all, the place and role that India's Northeast should have in its relations with its neighbor. Given the strategic importance of its northeastern frontiers bordering Tibet and Burma, India needs to decide whether they should be a gateway to both Southeast Asia and China — or merely a barrier. As long as India does not devise a clear strategy to open up its eastern frontier to its neighbors, Burma will be conceptualized as a maritime, instead of continental, gateway for India to Southeast Asia.

Also, India must invest in broader and more strategic infrastructure programs in Burma, rather than in localized and offshore ones. India could increase its economic opportunities by building extensive road networks, port facilities and railways, not only near its borders but also elsewhere in the country as China has done since 1988. To bolster their influence, New Delhi's policymakers must work harder to establish closer cultural and personal relationships with Burmese business communities of all ethnicities throughout the country, instead of relying primarily on Burmese Indians to re-establish economic and strategic footholds. Burmese of Indian origin — whether living in the country or exiled to India since the 1960s — are an important but largely informal and unreliable bridgehead from which Indian policymakers hope to develop closer commercial relations. Finally, Indian authorities can work, albeit cautiously and behind the scenes, to help secure the release of pro-democracy leader Aung San Suu Kyi from house arrest if they want to benefit from her support in the long run. Aung San Suu Kyi is known for her pro-Indian inclinations, having lived and studied in New Delhi and Shimla between

1960 and 1964 and then from 1986 to 1987. She has, in fact, kept an extensive network of friends in India, but these connections are ineffectual as long as she remains under house arrest in Rangoon without the ability to communicate with the outside world.

Indian diplomats can eventually restore a better image of India in Burma, even in dissident circles, by becoming more involved in regional and humanitarian matters. For example, the depoliticized humanitarian assistance offered by India in the aftermath of Cyclone Nargis in May 2008 helped improve India's image both in the Burmese ruling establishment and across the society.[88] The $200,000 donation to repair the Shwedagon pagoda in June 2008 also had a good local impact, though it was not well publicized. But in further-ing and consolidating more openly the rising Burmese civil society, which could benefit from the experience of India's own vibrant and dynamic civil society and educational system, India might be in a posi-tion to broaden its influence in a country which needs much basic assistance. In conclusion, India might lose an important opportunity to have effective, long-term strategic and economic leverage in the region if it does not adopt a stronger and clearly defined proactive policy toward Burma. Up to now, India has seen more frustration than satisfaction in its new approach to the Burmese military junta. New Delhi will need to change these results if it aims to gain a reputation as a global, responsible and proactive power.

---

[88] For details, see "India Sends Relief Ships to Cylone-Hit Myanmar", *Times of India*, May 6, 2008.

Chapter 12

Burma and ASEAN: A Marriage of Inconvenience

Stephen McCarthy

Abstract

Though Burma joined ASEAN with high hopes in 1997, the union has been a mutually disappointing one. Burma has not enjoyed the influx of FDI and general economic windfall it expected from joining, and ASEAN has been repeatedly embarrassed by SPDC human rights abuses. Yet there have also been benefits: the junta was inspired to release Aung San Suu Kyi (at least for a while) and to set forth the 7-step "roadmap" to constitutional government, while ASEAN became a more comprehensive regional organization and has augmented its diplomatic toolkit to deal with intransigently dissident members. How this uneasy relationship fares amid the 2010 elections remains to be seen.

Keywords: Constructive engagement; Treaty of Amity and Cooperation (TAC); Khin Nyunt; road map; national convention.

Introduction

In July 2005, Burma forfeited its turn to chair the Association of Southeast Asian Nations (ASEAN) in 2006, eight years after having joined the regional organization. The move came after intense Western pressure on ASEAN following events inside Burma in 2003 (e.g., the Depayin Incident), and a general failure on Burma's part to "keep its house in order" — as was promised by its leaders upon joining in 1997. Yet, the move was also reflective of a change in ASEAN's attitude toward the handling of domestic problems among its member states. Traditionally, ASEAN has adopted a posture of non-interference in the domestic politics of its member states and indeed this attribute was very attractive to Burma in 1997 as it sought regional alliances and legitimacy to counter the isolation imposed by the West. But as the ASEAN chairmanship rotated toward countries with more democratic agendas, or that could be more influenced by Western ones, Burma's membership in the organization has at times become uncomfortable for its generals and embarrassing for ASEAN.

Since its independence in 1948, Burma has adopted a neutralist stance in foreign relations, while at the same time attempting to balance competing interests of major powers in this strategically important region. The latter objective has required that it occasionally align itself toward one power in order to survive as an ostensibly independent nation. Indeed, it has been argued that Burma's foreign relations have been conditioned by a sense of survival since independence and that an officially non-aligned status has required a series of pragmatic short-term collaborations in order to achieve that survival.[1] It has also been argued that because of the country's size and underdeveloped status, Burma's foreign policy has naturally tended to be more reactive than proactive.[2] It is only relatively recently that Burma could be understood as being more proactive and directional in its foreign policies. Even here, regional interest in courting the Burmese leaders has grown because neighboring states view the generals' alliance with the People's Republic of China (PRC) as being possibly destabilizing. Because of its size and proximity, China has always figured highly in Burma's sphere of foreign relations — either as a potentially powerful enemy or as a strong ally, and more often than not Burma has had to consider China's possible reactions to its foreign policies.

---

[1] See Chi-shad Liang, *Burma's Foreign Relations: Neutralism in Theory and Practice* (New York: Praeger, 1990).

[2] Narayanan Ganesan, "Myanmar's Foreign Relations: Reaching out to the World", in *Myanmar: Beyond Politics to Societal Imperatives*, eds. Kyaw Yin Hlaing, Robert H. Taylor, and Tin Maung Maung Than (Singapore: Institute of Southeast Asian Studies, 2005), p. 30.

Burma joined ASEAN in 1997 after strengthening its relations with China. This has flavored not only the dynamics of the ASEAN–Burma relationship but also the relations that ASEAN has had with the West over Burma. This chapter looks at these various relations and the events leading to Burma's forfeiture of its ASEAN chairmanship in 2005, as well as developments in relations since then. It could be argued that in reference to its traditional foreign policy of neutrality and non-alignment, Burma's membership in ASEAN stands as an anomaly and that the uncomfortable position created, particularly from 2003 onward, has made the Burmese generals reconsider their regional friendships. Rather than viewing the country as a member of an inevitably globalized and increasingly democratized world, it is possible to consider that survival for the generals, given the nature of their regime, requires that they return to what could be their natural foreign relations position — neutrality coupled with pragmatic affiliations. Understanding Burma's foreign policy since independence may help in diagnosing the future of Burma's relations with ASEAN and the West.

Burma's Foreign Policy

Since independence, Burma has been ruled by a parliamentary democracy (1948–58 and 1960–62); by constitutional military rule (1974–88); and by direct military rule (1958–60, 1962–74, 1988 to the present). During the Cold War, particularly, Burma's foreign policy necessitated remaining neutral and non-aligned while strategically balancing the interests of major powers in the region. Survival required a counterbalancing foreign policy that was fashioned primarily by external events. The end of the Cold War brought increasing Western attention to developing countries riding the so-called wave of democratization.[3] In light of this heightened awareness, Western interest in Burma peaked following the junta's crackdown on pro-democracy demonstrators in 1988, and again following the State

---

[3] Samuel Huntington, *The Third Wave: Democratization in the Late Twentieth Century* (Norman: University of Oklahoma Press, 1991).

Law and Order Restoration Council's (SLORC) refusal to honor the elections of 1990 won by the National League for Democracy (NLD). Burma's turning toward China and then ASEAN in the late 1980s and 1990s was in large part brought about by the actions of the West in the post-Cold War climate. In order to assess whether Burma's membership in ASEAN was consistent with its traditional foreign policy objectives, and how China has figured highly in its foreign policy, it is necessary to consider the "neutralist" position adopted by Burma from 1948 to the 1990s. And since Burma's relations with China encouraged ASEAN's admission of Burma, we should also consider how Burmese–Sino relations have fluctuated over the years.

"Neutrality"

Because many of Burma's dealings with foreign countries from 1948 to 1961 were beyond its control, it could be argued that its most important external relations were not of its own making.[4] In 1949, for example, any hope that Burma may have held to forge alliances with the West was suppressed when the Chinese Communist Party (CCP) came to power. Burma quickly adopted a neutralist stance whereby it would pursue good relations with all countries and steer clear of aligning itself with power blocs. Prime Minister U Nu, furthermore, believed that aid should be accepted from all countries so long as the conditions were just and equitable and did not restrict or affect Burma's sovereignty. U Nu set about forging good relations with communist and non-communist countries alike, regularly making extensive tours in the process and participating in local and regional conferences, including the 1955 Asian–African Conference in Bandung, Indonesia, and the 1961 First Nonaligned Conference in Belgrade, Yugoslavia. Burma accepted aid from the US and Great Britain, as well as war reparations from Japan, and it engaged the Soviet Union and China through a series of barter trade agreements.

---

[4] Ganesan, "Myanmar's Foreign Relations", p. 32.

Following Ne Win's military coup in 1962, Burma embarked upon an autarkic economic program under the banner of the Burmese Way to Socialism. While all important sectors of the economy were nationalized, foreign relations with most countries were severely limited and those with the communist giants became particularly delicate following the Sino–Soviet split in 1960. Over the next decade, Ne Win sought to remain non-aligned by balancing the competing interests of the major regional powers — the Soviet Union, the US and the PRC. Burma accepted arms from both the Soviet Union and the US, students were sent to the Soviet Union for training and Soviet technicians were sent to Rangoon. Although Ne Win visited Moscow, Washington and Beijing, the latter would remain Burma's priority and for as long as Burma remained on good terms with China, Ne Win would remain careful in his arrangements with the Soviet Union and the US. Burma refused to be drawn into any new regional associations like the Asian Development Bank (ADB) in 1966 or the anti-communist ASEAN in 1967, and only supported a minimal presence in the movement of non-aligned nations.

After 1972, however, the warming of US–China relations, the failure of Burmese socialism and a possible cessation of hostilities in Vietnam persuaded Ne Win to soften Burma's isolationist posture toward the West and its regional neighbors. While continuing to offset relations between the Soviet Union and the PRC, Burma joined the ADB in 1973 and Ne Win embarked on a series of regional goodwill visits. The need for Burma to maintain some balance between the Soviet Union and the PRC was relaxed by Vietnam's invasion of Cambodia in 1978. Burma endorsed China's and ASEAN's opposition to the Soviet–Vietnam backed regime in Phnom Penh, and it resumed economic ties with the US in 1980. The effective withdrawal of a regional Soviet presence in the late 1980s meant that Burma could progress in two directions — toward China or the West. But following the West's reaction to the events of 1988 and 1990 in Rangoon, Burma was faced with few alternatives but to move closer to its most important neighbor — China.

Fostering Good Relations with China

Because of its geographical proximity, size and potential threat, China has always loomed large on Burma's "survival" horizon. Although the Burmese leadership has traditionally favored an official foreign policy stance of neutrality while balancing its position vis-à-vis the major powers, in practice, maintaining good relations with China has been its most important consideration. Under U Nu, Burma became the first non-communist country to recognize the PRC and regularly petitioned for the PRC's membership in the United Nations. Throughout the Cold War, Burma moved cautiously in its dealings with the Soviets and the US, being careful not to unnecessarily provoke China. Relations between Burma and China soured when the Cultural Revolution reached Rangoon in 1967; for example, arms shipments arrived from the Soviet Union and the US. Still, Burma chose to end US military assistance when its relations with China improved four years later.

Despite the fallout in 1967, Burma chose not to intimidate China further by joining ASEAN because the association had not recognized the PRC government. Relations between Burma and China significantly improved after 1979 when China promised to cut funding and stop shipping arms to the Communist Party of Burma (CPB) in return for Burma's cooperation against the Soviet Union. Burma opposed Vietnam's invasion of Cambodia, refused to recognize the new Phnom Penh government and boycotted the Moscow Olympics to register its opposition to the Soviet invasion of Afghanistan. Because ASEAN had also decided to oppose Vietnam's invasion of China's client state, for the first time Burma had no need to fear China's disapproval over having contact with the regional organization. Yet, while Burma had maintained good relations and trade with some ASEAN member states, it preferred not to seek membership and continued to balance the competing interests of the major powers. At least in theory, Burma remained a non-aligned socialist state.

The relationship between the PRC, Burma and ASEAN has undergone significant change since the end of the Cold War. Events leading to the collapse of the Soviet Union drew Burma and China ever closer together. The worldwide democracy movement of the mid to late 1980s burst onto Rangoon's streets in a series of protests culminating in 1988. Spurred as much by the failure of Burmese Socialist Program Party (BSPP) policies, plus financial mismanagement and economic collapse, pro-democracy demonstrators (students, monks, elements of the armed forces and the general public) took to the streets in search of political and economic change. Ne Win used the *Tatmadaw* (armed forces) to brutally crush the demonstrators and, to quell the possibility of reprisal, offered to stage free and fair elections for the first time in over 30 years. Across the border, China would deal with its own pro-democracy demonstrations in Tiananmen Square the following year. The elections won by the NLD in 1990 did not produce a transfer of power; instead, the military junta then ruling under the banner of SLORC declared the result to be merely a sign that a new constitution should be drafted and that a referendum would be held on it. Both Burma and China now faced intense criticism from the West including, in Burma's case, sanctions and a withdrawal of international aid funding.

In light of these circumstances, military, economic and diplomatic ties between Burma and the PRC blossomed in the 1990s, when cooperation in many areas began.[5] China became the *Tatmadaw's* primary supplier of military hardware — including training in the use of such hardware — and Burmese markets were flooded with Chinese products. China now saw India as a rival influence in Southeast Asia and did not want Burma to enter into a security agreement with New Delhi. It viewed closer relations with Burma as a means of gaining road and rail access to the Bay of Bengal, the Indian Ocean and the Strait of Malacca for shipping its products from the interior, and to encourage foreign investment. Burma was also seen as a source of raw materials, a market for Chinese goods from Yunnan Province and a means to gain access to a wider market in Southeast Asia. China assisted Burma in the development of ports, airfields, roads and civil infrastructure but it is doubtful that Burma also presented China with

---

[5] Donald Seekins, "Burma–China Relations: Playing with Fire", *Asian Survey* 37:6 (1997), pp. 525–40.

Stephen McCarthy

an opportunity to develop a naval presence in the Indian Ocean or intelligence gathering facilities on its western coast (see Egreteau's chapter).[6]

Burma's interest in having good relations with China was fostered not only to ensure the PRC would refrain from supporting insurgents inside Burma, but also by the prospects of increasing trade and securing an alternative to the Western markets now threatened by sanctions. Since the early 1990s, however, some have argued that Burma has become something of a Chinese client state (see Min Zin, Chapter 10).[7] Although China has indicated that it would not allow other countries to threaten Burma, Beijing's desire to stay clear of regional multilateralism and its long suspicion of ASEAN softened with its growing recognition that ASEAN was not dominated by the US.[8] Relations between China and ASEAN have improved markedly over the past decade, and today China sees itself as providing a regional counterbalance to the economic influence of the US, Japan and India.[9]

Burma Joins ASEAN

Burma's political and economic situation in the early 1990s made a partnership with ASEAN seem an attractive proposition. Facing diplomatic isolation and punitive sanctions from Western countries, Burma saw the advantages of ASEAN members having access to international funding (particularly the World Bank); a common voice

---

[6] See Andrew Selth, "Burma, China, and the Myth of Military Bases", *Asian Security* 3:3 (2007), pp. 279–307; Jurgen Haacke, *Myanmar's Foreign Policy: Domestic Influences and International Implications*, Adelphi Paper 381 (London: International Institute for Strategic Studies, 2006), pp. 26–28.

[7] Denny Roy, "Southeast Asia and China: Balancing or Bandwagoning?" *Contemporary Southeast Asia* 27:2 (2005), pp. 318–19.

[8] Alice Ba, "China and ASEAN: Renavigating Relations for a 21st Century Asia", *Asian Survey* 43:4 (2003), pp. 622–47.

[9] Michael Vatikiotis, "Catching the Dragon's Tail: China and Southeast Asia in the 21st Century", *Contemporary Southeast Asia* 25:1 (2003), pp. 65–78; Joseph Cheng, "Sino-ASEAN Relations in the Early 21st Century", ibid., 23:3 (2001), pp. 420–51.

in the UN; and a common posture on major policy issues and in negotiations with major powers — especially the US, the EU, India and Japan. Whereas local resentment in Mandalay toward the influx of Chinese traders may have also prompted the junta's desire to find alternative markets, Burma's neighbors in ASEAN as well as India were becoming acutely aware of a potentially destabilizing situation brought about by China's increasing military and economic presence in and its influence over Burma.[10]

In contrast to the Western approach, ASEAN justified its dealings with Burma through the principle of "constructive engagement" — introduced by Thailand's foreign minister, Arsa Sarasin, in 1991 as an Asian alternative to the "comprehensive engagement" concept coined by the Australian foreign minister, Gareth Evans, in the mid-1980s. By promoting trade, diplomatic and economic ties with an authoritarian regime, socioeconomic progress and the growth of a middle class would produce political liberalization. Yet, the middle class in Burma comprised military officers and Chinese businesspersons, all of whom stood to gain from maintaining the status quo. Despite the official line, most of the founding ASEAN member states also had their own reasons for engaging with Burma. Indonesia and Malaysia, for example, had strongly criticized the SLORC's forced repatriation of up to 200,000 Rohingya Muslims into neighboring Bangladesh. By engaging with Burma as per the ASEAN way, they could expect to exert greater influence over the generals than by criticizing them from a distance. Thailand, which was also dealing with a disputed border and a Burmese refugee influx, saw Burma's natural gas supplies as a potential solution to its looming energy crisis. Both Singapore and Thailand were attracted by the SLORC's new foreign investment law and began to invest heavily. All were aware of Burma's abundant natural resources — timber, gems and fish — and sources of cheap labor. Under the new SLORC regime, Burma was experimenting with a program of economic liberalization and was eager to accept foreign currency. This would bring it closer to ASEAN's ideals; the

---

[10] See J. Mohan Malik, "Myanmar's Role in Regional Security: Pawn or Pivot?" ibid., 19:1 (1997), pp. 57–60.

association's principle of non-interference in the domestic politics of member states seemed an attractive creed to the junta.

Burma attended the 1994 ASEAN meeting at the invitation of Thailand, where Rangoon declared that it would sign the Treaty of Amity and Cooperation (TAC). After releasing Aung San Suu Kyi in 1995, Burma was received as an official observer to the ASEAN meeting and joined the ASEAN Regional Forum (ARF) in 1996. In July 1997, facing intense pressure from the US to resist the granting of full membership, ASEAN finally admitted Burma on the recommendation of Prime Minister Mahathir Mohamad of Malaysia. The generals believed that in joining ASEAN they had achieved some form of political legitimacy, and they promised the organization to keep their house in order. The first step would be to change their name from the SLORC to the State Peace and Development Council (SPDC).

Burma's admission to ASEAN prompted a regional debate over how the organization could maintain its principle of non-interference when the domestic policies of one member state had cross-border implications. Of particular concern was the flow of refugees, illegal immigrants and drugs: opium production had soared under SLORC/SPDC rule. Reliable figures on the spread of HIV/AIDS were impossible to obtain. These concerns led Malaysia's then deputy Prime Minister, Anwar Ibrahim, to talk of "constructive intervention" in Burma. Relations between Burma and Thailand soured the following year after a series of incursions by the Burmese army and the Rangoon-backed Democratic Karen Buddhist Army (DKBA). In pursuit of the Karen National Union (KNU), the DKBA raided Burmese–Karen refugee camps on Thai soil. Thailand's Foreign Minister Surin Pitsuwan called on ASEAN to adopt a policy of "flexible engagement", which would allow member states to discuss and comment on the domestic policies of fellow members when they had cross-border implications.[11] The move was supported by the Philippines but rejected by Indonesia, Malaysia and Singapore because its meaning

---

[11] See Jurgen Haacke, "'Enhanced Interaction' with Myanmar and the Project of a Security Community: Is ASEAN Refining or Breaking with Its Diplomatic and Security Culture?" ibid., 27:2 (2005), pp. 188–216.

remained ambiguous and problematic. Of particular concern was that the move invited the possibility of ASEAN intervention in the domestic politics of any member state.

The ASEAN members were, however, more agreeable to the idea of "enhanced interaction", which meant that individual member states could comment on the domestic policies of other members but that ASEAN itself should not.[12] This new proposal did not in fact unleash a wave of criticism by member states against each other. But the concept would allow a number of initiatives to be undertaken in the wake of the financial crisis, including the exchange of economic information and the airing of mutual financial and macroeconomic concerns. Still, it remained unclear what "enhanced interaction" meant for member states like Burma — if intervention by ASEAN was not to become legitimate, their criticism could remain meaningless.

Estranged Bedfellows

In October 2001, the SPDC's then Secretary 1, Lieutenant-General Khin Nyunt, entered into secret talks with Aung San Suu Kyi that were brokered by the UN special envoy for Burma, Malaysian national Razali Ismail. While the content of the talks remained secret, they amounted to little beyond confidence building, although Suu Kyi was released from her second period of house arrest in May 2002. Yet only a year later, an incident occurred that would not only embarrass ASEAN but also test the boundaries of its "enhanced interaction" strategy.

The Depayin Incident

On May 30, 2003, a large number of pro-military Union Solidarity and Development Association (USDA) members ambushed Aung San Suu Kyi and her motorcade in Depayin, northwest of Mandalay,

---

[12] Ibid., pp. 189–90.

while they were returning from visiting her supporters in Kachin State. Numerous deaths occurred, and Suu Kyi was again arrested along with her entourage. On what charge? All NLD offices were closed and up to 200 members were arrested as well as at least 300 supporters across Burma. The arrests followed Suu Kyi's criticism of the SPDC for refusing to start serious talks. The SPDC's failure to release Suu Kyi attracted worldwide criticism — including that from the UN, Japan, the US and the EU. Britain persuaded the EU to toughen sanctions against Burma, issuing a travel ban on Burma's leaders and their families, freezing the assets of some 150 senior government officials and tightening the arms embargo. Japan again froze its financial aid to Burma and the US. Congress passed the Burmese Freedom and Democracy Act, banning specified Burmese imports, freezing the country's meagre financial assets held in US banks, and placing further visa restrictions on Burmese officials attempting to enter the US.

All of this activity placed ASEAN in an awkward position with respect to its principle of non-interference. While it may have been possible to argue that a member state's domestic policies had no direct cross-border implications for other member states, because of the heightened international indignation in this case, the SPDC's actions were an unnecessary embarrassment that impinged upon ASEAN's credibility as an organization. At their annual meeting of foreign ministers held in Phnom Penh in June, ASEAN issued an unprecedented joint statement calling for Suu Kyi's release.[13] This was the first time since Vietnam's occupation of Cambodia that the organization had taken a collective stand against one of its regional neighbors and, indeed, was more significant because Burma was now a full member. If "enhanced interaction" meant that ASEAN could begin to criticize its members' domestic policies, then what would be the incentive for Burma to remain a member and, perhaps just as important, why stop at Burma?

---

[13] ASEAN, *Joint Communique of the 36th ASEAN Ministerial Meeting*, Phnom Penh, June 16–17, 2003, Clause 18, available online at http://www.aseansec.org/14833.htm.

SPDC Chairman and Senior General Than Shwe responded by dispatching his foreign minister and deputy foreign minister to Thailand, Japan, Malaysia, Indonesia, Singapore, China, Bangladesh, Pakistan and India with a personal letter asserting that Suu Kyi and the NLD had been plotting an uprising and encouraging armed ethnic rebel groups to take part.[14] Mahathir Mohamad claimed that ASEAN nations had been forced to criticize Burma because its leadership had embarrassed its neighbors and added that if Suu Kyi was not released, as a last resort Burma could be expelled from ASEAN.[15] Thailand's then Prime Minister Thaksin Shinawatra rejected Mahathir's threat and urged ASEAN to give Burma's leaders more time to demonstrate their sincerity in returning to national reconciliation and the development of a democratic system.[16] Thailand would soon show what it meant by "enhanced interaction" with Burma.

Road Maps

At the Asia–Europe Meeting (ASEM) of foreign ministers in July, deflecting European criticism of the situation in Burma, Thailand's then foreign minister, Surakiart Sathirathai, proposed the idea of a road map designed to bring national reconciliation and democratic reform to Burma within three years — the country was due to chair ASEAN in 2006. The foreign minister then met with his Burmese counterpart, U Win Aung, and told him that his government must come up with its own road map. The Thai road map consisted of five steps[17]:

1. Release Aung San Suu Kyi from prison; free other opposition leaders from house arrest; reopen NLD headquarters and offices.
2. "Confidence building": Hold an investigation into the Depayin incident; cease the press campaign against Aung San Suu Kyi and

---

[14] "Burma Defends Suu Kyi Custody", *BBC News*, July 13, 2003, available online at http://news.bbc.co.uk.
[15] "Burma Faces ASEAN Expulsion", ibid., July 20, 2003.
[16] "ASEAN Split Over Burma", ibid., July 21, 2003.
[17] "Seeking a Way Out for Rangoon", *Bangkok Post*, August 9, 2003.

the NLD; release all political prisoners; sign truces with remaining ethnic groups still fighting the *Tatmadaw*; start peace talks.

3.   Draft a constitution involving the military, pro-democracy opposition and ethnic groups; adopt the draft constitution.
4.   Transitional period before holding elections; lifting of all international sanctions against Burma.
5.   Hold elections overseen by independent international monitors; hold an international conference on aid for Burma.

The following month, Khin Nyunt — who had just been appointed prime minister — announced Burma's new seven-point road map for "disciplined democracy"[18]:

1.   Reconvening of the National Convention that has been adjourned since 1996.
2.   After the National Convention, a step-by-step implementation of the process necessary for the emergence of a genuine and disciplined democratic system.
3.   Drafting a new constitution in accordance with basic principles and detailed basic principles laid down by the National Convention.
4.   Adoption of the draft constitution through national referendum.
5.   Holding of free and fair elections for *Pyithu Hluttaws* (People's Assemblies) according to the new Constitution.
6.   Convening of *Hluttaws* attended by *Hluttaw* members in accordance with the new Constitution.
7.   Building a modern, developed and democratic nation by the state leaders elected by the *Hluttaw*; and the government and other central organs formed by the *Hluttaw*.

A National Convention with the purpose of writing a new constitution was first proclaimed by the generals in 1992, a year before they established the USDA. Refusing to hand over power following the loss of the National Unity Party in the 1990 elections, the generals

---

[18] "Implementing the Seven-Point Road Map for the Future Nation," *New Light of Myanmar* (Rangoon), December 28, 2005.

had explained that the elections were merely a signal for constitutional change and that all major parties, or at least those members not still incarcerated, would be invited to attend a convention designed for that purpose. At the time, it was believed that the generals favored a regime that secured a permanent allotment for the military in parliament, along the lines of Indonesia's former model.

One of the objectives forming the framework of the "basic principles" alluded to in Step 3 of the SPDC's road map was laid down by the generals before the first meeting of the National Convention. It required that the *Tatmadaw* take the leading role in national politics in the future. The SPDC drafted a number of "basic principles" for a new constitution at its National Convention in 1993, and from 1994 to 1996 it drafted "detailed basic principles" that left little room for discretion or further drafting. The NLD walked out of, and was later expelled from, the National Convention in 1995, and in 1996 the SLORC issued Law 5/96 silencing any criticism of the convention and the Constitution after the NLD threatened to write its own. Prior to 2004, the National Convention had not been held in seven years. The NLD, along with some ethnic minority groups, chose to boycott the 2004 convention, the NLD citing the continued detention of Aung San Suu Kyi and the party's deputy chairman, Tin Oo. The SPDC pushed on regardless, citing the holding of the National Convention as a significant step toward the emergence of a genuine and disciplined democratic system.

Burma's new road map seemed, for the time being, to please most of the members of ASEAN, and the fact that the SPDC had moved Suu Kyi from detention to house arrest was a significant step in the right direction. In October 2004, however, prior to the ASEAN Summit in Vientiane, Prime Minister General Khin Nyunt was charged with refusing to obey orders and corruption — a common justification during a purge — and was placed under house arrest along with officers loyal to him. His intelligence apparatus was disbanded, and he was replaced by Than Shwe's protégé, General Soe Win, thought to be the one behind the planning of the Depayin incident. While Soe Win announced that the SPDC remained committed to the road map, the impact of Khin Nyunt's purge on Burma's foreign policy would prove to be significant. Among the top generals, he was regarded as the most pragmatic and outward-looking, being more aware of international sentiment toward the regime's policies. The government recalled more than a dozen ambassadors and 20 minister-counselors — nearly all of whom were associated either with Khin Nyunt or his military intelligence — and replaced these ambassadors with at least 11 brigadier generals.[19]

Burma remained off the official agenda at the 2004 ASEAN Summit, although disappointment was conveyed by some members over the announcement that Suu Kyi's house arrest would be extended for another year. Thailand's crackdown on Muslim separatists in the southern provinces had attracted international criticism prior to the summit. Prime Minister Thaksin had made it known that he refused to discuss the situation at the next ASEAN meeting and indeed threatened to walk out if it were raised. ASEAN could not censure Burma again on the one hand and avoid mentioning Thailand's activities on the other. While Bangkok had undergone a significant warming of relations with Rangoon under Thaksin's leadership, perhaps this incident was also his attempt to reestablish non-interference as the guiding principle for ASEAN's "enhanced interaction".[20]

Burma Forfeits its Chair

In 2005, with Suu Kyi still under house arrest and no tangible progress made toward democratic reform — by road maps or otherwise — ASEAN again faced intense pressure as Burma's chairmanship approached. The US and the EU as dialogue partners had threatened to boycott any ASEAN meetings chaired by Burma. In addition, the UN special envoy, Razali Ismail, had been denied access to the country. Some ASEAN governments — notably Malaysia, Singapore and Indonesia — began raising concerns over Burma's chairmanship and

[19] Ardeth Maung Thawnghmung and Maung Aung Myoe, "Myanmar in 2006: Another Year of Housekeeping?" *Asian Survey* 47:1 (2007), p. 198.
[20] See Haacke, "Enhanced Interaction", p. 199.

the lack of any substantive progress on its road map through various diplomatic channels, although Prime Minister Hun Sen of Cambodia supported Burma as chair. Mahathir, by now retired, called for Suu Kyi's release, and parliamentary debates were held and motions passed on the issue in Malaysia, the Philippines and Thailand. ASEAN made it clear that it would not force Burma to step down, lest this set a precedent, but noted that its chairmanship could severely affect the organization's international credibility. Burma had also caused a fair degree of embarrassment for ASEAN because the organization had argued that engagement with the regime would deliver the reforms that sanctions could not. It was clear that following the Depayin incident, the ASEAN governments had "experienced and articulated a new quality of irritation".[21]

In July 2005, at the ASEAN Foreign Ministers' Meeting in Vientiane, Burma's Foreign Minister U Nyan Win informed his colleagues that his government "had decided to relinquish its turn to be the Chair of ASEAN in 2006 because it would want to focus its attention on the ongoing national reconciliation and democratization process".[22] He explained that 2006 would be a critical year and that the government wanted to give its full attention to the process. The foreign ministers welcomed the decision and thanked Myanmar for not allowing its "national preoccupation to affect ASEAN's solidarity and cohesiveness".[23] Burma would be permitted to take its turn as the chair when it was ready to do so. Clearly relieved, ASEAN officials could now avoid unwanted international attention and, for the time being, suppress the issue of Burma. On Burma's side, the loss of prestige and enhanced legitimacy that would have accompanied holding the chair was compounded by the preparations already underway to host the event in Rangoon. The consequences of its forfeiture would play out in various ways the following year.

---

[21] Ibid., p. 209.
[22] ASEAN, *Statement by the ASEAN Foreign Ministers*, Vientiane, July 25, 2005, available online at http://www.aseansec.org/17590.htm.
[23] Ibid.

A Return to Isolationism or a Return to "Neutrality"?

For various reasons, it may be possible to argue that Burma retreated into an isolationist foreign policy. Yet, this interpretation must be balanced with Burma's proven ability to find friends with influence. That Burma has strengthened its bilateral ties with China, India and even Russia could be indicative of the fact that it views ASEAN differently from the organization it was attracted to join in 1997. Ten years on, ASEAN appeared to have fallen under a level of Western influence that had become increasingly uncomfortable for the Burmese generals. Indeed, forfeiting their chair had created mixed feelings toward some of their fellow member states. In addition, prior to the Kuala Lumpur Summit at the end of 2005, a group of Southeast Asian parliamentarians and a Malaysian cabinet minister had called for Burma to be expelled from ASEAN unless the regime improved its human rights record; they urged ASEAN to keep the Burma issue permanently on its agenda.[24] Indeed, in most countries throughout the region, civil society groups have assumed an increasingly visible and influential role in domestic politics, and particularly in Indonesia and the Philippines they have strongly promoted a regional commitment to democracy and human rights. The structural setting for policymaking in the region has also changed and political liberalization has had an impact on regional political agendas, with democratic norms diffusing from domestic to regional political spheres.[25] Groups from outside the executive branch have forced their governments to pay more attention to issues such as human security and human rights. In regards to Burma, the ASEAN Inter-Parliamentary Myanmar Caucus (a group of ASEAN legislators from Indonesia, Malaysia, Thailand, Singapore, the Philippines and Cambodia) have, since its founding in 2004, repeatedly raised Burma's human rights violations to ASEAN, the UN Security Council, and to national caucuses and parliamentary

---

[24] "ASEAN Urged to Tackle Burma Issue", *BBC News*, December 12, 2005, available online at http://news.bbc.co.uk; "U.N. to Hear Report on Burma Impact", ibid., December 3, 2005.

[25] Dosch, J. "ASEAN's reluctant liberal turn and the thorny road to democracy promotion", *The Pacific Review* 21: 4 (2008), p. 530.

groups outside ASEAN. In turn, ASEAN's engagement in a discourse on liberal norms and values has not resulted in an explicit strategy of democracy promotion, but it has begun to rethink its refusal to deal with issues that touch on domestic political orders.[26] Hence, together, through international pressure exerted over Burma as well as domestic pressure from civil society that has diffused into domestic and regional politics, democracy and human rights have been forced onto ASEAN's political agenda, forcing the organization to rethink its traditional position because of Burma.

At the 2005 Kuala Lumpur Summit, ASEAN noted the increased interest of the international community on developments in Burma. The Chairman's Statement called for the release of those placed under detention, encouraged the country to expedite its Road Map to Democracy, and welcomed Burma's invitation to Malaysia's foreign minister, Syed Hamid Albar, to learn firsthand of its progress.[27] Over the next few months, however, a delegation visit led by Syed Hamid was postponed twice because, according to the Burmese Foreign Minister Nyan Win, Burma was too busy moving its administrative offices to a new capital. The real reason for Burma's procrastination, however, may have been that unlike the state visits from Indonesia's President Susilo Bambang Yudhoyono and India's President A.P.J. Abdul Kalam, Syed Hamid had requested to meet with Aung San Suu Kyi and made this a prerequisite for future ASEAN solidarity.[28] The delegation finally arrived but was not permitted to meet with Suu Kyi, the NLD or Than Shwe, and the visit was cut short.

If one were to argue that the generals were retreating to their isolationism of the past, of the many indicators that could substantiate this thesis, perhaps the move to Pyinmana stands out. On November 7, 2005, foreign diplomats in Rangoon were notified that the capital had left town. They were informed by the Foreign Ministry that they

---

[26] Ibid, pp. 529–531.
[27] ASEAN, "Chairman's Statement of the 11th ASEAN Summit 'One Vision, One Identity, One Community'," Kuala Lumpur, December 12, 2005, Clause 34, available online at http://www.aseansec.org/18039.htm.
[28] Haacke, *Myanmar's Foreign Policy*, p. 57.

could write a letter if they needed to communicate with the Burmese government. For urgent matters, they could send a fax to Pyinmana.[29] The *Tatmadaw* had been developing a site for a number of years near remote Pyinmana Township, 240 miles (about 400 km) to the north (see detailed description below). The generals did not bother to inform their ASEAN neighbors of their intentions and the first public announcement was given by Information Minister General Kyaw Hsan the following day.

No official reasons were given for the move other than that the new capital was centrally located and had quick access to all parts of the country. Speculation on the generals' motives was rampant and generally centered on ensuring their survival. It is indicative of the lack of trust that the SPDC has in its own people that the generals may have desired to protect their administrative institutions by relocating them far from most citizens and from future mass demonstrations. In 1988, the pro-democracy demonstrations had brought Rangoon to a standstill and the government's administrative offices were unable to function. By moving their offices away from crowded and restive Rangoon, the SPDC could remain in control of its functions and coordinate an appropriate response.[30] The implications of the move were significant for foreign policy, not only because it left Rangoon-based foreign diplomats and non-governmental organizations (NGOs) in the dark but also because the new capital, located in the southern Mandalay Division, would be closer to the overland river and highway routes connecting Burma with China and India. The new capital — hundreds of miles from the sea — may have been isolated from the

---

[29] "Burma Shifts Capital to the Hills", *The Age* (Melbourne), January 1, 2006, available online at http://www.theage.com.au; "Burma's Confusing Capital Move", *BBC News*, November 8, 2005, available online at http://news.bbc.co.uk. The evacuation of government ministries by convoys of trucks laden with civil servants and their office furniture began at 6:37 a.m. on November 6, 2005 — an auspicious time according to Than Shwe's astrologers.

[30] The new location provides a geographically more convenient military headquarters from which troops could respond to trouble in Rangoon as well as the frontier areas of the Karen, Shan, Kayah and Chin. Pyinmana was also the location of General Aung San's wartime headquarters.

West and many ASEAN states, but it would be closer to the Asian continental powers most important to Burma's economy.

The SPDC planned to move all of its government ministries, military headquarters and a "parliament" to the new capital. It had begun a number of large projects in the area several years before, including the construction of a large airstrip, a military hospital, a five-star hotel, a golf course, mansions for the senior generals, apartments, a national headquarters for ethnic groups, government offices, and bunkers and tunnels (see Daniel Gomà, Chapter 7). The International Labor Organization (ILO) reported that extensive forced labor had been used on the projects and thousands of villagers had been relocated. Although the SPDC promised a tenfold rise in the salaries of civil servants, many were unhappy with the move.[31] On March 27, 2006 (Armed Forces Day), Burma's state television broadcast pictures of troops parading at the new site in the shadows of three massive statues — Kings Anawrahta, Bayintnaung and Alaungpaya, the three kings in Burmese history perhaps most noted for uniting the people and founding dynasties. The new capital was to be named Yanlon ("secure from strife") but Than Shwe officially named it Naypyidaw ("royal city" or "place of the kings"). By heeding the advice of astrologers and founding the new capital, Than Shwe was honoring tradition while effectively asserting his own "royal" legacy.

In 2005, movements were afoot at the UN to have Burma placed on the Security Council's agenda. Russia, China and Algeria had blocked an earlier attempt to get the Council to discuss Burma, but the presence of the Philippines, in its turn to sit on the Security Council, helped pass the proposal later that year. A report commissioned by Václav Havel and Desmond Tutu in 2005 had recommended that the Security Council pass a resolution for intervention.

---

[31] Because of a lack of accommodation for families in the new capital, single bureaucrats had been trying to find marriage partners to postpone their reassignment ("Retreat to the Jungle", *Irrawaddy*, December 2005, available online at http://www.irrawaddy.org; "Myanmar's Generals Build Their 'Xanadu'," *Asia Times*, July 22, 2005, available online at http://www.atimes.com).

This would require that Burma work with the secretary-general's office in implementing a plan for national reconciliation and a restoration of a democratically elected government; that the secretary-general remain vigorously engaged with the dispute resolution process and report back to the Security Council on a regular basis; that Burma ensure immediate, safe and unhindered access to all parts of the country for the UN and international humanitarian organizations to provide humanitarian assistance; and that Aung San Suu Kyi and all prisoners of conscience in Burma be immediately released.[32] The report was heavily criticized by the Burmese government. In December 2005, the Security Council finally heard a briefing by the undersecretary-general for political affairs, Ibrahim Gambari, and the members agreed to see how things progressed. No resolution for UN intervention in Burma was likely to be passed while Russia and China remained opposed.

In February 2006, Prime Minister General Soe Win traveled to Beijing to secure China's support for and future veto of any UN attempt to impose punitive economic and political sanctions via the Security Council. In April 2006, SPDC Vice Chairman Vice Senior General Maung Aye, accompanied by Foreign Minister General Nyan Win, traveled to Moscow to seek the same assurances from Russia. Maung Aye revived a project to build a center for nuclear studies — including the construction of a research nuclear reactor, laboratories and support infrastructure — signing a new cooperation agreement with the Kurchatov nuclear research center.[33] The project began in 2001, when Burma signed a deal with the Russian Ministry of Atomic Energy to build a 10-megawatt nuclear test reactor. Although personnel were sent to Russia for nuclear technology training, the project stalled because Burma was unable to finance the facility's construction.

---

[32] *Threat to the Peace: A Call for the UN Security Council to Act in Burma*, report commissioned by Vacláv Havel and Bishop Desmond M. Tutu, prepared by DLA Piper Rudnick Gray Cary, Washington, DC, September 20, 2005, available online at http://www.burma campaign.org.uk/reports/Burmaunscreport.pdf.

[33] "From Myanmar to Russia with Love", *Asia Times*, April 12, 2006, available online at http://www.atimes.com.

If Burma was snubbing ASEAN after forfeiting its chair, it clearly had a friend in China, and the SPDC was increasingly turning to Beijing for diplomatic advice. With time, any hope that ASEAN still could directly pressure Burma to resist China's aid and growing strategic influence in the region appeared remote. Indeed, unlike foreign investors in some ASEAN countries, China's investments in Burma were not driven solely by profit returns — China has regularly contributed to infrastructure development since the *Tatmadaw* turned to it in the late 1980s, and China views Burma as part of its strategic landscape. The Chinese government has criticized foreign interference in Rangoon's internal affairs, and Beijing hosts regular visits by Burma's generals and promotes further cooperation between the *Tatmadaw* and the PLA. Moreover, even as ASEAN remained apparently unaware of Rangoon's intentions in 2005, China assisted Burma to build hydropower plants near Pyinmana. ASEAN could only hope that by engaging directly with China in multilateral dialogues and agreements, it could at least attempt to control Chinese regional influence.[34]

In May 2006, the UN sent Ibrahim Gambari to Burma to raise human rights issues and the prospects for restoring democracy.[35] Gambari met with the three senior SPDC Generals — Than Shwe, Maung Aye and Soe Win — in their new capital. During his visit, Gambari became the first foreigner permitted to meet with Aung San Suu Kyi since Razali's visit in 2004. This was also unexpected because the SPDC had only recently accused the NLD of having links to terrorist groups and threatened to ban the organization. But because the generals were concerned about the Security Council possibly placing Burma on its agenda, the visit to Suu Kyi may have been a concession promoted by Beijing. Indeed, it is probable that Gambari's

---

[34] See Roy, "Southeast Asia and China", pp. 305–22.

[35] A Nigerian national, Gambari was the first UN envoy to visit the country since Indonesia's Ali Alitas in 2005. When Razali resigned in January 2006 because he had been denied entry for almost two years, he believed that Burma's road map had effectively come to an end with the arrest of Khin Nyunt in 2004. "United Nations Burma Envoy Quits", *BBC News*, January 8, 2006, available online at http://news.bbc.co.uk.

visit may have been permitted on the advice of Beijing, in order that China could continue supporting Burma at the UN.[36] Upon Gambari's return to the UN, Secretary-General Kofi Annan appealed to Than Shwe to release Suu Kyi, but the SPDC extended her detention the following day.[37] Her detention was extended for another year in May 2007 despite appeals for her release from ASEAN (in particular Malaysia, Indonesia and the Philippines), the UN, the EU and the US.[38]

A further possible sign that the generals had become increasingly isolationist was their attitude toward NGOs since the Khin Nyunt purge. Khin Nyunt had been more willing to work with international bodies, either by permitting NGOs access to remote parts of the country or at least not rejecting attempts at dialogues with special envoys. But following his sacking and arrest, the generals' xenophobia reemerged when they discovered how many foreigners and international agencies were operating inside Burma. The SPDC moved to introduce a new set of strict guidelines for UN agencies, international organizations and NGOs — local and international (INGOs).[39] The

---

[36] "Will Junta Show More Flexibility?" *Bangkok Post*, May 23, 2006, available online at http://www.bangkokpost.com.
[37] "UN Head Calls for Suu Kyi Release", *BBC News*, May 26, 2006, available online at http://news.bbc.co.uk; "Suu Kyi House Arrest Term Expires", ibid., May 27, 2006, available online at http://news.bbc.co.uk.
[38] "ASEAN Seeks Aung San Suu Kyi's Release", *International Herald Tribune*, May 22, 2007, available online at http://www.iht.com.
[39] The guidelines called for the registration of all NGOs; the submission of proposals, basic agreements, and Memorandums of Understanding for approval by the Ministry of National Planning and Economic Development (MNPED — the coordinating body) and the restriction of activities to the scope of the proposal; the consent of the MNPED on all international staff to be appointed; the coordination and approval of all internal travel by the MNPED as well as the accompaniment of government officials with UN/NGO/INGO personnel on internal travel; the setting up of Central-, State/Division- and Township-level Coordination Committees; and the monthly and quarterly reporting of activities by UN/NGO/INGO agencies to the MNPED (MNPED, *Guidelines for UN Agencies, International Organizations and NGO/INGOs on Cooperation Program in Myanmar*, February 7, 2006, available online at http://www.burmalibrary.org).

purpose of the new guidelines appeared to be near total control by the SPDC of all UN/NGO/INGO activities in the country, particularly in politically sensitive border regions.

Many NGOs found that they were unable to continue operating as before and canceled their projects. The new restrictions on travel and a refusal to renew licenses led to the withdrawal of a number of them, including the Geneva-based Center for Humanitarian Dialogue. Some that were critical of the regime, such as the ILO, became subject to threats. Although it was the wish of the generals that USDA officials accompany personnel of the International Committee of the Red Cross (ICRC) on their prison visit programs, the ICRC objected and canceled all such visits, as well as a planned trip to the country in December 2006, and reduced its foreign staff in Burma.

Coordination and monitoring of all UN/NGO/INGO activities per the new guidelines were made more difficult by the SPDC's decision to relocate all civil servants to their remote new capital. In March 2006, the French section of Doctors Without Borders (Médecins Sans Frontières — MSF) ended its medical programs and withdrew from Burma, citing unacceptable conditions imposed by the authorities on how to provide relief to people living in war-affected areas. The SPDC had imposed so many travel restrictions and applied such pressure on local health authorities not to cooperate with MSF teams that the organization realized it risked becoming merely a technical service provider subject to the political priorities of the junta.[40]

These are just some of the arguments that could be offered to support a case that Burma was retreating to an isolationist foreign policy. They must be balanced, however, with the realization that "isolation" here means seclusion from Western influence — particularly from the US, but increasingly from the EU and, more recently, from ASEAN itself. Retreating to an isolationist policy from Western

---

[40] "Prevented from Working, the French Section of MSF Leaves Myanmar (Burma)", press release/*MSF*, March 30, 2006, available online at http://www.doctorswithoutborders.org; "Prevented from Working, the French Section of MSF Leaves Myanmar", Voices from the Field/*MSF*, March 2006, available online at http://www.doctorswithoutborders.org.

influence meant that Burma had to strengthen its ties, or at least its short-term partnerships, with other rising regional powers, including China and India. Of particular concern to ASEAN in April 2007 was Burma's restoration of diplomatic relations with North Korea when Deputy Foreign Minister Kim Yong-Il visited Rangoon and signed an agreement with his counterpart, Kyaw Thu. This normalization, immediately approved by China, provided a further headache for ASEAN, whose ministers had just focused on the North Korean nuclear issue at the Cebu Summit in January 2007.

In the wake of North Korea's successful nuclear test in October 2006, Burma's courting of Pyongyang meant that an ASEAN member state had dealings with an apparently nuclear pariah state. This would have been of particular concern for ASEAN as it came despite Burma's having signed ASEAN's Treaty on the Southeast Asia Nuclear Weapon-Free Zone. There was speculation that North Korea was seeking access to Burma's natural resources, while the *Tatmadaw* could gain access to military equipment blocked by US and EU sanctions. Since both Asian countries faced condemnation from the West and particularly the US, the improvement in their bilateral ties was seen by some as a natural attraction of pariah states. Following a second nuclear test by North Korea in May 2009, followed by a series of short-range missile tests, the UN Security Council imposed new sanctions on North Korea, tightening an arms embargo and authorizing ship searches in an effort to curb its nuclear and ballistic missile programs. In July 2009, a North Korean ship headed for Burma was tracked by the US Navy and turned around on its own accord. Though denied, the vessel was suspected of carrying weapons for the regime and would have faced possible inspection under the new UN sanctions resolution. Although a nuclear relationship has yet to manifest itself in any tangible detail, North Korea has long been suspected of providing tunneling expertise to the SPDC. However, that Burma could turn to nuclear Russia while developing bilateral relations with North Korea and other regional neighbors (in spite of Rangoon's differences with ASEAN) could indicate, if anything, that Burma has merely returned to its natural reactive foreign policy posture. This is a form of neutralism whereby the generals prefer bilateral dealings to multilateral ones and continue to balance the competing interests of major (and nuclear) powers in the strategically important region through a series of pragmatic endeavors aimed at achieving their own survival.

Survival in the Face of Domestic Strife and Natural Disaster

The mass demonstrations of September 2007 attracted unprecedented worldwide attention from foreign governments, parliaments, NGOs and the media. Much of the attention could be attributed to the increased availability of Internet and satellite coverage of the events recorded by amateurs armed with mobile technologies. Notwithstanding the regime's best efforts, pictures of the demonstrations were recorded and sent to the international media for worldwide broadcast, including inside Burma. Calls for restraint on the part of the Burmese authorities, as well as for the release of detained protesters, came from multiple corners including the UN, the EU, the European Parliament and some ASEAN countries. Notably, some Western governments turned to Beijing in the hope that Chinese officials might exercise their influence over the regime's leaders and persuade the SPDC to act with restraint. Following the crackdown on September 26, ASEAN foreign ministers issued a statement deploring the violent suppression of the demonstrations, as did the UN Human Rights Council. Gambari was sent to Burma on the first of several visits to meet with Than Shwe and Aung San Suu Kyi. With Chinese and Russian approval, the Security Council also issued a moderated statement urging the SPDC to address the human rights, humanitarian and economic concerns of its people. Travel and financial transaction restrictions were increased on SPDC officials and their families by the US, UK, Australia, Canada and the EU. Further calls were made to release all political prisoners and open a dialogue with Aung San Suu Kyi — prompting the SPDC to appoint a special liaison officer to manage relations with her.

Amid the demonstrations, the SPDC announced the completion of its National Convention on a new constitution and claimed that the protesters were undermining the road map to democracy. In October 2007, the regime held a 60,000-person-strong ceremony to support the National Convention in Hpa-an, Kayin State. In February 2008, officials announced that a referendum would be held on the new constitution draft and scheduled general elections for 2010. The news was welcomed by China, Russia and India. The SPDC may have hoped to diffuse the unrest of 2007 with these pronouncements but upholding its referendum promise in May 2008 again drew widespread international condemnation from states, politicians and legislatures, INGOs, and international aid organizations alike. This was not only because the referendum was viewed as a contrived entrenchment of future military rule but also because it drew attention and resources away from the devastation caused by Cyclone Nargis in the Irrawaddy Delta. Despite Nargis, the authorities pushed ahead with their referendum, only postponing it for two weeks in areas most affected by the cyclone. Official results for the first round showed that the new constitution draft was passed by a remarkable 92.4% of voters.

While the regime's handling of Cyclone Nargis drew international criticism, it also presented an opportunity to ASEAN. Although multiple offers of humanitarian assistance were initially made to the regime, the SPDC refused to grant entry visas to aid agencies and workers (per the new guidelines set for NGOs) or to allow foreign (US, UK and French) warships loaded with aid to dock and unload their cargo. Calls for humanitarian intervention based on the UN's "Responsibility to Protect" principle, endorsed at its World Summit in 2005, were proffered by humanitarian and pro-democracy advocates, supported by some officials, including French Minister for Foreign and European Affairs Bernard Kouchner, as well as more conservative journalists. The authorities gradually relaxed their stand and allowed some aid flights into Rangoon but would not permit unfettered access or distribution of aid, offering instead to distribute the aid themselves. Some three weeks after Nargis struck, UN Secretary-General Ban Ki-moon met with Than Shwe in Naypyidaw; ASEAN officials had also been mediating to allow international aid and aid workers into the country. The SPDC eventually acquiesced on the workers. Unfettered access to foreign aid workers was granted and Burma agreed to join ASEAN and the UN in a Tripartite Core Group (TCG) to coordinate the international assistance.[41] Although ASEAN would later claim a minor victory, enhancing its status and reputation, from these negotiations at its next Ministerial Meeting in Singapore, the international attention and criticism of Burma would only subside following the subsequent earthquakes in China.

At its Ministerial Meeting in Singapore in July 2008, ASEAN was in a rare position to issue a strong rebuke to Burma, following the SPDC's extension of Aung San Suu Kyi's detention in late May. At the same time, the association could trumpet its successful mediation efforts described above. Also attending the meeting, US Secretary of State Condoleezza Rice described the SPDC's plans to restore democracy gradually as a "mockery"; the US and UN had earlier criticized the SPDC's decision to extend Aung San Suu Kyi's detention and President Bush had extended sanctions for another year. The Singapore meeting was, moreover, noteworthy for Burma's signing on to the new ASEAN Charter, with its provision for establishing an ASEAN Human Rights Body (HRB), the terms of reference for which were to be determined at the Foreign Ministers Meeting.[42] By October, all member states had ratified the charter, despite lawmakers in Thailand, the Philippines and Indonesia expressing concerns over the parameters of, among other things, the human rights body, particularly with respect to Burma; these concerns would continue to be negotiated before the Bangkok Summit in December. A High Level

---

[41] Although this allowed the aid presence to increase dramatically, the SPDC still tried to control the movements of foreign aid workers and reports of the siphoning of aid supplies by local authorities was common. The regime continued to place major obstacles in the way of foreign relief workers and delayed the granting of visas to foreign nationals seeking access to the delta region. The most effective distributors of aid in the delta region were Buddhist monks and their monasteries which provided shelter and relief to large numbers of displaced persons as well as children who had been orphaned by the cyclone.

[42] Article 14, *The ASEAN Charter* (Jakarta: ASEAN Secretariat, 2008), available online at http://www.asean.org.

Panel (HLP) was set up to draft the terms of reference for the HRB and delivered its first draft to the Foreign Ministers Meeting at the Summit in Cha-am, Thailand, in March 2009.

What relevance this human rights body will have for Burma, however, must remain questionable. The UN's new human rights envoy, Toma Ojea Quintana, arrived in Burma for his first visit in August 2008, replacing Paulo Sergio Pinheiro. Given the junta's fickle treatment of UN. envoys in recent years, the prospects for any ASEAN-led investigative human rights envoys achieving meaningful concessions would appear to be slim at best — particularly if the world's attention is not focused on Burma as it was in 2007–08. In addition, at the Foreign Ministers Meeting, Burma and Cambodia blocked civil society representatives from their own countries from attending the meeting. In a 2008 meeting of the HLP, Burma's foreign minister, Nyan Win, indicated that Burma would oppose any effort to give the HRB the power to monitor or investigate human rights violations, and that the HRB should uphold ASEAN's policy of non-interference. Burma would prefer that the HRB only served as a "consultative mechanism" and not "shame or blame" any ASEAN nation.[43] Although the idea of human rights envoys having free access inside Burma may not sit comfortably with either the SPDC or with Beijing, a perception of cooperation could for the time being define the parameters that both parties are willing to promote, or accept, in their multilateral dealings with the region and the world. The same, of course, might readily be said of other ASEAN nations. Yet granting access to HRB personnel, even with limited powers, may be the trade-off Burma must make to at least appear to be willing to cooperate with ASEAN and, in turn, allow ASEAN to show the world that it is taking human rights seriously. Bangkok said that it wished the draft to be finalized during its tenure as chair (2009) and that the HRB will begin operating in the same year.[44] The matter was, it seemed, to be of some urgency because

---

[43] Jim Gomez, "Myanmar Opposes Investigative Powers of ASEAN", *The Irrawaddy*, July 22, 2008, available online at http://www.irrawaddy.org.
[44] Xinhua News, "Thailand Expects ASEAN Human Rights Body to be Set Up Around End of 2009", February 27, 2009, available online at http://news.xinhuanet.com.

the next ASEAN chair, Vietnam, would not have the same motivations for making human rights progress in Burma.[45] The extension, at the Hua Hin Summit, of ASEAN's humanitarian taskforce and the TCG in Burma through to 2010 also provided an implicit witness mechanism and possible restraint on any future acts of mass violence there.

Aung San Suu Kyi was accused of breaking the terms of her house arrest in May 2009, when a US national, John Yettaw, swam across Inya Lake to her house on University Avenue and stayed for two nights before being caught by the authorities upon his departure. Since the current period of her house arrest was due to expire in May (the 1975 State Protection Law permits a maximum of 5 years renewable arrest), and with elections scheduled for 2010, the uninvited guest gave the SPDC a timely reason for continuing her incarceration. She was moved to Insein Prison and committed to trial, being charged under the law "Safeguarding the State from the Dangers of Subversive Elements". Although she pleaded her innocence, she would undergo a closed trial inside the prison scheduled for June–July 2009. International condemnation followed the SPDC's committal for trial of Aung San Suu Kyi. ASEAN issued a rare statement expressing "grave concern" about the trial and that, with the world watching, "the honour and credibility of the Government of the Union of Myanmar are at stake" and that, as a member of ASEAN, Burma has the responsibility to protect and promote human rights.[46] Following this latest statement from ASEAN, the Burmese government accused Thailand (as chair of ASEAN) of interfering in Burma's domestic affairs by releasing the statement. At the Asia–Europe meeting (ASEM), European ministers called for the immediate release of Suu Kyi.

---

[45] Asia Times Online, "ASEAN Makes Fragile Myanmar Progress", March 5, 2009, available online at http://www.atimes.com.
[46] ASEAN Secretariat, "ASEAN Chairman's Statement on Myanmar, Ministry of Foreign Affairs of Thailand", May 19, 2009, Thailand, available online at http://www.aseansec.org.

Ibrahim Gambari visited Burma as a precursor to a visit by the UN Secretary General. This visit followed in June 2009, when Ban Ki-moon met with Than Shwe in Naypyidaw at the same time as Aung San Suu Kyi's trial was underway. He requested but was refused a visit to Aung San Suu Kyi, prompting UK Prime Minister Gordon Brown to threaten the possibility of further sanctions against Burma. The court delayed issuing a verdict on Suu Kyi's trial, possibly to avoid attracting further attention and condemnation at the 16th ASEAN Regional Forum (ARF) meeting at the same time. While US Secretary of State Hillary Clinton had suggested that Burma be expelled from ASEAN if Aung San Suu Kyi was not released, the ARF members officially offered to work with Burma to promote democracy, human rights and the well-being of its people.[47] In August 2009, the court found Suu Kyi guilty and sentenced her to a three-year jail term which was commuted by Than Shwe to a 18-month house arrest. Yettaw was sentenced to seven years' imprisonment, although his release was negotiated by US Senator Jim Webb who visited Than Shwe in Naypyidaw several days afterwards. The ASEAN chair, Thailand, issued a statement expressing "deep disappointment" upon learning of Suu Kyi's sentence and reiterated the calls made by the ASEAN foreign ministers attending the 42nd Foreign Ministers Meeting and the 16th ARF meeting for the immediate release of all those under detention, including Aung San Suu Kyi, to enable them to participate in the 2010 general elections. According to the statement, the chair believed that "only free, fair and inclusive general elections will then pave the way for Myanmar's full integration into the international community". Nevertheless, the organization claimed that it would stand ready to cooperate with the Myanmar government in its efforts to realize the seven steps to democracy, that it would remain constructively engaged with Myanmar, and urged Myanmar's full cooperation with the United Nations.[48]

---

[47] Kittipong Thavevong, "ASEAN offers to help Burma", *The Nation*, Bangkok, July 24, 2009, available online at http://www.asianewsnet.net.

[48] ASEAN Secretariat, "ASEAN Chairman's Statement on Myanmar", August 11, 2009, Bangkok, available online at http://www.aseansec.org.

Conclusions

Burma's foreign policy motivations in recent years should be considered within the context of ensuring the SPDC's self-preservation and the regime's survival. It is often difficult, even impossible, to know the real motivations that lie behind the veil of secrecy that surrounds Than Shwe's inner circle. The generals' move to their new capital, as well as their response to the events of 2007 and Cyclone Nargis, reflects a siege mentality — both at home and abroad — that motivates their behavior and accompanies the general lack of internal and external legitimacy of their regime. In the eyes of the West, the regime will remain illegitimate so long as free and fair elections are withheld and the state fails to deliver basic goods and services to its people. This problem has been exacerbated by the SPDC committing Burma's limited resources to building the new capital; purchasing weapons to enforce domestic policies and suppress public demonstrations; and staging unmonitored constitutional referendums at the expense of meeting basic aid, health and infrastructure needs. That the generals cannot trust their own people, let alone Western foreigners, must today figure highly in the internal political dynamics behind the SPDC's foreign policy.

It can be argued that Burma's domestic politics causes cross-border problems and that these create regional instability for a number of reasons. Among these are drug production and addiction; the possible pandemic spread of HIV/AIDS and unrecorded bird flu outbreaks; and border area conflicts, forced relocations, destitution and suppression of dissent, creating a steady flow of illegal immigrants or refugees into neighboring countries. One would think that for these reasons alone, ASEAN should be concerned with Burma's internal politics. But international pressure on Burma has added another dimension to the ASEAN–Burma relationship and an increased international awareness of some events inside Burma has caused headaches for ASEAN, particularly since 2003.

It can also be argued that joining ASEAN in 1997 may have been against Burma's long-held tradition of foreign relations neutralism — in its various forms — since independence. As a member of ASEAN in a new age of multilateralism, Burma has discovered that it is part of an

organization that responds to outside pressure from its dialogue partners — the US, the EU and the UN. This makes Burma feel uncomfortable and it has increasingly embarrassed ASEAN. Yet, it could also
be said that Burma was pressured into joining ASEAN, as well as forging a closer alliance with China, because of the sanctions imposed by the
West. If this is the case, then it should not be surprising that the generals may have felt uneasy in ASEAN because they must have perceived
that the original terms of their membership agreement had changed.
The new ASEAN Charter may only reinforce this perception.

Although Burma sought ASEAN membership as a means to gain
prestige and political legitimacy, access to markets and foreign currency, it is doubtful that the junta ever intended to introduce substantial economic liberalization and adopt the free-market reforms that
may have, in theory, helped to encourage some long-term economic
growth. More likely, the generals were in search of quick friends and
some ASEAN members were more than happy to gain access to
Burma's natural resources. Yet many foreign investors discovered over
time that, aside from intense lobbying by democracy activists, the
country's rules and regulations, corruption and lack of infrastructure
all severely limited their profit margins. As investors withdrew and
Western pressure increased, the hidden attraction of "constructive
engagement" for ASEAN became overshadowed by the awkward
redefining of "enhanced interaction" toward Burma.

In a climate where the generals are far more concerned with maintaining their monopoly on political power than responding to economic
pressures or incentives, the debate over sanctions or engagement has
become increasingly irrelevant — especially if their ultimate objective was
to bring about a change in the regime.[49] That any shift in the balance of
power between state and society is unlikely to occur soon is reflected in
the SPDC's attitude toward international agencies and NGOs, an attitude that required intense negotiations before it could be relaxed in the
wake of Cyclone Nargis. In foreign relations, neutrality may be where
the generals feel most comfortable, following a policy that minimizes

---

[49] Donald Seekins, "Burma and U.S. Sanctions: Punishing an Authoritarian Regime,"
Asian Survey 45:3 (2005), pp. 437–52.

adverse multilateral influences and promotes bilateral dealings and the selective balancing of various countries' interests against their own.

Burma's recalcitrance should inform ASEAN and the West that their positions have not brought about political change and that perhaps it is time to adjust their strategies, or at least their goals.[50] The generals have proved adept at adapting to external isolationist policies and indeed for much of their history have welcomed them. For the junta, economic liberalization has always been an experiment that could be withdrawn if it threatened political stability. It would be hard for the generals, therefore, to envisage that sanctions were punitive measures designed to instigate political reform. Within the context of Burma's reactive form of neutrality, withdrawing from Western influence means promoting and strengthening diplomatic, economic and possibly future military ties with alternative major regional powers: Burma maintains alternative trade markets in China and India[51] as well as significant investments and trade with Thailand and Singapore.[52]

---

[50] Through a number of initiatives in 2009, including Secretary of State Hillary Clinton's signing of ASEAN's Treaty of Amity and Cooperation after the 42nd ASEAN Ministerial Meeting in July 2009, the Obama administration signaled a desire on the part of the United States to increase its presence in the region. After the sentencing of Aung San Suu Kyi in August 2009, the chair of the US Senate Foreign Relations subcommittee on East Asia and Pacific Affairs, Senator Jim Webb, also visited Naypyidaw to meet with Than Shwe. Although the Obama administration claimed it would review its policy on Burma, whether this translates into a fundamental shift away from sanctions against Burma remains to be seen. (See ASEAN Secretariat, "US Signs Treaty of Amity and Cooperation (TAC)", Press Release, Phuket, Thailand, 22 July 2009, available online at http://www.aseansec.org).

[51] In December 2008, the SPDC also signed an agreement with a consortium of four firms from South Korea (Daewoo and Korea Gas Corporation) and India (ONGC Videsh and GAIL) to pipe natural gas from Burma's northwestern coast to China. The 30-year deal will provide natural gas to China's National United Oil Corporation.

[52] This remains the case, despite the remarks of former Prime Minister of Singapore, Goh Chok Tong, after a visit to Myanmar in June 2009. Goh had claimed that no Singapore investor would enter in a big way before the move towards democracy yielded results, and that he had urged the generals to make the 2010 elections fair, transparent and inclusive, with all parties wanting to contest being allowed to do so (see Nopporn Wong-Anan, "Singapore Links Investment to Myanmar Democracy", *Reuters*, available online at http://in.reuters.com/article/southAsiaNews).

ASEAN's engagement policy, on the other hand, seems to have deteriorated into a hazardous exercise of redefining the boundaries of "enhanced interaction" toward Burma. This appears to involve a game of ASEAN officials or states occasionally criticizing the domestic policies of a member state (and hence, breaching the rule of non-interference) while appearing as if they were *not* criticizing the domestic policies of a member state.[53] Because this game could easily backfire on other ASEAN members, their hesitancy is understandable, but pressure — both internally from new democracies in the region, as well as from outside forces — kept them pushing the concept nonetheless. What difference their new charter will make toward the evolution of this concept remains to be seen.

It does seem inevitable, though, that if ASEAN's international credibility is again threatened by Burma's actions, it will continue to criticize Burma's leaders, and perhaps it is more important for ASEAN to be seen criticizing them than doing nothing. That the generals may not wish to remain a member of an organization that heaps criticism on them and not on other member states is understandable. Yet, it is becoming more important for ASEAN to keep the country inside the organization rather than outside. ASEAN may increasingly turn to the UN to take more responsibility for Burma's "democratization", and by so doing may deflect some criticism from the West over its own lack of success. Indeed, any recent successes there have been in negotiating concessions from the junta would seem to indicate that the UN is needed to add weight to ASEAN's voice, if only because China as a member of the Security Council finds it difficult to defend Burma's interests there without the generals at least appearing to cooperate.

---

[53] Three notable exceptions to this general rule occurred in 2007, when all ASEAN states expressed their "revulsion" at Burma's crackdown on the demonstrating monks; in 2009, in regards to the trial of Aung San Suu Kyi, when ASEAN warned the regime that "the honour and credibility of the Government of the Union of Myanmar are at stake"; and again, upon learning of her sentence in 2009, when the ASEAN Chair expressed "deep disappointment". It remains to be seen whether these kinds of exceptions will become the norm.

Chapter 13

Conclusion

Lowell Dittmer

Abstract

In order to have a successful national identity — one capable of facilitating a successful national developmental trajectory — a country needs a felicitous combination of an inclusive political structure, an integrated (but reasonably tolerant) national culture, and a respected international status. Which of these elements Burma is endowed with and which ones are missing and why? These are some of the questions explored in this concluding chapter.

Keywords: Constitution; pacted transition; neutrality.

Burma, we have argued, is a country in which for various reasons a sense of cohesive and inclusive national identity has been unusually slow to evolve. And this continuing deficit has in turn impeded the achievement of more conventional indices of political and economic development as well. Identity had already become confused during the colonial era by the imperial incorporation of geographically arbitrary fragments of ethnic minorities (and by the exclusion of others) and then by the immersion of this mélange into British India, where some were treated more favorably than others, exacerbating inter-group rivalries. Independence came without a national revolution, the type of cauterizing event which, however destructive, by engaging the populace on behalf of a common cause can help, if successful, to fuse a sense of shared identity. The next half century was littered with the wreckage of unsuccessful attempts to resolve the problem. The initial democracy, beleaguered by minority nationality revolts and an ethnically impacted communist insurgency, first invited and eventually succumbed to a military takeover. The subsequent military regime, while more successful at suppressing internal divisions, thereby opened up an even more rancorous vertical cleavage between the central government and civil society. But the SLORC/SPDC tacitly recognized the incompleteness of this resolution, in taking a series of steps to move beyond dictatorship to a more legitimate and inclusive framework. For reasons to be discussed below, these efforts have heretofore proved inadequate, and there is serious reason for concern that they will be no more successful in the foreseeable future. The current military leadership's commitment to the realization of an inclusive national identity is at war with its interest in the status quo and its fear that concessions will lead even the present tenuous balance to unravel completely.

A coherent national identity, if not absolutely *sine qua non,* is a very useful attribute for a new nation-state to have, allowing it to move on to other pressing national needs and developmental tasks without being unnerved or diverted by internal splits or external irredentism. We submit that there are at least three basic prerequisites for the formation of such an identity. First, an *inclusive political structure* must be constructed that defines the criteria for participation in a sufficiently precise way that all constituents of the nation have the opportunity to participate while being entitled to retain vital differences endemic to their elective sub-cultures. Second, a *national culture* should function to define the values, history, myths, normative rules and criteria for distributive justice that the nation has in common and is willing to defend. Third, the government must construct an *international status* that defines the nation's role in the world, facilitating good relations with those countries whose support is vital to the "national interest" while negotiating differences with those threatening to dismember the country. Let us briefly reconsider Burma's experience in meeting each of these criteria.

Political Structure

Burma has had, in its relatively brief modern history, no less than three constitutions. The first, the "independence constitution" adopted and enacted in September 1947, provided for the establishment of a parliamentary democracy, safeguarding the rights of national minorities in the 'Union of Burma'; this was also provided for in the January 1947 agreement between General Aung San and British Prime Minister Attlee, as well as in the historic February 1947 Panglong Agreement between Burman leaders and other national groups. The 1947 Constitution created a two-house legislature and an independent judiciary and defined the rights of the people and the state. And, as a "union", it allowed each nationality to be represented in a national Chamber of Nationalities. But the constitution explicitly recognized only four subsidiary states for the largest ethnic groups (*viz.* Karen, Karenni, Shan and Kachin), only two of which (Shan and Karenni) were granted the right to secede—after 10 years. No territory was provided to the other nationalities, many of which saw in this a continuation of the colonial practice of playing nationalities off against each other. By treating different groups differently and not giving real autonomy to any, the constitution gave rise to minority discontent. First to revolt were the Karen in 1949, who (like the Tamils in Sri Lanka) had been treated favorably under the Raj. The Shan also complained about being unfairly treated by the constitution and some advocated exercising their right of secession. A second, related constitutional flaw was the failure to delimit the political role of the military. Prime Minister U Nu convened a seminar on federalism to discuss ways of resolving the minority dilemma, but the Burman-dominated War Office viewed federalism as a threat to the unity of the nation and before the meeting could complete its work the military seized power on March 2, 1962, bringing down u Nu's regime.

Democracy was replaced by a Revolutionary Council consisting of 17 senior military officers, who issued a 28-point manifesto, "The Burmese Way to Socialism", a distinctive amalgam of socialist economics, nationalism and Buddhism, and exercised power through a hierarchy of Security Administrative Councils, manned by a combination of military, police and administrative officials, reaching from Rangoon to the remotest village. Hoping to put the regime on a more secure footing, the Revolutionary Council created its own exclusive political party, the Burma Socialist Programme Party and, following the first BSPP Congress, assigned the party to write a new constitution. A few months later, the Revolutionary Council gave way to the creation of the Government of Burma, with most of the same leaders as before, now retired from military to nominal civilian positions. Following a referendum at the end of 1973, a new constitution was formally adopted in January 1974, followed by an election for seats in the new government, the Socialist Republic of the Union of Burma, held in the spring of 1974. A unicameral legislature was created, the *Pyithu Hluttaw* (People's Assembly), under two administrative bodies: a Council of State, with a Union President; and a Council of Ministers. In the 1974 Constitution the state made provision for nominal minority nationality autonomy, with the state divided into 14 sub-units called divisions and states bound together in the national parliament by the principle of democratic centralism, but the rights of secession and autonomy of local states were abolished and all divisions were Burman-dominated. Indeed, although the constitution promised rights it also added obligations and set the national interest before the rights of individuals or groups. Again, it failed to specify the political role of the military, perhaps unnecessary in view of its continued informal dominance.

But although the promise of rights was heavily qualified, it did have the consequence that people believed in and demanded those rights, particularly in the wake of Burma's economic downturn at the end of the 1980s (according to IMF statistics, after a modest 3.85% growth rate in 1985, the nation incurred negative GDP growth in 1986, 1987 and 1988). The famous Four Eights protest was specifically motivated by the government's withdrawal of all high-valued kyat notes in circulation, to be replaced by a new currency denominated on the base of 9 (considered a lucky number by Ne Win's fortunetellers), wiping out many people's savings. Protests escalated in a confrontation with the military, culminating in a massacre of thousands in the summer of 1988. Ne Win's socialist rule was replaced by the State Law and Order Restoration Concil (SLORC) in a stage-managed coup d'etat (in which he however continued to play an influential role, at least until 1998). The promised elections were held by the SLORC in May 1990, resulting in the quite unexpected but convincing victory of the NLD under Aung San Suu Kyi and Tin

Oo, even though Suu Kyi was under her first house arrest and Tin Oo was in prison during the elections. The SLORC however refused to honor the elections results and cracked down on the NLD by imprisoning dozens of NLD MP-elects. To compensate for its damaged ideological legitimacy, the size of the army was doubled, with nearly half the state budget allocated to the security sector. The junta however sought future popular legitimation by promising new elections after setting up a national convention to draft a new constitution, which first convened in early 1993; the democratic opposition first took part in the convention then boycotted it in 1995 and was later barred from participating in 2004. The national convention deliberated inconclusively for so long it risked losing credibility, finally emerging after 14 years with a much-revised 194-page draft constitution in September 2007. The constitution was put to a referendum in May 2008, despite Cyclone Nargis, and was passed by 92.4% of the vote (with a 98% turnout). General elections are scheduled for 2010, bringing the seven-step "road map to disciplined democracy" within view of completion. The new constitution returns to a bicameral legislature consisting of a National Assembly (*Amyotha Hluttaw*) and a People's Assembly (*Pyithu Hluttaw*); there are also regional legislative bodies with limited powers. The government remains essentially central with limited degrees of federal autonomy: there are seven regions and seven states, within which are six "self-administered areas". One quarter of the seats in all legislatures are reserved for military personnel appointed by the commander-in-chief, who will vote under army discipline. The president is both head of state and head of government but not head of the military, over which he has little control. The commander-in-chief of the military has the right to declare emergency rule as he sees fit, and to appoint key cabinet ministers (including defense, border affairs and home affairs ministers) without legislative approval. There is a Supreme Court, but it has no jurisdiction over the military. The legal framework for the 2010 election remains elliptical, leaving even the date unspecified (as of mid-July), but Aung San Suu Kyi is specifically excluded (in Section 59) as are members of religious orders (e.g., Buddhist monks) and any with criminal convictions. Under these restrictions, which barred most of its leaders from running, (and some 2000 political prisoners from voting), the NLD refused to register and was hence disbanded in May 2010, though a splinter party, the National Democratic Force, split off to contest the elections.[1]

The end-state of the "pacted transition" toward which the SPDC is attempting to move very much resembles the Indonesian "guided democracy" under Soeharto, and it is not implausible that it will succeed — at least more than previous attempts in 1947 or 1974. Burma could well become another Southeast Asian petro-state as recent offshore discoveries come on stream, giving the military leadership a source of funding proof against both international humanitarian sanctions and domestic protest. But there are several reasons to doubt that the future of "disciplined democracy" will be quite so rosy. Indonesia's New Order was a form of institutionalized personalism anchored to Soeharto's charismatic leadership, but as Kyaw Yin Hlaing makes plain, Burma's current *primus inter pares,* Senior General Than Shwe, is hardly charismatic, and moreover is 77 years of age (born 1933) with serious health issues and no clear line of succession.[2] Since the purge of Khin Nyunt and his intelligence corps in October 2004, the leadership's feedback loop seems to have deteriorated. Whereas Soeharto enjoyed US support in the Cold War framework, Burma's most reliable supporter is China, a patron never fully trusted. But of course the biggest hurdle is that "disciplined democracy" is not inclusive. In fact a large proportion of the country's population and power base are not signatories to the "pact". For, as outlined in the introduction, Burma is a nation with a long history of divided identity, and the new constitutional structure is so engineered as to exclude those categorized as beyond the pale. Burma's "other half" is in many ways the mirror image of its official identity: disorganized, pluralistic, spontaneous, even chaotic while the junta is calculating, punitive, autocratic and hierarchically organized. Relations

---

[1] The Constitution was published in draft form in Burmese in April 2008, and an English translation was published by the Myanmar Ministry of Information in September 2008. Only the Burmese text is authoritative.
[2] On the Indonesian "New Order," see R. William Liddle, "Soeharto's Indonesia: Personal Rule and Political Institutions," *Pacific Affairs* 58:1 (Spring, 1985), pp. 68–90.

between these two halves of Burma's split identity are of course anti-thetical and zero-sum, yet at the same time oddly symbiotic. Although Burma's shadow half has lost every confrontation to the more cohesively organized and well-armed establishment, it has also demonstrated impressive resilience, repeatedly erupting after suppression and years of dormancy (e.g., in 1962, 1969–1970, 1974, 1988, 1996, 2007). In 2005 a respected Burma analyst reported on the basis of his surveys and interviews that political activism among the general public had apparently died out, with no visible trace of support among the *sangha*, the students or the intelligentsia: "most ordinary people are not prepared for active involvement in organized protest movements".[3] And yet two years later, some 200,000 protesters paraded through the streets of Yangon in the so-called Saffron Uprising. While Burma's shadow half has been far less successful at gaining or exercising power than the establishment due to the power imbalance and its own chronic disorganization and disunity, it has been able to force periodic crises and political reorganizations, and if completely ignored in the junta's new order it is quite conceivable it will do so again.

National Culture

A coherent political identity presupposes not only an inclusive political structure but a set of shared ideas about the nature and proper destiny of the nation-state. Having inherited a fragmented tradition, Burma's leadership attempted to forge a coherent national culture out of three elements: a socialist form of developmentalism, Theravada Buddhism, and a militaristic centralism.

In all post-colonial developing countries, growth is at the top of the political agenda and if successful it can help instill a sense of collective pride and purpose. Very few new nations have approached the latter with *laissez-faire* dispositions, fearing an untrammeled market

[3] Kyaw Yin Hlaing, "Myanmar in 2004: Why Military Rule Continues," in *Southeast Asian Affairs*, eds. Chin Kin Wah and Daljit Singh (Singapore: Institute of Southeast Asian Studies, 2005), pp. 231–256.

would tear society apart and preferring a more proactive governmental role, but efforts at socialist planning have not always been smooth sailing either. In any case, new states usually attempt to stimulate growth with some mixture of market stimulation and central planning, hoping to augment national unity with performative legitimacy. Part of the reason for the long failure of Burma's leadership to resolve their country's identity quandary is that the specific variant of market socialism they have assembled, unlike that of China or even the former Soviet Union, has consistently failed either to generate economic growth or to provide for the general welfare, providing a ready grievance for political opposition.

Burma had no communist revolution but the young men who led the independence movement were influenced by the revolutions *qua* national liberation wars in China and, later, French Indochina and Malaysia. Many of them, including Aung San, were initially members of the CPB, so it is not surprising that the government's economic construction formula initially embraced socialist planning. But the socialism that was practiced, rhetorically under Nu and more systematically under Ne Win's "Burmese way to socialism", involved the nationalization of the economy without any clear notion of how to grow it. There was no revolutionary "breakthrough" to incentivize a massive public investment strategy and no socialist patron state to guide this resolutely neutralist economy.[4] Though Ne Win never engaged in the kleptocratic plunder of a Marcos or Soeharto, his appointments were based on loyalty rather than competence and corruption was rife in the BSPP. The stagnating economy did not directly cause rebellious or fissiparous tendencies but provided little incentive for national integration. After the 1988 protests and ensuing crackdown, the SLORC opened the economy to foreign extraction of resources, abandoning socialist planning in favor of the market (albeit without much privatization), and the frontier regions were given somewhat greater autonomy. But while the economy was unquestionably stimulated by the influx of profits from gas and oil extraction (by 2007, 40% of all export earnings came from natural gas, abruptly

---

[4] See Kenneth Jowitt, *Revolutionary Breakthroughs and National Development: The Case of Romania, 1944–1965* (Berkeley, University of California Press, 1971).

shifting the country's trade deficit into a surplus), this has involved clear symptoms of a "resource curse" as Turnell points out, with 30–40% inflation rates and an atrophied industrial sector. Thus economic development has failed to serve as an adequate functional substitute for a coherent sense of national identity, and the regime has repeatedly turned to retrieving elements of the traditional belief system.

Buddhism, as the religion practiced by over 80% of the population, was the obvious choice to provide both a cognitive template and normative guidelines for the government to construct a national culture. And yet it has proved a problematic integument for binding the nation together. In the past, the nexus between religion and political power was very close: though in theory the king was ritually inferior to the monkhood, he was viewed as the protector of Buddhism and its highest secular officiant; the head of the *sangha*, who alone had authority to discipline the monks, served at the pleasure of the king and his religious council. When the British finally conquered Burma in 1886 and sent King Thibaw into exile, no new governing body of the monks was established and discipline in the religious orders deteriorated.[5] The introduction of Western schools reduced the need for traditional education, depriving the *sangha* of this vital social function. "Having lost a central source of discipline and one of their principal occupations, many monks assumed a new role — that of political leaders — filling the void created by the colonial government's displacement of the traditional hereditary leaders. Political monks became a major force in the nationalist movement."[6] Young, politically active monks supported the anti-tax movement of local village committees and set up their own Young Men's Buddhist Association and other liberation organizations. The more active political role of the monkhood in some ways contradicted traditional prescriptions of Buddhist religious roles, though in its rejection of imperialism there is perhaps an elective affinity. Theravada Buddhism

---

[5] Donald Smith, *Religion and Politics in Burma* (Princeton: Princeton University Press, 1965), Chap. 2.
[6] Josef Silverstein, *Burma: Military Rule and the Politics of Stagnation* (Ithaca, NY: Cornell University Press, 1977), p. 24.

places responsibility for enlightenment upon the individual, viewing politics not as a solution to life's problems but essentially as an extraneous burden, one of the "five evils" all men must endure.

Though perhaps well suited for a national liberation movement, Burmese Buddhism was to prove a difficult bedfellow for a postcolonial regime, for two reasons. First, although most Burmans are Buddhist, not all of them are, and those who are not Buddhist opposed using religion as a national common denominator. About 4% of the population is Christian (most of the Karens) and about 4% are Muslim, many of them Rohingya who are discriminated against (some 200,000 have emigrated to Bangladesh since 1978). Prime Minister U Nu strongly emphasized Buddhism as a uniting force during the constitutional period, founding the Buddha Sasana Organization as the central organization representing Buddhists in the country. He also established government-sponsored ecclesiastical courts to restore order within the *sangha* and founded Pali University, where standards for teaching Buddhist scriptures were regularized.[7] But when he pushed through a law making Buddhism the state religion, following a campaign promise made during his 1960 electoral campaign, several minority groups started secessionist movements — precipitating Ne Win's *coup d'état*.[8] Some 300,000 Burmese Indians emigrated from the country in 1964, complaining of racist or religious persecution and the nationalization of private property. While the military-led government subsequently opted to give the minority governments somewhat greater autonomy in ceasefire agreements rather than fight them, the latter's reluctance to subordinate themselves to the central government has continued to be based ideologically on the latter's implicitly Buddhist "Burmanization" (*bama san-gyin*) campaign.

---

[7] John Cady, "Religion and Politics in Modern Burma," *Far Eastern Quarterly* 12:2 (1953), pp. 158–160.
[8] Stephan Engelkamp, "Moral Authority in Burmese Politics," *Asien* 109 (October 2008), pp. 37–53.

Second, at least since the fall of Ne Win, the *sangha* has reverted
to its colonial-era involvement in political resistance on behalf of the
poor and oppressed as well as its own corporate interests, while the
SLORC/SPDC in turn has sought in vain to assert its political
authority over religion, vacillating between benign patronage and
harsh discipline. Ne Win's Revolutionary Council, while emphasizing
the analogies between Burmese socialism and "traditional values",
halted state support for Buddhism and voided all laws and state sub-
ventions, barred monks from political participation and otherwise
suppressed Buddhist political activities. In 1980 the state organized a
sangha congregation designed to bring the Buddhist orders under
greater state control.[9] Still, Ne Win contended that "he personally
was a good Buddhist" and sought in the traditional manner to earn
merit by religious benefactions, building for example a pagoda right
beside the Shwedagon Pagoda in Rangoon.[10] In the wake of the
1988–1990 turmoil, the military invaded monasteries and pagodas to
cleanse the clergy of "political" elements, establishing an All-Nikayas
Council under the Ministry of Religious Affairs to impose institutional control over the *sangha*. But at the same time, Than Shwe built
two pagodas and refurbished many others, making public obeisance
and paying homage to the order, asserting that SPDC policies were
enforced with "goodwill" (*cetana*).[11] The monkhood first became
explicitly involved in public protests in 1974 when U Thant was not
given a proper burial, and again in 1990 to protest the shooting of a
highly respected (*tipitaka*) monk during a peaceful protest, several
times in the late 1990s, then again of course in the 2007 Saffron

[9] Robert Taylor, *The State in Burma* (Honolulu: University of Hawaii Press, 1987),
pp. 358–359.
[10] Ne Win seems to have also relied on religious superstition, as in numerology and
spirits, for supernatural protection. See Bruce Matthews, "The Present Fortune of
Tradition-Bound Authoritarianism in Myanmar," *Pacific Affairs* 71:1 (1998),
pp. 19–20.
[11] David Steinberg, *Burma: The State of Myanmar* (Washington, DC: Georgetown
University Press, 2001), p. 42.

Uprising, provoked by the sudden hike in fuel prices. The upshot is that while all Burmese political elites have sought legitimacy and unity in Buddhism, the opposition too speaks the language of religious piety, and the monkhood has tended over time to side with the latter, based not only on its own interests but the interests of the common people who are its ultimate base of support.

The ethnic issue is distinct but related to the leadership's exclusive reliance on Buddhism for ideological legitimation. While the SLORC was more successful than U Nu or even the BSPP in negotiating ceasefires with 17 of the largest and most powerful of these ethnic groups, this did not assuage their suspicions of the center and they have continued to field their own armies. Only a few minor groups have thus far accepted the SPDC's proposal to deal with the problem, i.e., the absorption of all ethnic armies into a national Border Guard Force. Meanwhile, the military's general approach to ethnic splits — enforced centralism — created another, even more rancorous one, that of superimposed centralized authoritarianism. Burma never had a revolution whereby such enforced centralization could be popularly legitimated — power was seized from the top down. The price has been a pervasive degradation of human rights that soon generated its own indigenous opposition, inspired by somewhat idealized memories of the nation's democratic origins. This is by no means necessarily a fatal drawback; many countries have achieved a cohesive national identity by duress, among them modern Germany and Japan, South Korea and Taiwan; even the United States during its Civil War imposed by force its regime on a part of its national constituency that fundamentally disagreed with it. But aside from the nationalism often dangerous to its neighbors that such top-down solutions may evoke, the problem peculiar to Burma's military dictatorship, whether under the "Burmese way to socialism" or the subsequent SLORC and SPDC regimes, has been the relative lack of compensating benefits for the forfeiture of civil liberties. Germany, Japan, Taiwan, South Korea and the PRC were able to build competent national bureaucracies, introduce modern educational institutions, welfare states and other public infrastructure and, certainly not least, generate rapid economic growth, thrusting their countries willy-nilly into economic modernity. The failure of the Burmese military state to do so has no doubt been one of the reasons for the unusual tenacity of the democratic opposition, despite its repeated brutal suppression.

International Status

The nation-state's place in the international arena also contributes to its national identity in a number of ways: its relative size, geographic shape and position, population, military and economic power, diplomatic skills and its role in international organizations all affect what it can and cannot do in the world and how it is treated by other states. Burma is well-endowed with fertile farmland and fisheries and other natural resources and has the second-largest area and the longest land borders in Southeast Asia. It is bordered by China on the northeast, Laos on the east, Thailand on the southeast, Bangladesh on the west, India on the northwest and the Bay of Bengal to the southwest with the Andaman Sea defining its southern periphery. One-third of Burma's total perimeter (1,930 km or 1,199 mi), forms an uninterrupted coastline. Its most powerful and important neighbors have been China and India, the relations with which have been capably analyzed by Min Zin and Renaud Egreteau respectively. Although over 80% of its population is Buddhist, historically Burma inherits a reputation as a predatory kingdom, particularly in Thailand. It still fields the second-largest army in Southeast Asia after Vietnam. The most important international organizations to which it belongs are the United Nations and, more recently, ASEAN. In its first decade Burma played a significant international role: U Thant became UN General-Secretary, and together with Indonesia, Yugoslavia, China, Egypt and India, Burma helped define a "third way" for developing countries between the two ideological blocs. In the 1960s, however, the country's diplomatic significance faded as Ne Win hewed to a neutralist and isolationist foreign policy.

During the Cold War, Burma's pursuit of a neutral course between the ideological camps seemed well-conceived, enabling Rangoon to maintain cordial relations with China even as its protracted war against the domestic communist insurgency endeared it to advanced

Western democracies. But since the fall of the communist bloc at the end of the Cold War, the SLORC's brutal crackdown on demonstrations and refusal to honor the results of the 1990 elections, plus the West's shift from a legitimating ideology of anticommunism to one of international human rights, have precipitated the invocation of sanctions and the country's reputation as a "hermit kingdom". Actually, the country has by no means been completely isolated, as Jalal Alamgir points out; one of the distinguishing features of the SLORC/SPDC regime has been its openness to trade and foreign direct investment. China, Singapore and Thailand (particularly under Thaksin) have consistently maintained reasonably cordial economic relations, and this has provided moral cover for other countries, notably Japan and India. But even Alamgir concedes that the nation's economic globalization remains significantly less than that of its East Asian or Southeast Asian neighbors, as has, not coincidentally, its GDP growth and per capita income (e.g., as of 2003, the ratio of foreign trade to GDP was 5.6%, vs. an average of 96.6% for the other nine members of ASEAN — even when clandestine trade is taken into account, Burma's trade ratio remains well below its neighbors).

Thus it would appear that if by national identity we mean a country's realization of the full potential implicit in its geophysical endowment, demographic attributes, political culture and other assets, Burma has not yet consolidated a cohesive identity. The military government, apparently apprehensive lest opening up to the outside world exacerbate fissiparous propensities, has been inclined to defer further opening until internal cohesion can be ensured. And yet the attempt to create a unified national identity by forcing conformity has only protracted and embittered cleavages. Not even Beijing is fully satisfied with the domestic political situation, as the revival of minority conflict threatens to spill over into China. Only through dialogue and voluntary cooperation is true unity possible (i.e., a unity that does not explode once force is relaxed). To fully realize the country's economic potential will also entail opening up the economy — but unlike China in 1978, this may not be enough because of the sanctions imposed by the West. To get the sanctions lifted will require completion of the seven-step road map, but in a way that also allows the opposition into the process. If the opposition is shut out, they will become a time bomb. Western reservations about deepening their involvement are not based solely on human rights concerns; there must be a favorable political climate in which to conduct business, meaning the SPDC or whatever new government is established in the light of the 2010 elections must have sufficient support from the opposition and ethnic minorities to be able to govern without the threat of riots or civil war. If the post-2010 settlement can sufficiently satisfy the other major players in the political arena to achieve domestic tranquility, it is likely that the country's major potential trade partners will condone it as well.

Will the SPDC yield? At this point it seems unlikely. Unfortunately, it is conceivable that the SPDC sees greater peril in responding reasonably to its major grievants than in keeping the lid on — its opponents would take any concessions as license to push their agenda further, the junta anticipates, generating a more lively but conflictual political scene that the authorities would find difficult to control, particularly if encumbered by human rights procedural constraints. Whereas unconditional suspension of sanctions would be welcome, continuing to trade only with those countries imposing no political preconditions is also quite acceptable to them. Human rights conditionality, on the other hand, would be intolerably risky. Thus it is possible that the "pacted transition", conducted top-down without pacted partners, will arrive at an end-state very much like the status quo. Burma's struggle for national identity, so tantalizingly close to completion, would thus be deferred, subject to further misadventures.

Index

www.ingramcontent.com/pod-product-compliance
Lightning Source LLC
Chambersburg PA
CBHW051948270326
41929CB00015B/2573